THE CAMBRIDGE COMPANION TO
ANCIENT MEDITERRANEAN RELIGIONS

In antiquity, the Mediterranean region was linked by sea and land routes that facilitated the spread of religious beliefs and practices among the civilizations of the ancient world. *The Cambridge Companion to Ancient Mediterranean Religions* provides an introduction to the major religions of this area and explores current research regarding the similarities and differences among them. The period covered is from the prehistoric period to late antiquity, that is, c. 4000 BCE to 600 CE. Part I of the volume offers nine essays providing an overview of the characteristics and historical developments of the major religions of the region, including those of Egypt, Mesopotamia, Syria-Canaan, Israel, Anatolia, Iran, Greece, Rome, and early Christianity. Part II contains five essays dealing with key topics in current research on these religions, including violence, identity, the body, gender, and visuality, taking an explicitly comparative approach and presenting recent theoretical and methodological advances in contemporary scholarship.

Barbette Stanley Spaeth is Associate Professor of Classical Studies and Co-Director of the Institute for Pilgrimage Studies at the College of William and Mary. Her specialty is Greek and Roman religion. She is the author of *The Roman Goddess* (1996) and of articles in *Daughters of Hecate: Women and Magic in the Ancient World* (forthcoming), *Rome and Religion: A Cross-Disciplinary Dialogue on the Imperial Cult* (2011), and *Sub Imagine Somni: Nighttime Phenomena in Greco-Roman Culture* (2010). Her work has been published in the *American Journal of Archaeology*, *Hesperia*, *Historia*, and *Classical World*. Spaeth has held fellowships at the American School of Classical Studies in Athens and the American Academy in Rome. She has received grants from the National Endowment for the Humanities, the Loeb Classical Library Foundation, the Center for Hellenic Studies, and the Memoria Romana Project of the Max-Planck Society. She is co-founder and past president of the Society for Ancient Mediterranean Religions, as well as past president of the Alumni/ae Association of the American School of Classical Studies at Athens.

CAMBRIDGE COMPANIONS TO RELIGION

This is a series of companions to major topics and key figures in theology and religious studies. Each volume contains specially commissioned chapters by international scholars, which provide an accessible and stimulating introduction to the subject for new readers and nonspecialists.

Other Titles in the Series

AMERICAN ISLAM *Edited by* Juliane Hammer and Omid Safi

AMERICAN JUDAISM *Edited by* Dana Evan Kaplan

AMERICAN METHODISM *Edited by* Jason E. Vickers

KARL BARTH *Edited by* John Webster

THE BIBLE, 2ND EDITION *Edited by* Bruce Chilton

BIBLICAL INTERPRETATION *Edited by* John Barton

DIETRICH BONHOEFFER *Edited by* John de Gruchy

JOHN CALVIN *Edited by* Donald K. McKim

CHRISTIAN DOCTRINE *Edited by* Colin Gunton

CHRISTIAN ETHICS *Edited by* Robin Gill

CHRISTIAN MYSTICISM *Edited by* Amy Hollywood and Patricia Z. Beckman

CHRISTIAN PHILOSOPHICAL THEOLOGY *Edited by* Charles Taliaferro and Chad V. Meister

CLASSICAL ISLAMIC THEOLOGY *Edited by* Tim Winter

JONATHAN EDWARDS *Edited by* Stephen J. Stein

FEMINIST THEOLOGY *Edited by* Susan Frank Parsons

THE JESUITS *Edited by* Thomas Worcester

JESUS *Edited by* Markus Bockmuehl

C. S. LEWIS *Edited by* Robert MacSwain and Michael Ward

LIBERATION THEOLOGY *Edited by* Chris Rowland

MARTIN LUTHER *Edited by* Donald K. McKim

MEDIEVAL JEWISH PHILOSOPHY *Edited by* Daniel H. Frank and Oliver Leaman

MODERN JEWISH PHILOSOPHY *Edited by* Michael L. Morgan and Peter Eli Gordon

MOHAMMED *Edited by* Jonathan E. Brockup

POSTMODERN THEOLOGY *Edited by* Kevin J. Vanhoozer

PURITANISM *Edited by* John Coffey and Paul C. H. Lim

THE QUR'AN *Edited by* Jane Dammen McAuliffe

KARL RAHNER *Edited by* Declan Marmion and Mary E. Hines

REFORMATION THEOLOGY *Edited by* David Bagchi and David Steinmetz

RELIGIOUS STUDIES *Edited by* Robert A. Orsi

FREIDRICK SCHLEIERMACHER *Edited by* Jacqueline Mariña

SCIENCE AND RELIGION *Edited by* Peter Harrison

ST. PAUL *Edited by* James D. G. Dunn

THE TALMUD AND RABBINIC LITERATURE *Edited by* Charlotte E. Fonrobert and Martin S. Jaffee

HANS URS VON BALTHASAR *Edited by* Edward T. Oakes and David Moss

JOHN WESLEY *Edited by* Randy L. Maddox and Jason E. Vickers

THE CAMBRIDGE COMPANION TO

ANCIENT MEDITERRANEAN RELIGIONS

Edited by Barbette Stanley Spaeth
College of William and Mary

CAMBRIDGE
UNIVERSITY PRESS

CAMBRIDGE
UNIVERSITY PRESS

University Printing House, Cambridge CB2 8BS, United Kingdom

One Liberty Plaza, 20th Floor, New York, NY 10006, USA

477 Williamstown Road, Port Melbourne, VIC 3207, Australia

4843/24, 2nd Floor, Ansari Road, Daryaganj, Delhi - 110002, India

79 Anson Road, #06-04/06, Singapore 079906

Cambridge University Press is part of the University of Cambridge.

It furthers the University's mission by disseminating knowledge in the pursuit of education, learning and research at the highest international levels of excellence.

www.cambridge.org
Information on this title: www.cambridge.org/9780521132046

© Cambridge University Press 2013

This publication is in copyright. Subject to statutory exception and to the provisions of relevant collective licensing agreements, no reproduction of any part may take place without the written permission of Cambridge University Press.

First published 2013

A catalogue record for this publication is available from the British Library

Library of Congress Cataloging in Publication data
Spaeth, Barbette Stanley.
The Cambridge companion to ancient Mediterranean religions / Barbette Stanley Spaeth, College of William and Mary.
    pages   cm. – (Cambridge companions to religion)
Includes bibliographical references and index.
ISBN 978-0-521-11396-0 – ISBN 978-0-521-13204-6 (pbk.)
1. Mediterranean Region – Religion.   I. Title.
BL687.S63   2013
200.937–dc23   2012049271

ISBN 978-0-521-11396-0 Hardback
ISBN 978-0-521-13204-6 Paperback

Cambridge University Press has no responsibility for the persistence or accuracy of URLs for external or third-party internet websites referred to in this publication, and does not guarantee that any content on such websites is, or will remain, accurate or appropriate.

Contents

List of Illustrations   *page* ix
List of Contributors   xi

Introduction   1
BARBETTE STANLEY SPAETH

Part I

1 Egypt   13
EMILY TEETER

2 Mesopotamia   33
BEATE PONGRATZ-LEISTEN

3 Syria-Canaan   55
SHAWNA DOLANSKY

4 Israel   76
MAYER I. GRUBER

5 Anatolia   95
BILLIE JEAN COLLINS

6 Iran   116
W. W. MALANDRA

7 Greece   136
JENNIFER LARSON

8 Rome   157
CELIA E. SCHULTZ

9 Early Christianity   177
H. GREGORY SNYDER

Part II

10 Violence   199
BRUCE LINCOLN

11 Identity 220
KIMBERLY B. STRATTON

12 The Body 252
ELIZABETH A. CASTELLI

13 Gender 281
ROSS SHEPARD KRAEMER

14 Visuality 309
ROBIN M. JENSEN

Index 345

List of Illustrations

Figures

1.1 Ramesses IV offering food to the god Khonsu. Relief from the Khonsu Temple, c. 1153–1147 BCE. *page 24*

8.1 So-called Tellus Relief of the Ara Pacis Augustae, 13–9 BCE. 161

10.1 Graph of conquest as divinely sanctioned. 206

10.2 Graph of defeat as humiliation. 207

10.3 Graph of millennarian revolt. 207

10.4 Graph of mortification of the flesh. 208

14.1 Statue of Minerva, known as the Athena Giustiniani. Antonine era copy of a fourth-century BCE Greek original. 321

14.2 Vision of Ezekiel. Wall painting from the Dura Europos Synagogue, c. 239 CE. 325

14.3 Jesus enthroned with apostles. Apse mosaic from the Church of Sta. Pudenziana, c. 400–410 CE. 327

14.4 Jesus walking on the water. Wall painting from the Christian baptistery in Dura Europos, c. 240 CE. 330

14.5 Apse mosaic from the Church of Ss. Cosmas and Damian, c. 526–30 CE. 331

14.6 West wall and Torah niche from the Dura Europos Synagogue, c. 239 CE. 332

14.7 Zodiac mosaic floor panel from the Beth Alpha Synagogue, sixth century CE. 333

14.8 Wall paintings from the Villa of the Mysteries, first century CE. Pompeii. 335

14.9 Abraham's hospitality, offering of Isaac. Sanctuary mosaic from the Church of San Vitale, c. 547 CE. Ravenna. 337

14.10   The so-called Two Brothers Sarcophagus,
          mid-fourth century CE.   338
14.11   Ara Pacis Augustae, 13–9 BCE.   339

Table

10.1   Martyrological inversion of imperial narratives.   211

Map

Map of the Mediterranean world.   xii

List of Contributors

Elizabeth A. Castelli, Professor, Department of Religion, Barnard College, Columbia University

Billie Jean Collins, Instructor, Department of Middle Eastern and South Asian Studies, Emory University

Shawna Dolansky, Adjunct Research Professor, College of the Humanities, Carleton University, Canada

Mayer I. Gruber, Professor, Department of Bible Archaeology and the Ancient Near East, Ben-Gurion University of the Negev, Israel

Robin M. Jensen, Luce Chancellor's Professor of the History of Christian Art and Worship, Vanderbilt University

Ross Shepard Kraemer, Professor of Religious Studies and Judaic Studies, Brown University

Jennifer Larson, Professor, Department of Modern and Classical Language Studies, Kent State University

Bruce Lincoln, Caroline E. Haskell Distinguished Service Professor of History of Religions, University of Chicago

W. W. Malandra, Professor Emeritus, Department of Classical and Near Eastern Studies, University of Minnesota

Beate Pongratz-Leisten, Professor, Institute for the Study of the Ancient World, New York University

Celia E. Schultz, Associate Professor, Department of Classical Studies, University of Michigan

H. Gregory Snyder, Professor, Department of Religion, Davidson College

Barbette Stanley Spaeth, Associate Professor, Department of Classical Studies, College of William and Mary

Kimberly B. Stratton, Associate Professor of Religion, College of the Humanities, Carleton University, Canada

Emily Teeter, Egyptologist and Research Associate, Oriental Institute, University of Chicago

Map of the Mediterranean world.

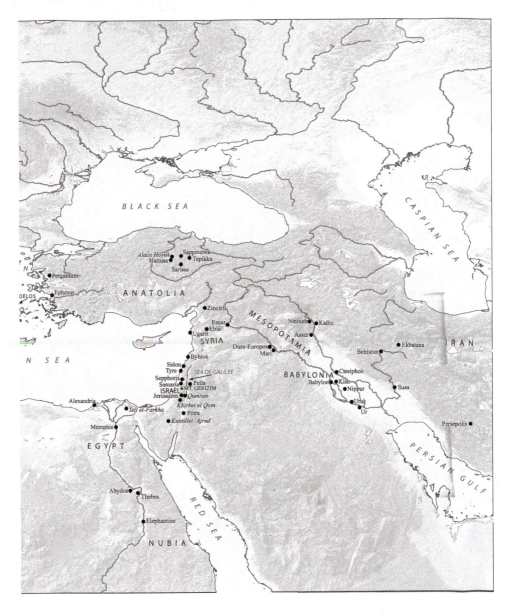

BLACK SEA

CASPIAN SEA

N

Pergamum

Ephesus

DELOS

N SEA

ANATOLIA

Alaca Höyük   Sappinuwa
Hattusa   Tapikka
        Sarissa

Zincirli

Emar
Ebla
Ugarit
SYRIA

Byblos
Sidon
Tyre
Sepphoris   SEA OF GALILEE
Samaria   Pella
ISRAEL   MT. GERIZIM
Jerusalem   Qumran
Khirbet el Qom
Petra
Kuntillet 'Ajrud

Dura-Europos
Mari

MESOPOTAMIA

Nineveh   Kalhu
Assur

BABYLONIA
Babylon   Kish
        Nippur
        Uruk
        Ur

Ctesiphon

Behistun   Ekbatana

IRAN

Susa

Persepolis

Alexandria

Tell el-Farkha

Memphis

EGYPT

Abydos
Thebes

Elephantine

NUBIA

RED SEA

PERSIAN GULF

Introduction

BARBETTE STANLEY SPAETH

Over the past few decades, scholars have come to recognize ever more clearly that the cultures of the ancient Mediterranean world were interconnected in complex ways and therefore should be studied with an interdisciplinary methodology that both probes significant similarities among cultures and yet recognizes important differences among them as well.[1] Nowhere is this interdisciplinary and comparative approach more fruitful than in the study of ancient Mediterranean religions.[2] Religious beliefs and practices permeated all aspects of life in the ancient Mediterranean world.[3] To be sure, some scholars have argued that the term "religion" is not applicable to antiquity, since it reflects a post-Reformation dichotomy between a pursuit viewed as purely "spiritual" and other more pragmatic human activities, such as politics and economics, whereas in antiquity these activities were closely bound together.[4] Nevertheless, it seems clear that phenomena that we would categorize as "religious" did exist in the ancient Mediterranean, including such things as beliefs about divine beings, rituals devoted to these beings, and institutions connected with the performance of those rituals. In some cases, religious phenomena were transmitted across cultural boundaries, resulting, for example, in the spread of specific cults across the Mediterranean world, such as those of the Egyptian Isis and the Phrygian Cybele. In other cases, religious phenomena helped to define cultural identity through reinforcing perceptions of difference from surrounding cultures, as in the focus on monotheism in ancient Judaism. The study of ancient Mediterranean religions thus provides an unparalleled opportunity to explore issues of cultural diffusion and hybridity, investigate problems of ethnicity and identity, develop new theoretical approaches to comparative religion, and further the study of individual cultures in the matrix of ancient Mediterranean civilization.

The academic discipline of the study of ancient Mediterranean religions, however, is still in its nascent stages. The relatively recent development of this field may be attributed to a variety of factors. First, the trend toward academic specialization in the twentieth century has meant that until recently most scholars have been traditionally trained in fields that have had relatively rigid boundaries. In classical studies, for example, my own field, scholars are trained in one of three major disciplines: Latin and Greek language and literature, ancient history, or classical art and archaeology. Since the study of Greek and Roman religions crosses these disciplinary boundaries, training in this area is absent from the curricula of many graduate programs in classical studies, and so few scholars tend to specialize in this area. Second, the problem of academic specialization is compounded when one considers the large number of scholarly fields that comprise the study of ancient Mediterranean religions, among them classical studies, Near Eastern studies, biblical studies, Egyptology, art and art history, history, archaeology, and religious studies. Scholars are often uncomfortable stepping outside of their own fields and into comparative or interdisciplinary work, and hence often do not attempt research that requires such work. Finally, communication among scholars who work on different aspects of ancient Mediterranean religions has been limited. Scholars tend to associate with others in their field, and so do not come into dialogue with those in other areas. This is signaled, for example, by the fact that very few classicists attend the annual meeting of the Society of Biblical Literature and few scholars of biblical studies attend the annual meetings of the American Philological Association and the Archaeological Institute of America.

There are signs recently that this artificial division born of academic specialization is breaking down. Interest has been growing in the interdisciplinary and comparative study of the ancient Mediterranean world and of the role of religion within that world. This interest is marked, for example, by the formation of new scholarly organizations, such as the Midwestern Consortium on Ancient Religions (2002), the Joukowsky Institute for Archaeology and the Ancient World (2004), the Colloquium on Material Culture and Ancient Religion (2008), and the Society for Ancient Mediterranean Religions (2008). Numerous scholarly conferences have also been held on various aspects of the religions of the ancient Mediterranean, for example, "Sanctified Violence in Ancient Mediterranean Religions" (University of Minnesota, 2007), "Ways of Seeing: Visuality in Late Antique Material Religion" (University of Kentucky, 2008), and "What's Religious about Ancient Mediterranean Religions?" (Pontifical Biblical Institute, Rome, 2009). Moreover, undergraduate and graduate courses are now offered in this field at a number of colleges and universities, and new graduate programs have been formed to serve a rising interest in this area, such as the interdisciplinary specialization in the Religions of the Ancient Mediterranean in the Department of Classical Studies at Ohio State University, the specialization in Ancient Mediterranean Religions in the Department of Religious Studies at the University of North Carolina at Chapel Hill, and the concentration in Religion in the Ancient Mediterranean in the Department of Religious Studies at the University of Texas at Austin. Ancient Mediterranean religion is thus coming to be recognized as an academic discipline in its own right.

Because of its relatively recent development as an academic discipline, there are few published works that focus on ancient Mediterranean religions, particularly at an introductory level.[5] This *Cambridge Companion* is intended to fill this gap: to introduce advanced undergraduates, graduate students, scholars in related fields, and interested general readers to a new and burgeoning discipline. The volume provides an introduction to major religions of the ancient Mediterranean from the prehistoric period to late antiquity, that is, from around 4000 BCE to 600 CE, and explores current research regarding the similarities and differences among them. The book is intended to be useful for upper-level undergraduate courses in the field, as well as to serve as a reference for graduate students and faculty in a variety of disciplines. It also is intended to open up more dialogue among the scholars who work on the different religions of this region from a variety of theoretical and methodological perspectives.

The format of the *Cambridge Companion* as an edited collection of articles suits the field of ancient Mediterranean religions quite well. Since the disciplinary boundaries remain strong, experts in the various disciplines that make up the field can contribute their particular expertise to provide an overview of the field as a whole. In recognition of this strong disciplinary focus, this *Companion* is divided into two parts. Part I offers nine essays that provide an overview of the historical development and characteristics of the major religions of the lands and peoples of the ancient Mediterranean and are written by experts in these fields, including Egypt (Emily Teeter), Mesopotamia (Beate Pongratz-Leisten), Syria-Canaan (Shawna Dolansky), Israel (Mayer I. Gruber), Anatolia (Billie Jean Collins), Iran (W. W. Malandra), Greece (Jennifer Larson), Rome (Celia E. Schultz), and early Christianity (H. Gregory Snyder). The religions covered obviously do not comprise all those that were practiced in the ancient Mediterranean, but they do represent the core of this vast field. The regional organization of this section is based not only on scholarly tradition, but also on the current intellectual interest in the interrelationship of religion and landscape, the use of religion as a marker of geographical and ethnic boundaries, and the reciprocal connections among religion, society, and ecology. Part II of this volume contains five longer essays that deal with key topics in current research on ancient Mediterranean religions: violence (Bruce Lincoln), identity (Kimberly B. Stratton), the body (Elizabeth A. Castelli), gender (Ross Shepard Kraemer), and visuality (Robin M. Jensen). The chapters in this section take an explicitly comparative approach to these topics and set them in the context of recent theoretical and methodological advances in contemporary scholarship.

To facilitate comparison of each religion with the others covered in the volume, the contributors to Part I of the volume were asked to follow a common outline. First, each contributor was asked to provide a brief introduction to the geographical, ethnic, and chronological reach of the religion under discussion. Then, he/she was to outline its historical development, including the effects of contact with other Mediterranean cultures on its evolution and its own effects on the religions of other Mediterranean cultures. The important characteristics of the religion were to be outlined next: its beliefs (divinities, cosmology, eschatology), practices (prominent rituals, concepts of sacred time and sacred space, structural organization), and social context (role of social divisions in the practice of the religion, relationship of the religion to other aspects of society, especially politics, and role of ethics and philosophy in the religion). Finally, each contributor was asked to consider the state of research on the religion (major sources for our knowledge of the religion, historical development of scholarship on the religion, current questions being asked by scholars about the religion). In addition, each contributor was to provide a brief description of works that they would recommend to non-specialists to direct further reading on the topic, a chronological chart for the historical development of the religion, a list of works cited in the chapter, a glossary of terms and names of divinities that might be unfamiliar to the non-specialist, and a list of important sites related to the religion to appear on a map of the Mediterranean world at the front of the book. Of necessity, this map does not cover a specific historical period, but rather shows a variety of sites that existed at different periods, in order to orient the readers to the geographical locations associated with each religion covered in the volume. The names of the regions on the map correspond to the titles of the chapters in the volume. In order to accommodate the diversity of the religions in the ancient Mediterranean, the authors in this section were allowed some flexibility within the set outline of topics, in that they could choose to skip or compress certain topics in order to focus on others more germane to the religion in question. Although the project of comparison is not explicit in this first section of the *Companion*, I hope that the reader will find many points throughout useful for understanding both the similarities and differences among the various religions covered.

The authors of the chapters in Part II of this volume take a more explicitly comparative approach to the study of ancient Mediterranean religions. The authors of these essays were asked to focus on a particular aspect of ancient Mediterranean religions that crosses cultural boundaries and engages new theoretical and/or methodological perspectives. Each author was requested to branch out from his/her particular field of expertise to embrace the study of at least three different ancient Mediterranean religions and to incorporate a variety of types of evidence, such as texts, archaeological remains, and inscriptions, in their consideration of the topic at hand. Again, at the end of their essays, the contributors were asked to provide a brief description of works recommended to non-specialists for further reading on the topic, a list of works cited in the chapter, and a glossary of specialized terms. Since the chapters of this section of the volume do not follow a common organizational scheme, and their approaches to the topics under consideration are quite varied, I summarize each of these chapters in the following paragraphs.

In the first chapter of Part II, Bruce Lincoln theorizes the role of violence in ancient Mediterranean religions. Lincoln first addresses the nature of violence and its relation to domination, defining the former as the deployment of physical force to convert human subjects into depersonalized objects and the latter as the cultivation of fear through the threat of violence in order to produce a semi-objectified state among the fearful. He then outlines four relatively common ways that violence was invested with religious significance in the ancient Mediterranean: (1) Conquerors viewed their conquest as divinely sanctioned; (2) the conquered saw their defeat as salutary humiliation bringing them closer to the divine from which they had become estranged; (3) the conquered engaged in millenarian revolts sanctioned by the divine and led by a salvific hero; and (4) ascetics on a more individual level practiced mortification of the flesh to liberate themselves from base matter in order to come closer to the divine. Lincoln closes his discussion of this topic by examining martyrdom, which he sees as the embracing of violence by its victims to discredit and delegitimize their adversaries and to elevate their own moral and religious status, thus rejecting the objectifying effects of violence and preserving and enhancing their own roles as subjects.

The next essay, by Kimberly B. Stratton, investigates how new theoretical and critical approaches can be applied to the construction, negotiation, and representation of religious identity in the ancient Mediterranean world. Her investigation concentrates on two fundamental modes by which religious identity was expressed, inculcated, and maintained: narrative and performance. Under narrative, she considers how myths about one's group or others might be understood to be defining, either by creating an idealized past around which a social group could rally, or by constructing an "other" as a foil upon which unwanted characteristics could be projected. Under performance, Stratton discusses how ideas of self and community were constructed through actions that moved the individual body through space and place in socially meaningful ways. She also considers how the type of gods worshipped, as well as the geographical location in which they were worshipped, affected concepts of identity, and how religious actions could either sharpen or blur the boundaries around which collective identities coalesced.

The essay by Elizabeth A. Castelli explores the role of the body in ancient Mediterranean religions, alternating between representations of the body (the body as signifier, metaphor, and ideological construction) and bodily enactments (performances, rituals, and other embodiments), and noting instances when the two overlap or intersect. The issues she considers include the nature of the divine body and its connection with the human body, the reciprocal relationship between the macrocosm of the cosmos and the microcosm of the human body, the use of the body as metaphor and as allegory in religious discourse, the role of bodily purity and pollution in the performance of ritual and the preservation of sacred space, the use of religious and magical practices to heal the ailing body, the application of ascetic practices in the service of religious devotion, and the nature of the resurrected body.

Gender is the theme of the chapter by Ross Shepard Kraemer. Kraemer begins by examining gender-specific religious practices in the ancient Mediterranean and their role in bringing about the cultural production of properly gendered persons, both female and male. She also considers how attention to gender and its relation to social hierarchy illuminate other religious practices, such as prayer, prophecy, baptism, and the holding of cultic office. She follows with a discussion of the central role of gender in the cosmology and cosmogony of ancient Mediterranean religions. Finally, Kraemer takes a brief look at the effects of Christianization on gender construction in the region in late antiquity.

Finally, in the last essay of this volume, Robin M. Jensen explores the role of visuality in ancient Mediterranean religions, focusing on images as reflective and performative instruments of religiosity. Jensen begins by outlining the role of visual studies in the history of religions, and then considers the question of reality and illusion that is central to religious visual practice through examining ancient theories of sight and the reliability of the senses. She then turns to examining the ways that the peoples of the ancient Mediterranean perceived the visual images of their gods and how they imagined their gods to look. She also investigates the problem of divine visibility or invisibility, particularly in ancient Judaism and early Christianity. Jensen finally considers how pictorial narratives were produced and how sacred stories were transmitted and interpreted through visual art.

I hope that this *Cambridge Companion* will introduce readers to the exciting new work that is being done in ancient Mediterranean religions. My own interest in the topic was kindled by a seminar on Roman religion sponsored by the National Endowment for the Humanities at the American Academy in Rome in 2002 and led by Karl Galinsky, in which I came in contact with a number of scholars of early Christianity and Judaism, including Greg Snyder, Nicola Denzey, Jonathan Reed, and Jeffery Brodd, and learned how their work could help inform my own. I furthered my interest in this topic by participating in two conferences that Steve Friesen, Dan Showalter, James Walters, Christine Thomas, and John Lanci organized on the religious and social landscape of ancient Corinth in 2007 and 2010 at the University of Texas at Austin, and in two of the Colloquia on Material Culture and Ancient Religion that this group of scholars led in 2010 in Israel and 2011 in Greece. In 2008, Eric Orlin and I co-founded the Society for Ancient Mediterranean Religions (SAMR), which has rapidly expanded over the past five years to more than 200 members. I have profited greatly in my own work from the exchange of ideas among scholars of many different disciplines that SAMR has helped to promote. I hope that this volume will generate even more interest in the field of ancient Mediterranean religions and help it gain the wider recognition that it deserves.

A volume such as this one represents the work of many different people who have come together for a collaborative interdisciplinary exercise. I would like to thank the fourteen contributors to this volume for lending their knowledge and expertise to this project and also for their patience and good humor over the period of time it took for it to come together. I also wish to express my gratitude to the various editors and editorial assistants at Cambridge University Press who worked with me to see this volume to completion, including Andrew Beck, Jason Przybylski, Emily Spangler, Amanda Smith, Isabella Vitti, Elise M. Oranges, and Beatrice Rehl. I am also grateful for the suggestions that my friends and colleagues offered for this work, including William Hutton, Linda Reilly,

Naama Zahavi-Ely, John Oakley, and Molly Swetnam-Burland. Finally, I would like to thank my husband Bob for his support and encouragement while I worked on this volume, without which it certainly would never have been completed.

Notes

1   On the study of "Mediterraneanism," especially for the ancient Mediterranean, see Chambers 2008, Horden and Purcell 2005, Harris 2005, Malken 2005, Morris 2005, Braudel 2001, and Horden and Purcell 2000. For the concept of Mediterraneanism in general, see the seminal work of Braudel 1995, originally published in French in 1949.
2   On the history of the study of ancient Mediterranean religions, see most recently Johnston 2007:viii–ix.
3   On defining what is "Mediterranean" about ancient Mediterranean religions, see Graf 2007, Woolf 2005, Chaniotis 2005, and Horden and Purcell 2000:403–460. On defining what is "ancient" about ancient Mediterranean religions, see Lincoln 2007.
4   On the problem of defining "religion" as a category for pre-modern or non-Western societies, see Asad 1993, Fitzgerald 2000, and McCutcheon 1997.
5   Other recent works that treat ancient Mediterranean religions include Johnston 2004 (an encyclopedic reference work), Johnston 2007 (a condensed version of the encylopedia), and Hinnells 2007 (a survey of a variety of ancient religions across the world).

Works Cited

Asad, Talal. 1993. "The Construction of Religion as an Anthropological Category." In *Genealogies of Religions: Discipline and Reasons of Power in Christianity and Islam*: 27–54. Baltimore and London.

Braudel, Fernand. 2001. *Memory and the Mediterranean*. Trans. by Sian Reynolds. New York.

———. 1995. *The Mediterranean and the Mediterranean World in the Age of Philip II*. Vols. 1 and 2. Trans. Sian Reynolds. Berkeley.

Chambers, Iain. 2008. *Mediterranean Crossings: The Politics of an Interrupted Mediterranean*. Durham, NC, and London.

Chaniotis, Angelos. "Ritual Dynamics in the Eastern Mediterranean: Case Studies in Ancient Greece and Asia Minor." In *Rethinking the Mediterranean*. Ed. W. V. Harris, 141–166. Oxford, New York, et al.

Fitzgerald, Timothy. 2000. *The Ideology of Religious Studies*. New York and Oxford.

Graf, Fritz. 2007. "What Is Ancient Mediterranean Religion?" In *Ancient Religions*. Ed. Sarah Iles Johnston, 3–16. Cambridge, MA, and London.

Harris, W. V., ed. 2005. *Rethinking the Mediterranean*. Oxford, New York, et. al.

Hinnells, John R. 2007. *Penguin Handbook of Ancient Religions*. London, New York, et al.

Horden, Peregrine and Nicolas Purcell. 2005. "Four Years of Corruption: A Response to the Critics." In *Rethinking the Mediterranean*. Ed. W. V. Harris, 348–376. Oxford, New York, et al.

———. 2000. *The Corrupting Sea: A Study of Mediterranean History*. Oxford, England and Malden, MA.

Johnston, Sarah Iles. 2007. "Introduction." In *Ancient Religions*. Ed. Sarah Iles Johnston, vii–xii. Cambridge, MA, and London.

Johnston, Sarah Iles, ed. 2004. *Religions of the Ancient World: A Guide*. Cambridge, MA, and London.

Lincoln, Bruce. 2007. "Epilogue." In *Ancient Religions*. Ed. Sarah Iles Johnston, 241–252. Cambridge, MA, and London.

Malken, Irad, ed. 2005. *Mediterranean Paradigms and Classical Antiquity*. London and New York.

McCutcheon, Russell T. 1997. *Manufacturing Religion: The Discourse on Sui Generis Religion and the Politics of Nostalgia*. New York and Oxford.

Morris, Ian. 2005. "Mediterraneanization." In *Mediterranean Paradigms and Classical Antiquity*. Ed. Irad Malken, 30–53. London and New York.

Woolf, Greg. 2005. "A Sea of Faith?" In *Mediterranean Paradigms and Classical Antiquity*. Ed. Irad Malken, 126–143. London and New York.

Part I

1 Egypt

EMILY TEETER

According to Herodotus (*Histories* 2.37), the Egyptians were "religious to excess, beyond any other nation in the world." This can be seen in the way that theology was incorporated into every aspect of their culture, a tradition that continued to be a feature of Egyptian civilization for more than 3,000 years.

The following remarks are based on information dating primarily from the Old Kingdom through the Late period (ca. 2600–332 BCE), although references and comparisons are made to beliefs of the following Ptolemaic and Roman periods (to about 250 CE). Much of the evidence is derived from monuments in the Nile Valley from the ancient southern boundary at Elephantine (modern Aswan) to the Mediterranean.

I. HISTORICAL DEVELOPMENT

The origins of Egyptian religion are largely unknown, for there is a very short interval between the emergence of the culture and the appearance of the basic patterns of religious belief (the concept of life after death, offering cults, mortuary practices, the relationship of the king and the gods). These features present themselves in the early Old Kingdom and remain in their basic form throughout the 3,000 years of the Dynastic period. This retention of patterns was based on the respect for the "earliest times," which, as a creation of the gods, was considered to be perfect. Moving away from those patterns was not viewed as progress, but as corruption.

However, within these essential characteristics, there was considerable change over time, especially in the increasing complexity of rituals and iconography. Alternate representations and explanations of theological issues and deities were developed. The old conceptions were retained and mixed and layered with the new, emphasizing the lack of set doctrine in Egyptian religion. To the Egyptians, these resulting contradictory images added to the diversity of theology. What the Greeks and Romans derided as confusion was, to the Egyptian mind, a rich and complementary explanation of their cosmos.

Egypt's geographic isolation and the Egyptians' sense of cultural superiority ensured that most features of their religion were unaffected by foreign influence until the New Kingdom, when Egypt had more consistent contact with Western Asia. From that time, Levantine gods (Astarte, Anat, Baal, Reshep, and Qudshu) were incorporated into the pantheon. The belief in, and reverence for, foreign deities is suggested by King Amunhotep III's request to Mitanni (now northern Syria) King Tushratta for a statue of Ishtar of Nineveh to alleviate an illness (c. 1350 BCE).[1] Although foreign deities are attested, they were not widely popular, and few temples were dedicated to them. In contrast, Egyptian gods were widely exported to neighboring regions. Amun, a god closely associated with the state and the king, was adopted by the Nubians, and he became their chief deity, remaining so through the Meroitic period, first century CE.

Ptolemaic and Roman period rulers adopted Egyptian cults and royal ideology and iconography as part of the political process of ruling the Nile Valley. This imitation of Egyptian ways was politically expedient, but it also reflected deep reverence for the ancient traditions of Egypt. Egyptian cults were exported to Europe in the Ptolemaic period. By the fourth century BCE, temples dedicated to Isis were established on the islands of Delos, Rhodes, Kos, Samos, Lesbos, and Cyprus as well as in Ephesus on the mainland of Asia Minor. In the next centuries, sanctuaries of the goddess were built throughout the Roman Empire.[2] Similarities between Egyptian Maat and Greek Metis of the *Theogony* suggest that its author Hesiod was influenced by Egyptian myth.[3] Serapis, a form of Osiris-Apis identified with Jupiter and Zeus, was worshipped in Greece and Rome, and the cult of that god as well as of Isis were the foundation of a Greek mystery religion. It has been claimed that early Christian iconography of Mary holding Jesus was influenced by compositions of Isis and her son Horus.[4] Features of second- and third-century CE Gnosticism, especially Nun as the mother of a deity who is associated with God of the Old Testament, and the adoption of the ogdoad (group of eight gods), are rooted in ancient Egyptian tradition.[5] Finally, the marked similarities between the New Kingdom composition of the "Instructions of Amenemope" and Proverbs 22.17–24.22 have been ascribed to direct influence.[6]

2. BELIEF

Egypt was profoundly polytheistic, and by the New Kingdom and later there were thousands of deities. The core pantheon was developed in the earliest centuries of Egyptian history, and over time the number of gods greatly increased.

The development of the iconography of the gods is not entirely clear. Among the earliest depictions are animals (a cow representing Bat, a bull as Horus) shown on Predynastic ceremonial stone palettes. These animals refer to the power of the animal inherent in the god rather than the sacredness of the animal itself, just as the earliest kings are named for animals (Catfish and Scorpion). Animal, anthropomorphic, and mixed forms occur at roughly the same time. For example, the Dynasty I deposit at Tell el-Farkha includes figurines of a falcon-headed feline and a figurine of a serpent with a woman's face.[7] The colossal statues of the god Min shown wholly in human form are among the earliest anthropomorphic images of a deity (although the dating to Dynasty I has been disputed). A single god could assume a multiplicity of forms. For example, Thoth could be shown as an ibis, an ape, or an ibis-headed man. A few gods, such as Ptah, were never shown in animal form. Each of the various representations was considered to be an equally valid way of portraying the deity.[8]

Gods could be identified by attributes, especially headdresses, although they rarely have any direct reference to the god's "power." Often, these attributes are shared by several gods, so if there is no accompanying text, identifying a god can be problematic. For example, a woman with a lyre-horned sun disk on her head can be Isis or Hathor or a non-divine queen.

Only a few features of nature were personified as gods: the Nile as Hapy; the sun as Re, Horus, or the Aten; and the western hills of Thebes as a form of Hathor. Some gods have closely defined spheres of influence. For example, Ptah was a creator god who was associated with wisdom and craftsmen, and Thoth was a creator god and the patron of writing. Others had very vague realms. For example, Hathor was associated with music, singing, dance, love, and the necropolis. The realms of gods overlapped: Ptah, Atum, Khnum, and Nofertum were all credited as being creator gods.

The number of gods was seemingly endless through the forces of syncretism. This temporary indwelling of one god within another expressed the multifaceted nature of the god. For example, Ptah (a creator god) joined with Sokar and Osiris (both deities of the underworld) to form Ptah-Sokar-Osiris, a distinct god of the afterlife, and Amun joined with Re to form a third deity Amun-Re. A single god could be divided into multiple aspects. For example, where there were many forms of Amun at Thebes, including Amenemope (Amun of Luxor), Amun-Re of United-with-Eternity (of the temple of Medinet Habu), Amun of the Valley,

Amun of Pa-Khenty, and Amun of Bukenen, all of whom were independent deities. Although some gods were especially associated with one
geographic area (Khnum with Elephantine, Amun with Thebes, Ptah
with Memphis), they had temples throughout the country.

The Egyptians believed that the world was created "the first time"
from the undifferentiated primordial mass (Nun). Various myths relate
how the undifferentiated became one and then developed into many.
The "many" are frequently expressed in pairs: the contrast of Nun to the
created world, light to dark, earth to sky, order to chaos.

The universe was composed of the heaven, the earth, and the underworld. The earth was suspended in and surrounded by Nun. The heaven
above was conceptualized as the arched body of the goddess Nut whose
hands were on the western horizon and her feet on the east. The sun
traveled across the arch of her body. At dusk she consumed the sun,
and at dawn, after passing through her body, it emerged again from her
vulva. By the New Kingdom, conceptions of solar and chthonic theology
merged with images of the sun in the form of a ram-headed god (Atum)
who descended into the underworld to traverse the twelve hours of the
night until emerging at dawn in the form of a scarab. Both these views of
the cosmos operated simultaneously in this later period.

Gods inhabited the land, the heaven, and the underworld. Generally,
heaven was the realm of the sun god Re and the underworld that of
Osiris, but by the New Kingdom, there was a blurring of the boundaries
with the conception that Re and Osiris together completed the cycle of
rebirth. For example, in the tomb of Nofertari (Dynasty 19), an image
labeled "This is Re who rests in Osiris; This is Osiris who rests in Re"
expresses the unity of the solar cycle – the travels of the sun (Re) through
the realm of Osiris, and Osiris' reciprocal travel through the day sky.

A variety of myths recount the creation of the gods and the world.
The version from Heliopolis relates that the god Atum, through an act of
masturbation (because he had no female counterpart), created the gods
Shu and Tefnut, who represent air and moisture. They in turn bore Geb
and Nut (earth and sky) and their offspring, the siblings Isis, Osiris, Seth,
and Nephthys. Each god personified a paired and contrasting aspect of
the world. In the tradition of Memphis, Ptah created the gods through
his heart (intellect) and his speech.

Belief in life after death was fundamental to Egyptian beliefs, and
as early as the Predynastic period, burials were furnished with grave
goods for the use of the deceased. Royal pyramid tombs, symbols of the
mound of creation and also of a stairway to the heavenly realm of the
gods that appear in Dynasty 3 attest to the growing solar associations

of the afterlife. By the end of Dynasty 5, the interior chambers of the king's pyramid were incised with Pyramid Texts, a series of "utterances" (presumably of a much earlier date of composition) that describe the ascent of the soul of the king to the sky. The Coffin Texts of the First Intermediate period and Middle Kingdom, which were used for private burials and which incorporate Pyramid Texts, reflect the "democratization" of the afterlife. These texts express the growing influence of chthonic beliefs focused on the god Osiris, the mythical first king of Egypt who ruled the underworld realm of the afterlife.

By the New Kingdom, funerary beliefs reflected the duality that is so evident in so many other aspects of Egyptian thought – in this case, the fusion of Osirian and solar conceptions of the afterlife. In this synthesis, which is expressed in both royal and non-royal contexts, the soul of the deceased was judged by a panel of judges before Osiris. The deceased recited a "negative confession" that he or she had not committed a series of transgressions against the state, the gods, or society. If the confession was judged to be true, the soul of the deceased became a transfigured spirit (*akh*) who was associated with Osiris. In the *akh* form, the soul eternally joined the cycle of the sun and accompanied the god in his solar bark traversing the depths of the twelve dark caverns or hours of the underworld ruled by the gods Sokar and Osiris to re-emerge reborn into the realm of the solar god.

This judgment by the gods indicates that an individual's fate was determined by actions while on earth, not by any sense of predestination. There was a strong sense of responsibility for correct personal behavior because all actions supported or undermined the societal notions of order inherent in the concept of "maat" that was personified by a woman with an ostrich feather in her hair. *Maat* was an interconnected sense of balance, fairness, and truth that was juxtaposed to *isfet* or disorder. *Maat* and *isfet* created a tension of opposites whose balance had to be maintained through the correct actions of every individual. The concept of *maat* encompassed an individual's behavior such as fair dealing in the marketplace, respect for elders, and correct performance of rituals, as well as the fundamental cycles of nature – the rising and setting of the sun and the annual inundation of the Nile. Through their actions, each member of the society was personally responsible for the maintenance of *maat*. If *maat* was not maintained on any single level, *isfet* could emerge triumphant, and the universe would descend into chaos.

The Egyptologist Jan Assmann has posited that in the post-Amarna period (Dynasties 19–20), one's actions and fate were disassociated, and that the fate of the deceased was arbitrarily decreed by the gods.[9] In this interpretation, the post-Amarna texts that refer to striving for the blessings and mercy of the gods reflect a new sense of uncertainty and humility that replaced the traditional self-confident behavior dictated by acting in accordance with accepted social patterns and rules inherent in *maat*.[10] This "personal piety" is attested by a small number of texts, mainly from Dynasties 19 and 20.

3. PRACTICE

It has been suggested that Egyptian theology, with its lack of set doctrine and emphasis on performative actions, was a collection of rituals rather than a true religion. The most important of these were offering rituals, which were enacted in funerary and non-funerary contexts, on both a state and a private level. The prominence of offering rituals is based on two beliefs, the first being that the gods had the same material needs as people. As a result, the deity required food, drink, clothing, and rituals of purification. Second, in the private funerary cult the deceased, who dwelled eternally in the afterlife, needed food and drink and objects of daily life. The focus of the temple cult was a statue of the deity that resided in a *naos* in the temple sanctuary. Three times daily an elaborate ritual was enacted that cared for the needs of the god. This ritual is detailed in three Third Intermediate period papyri and in less well-ordered series of temple reliefs. The main priest of the temple entered the sanctuary and cleansed the room with incense. He opened the doors of the *naos*, awakened the god, and placed the divine statue on a layer of clean sand. He removed the god's linen garments; cleaned and purified the statue; offered lengths of cloth, perfumes and ointments, and eye cosmetics; and finally wrapped the god in fresh linen and adorned it with bracelets, necklaces, and the appropriate headdress. Food and drink were then presented to the deity. After the god "consumed" a sample of the offerings, the food, called reversion offerings, was distributed to the temple staff as their wages. It is clear that the food laid before the god was only a sample of the daily offering. For example, 2,345 liters of grain, 30 birds, 20 baskets of fruit, 100 bundles of vegetables, 20 bulbs of onions, and liters of honey and fat and other foods made up the daily offering in the temple of Medinet Habu in western Thebes.[11] It has been estimated that 150–166 priests worked in that temple and shared the food offering.[12]

In the funerary context, offerings to the dead were placed before a statue that represented the *ka* or physical aspect of the deceased and that required sustenance. As in the divine cult, the food offerings would later be consumed by priests who served that cult. However, in both funerary and temple contexts, foodstuff and other offerings could also be supplied eternally by images that were painted and carved on the temple or tomb walls or on and inside the coffin.

Purification rituals were essential for priests of temple and funerary cults. Before a priest entered the temple, he (or she) was compelled to be "pure," although the actual physical meaning of the term is vague. Herodotus (*Histories* 2.37, 40, 64) relates that priests shaved their bodies, rinsed their mouths with natron, avoided sex, and refrained from eating certain foods, such as fish, but it is unclear how accurate this is. It is probable that the idea of "pure" was variable depending on the time period, place, and cult.

Votive offerings were an important part of the private mortuary and non-mortuary cult. What are among the earliest votive figurines date to early Dynasty 1. This deposit, from Tell el-Farkha in the Delta, consisted of ivory, pottery, and stone figurines of men, women, women with children, dwarves, bound captives, deities, and baboons.[13] The same general types of objects have been recovered from temples, tombs, and remains of houses throughout most of Egypt's history. Figurines of phalluses, ears, animals, deities, and cult objects such as *sistra* (ritual rattles) and *situlae* (containers for liquid offerings) associated with deities have been recovered in great numbers from temples.[14] They appear to have been votives (models) made specifically for offering rituals.

Human sacrifice played a minor role in Egyptian religion. In Dynasty 1, the royal tombs at Abydos were accompanied by subsidiary burials for, in some cases, hundreds of sacrificed retainers.[15] This practice was discontinued at the end of the dynasty. By the middle of the Old Kingdom, the walls of tombs and memorial temples were covered with scenes of offering bearers, indicating that these representations of servants, rather than the servants themselves, were believed to be able to provide service in the afterlife. The entrance pylons of most New Kingdom temples are decorated with scenes of the king dispatching groups of foreigners before an approving god (usually Amun, Amun-Re, or Montu). It is assumed that this is a timeless non-specific representation of the king's power rather than an image of a state-sanctioned sacrificial activity that ensured the success of the Egyptian armies.

In the first millennium BCE, the ritual sacrifice of animals became very common. The animal that was thought to represent the spirit (*ba*) of the resident deity of the temple was raised on or near the temple grounds (baboons for Thoth, hawks for Horus or Re, crocodiles for Sobek, etc.). Priests periodically culled the flocks and herds and mummified the sacrificed animals. The resulting votive mummies were then apparently sold to pilgrims who visited the temple. The mummies were then rededicated to the deity and returned to the priests who buried them in vast catacombs. The temple of the mummified falcons at North Saqqara is estimated to hold 4 million bird mummies, a good indication of the popularity of the cult down into the Roman era.

The mummification of birds and parts of larger animals (mainly joints of beef) to serve as food offerings for the deceased is attested from the Predynastic period into the Third Intermediate period.[16] These were often placed in wood containers and stored in the tomb.

A third type of animal sacrifice is referred to in an episode of the Opening of the Mouth (New Kingdom and later) ritual. It calls for the leg of a calf (the form of the hieroglyph for "to have power") to be severed in the presence of its mother (whose mooing was equated with the sound of mourners who grieved for Osiris) and carried, still dripping blood, to the cult statue.[17] The offering was thought to restore the vitality of the deceased and to symbolize the defeat of any enemies of the deceased.

Meat offerings have a prominent role in the funerary offering cult, but judging from scenes in Old Kingdom tombs showing butchers at work, the offerings appear to have been prepared within a temporary structure or in the open air, which may be more of an industrial slaughter-yard rather than a sacred space. However, some temples appear to have had designated slaughter and preparation areas.[18]

The Egyptians did not need to be in a designated sacred space to worship their gods because their deities were omnipresent. However, there were defined sacred spaces. Temples were typically within a walled enclosure. The temple architecturally imitated the cosmos. It was normally built on a platform that evoked the mound of creation, and its series of pylon gateways imitated the horizon. The ceilings were decorated with the stars of the heaven. The columns of the hypostyle halls imitated papyrus or lotus plants growing from a marsh. The sanctuary was marked as being the focus of the temple by the rising floor level and the lowering of the ceiling level as one drew near it. It was dimly illuminated by directed beams of light.

The hypostyle halls and courtyards of the temple provided a setting for rituals and processions. Parts of the temple, generally the first courtyard, were accessible to worshippers. This may be indicated by brief texts on walls or architraves that state that "people" adored the king or the god in that area.[19] But other areas were accessible only to the highest ranks of priests and the king himself. Markings on doors of some Theban temples suggest there was an escalating level of purity that indicated who could enter certain parts of the temple. For example, a door leading to the Hypostyle Hall at Karnak states that "Everyone who enters this temple shall be four times pure," which may reflect a specific sequence of purification actions. But even if denied entrance to the more sacred parts of the temple, it seems likely that people were aware of the rituals that were enacted therein, because the walls of the accessible areas were covered with scenes showing the rituals that were performed in the sanctuary. Although a large structure like the Karnak Temple was dedicated to the resident god Amun, the complex included temples to his consort Mut, their child Khonsu, and also other gods, including Ptah, Montu, Opet, a variety of forms of Osiris, and past king(s).

In the course of festivals, the god left the sanctuary. On such occasions, the statue of the god was placed in a shrine and mounted on a boat that was supported on poles carried by priests. Rows of sphinxes defined the processional ways that linked temples, and small kiosks located along the route allowed the boat of the god to rest and be viewed by the community.

Sacred space in the mortuary sphere was also defined by architecture. Most non-royal tombs were composed of a subterranean and inaccessible burial chamber and a chapel decorated with offering scenes that accommodated visits by the family and friends of the deceased (as well as by strangers). By the New Kingdom, the private tomb assumed the form of a temple with its own forecourt and pylon gateways.

Sacred time was conceived in both cyclic (*neheh*) and linear (*djet*) terms. Cyclic time comprised eternal repetitions of an event, such as the cycle of the sun or the annual inundation of the Nile. *Djet* is typified by progressions such as the emergence of the world from chaos, the emergence of the creator god(s), the rule by gods, and finally the rule by kings.[20] These two conceptions of time functioned simultaneously, embedded in each other, with the cyclic events moving along the linear. The essential pairing of the two different types of time is most clearly expressed by the wish that one might live "forever and ever" (*neheh* and *djet*). Sacred time was also organized by festivals that marked the year. These could be annual (Opet, Feast of the Valley) or more frequent, such as the Decade Festival that was celebrated every ten days in Thebes.

Most of the cults that served the gods, the semi-divine king, and the private and royal mortuary cults were quasi-independent entities with their own priests and landholdings or other resources that supported the construction and maintenance of the temple or tomb and paid for the staff and the offerings. There was cooperation between cults. For example, at Thebes, the resources of the temple of Karnak could be transferred to other temples, and other temples, in turn, provided for Karnak, perhaps due to co-ownership of the field and other resources.[21]

4. SOCIAL CONTEXT

Texts and the archeological records document the religious practices of the elite of the society – those who had the resources to leave documents of their faith. As a result, religious beliefs of the non-elite are essentially unknown, although it is speculated that they were similar to those of the elite.

A large percentage of the elite population, both male and female, served as some category of priest/priestess/temple musician. Even among the upper ranks, these individuals married and had children. Part-time priests reverted to their other occupation(s) when off duty. Strings of titles in genealogical texts show that a priest could also serve in professions such as the Overseer of the Store Rooms, Seal Bearer, or a scribe. This combination of a quasi-secular with a priestly title is a reflection of the way that religion was embedded into the overall society.

Hundreds of priests worked in the temples. In theory, Egypt was a meritocracy and advancement was due not to class but to ability. Autobiographical texts refer to promotion from one rank to the next, sometimes after a number of years in a single position.[22] Yet, in practical terms, being from a privileged background was an important factor, as indicated by references in these texts to the king installing priests from "families that are known." Genealogical texts document that a son commonly assumed the post of his father, suggesting that jobs were kept within specific social circles or families.

The priesthood was inclusive, employing a great number of men and women, some of them in posts that seem to have required a very low level of specialized training or literacy. The priesthood was bureaucratic, being composed of levels of priests and priestesses with specific duties in the temple or mortuary cult. The best-documented organization is the domain of Amun at Thebes that was headed by the First Priest, who served as the highest officiant in the cult. He, or another ranking priest, was deputized by the king to act for him in the daily offering ritual. Immediately below the First Priest were the Second, Third, and Fourth Priests, then ranks of other priests such as God's Father, and then Lectors. Each group had its own supervisor. Priests had administrative as well as sacred duties, an indication of how little separation there was between the secular and sacred worlds.

Priests were not ordained for life. Until the New Kingdom, most worked part time for a specific cult (or cults). They were organized into four or five (depending on the time period) service groups or *saw* (translated as *phyle* from the Greek), who served in rotation for thirty days (the duration of the Egyptian month). As indicated by strings of professional titles, priests could work for several cults, presumably rotating among them in the *phyle* system. Some priestly titles appear to have been de facto hereditary, although there are references to priests being appointed to specific posts by the king.

Although men and women had the same legal rights, gender and class placed restrictions on women's involvement in religious rituals. In the Old and Middle Kingdoms, elite women appear with the title Priestess of Hathor. Others appear with the more modest priestly title "pure one." By the New Kingdom, few women had priestly titles, but many elite women, some of them of the royal house, served as priestess-singers whose music was believed to placate and amuse the god(s).

From early Dynasty 18, the daughter of the First Priest of Amun appeared with the title "God's Wife of Amun." These women are shown primarily officiating at a variety of rituals, but their actual duties are unclear. Thereafter, the title was held by females of the royal family.[23] In the Third Intermediate period, the God's Wives of Amun were princesses who acted as the virtual rulers of Thebes, controlling huge economic resources. Although these women were considered to be the spouses of Amun, it is debated whether they had mortal husbands.

Gender was not an impediment for women even becoming pharaoh. In the Dynastic period, at least four women claimed that office, the best-documented being Hatshepsut (r. c. 1473–1458 BCE), who was the daughter and the wife of pharaohs.

Although images of ithyphallic gods in temples and references to regeneration are very common, there is no tradition of temple sex or sacred prostitution for either women or men. As already mentioned, there was no prohibition against priests and priestesses marrying and having children. But this tradition changed dramatically in the late third century CE with the rise of the monastic movement with the desert fathers (and some sisters) who removed themselves from society.

Religion and politics were completely interwoven. Most fundamentally, the living king was the earthly incarnation of the solar god Horus. Upon death, he assumed the identity of Osiris, the father of Horus, thereby creating an unbroken succession of father-son regardless

Figure 1.1. Ramesses IV offering food to the god Khonsu. Relief from the Khonsu Temple, c. 1153–1147 BCE. Photo: Emily Teeter. Ramesses IV offers a tray of food (geese, bread, fruits, and vegetables) to the god Khonsu. Four trussed oxen surrounded by more food offerings are laid before the god. The texts relate that Khonsu granted the king "a lifetime as king." The king's text reads "Presenting things to his father Khonsu Nefer-Hotep. May he [the god] make [a state of] given life for the king."

of the actual biological ties of the king to his successor. The gods supported the semi-divine king and, in return, the king promised the gods that he would rule justly and support the cults of the gods. The nature of this reciprocal relationship is illustrated by offering scenes.[24] These scenes are normally narrated by three brief formulaic inscriptions. The first is the recitation by the god, "It is to you that I have given life...," which indicates that the god created (past tense) the king, enabling him to rule and, in turn, to honor the gods. The king's offering is framed in the active: "Giving to him...." In the third text, the god reciprocates by promising the king continued life: "May he (the god) make the state of 'given life' (for the king)."

One of the king's main obligations to the god was to rule the land in accordance with *maat*, the interconnected concept of cosmic balance and truth that was personified by the goddess Maat. This commitment to *maat* is illustrated by offering scenes where the king presents a figure of the goddess Maat to the deities as a visible affirmation of his just rule and the acknowledgment that he will uphold the tenets inherent in *maat*. In the New Kingdom, the king's coronation name was often compounded with Maat, another indication of the association of the king and principle of truth. Some New Kingdom kings are shown presenting a rebus of their name captioned "presenting Maat," suggesting that the king himself was imbued with, or personified, Truth.[25]

The judicial system was also heavily influenced by religion. The king was a semi-divine ruler from whom all policy and laws emanated. In the New Kingdom and later, divine oracles became an important adjunct to the judicial system when dealing with civil matters such as theft, inheritance, and business dealings, and rarely even to confirm the royal succession. Oracles were delivered by the god (the most common at Thebes are of Amun) when the god left the temple in procession, either in the course of festivals or specifically for the purposes of giving a judgment. Oracles could be posed in the form of written yes/no questions, or by the recitation of the names of the accused. The boat that carried the image of the god in processions could move toward or away to indicate yes or no, or the divine will could be made known by the god causing the priests at the bow of the boat to bend down, or by the entire boat shaking when the god became agitated.

There is no tradition of divination by extispicy or augury, of priests using other omens to advise the king, or of court astrologers. In only a few instances the king claimed that the god came to him in a dream during the course of a battle promising to give him strength (Amunhotep II and Merenptah), or that he would accede to the throne (Prince Thutmose).[26] Success on the battlefield was often attributed to the help and favor of the gods, and in the New Kingdom, failure in war was ascribed to the gods "turning their backs against the land."

The Egyptians were not philosophers in the same manner as the Greeks. They had no tradition of discourse and debate. It was not in their nature to ask "why?"; rather, their question was "how?" This resulted in a very clear, but superficial, understanding of the workings of the universe expressed through analogies with visible physical phenomena rather than with the unseen philosophical world.

5. RESEARCH

Sources for research on ancient Egyptian religion include written sources such as Pyramid Texts, Coffin Texts, Books of the Dead, Underworld Books, prayers, hymns, mythological papyri, autobiographies, and historical and literary texts. Wall reliefs and paintings in temples and tombs provide copious data for the performance of offering ceremonies, purification rituals, divine processions, and festivals. These sources are augmented by statues that functioned in the cult, objects from offering ceremonies and funerary cults (mummies, artifacts related to embalming and burial and amulets) and materials that reflect magical practice (magic rods, knives, engraved gems). These texts and objects are contextualized by the remains of temples, tombs, and chapels that provide the setting for religious practice. Our understanding of Egyptian religion is constantly being sharpened by the discovery of new texts, and especially by the reinterpretation of already known sources.

The study of Egyptian religion started in antiquity. Herodotus' accounts are of variable reliability. Assessments given by some classical writers such as Juvenal and Lucian are often unflattering and reflect a lack of understanding of the underlying theology that they criticize or ridicule. Religious practices of the Isis cults of Italy in the Classical Age are so far removed from the original Egyptian theology that they are not helpful for interpreting the original tradition.

More recently, one of the recurring questions about Egyptian religion is whether monotheism underlay the evident polytheism.[27] Le Page Renouf (1880) viewed this in evolutionary terms, suggesting that Egyptian religion was initially monotheistic, and only later became a degenerate polytheistic system. The "neo-monotheism school," led by Etienne Drioton, posited the opposite – that monotheism grew out of polytheism. Most recently, Jan Assmann has suggested that a single transcendent god arose in the New Kingdom.[28]

Closely related to this still-ongoing discussion is the nature of the religion of the Amarna period (late Dynasty 18) and its relationship to the theology of earlier and later periods. Over the years, the interpretation of Amarna theology as monotheism has been tempered by growing awareness of the movement's goal of proclaiming the divinity of the king and queen as a feature of their relationship to the Aton. The concept of henotheism, which was first championed in the early nineteenth century, has again come to the forefront of the argument. In 1989, James Allen described the Amarna theology as a philosophy rather than as a belief system.

A third line of current inquiry is in regard to the growth of personal piety in the New Kingdom, specifically how widespread the trend was and whether it was an outgrowth of the Amarna experience, while others have questioned how pervasive personal piety was in any period.[29]

FURTHER READING

Fundamental works are Hornung 1982 and Morenz 1973. A new approach that compares Egyptian religion in the Dynastic period to the Ptolemaic and Roman can be found in Dunand and Zivie-Coche 2004. Many of Jan Assmann's influential monographs have now been translated into English (1995, 2001). Many of his works touch upon the idea of the existence of a transcendent god and the erosion of the concept of *maat* in the late New Kingdom as a result of the Amarna period. For the Underworld Books of the New Kingdom, Hornung's volumes (1990, 1999) cannot be equaled for their clarity. For a thorough treatment of funerary beliefs based on the textual (and archaeological) evidence, see Assmann 2005. For types of priests, a handy summary is Sauneron 1980, and more updated and detailed information can be found in Teeter 2011. For sacred space and rituals, see Bell 1997 and Haeny 1997. Borghouts 1978 and Ritner 1993 are the best sources for magical texts and practice. For temple cults, see Lorton 1999 and Teeter 2007. Haring 1997 is an invaluable source for economic aspects of temple cults. For the concept of hell, see Hornung 1994, and for ethics Lichtheim 1992, 1997. The best source for popular religion is Sadek 1987, and see also Teeter 1993, 2011. Pinch 1993 is the authority on votive offerings. For Roman religion in Egypt, a topic largely outside this discussion, see Frankfurter 1998 and Dunand and Zivie-Coche 2004. For connections between Maat and the Greek Metis see Faraone and Teeter 2004. The impact of Egyptian religion and culture on the West into modern days is appraised by Hornung 2001. The many works of E. A. W. Budge should be avoided.

CHRONOLOGY

Note: All dates prior to 664 BCE are approximate.

4000–3100 BCE	PRE-DYNASTIC PERIOD	Burials furnished with offerings attest to the belief in life after death. Votive figurines of animal, human, and divine figurines deposited in tombs.
3100–2705 BCE	EARLY DYNASTIC PERIOD or ARCHAIC PERIOD (Dynasties 1–2)	Consolidation of the Egyptian state. First funerary offering texts, funerary stelae, and images of the king.

2705–2250 BCE	OLD KINGDOM (Dynasties 3–6)	
2705–2630 BCE	Dynasty 3	First large-scale stone funerary monuments for kings and stone mastaba tombs for nobility. Elaboration of funerary stelae.
2630–2524 BCE	Dynasty 4	Construction of pyramids in Lower Egypt. Increase in documentation for religion and culture through wall reliefs and written texts.
2524–2400 BCE	Dynasty 5	Appearance of Pyramid Texts that explicate the king's afterlife largely in a solar context. Elaboration of private tombs, wall reliefs, and tomb furnishings. Redefinition of the divinity of the king as reflected by new elements of the titulary.
2400–2250 BCE	Dynasty 6	Height of Old Kingdom tomb decoration with elaborate paintings and reliefs.
2250–2061 BCE	FIRST INTERMEDIATE PERIOD (Dynasties 7–11)	Appearance of Coffin Texts in private tombs.
2061–1784 BCE	MIDDLE KINGDOM (Dynasties 11–12)	
1991–1784 BCE	Dynasty 12	Rise of the god Amun at Thebes.
1784–1550 BCE	SECOND INTERMEDIATE PERIOD (Dynasties 13–17)	Incursion of people from Western Asia into Lower Egypt.
1550–1070 BCE	THE NEW KINGDOM (Dynasties 18–20)	The "Golden Age" of ancient Egypt. Foreign conquest, great building projects in Egypt and Nubia. Very detailed documentation of religion and funerary beliefs in decorated tombs, papyri, and funerary objects. Growing Osirianization of funerary religion.

1570–1293 BCE	Dynasty 18	Period of great building and expansion of the temples in Thebes. Establishment of royal tombs in the Valley of the Kings and Queens. Appearance of the Book of the Dead and Underworld Books. Amarna period with elevation of the Aton above all other deities.
1293–1185 BCE	Dynasty 19	Expansion of the Karnak and Luxor Temples. Increased solar references in the architecture of tombs in the Valley of the Kings. Increase of imagery of deities and religious rituals in private tombs. Architecture of private tombs imitates temples.
1185–1069 BCE	Dynasty 20	Last period of use of the Valley of the Kings as a royal cemetery.
1070–656 BCE	THIRD INTERMEDIATE PERIOD (Dynasties 21–25)	Period of fine coffins, elaborate mummification procedures, mythological papyri, and rise of animal cults. Tombs commissioned for a man and wife generally replaced by cache tombs for an entire family; decoration that had been on tomb walls transferred to coffins. Nubians, who had adopted the worship of Amun, rule Egypt in Dynasty 25.
664–525 BCE	SAITE PERIOD (Dynasty 26)	Period of renaissance in arts and building. Construction of large private tombs at Thebes with walls covered with archaizing images.
525–332 BCE	LATE PERIOD (Dynasties 27–31)	
332–30 BCE	PTOLEMAIC PERIOD	Egypt ruled by Macedonian Greeks (Ptolemies). Period of multiculturalism. Continuation of most religious traditions. Rise

| | | of the cults of Serapis and Apis and widespread popularity of animal cults. |
| 30 BCE–395 CE | ROMAN PERIOD | Egypt annexed to the Roman Empire. Rise of Isis cults and mystery cults. Order of Theodosius that all temples be closed (393 CE). Advent of Christianity and monasticism. |

GLOSSARY

akh: A "transfigured spirit," the form assumed by the deceased upon rebirth in the afterlife.

Amun: A deity with whom the king was associated in the New Kingdom and later periods; known as "the king of the gods."

Atum: A primordial god who existed alone at the beginning of the world. In the tradition of Heliopolis, he is credited with creating the first generation of gods.

ba: An aspect of the human soul that represented the life energy and personality.

maat: The concept of cosmic balance and order personified by the goddess Maat.

Osiris: Legendary first king of Egypt; major deity of the afterlife with whom all people were associated after death.

Notes

1 Redford 1992:231.
2 Hornung 2001:67.
3 Faraone and Teeter 2004.
4 Hornung 2001:75.
5 Ibid., 43, 46.
6 Redford 1997:56.
7 Cialowicz 2007.
8 Hornung 1982:112–113.
9 Assmann 1995:196.
10 For primary sources see Assmann 1975:349–417. For further interpretation see Assmann 1995:190–210.
11 Haring 1997:76.
12 Ibid., 79.
13 Cialowicz 2007.
14 Pinch 1993.
15 Most conveniently, O'Connor 2009:148

16 Ikram 1995:262–64. The latest examples are from the tomb of Queen Isitemkheb D (Dynasty 21).

17 Assmann 2005:324.

18 Ikram 1995:81–108.

19 Teeter 1997:4–5.

20 Assmann 2002:18–19 and Pinch 2002.

21 Haring 1997:383–88.

22 Frood 2007:41.

23 Robins 1993:149.

24 Teeter 1997:81–2. This pattern changed in Dynasties 19–20.

25 Teeter 1997:78.

26 Szpakowska 2003:47–54.

27 See Hornung 1982:15–32 for a detailed history of this debate.

28 Assmann 2001:230–244.

29 Assmann 1989, 2001:198–237 for greater influence of personal piety; Lichtheim 1992:99–102 and Teeter 1997:83–87 for lesser influence.

Works Cited

Allen, James. 1989. "The Natural Philosophy of Akhenaten." In *Religion and Philosophy in Ancient Egypt*. Ed. W. K. Simpson, 89–101. Yale Egyptological Studies 3. New Haven, CT.

Assmann, Jan. 1975. *Aegyptische Hymnen und Gebete*. Zurich.

———. 1989. "State and Religion in the New Kingdom." In *Religion and Philosophy in Ancient Egypt*. Ed. W. K. Simpson, 55–88. Yale Egyptological Studies 3. New Haven, CT.

———. 1995. *Egyptian Solar Religion in the New Kingdom: Re, Amun and the Crisis of Polytheism*. London and New York.

———. 2001. *The Search for God in Ancient Egypt*. Ithaca, NY, and London.

———. 2002. *The Mind of Egypt: History and Meaning in the Time of the Pharaohs*. New York.

———. 2005. *Death and Salvation in Ancient Egypt*. Ithaca, NY, and London.

Bell, Lanny. 1997. "The New Kingdom 'Divine' Temple: The Example of Luxor." In *Temples of Ancient Egypt*. Ed. Byron Schafer, 127–84. Ithaca, NY, and New York.

Borghouts, Joris. 1978. *Ancient Egyptian Magical Texts*. Religious Texts Translation Series: NISABA 9. Leiden.

Cialowicz, Krzystof. 2007. *Discoveries in Tell el-Farkha (the Nile Delta)*. Poznan.

Dunand, François and Christiane Zivie-Coche. 2004. *Gods and Men in Egypt 3000 BCE to 305 CE*. Ithaca, NY, and London.

Faraone, Christopher A. and Emily Teeter. 2004. "Egyptian Maat and Hesiodic Metis." *Mnemosyne* 58: 117–208.

Frankfurter, David. 1998. *Religion in Roman Egypt: Assimilation and Resistance*. Princeton, NJ.

Frood, Elizabeth. 2007. *Biographical Texts from Ramessid Egypt*. Atlanta.

Haeny, Gerhard. 1997. "New Kingdom 'Mortuary Temples' and 'Mansions of Millions of Years'." In *Temples of Ancient Egypt*. Ed. Byron Schafer, 86–126. Ithaca, NY, and New York.

Haring, B. J. J. 1997. *Divine Households: Administrative and Economic Aspects of the New Kingdom Royal Memorial Temples in Western Thebes.* Egyptologische Uitgaven 13. Leiden.

Hornung, Erik. 1982. *Conceptions of God in Ancient Egypt: The One and the Many.* Ithaca, NY, and New York.

———. 1990. *The Valley of the Kings.* New York.

———. 1994. "Black Holes Viewed from Within: Hell in Ancient Egyptian Thought." *Diogenes* 42(1): 133–56.

———. 1999. *The Ancient Egyptian Books of the Afterlife.* Ithaca, NY, and London.

———. 2001. *The Secret Lore of Egypt: Its Impact on the West.* Ithaca, NY, and London.

Ikram, Salima. 1995. *Choice Cuts: Meat Production in Ancient Egypt.* Leuven.

Lichtheim, Miriam. 1992. *Maat in Egyptian Autobiographies and Related Studies.* Orbis Biblicus et Orientalis 120. Freiburg and Göttingen.

———. 1997. *Moral Values in Ancient Egypt.* Orbis Biblicus et Orientalis 155. Freiburg and Göttingen.

Lorton, David. 1999. "The Theology of Cult Statues in Ancient Egypt." In *Born in Heaven: Made on Earth: The Making of the Cult Image in the Ancient Near East.* Ed. M. B. Dick, 123–201. Winona Lake, IN.

Morenz, Siegfried. 1973. *Egyptian Religion.* Ithaca, NY.

O'Connor, David. 2009. *Abydos: Egypt's First Pharaohs and the Cult of Osiris.* New York.

Pinch, Geraldine. 1993. *Votive Offerings for Hathor.* Oxford.

———. 2002. *A Handbook of Egyptian Mythology.* Santa Barbara, Denver, and Oxford.

Redford, Donald. 1992. *Egypt, Canaan, and Israel in Ancient Times.* Princeton, NJ.

———. 1997. "Egypt and the World Beyond." In *Ancient Egypt.* Ed. David Silverman, 40–57. London.

Renouf, P. le Page. 1880. *Lectures on the Origin and Growth of Religion.* London.

Ritner, Robert. 1993. *The Mechanics of Ancient Egyptian Magical Practice.* Studies in Ancient Oriental Civilizations 54. Chicago.

Robins, Gay. 1993. *Women in Ancient Egypt.* London.

Sadek, Ashraf I. 1987. *Popular Religion in Ancient Egypt.* Hildesheimer Ägyptologische Beiträge 27. Hildesheim.

Sauneron, Serge. 1980. *The Priests of Ancient Egypt.* New York.

Szpakowska, Kasia. 2003. *Behind Closed Eyes: Dreams and Nightmares in Ancient Egypt.* Swansea, Wales.

Teeter, Emily. 1993. "Popular Religion in Ancient Egypt." *KMT: A Modern Journal of Egyptology* 4: 28–37.

———. 1997. *The Presentation of Maat: Ritual and Legitimacy in Ancient Egypt.* Studies in Ancient Oriental Civilizations 57. Chicago.

———. 2007. "Temple Cults." In *The Egyptian World.* Ed. Toby Wilkinson, 310–24. London and New York.

———. 2011. *Religion and Ritual in Ancient Egypt.* New York.

2 Mesopotamia

BEATE PONGRATZ-LEISTEN

The religions that developed in the "land between the rivers," approximately corresponding to modern Iraq and northeastern Syria, belonged to a variety of people over several thousand years of history, beginning in the Preceramic Neolithic period (from c. 9500 BCE) and ending with the Late Babylonian period (from 539 BCE). These people included the non-Semitic Sumerians and Semitic Akkadians (c. 3800–2000 BCE), the Assyrians and Babylonians (c. 2000–539 BCE), and other groups such as the Amorites (1810–1760 BCE), the Kassites (1600–1000 BCE), and the Arameans (from 1200 BCE). Moreover, since later territorial and imperial states in the region of Mesopotamia either developed out of an individual city-state, such as Assyria, or were created out of a conglomeration of city-states having a long history as cultural and cultic centers in their own right,[1] such as Babylonia, Mesopotamian religion was primarily local in its character. Only through institutional efforts (such as the foundation of palaces and temples) and theological systematization did religion gain regional and supra-regional features. Notwithstanding the local character of religion in Mesopotamia, archaeological and textual evidence attests to a religious system that was intended to foster cultural cohesion.

I. HISTORICAL DEVELOPMENT

The emergence of religion in human history is a topic hotly debated among biologists, behavioral scientists, paleontologists, and anthropologists.[2] In the ancient Near East, before the emergence of writing, evidence for religious behavior and a religious world view is provided by burials, monumental architecture, and artifacts found in archaeological contexts. The earliest evidence for ritual behavior can be detected in the cave of Shanidar (in today's Kurdistan), as well as in the monumental remains of the hillside sanctuaries in the region of Urfa, that is, Göbeklı Tepe and Nevalı Çori, dating to around 9500 BCE and 7000 BCE, respectively.[3] These sanctuaries displayed large pillars, some of them carved with images of animals, and sculptures, including a more than life-sized human head with a snake. Hundreds of clay figurines discovered at these sites have been interpreted as votive offerings.

With the emergence of urbanization in the alluvial lowlands of southern Mesopotamia during the fifth millennium BCE, the remains of temple structures attest to an anthropomorphic concept of the divine: the deity was thought to inhabit the temple as if a house and to preside over it as head of a household.[4] It is during this early period of urbanization that conventions of the iconographic repertoire reflecting ritual behavior, as well as conceptions of divine agency, were developed: these conventions carried into the historic periods until the demise of the Assyrian and Neo-Babylonian Empires in the first millennium BCE.[5]

Earlier scholarly studies took an evolutionary approach to the conception of the divine in Mesopotamian religion.[6] More recent studies, by contrast, have acknowledged that divine agency always acted on a variety of planes – cosmic, mythic, and ritual – and can be distributed into a variety of modes – astral body, statue, emblem, standard, name – evidence for all of which dates to the beginning of writing, if not earlier.[7] Archaeologically, the composite texture of the divine translates into a sacred precinct that combines the temple with a temple tower or ziggurat. Such temple towers grew out of raised temple terraces, the first ones being the White Temple dedicated to the sky god Anu (Ubaid – Jemdet Nasr Periods) as well as the Eanna complex dedicated to Inanna/Ishtar, goddess of love and war, in Uruk (Uruk–Late Babylonian periods). Toward the end of the third millennium, the kings of the dynasty of Ur III founded ziggurats for the patron deities of every major city, and these structures were repeatedly restored throughout Mesopotamian history. The ziggurat as a monumental emblem of the Babylonian chief god Marduk survived Babylonian history into modernity as a symbol of colossal architecture, human hubris, and sin. The iconography of the early Mesopotamian glyptic and other artifacts shows banquet scenes and combat scenes with the divine hero smiting wild animals. The latter reflects the notion that cosmic stability is obtained through warfare, a concept that not only accounts for the dynamic aspect of creation but also explains the visual space devoted to this theme on the royal steles of the Early Dynastic period[8] and on steles and reliefs of the later periods. Attempts have been made to find allusions to myth in the iconography of the cylinder seals but, to a large extent, visual arts resist the Western idea of mimetic representation[9] and the illustration of mythological and other narratives in this early period. The famous Uruk Vase (Uruk period), which shows the procession of numerous people and animals for the offerings of the goddess Inanna, is the earliest surviving visual reference to ritual practice. Boat scenes in cylinder seal impressions may reflect the ritual journey of the gods from one city to another on festive occasions;[10] steles of Gudea and Urnamma refer to the building ritual of a temple.[11] Foundation deposits found below the corners of temples, palaces, and private houses attest to the existence of a building ritual initiating the building process from as early as the Late Uruk period.[12] Later plaques making visual reference to rituals performed against the demon-goddess Lamashtu take a mythologizing approach, representing the exorcist in the garb of the mythic sage and referencing the success of the purification of the patient through the representation of Lamashtu being exiled to the netherworld.[13] This evidence attests to the existence of a religious system of which the production and organization from very early on lies in the hands of professional experts.

Given the central position of Mesopotamia in the geography of the ancient Near East, it is not surprising that throughout its historical development Mesopotamian religion participated significantly in the intercultural dialogue of the region. Divided between the northern rolling plains that comprised Assyria and are still part of the rainfall zone and the southern alluvium in which Sumer and later Babylonia were located, Mesopotamia was bounded by the Iranian mountains to the east, the Persian Gulf to the south, the Arabian desert to the southwest, the Syrian steppe to the northwest, and the Anatolian mountains to the north. Migrations due to drought and famine, shifts in the watercourses of the Tigris and the Euphrates, trade, and massive deportations, these latter particularly undertaken during the period of the Assyrian and Babylonian Empires, entailed repeated and substantial demographic shifts. Commerce and diplomacy encouraged the interconnectivity of the various powers and promoted the circulation not only of elite goods and iconographic motifs but also of religious experts, religious texts, and divinities as carriers of identity. Indeed, statues of gods and cultic paraphernalia made of exotic valuable materials such as metals and semi-precious stones are the products and indicators of trade relations. Cuneiform culture, which rapidly spread from southern Mesopotamia into the entire ancient Near East, not only served as a tool of communication and of external storage of the human memory, but also developed into a medium of scholarly prestige and erudite lore. God lists developed as part of that tradition and demonstrate the in-depth exploration and knowledge of the writing system.[14] Additionally, the dynamics of the cultural encounters described previously, as well as the co-existence of Sumerians and Semites in southern Mesopotamia, required a continual systematization of the local, regional, and supra-regional pantheons and resulted in bilingual or even multilingual god lists. Originating in the Early Dynastic period[15] these god lists culminated in the great list AN (=Anum), a compilation of seven tablets listing about 2,000 god names organized in hierarchical order and headed by the former triad of Anu, Enlil, and Ea, each of whom is introduced with his divine court including consort, children, and a retinue of servants.[16] Driven by an *esprit collectionnaire*, these encyclopedic lists differ significantly in their organizing nature and intention from Mesopotamian myth in which we might find the strategy of deranking and killing foreign gods as forms of reorganization. Such is the case in the Old Babylonian myth of *Girra and Elamatum*, for example, in which Enlil transforms into a celestial body, the goddess Elamatum ("woman of Elam"), held responsible for famine and the failure of the herds to breed and therefore killed by the fire god Girra.[17] This transformation is reminiscent of Marduk's use of the body of Tiamat as the structural elements for creating the universe in the *Creation Epic* in the first millennium BCE. In the purification ritual *Šurpu*, Elamatum survives as an evil force among the sorceresses listed – the women of Gutium, Sutium, Lullubu, and Hanigalbat – who are to be exorcised by fire, that is, by Girra.[18] Distinctive forms of knowledge such as treaty-making required the engineering of the trans-local or international involvement of gods of the respective parties and contributed to the trans-regional systematization of the pantheon.

The periodic expansion of political control could generate not only the transfer of roles and functions from one deity to another but also actual identifications. Such is the case with the identification of the Sumerian Inanna with the Semitic Ishtar, of the Sumerian moon god Nanna with Sin, and of the Sumerian sun god Utu with Shamash. Such identifications culminated in the transfer of the Enlilship, that is, the divine rulership, of the Sumero-Babylonian chief god Enlil,[19] to Marduk as he rose into the position of the chief god of the Babylonians.

Close intercultural contact between Mesopotamia and the Syrian-Anatolian realm is apparent in the existence of the Ishtar hypostasis Ishkhara[20] and the Hittite Kubaba,[21] as well as the Hurrian Ishtar Shawushka in Arbail. Another hypostasis of the Hurrian Shawushka is Shawushka of Nineveh.[22]

2. BELIEF

In Mesopotamian religion, the notion of the divine was fluid in nature. In cuneiform writing the classifier *dingir*, "god," could be assigned to heroes, to living and dead kings, as well as to ancestors in general, the temple, cultic paraphernalia,[23] statues of the king, divine symbols and celestial bodies, and, of course, gods and monsters. What linked all of these was their intentionality and agency. In Mesopotamia, divinity thus reached far beyond a single agent imagined in an anthropomorphic form, and, instead, the potentiality of having agency, that is, anthropomorphism, was extended to anything possessing divine quality. Roles and functions could fluctuate between deities and so could their emblems. Thus Marduk, when adopting the role of the warrior-god Ninurta, also appropriated his weapon Sharur, which again, in the myth *The Exploits of Ninurta*, could take on agency in his own right and act as his messenger. The *mushkhushshu*-dragon, for example, could accompany the weather god Adad, the Babylonian chief god Marduk, or Marduk's son Nabu.

Divinity was conceived as a multifaceted assemblage of parts: in addition to the secondary agents listed previously, divine body parts, names, auras, and voices could operate as independent centers of activity.[24] The "hand of the god," for instance, was often said to afflict individuals. Names such as Inanna-morning star or Inanna-evening star clearly link the planet Venus as a secondary agent to the goddess Inanna of Uruk, testifying to a belief system in which a particular celestial body was associated with and acted on behalf of the divinity. Divinity, as personhood, was primarily relational, defined by the functions and roles given in relation to others. Moreover, gods were assigned non-standard cognitive properties such as omniscience, omnipotence, omnipresence, and immortality.[25] As told in succession myths[26] and cultic commentaries[27] gods could still be killed; their deaths, however, did not signify complete annihilation; rather, divine death functioned as a cultural strategy to relegate particular gods to a minor position or, in a process of transformation, their flesh and blood served to create humankind (*Atrahasis Myth* and *Creation Epic Enuma Elish*).

As the Mesopotamian concept of the divine was patterned after a sociomorphic understanding of the world, gods were part of a social network, independent of their form or appearance, whether anthropomorphic, theriomorphic, or hybrid. The gods' actions were defined by their functions and by roles that were based on Mesopotamian social organization. Religion thus reinforced the structure of Mesopotamian society.

Moreover, divine interaction within the polytheistic system guaranteed the cosmic order. Every city had its patron deity who presided over the local pantheon. The close relationship between the city and its deity is reflected in the writing of city names, which might use the same signs or sign as for its patron deity. The divine name Ishkur can thus be read not only as a name for the weather god but also as the name of his city Karkar.[28] On a local level, the multitude of Mesopotamian gods was organized according to human-style kinship and social patterns, so that patron deities were attributed with spouses, children, households, and courts. On a regional level, an overarching cultural-religious tradition strove to integrate the multitude of local gods into a hierarchical system, which comprised the supra-regional pantheon recorded in god lists and myth.

While the Sumero-Babylonian supra-regional pantheon centered on Enlil until the Old Babylonian period, in Babylonia during the Middle Babylonian period, Marduk of Babylon replaced Enlil as the divine leader.[29] In northern Mesopotamia, the growth of Assur into a city-state similarly was associated with the god Assur's rise to become the patron deity of the city and later chief god of the Assyrian pantheon; this happened at the expense of the goddess Ishtar, whose temple, which was constructed at the beginning of the third millennium BCE, antedates the Assur temple by c. one millennium.[30]

Gods of the netherworld include Queen Ereshkigal and her court. Later tradition turns her spouse Nergal, god of pestilence, into the king of the netherworld. Associated with them is the god Erra, likewise a god of pestilence and warfare. Some deities functioned as patron deities of particular "guilds," such as the goddess Nisaba and the god Nabu for the scribes.

In addition to these ideas about divinity, Mesopotamian religion also includes beliefs about the origins and development of the universe, that is, cosmology. In Mesopotamia, no cosmogonic account exists in its own right. Textual tradition does not reflect a primary concern with considering the cosmos solely for the sake of elucidating its origins. Instead, cosmogonies function as analogies and etiologies for a particular plot, figure, or goal of a text or ritual. As such, they typically appear as prologues to larger poems and songs revolving around a specific hero or tool, as well as to dialogues, songs, and omen series. Further, they play a major role in those building rituals and healing rituals that are meant to reestablish a primary state of perfection. The link with a primordial state or figure always signals contact with perfection and anchorage in tradition. Cosmology in Mesopotamia consequently provides the key metaphor and conceptual framework for change and innovation. Even the so-called Babylonian *Creation Epic*, once popularized as a cosmogonic composition, is not concerned so much with the origins of creation as with explaining and justifying Marduk's ascension to the kingship of the Babylonian pantheon. Marduk's creation of the universe, including the firmament, constellations, sun and the phases of the moon for time-reckoning, the rivers and mountains of the earth, as well as humankind, ultimately serves the building of his cultic abode and the creation and maintenance of the cult of the gods. Written in the second half of the second millennium BCE, it originally presupposes a cosmos centered on Babylon;[31] under the Assyrian king Sennacherib, however, it was transferred to the city of Assur and rewritten as a theological statement about the Assyrian chief god Assur.[32]

The contrast of the flat alluvial plain bounded by the Tigris and the Euphrates with the mountainous regions and the steppes and deserts had a deep impact on the mental maps and worldviews of the Mesopotamians. In a systematic thought process of inversion, urban elites conceived of "city life as inherently superior to life in the countryside"[33] and allocated the Other and the enemy to these regions peripheral to the alluvial plain.[34] Sumerian cosmogonies in particular emphasize the technological achievements of irrigation and agriculture, as well as the invention of writing, all products of urban culture. Cosmogonies, therefore, define the city as the central element of divine creation.

Since for Mesopotamian culture the idea of "beginning" harbors the notion of structural instability, which potentially allows for a variety of solutions over time, cosmogonies favor the idea of a creator god as represented by Enki/Ea, who is assisted by the goddess Belet-ili in the *Atrahasis Myth*.[35] In Sumerian cosmogonies, these divine creator figures are not necessarily identical with the divine leader figure: the Sumero-Babylonian chief god Enlil thus separates heaven and earth but leaves the creation of humankind to the deities just mentioned. Only with the rise of territorial states in the second half of the second millennium BCE are these various functions united in the chief deity to enhance and foster the image of the leader's superiority. Already in the Old Babylonian period, Sumerian and Babylonian cosmogonies turn into narratives about the cosmic battle, shifting their focus to the binary perspective of the known/controlled territory versus the unknown/uncontrolled world, and bring the conflict to the fore. The turn toward a divine leader figure as epitomized by Marduk in the Babylonian *Creation Epic*[36] is a reflection of the necessity of legitimizing strong military leadership and the privileges of a few at the expense of the larger population.

Early Sumerian cosmology viewed the world as a horizontal construct in which the netherworld was mapped in the mountains to the east of the alluvial plain and could be reached either via a road, as told in *Ur-Namma's Death*,[37] or a ship, as described in *Gilgamesh, Enkidu and the Netherworld*.[38] This notion is abandoned later in favor of a vertically three-tiered cosmos, comprising the heavens above, the earth swimming upon the freshwater ocean in the middle, and the netherworld below. The upper hemisphere and the lower hemisphere are seen as virtually identical counterparts of one another, expressed in the terms Heaven–Earth, wherein Earth includes both the terrestrial and subterranean levels. All of these realms are surrounded by the saltwater ocean, beyond which lies unchartered space represented in the *Babylonian Map of the World* by triangles.[39] The direct and unbreakable link between the heavens and the lower realms was guaranteed by the cosmic mooring rope that bound the two hemispheres together. Cities and temples can be seen as the physical location where these two spheres were held together by the cosmic bonds, as is Nippur with the Enlil Temple and later Babylon with the Temple of Marduk.[40] Such conceptualization importantly implies that neither on earth nor in heaven can anything happen without affecting the other sphere, a notion that explains the central role of divination in Mesopotamian life.[41]

Mythology furthermore presents a binary perspective of center and periphery in which the center is controlled by the anthropomorphic gods, while the periphery, that is, everything beyond the city walls, is perceived as the home of the demons. The world beyond is the home of the monsters that have to be battled by the warrior-gods as described both in Sumerian poems such as *Ninurta's Exploits* and *Ninurta's Return to Nippur*[42] and in Babylonian compositions such as the *Anzû Epic* and the *Creation Epic*.[43] In addition to pushing any potential threat to the margins of the controlled or known world, this spatial model also includes the Below as part of the extra-human world, a home to demons, netherworld gods, and spirits of the ancestors. Even the heavenly gods are not allowed to transgress the boundaries of the Below. When a god did trespass, as told in the Sumerian and Babylonian versions of *Inanna's/ Ishtar's Descent to the Netherworld*,[44] he or she had to provide a substitute for the time when they wanted to leave the netherworld. Although visualized as a city with a palace and a social structure, Mesopotamian tradition conceived of the afterlife as an inversion of life where food was dust and water was salty. Only privileged conditions in life, such as being blessed with several sons and attaining a superior rank in society, could alleviate the gloomy situation in the netherworld, a reason why we might find lavish displays of goods and former possessions as well as equipment for the afterlife in graves and tombs.[45]

3. PRACTICE

Knowledge about Mesopotamian ritual can be gleaned not only from ritual prescriptions but also from prayers, hymns, letters, and royal inscriptions, all of which might contain references to ritual performance. Offering lists and administrative texts with dates of festive rituals and hints to locations of the performance of the offering might help to reconstruct a ritual to some extent. While Sumerian ritual prescriptive texts do not exist, short subscripts at the end of liturgical texts and incantations with regard to their performance indicate their ritual context. By contrast, Eblaite and Akkadian literature provides rich material for ritual texts. Rituals required the presence of professional experts, as their efficacy was based on the correct sequential performance of ritual actions and recitations of prayers and incantations. This applied to the performance of extispicy and healing rituals as well as the daily cult in the temple. All rituals had to be performed in a place segregated from daily life – either defined by means of a circle of flour, contained within a reed hut, upon the roof of a house, or in the temple. Setting up figurines later to be buried or ritually discarded could also serve to define sacred space. Prerequisite to serving the gods was a perfect integrity of the body and a state of absolute purity,[46] to be obtained by means of ritual procedures, the observance of eating taboos, and the following of regulations regarding clean clothing.[47] Washing of the mouth before communicating with the divine could also be part of the purification rites.[48] Furthermore, the speech of the ritual performer had to be clear, the breath agreeable (eating taboos), and the person had to be physically intact.

Daily ritual actions in the temple included the awakening of the temple, the opening of the gates, the sprinkling of water, the preparation of the offering table, and the greeting and clothing of the deities. Newly fashioned statues of gods and cultic paraphernalia were subject to the mouth-washing ritual in order to segregate them from their human origins and simultaneously "animate" them in a way that allowed them to interact with humans on behalf of the divine.[49]

Beyond the performance of the daily cult in the temple, a large body of texts includes purification rituals of elimination and substitution with lengthy incantations.[50] Eliminatory rites often work by analogy to purify somebody from having transgressed any taboos or offenses against a deity.[51] The ritual of the substitute king, triggered by solar and lunar eclipses and interpreted as an expression of divine wrath, is attested primarily in Neo-Assyrian contexts. It represents a particular case of eliminatory rites in which, instead of a living or dead animal, a human being (prisoner of war, criminal) had to assimilate negative elements and events threatening the real king and take them down to the netherworld. While the substitute king was supposed to sit on the throne for the prescribed period of threat, the real king retired to a separate structure, where, in the guise of a "farmer," he would continue to exercise his royal duties while performing numerous purification rites to reestablish his communication with the gods and to maintain the cosmic order.[52] Beyond the corpus of purification rituals there are the building rituals, which exist as ritual prescriptive texts[53] as well as woven into the literary narrative of a building hymn.[54]

Sacred time and space played an important role in Mesopotamian religious practice. Time was imagined in two complementary models: linear, as in the case of human life or history, and cyclical, as determined by nature, such as day and night, and lunar months and solar years.[55] The division of the month into lunar phases such as new moon on day 1, first quarter on day 6/7, and full moon on day 14/15 marked prominent days in the cultic calendar and gave rise to monthly festivals. The disappearance of the moon at the end of the month was considered dangerous for the king, who had to undergo purification and mourning rites. The agricultural year was marked by the annual flooding of the rivers, which occurred in spring (April/May), the time of harvest. Seeding took place in autumn (October/November). Autumnal and vernal equinoxes determined the semi-annual celebration of the *akītu*-festival. The life and death of the vegetation defined the Dumuzi cycle, and the dead were remembered during the festival/month of the summer month Abu.[56]

Particular places in nature, such as mountains, rivers, or trees, as well as in the city, such as city walls and streets, could be considered controlled by a deity, as reflected by the ceremonial names given to such entities, most of which were listed in topographical texts.[57] In addition, sacred space included constructed localities such as temples, mausolea, and terraces and temple towers dedicated to deities, as well as temporary structures, such as reed huts or circles defined by a sprinkle of flour for use in purification rituals. The temple encoded cultural identity, a phenomenon apparent in the city laments, which deplore the gods leaving their temple in times of crisis. The ground plan of the temple had to be revealed by the gods, and its building or restoration was preceded by dream messages and extispicy to ensure divine origins. Foundation rites and purification rites marked the temple as sacred. Visually, the sacred precinct was set off from its surroundings by its monumentality, as well as by a wall surrounding it. The exterior walls of sacred buildings were characterized by their alternating niches and buttresses.

Responsibility for the maintenance of the temple cult was vested in the institution of kingship. Among the Sumerians, the king could adopt a priestly title such as the "Purification Priest of Anum." In contrast to Assyria, however, where the king was the First Priest of Assur and acted accordingly in the state rituals, Sumerian and Babylonian kings never assumed a central role in the state cult. Even during the Babylonian New Year festival the king did not perform any regular cultic duty. Performing the negative confession to assure the god that he had not violated the privileges of the citizens of Babylon and taking the god Marduk by the hand to invite him to perform the procession to the festival house was a signal of the king's legitimate right to rulership over Babylonia, but otherwise he did not engage in any cultic activity. The Sacred Marriage (hierogamy) envisioned to be performed between the king and the goddess Inanna/Ishtar in Sumerian and Old Babylonian love poetry and the theogamy ritually performed between a male deity and his consort (third to first millennia BCE) served as a setting to approve the king in his cultic care for the gods and in providing abundance and justice for the land, to confer divine knowledge and divine blessing.[58]

Kings could appoint their daughters as high priestesses chosen and confirmed by means of oracular procedure to a deity.[59] The installation of a high priestess was treated analogously to marriage rites, as can be gleaned from the ritual of the *entu* priestess in Emar.[60] Similarly, ordinary families could dedicate their daughters to the service of a divinity, as in the cases of the Old Babylonian *nadītu*-women in Sippar[61] and the *ugbabtu*-women in Nippur, Mari, and Susa.

Other religious personnel involved in the temple cult included large numbers of cultic specialists and temple officials engaged in the performance of the daily cult and maintenance of the temple. The duties of the personnel were clearly defined and limited to specific tasks. The competence of the cultic personnel did not extend beyond the enclosure walls of the temple, and they were not typically involved in the communication between ordinary people and the divine. Instead, their activities during the daily cult were confined to formal ritualism, including feeding and clothing the gods, performing prayers and offerings, and examining the entrails of sacrificial animals for omens. Religious personnel lived off of allocations and a portion of the offerings that were distributed after the god's meal. Over time the temple offices were passed on by inheritance, sale, or rentals and thus were turned into prebends. High-ranking administrators were also among the recipients of royal grants that included estates and other goods.

4. SOCIAL CONTEXT

Ancient Near Eastern societies did not make a distinction between religious and secular power. Their cultural discourse sacralized kingship and the sociopolitical hierarchy, which was thought to have been established by the gods. Myth imagined the king to be made of the flesh of the gods, equipped not only with surpassing wisdom and knowledge but also physical perfection and extraordinary strength.[62] He was considered to partake in the divine scheme and bridge the division between mortals and immortals. With the first imperial vision emerging during the Akkad Dynasty, for a short time, the king's distinct status was expressed in writing the royal name with the classifier for god. Later, tropes such as kinship relations and other alliances with the gods prevailed. Communication with the gods by means of divinatory practices – astrology, extispicy, dream oracles, and prophecy – secured proper royal action in harmony with the divine scheme. In image and ritual performance, the perfection of the body of the king visualized and mediated in its perfection the notion of cosmic order. Iconic tropes such as the king trampling on the enemy, stabbing the lion, holding a domesticated animal, and carrying a basket of bricks created the *body politic* of the king and exhibited him in his various roles: as warrior, shepherd of his people (an image adopted from the gods Ninurta and Shamash), and caretaker of the cult. This visual repertoire transformed the body of the king into a signifier for the existing social order and value system. Public ceremonials during which the king appeared in the company of the gods and his triumphal procession after a victorious campaign into the temple of the chief deity added to the demonstration of royal power and status.

Spatial dimensions marked the ceremonial representations of political life and were instrumental in producing power and legitimacy as well as a sacred topography of the empire that created a relational space bonding with the political center.[63] During the Ur III period, shrines with statues of the king were dispersed throughout the controlled territory to secure the loyalty of the provinces. In the first millennium, steles showing the king in the company of the gods were set up at the gates of cities in conquered territories to evoke the constant presence of the king, and rock reliefs serving the same purpose of expressing the dominance of the Mesopotamian kings at the command of the gods were carved at great distances from the center. State rituals and festivals had a strong spatial component and were instrumental in producing not only power and legitimacy but also coherence and solidarity between the center and the provinces under its control. During the New Year Festival in Babylon, the gods from other cultic centers traveled to Babylon to honor the chief god Marduk and to take part in the assembly of the gods to determine the destinies of the king and the land, thus reflecting on a divine level the allegiance of the major Babylonian cultic centers to the capital. Beyond Assur, which demonstrates some similarities with Babylon, the *akītu*-festival was also performed in those provincial centers of Assyria that were strategically important to the control of the periphery of the Assyrian Empire. In those cases, the festival was performed on one day only and centered on the procession of the king, who was represented by his garments in the company of the city god.[64] The banquet–ritual *tākultu*, with its blessings to be spoken by every city in favor of king, god, and the city of Assur, aimed at creating an identity predicated on faith in the universality of the Assyrian chief god Assur.[65]

Just as government (in the person of the king) was closely integrated with Mesopotamian religion, so too was ethics. Indeed, religion in terms of "fear of the god" was concerned with proper cultic and social behavior rather than propositional belief. Support of the personal god was guaranteed if the individual attended to the god's wishes and showed comparable kindness to his fellow humans, as illustrated by the Old Babylonian poem *Man and his God*.[66] Various corpora of Mesopotamian literature contain statements about moral concerns and proper human conduct. Among these texts are law corpora more concerned with attesting to the king's awareness of exercising justice among his people, which represent part of the larger corpus of royal inscriptions rather than prescribed legislation;[67] wisdom literature such as proverbs and the *Instructions of Shuruppak*;[68] purification rituals such as *Šurpu*, which in its second tablet lists social misdeeds and cultic offenses;[69] and omen series concerned with human behavior and dream omens. All these texts belonged to the stream of tradition and were aimed at preserving the existing social order, that is, the social hierarchy and the social framework of the family.[70] Adoption and inheritance documents reflect a son's obligation to care for his elderly parents and to continue this care after death by performing the proper funerary rites and regular mortuary cult. Moral standards included the prohibition of homicide, honesty in commercial relations, and the reliability of the spoken word. Sexual ethics treated women within the framework of property rights: in cases of rape of an unmarried free woman or a slave girl, for example, the rapist was sentenced to compensate her father as owner through payments. Some infractions were considered a taboo of a particular deity and were thought to undermine cosmic stability. Although there was a belief in the equation between transgressions and suffering, several texts ponder apparently arbitrary divine inflictions and punishment.[71]

5. RESEARCH

The textual sources for Mesopotamian religion include a great variety of categories, such as economic records concerned with the administration of the temples, offering lists, liturgical calendars, rituals and commentaries on them, hymns, prayers, letter-prayers, myths, dialogues and disputations, compendia of omens, hemerologies, menologies, divinatory reports based on extispicy or astrology, oracles transmitted as reports or worked into letters and literary narratives, dream oracles, the epistolary literature between religious experts and the king, and historiographic sources, such as chronicles and historical narratives. Beyond the textual sources the archaeological record has yielded the architectural remains of temples and palaces, as well as tombs, burials, iconography, statues, figurines, and cultic objects of all kinds that encode information about religion in Mesopotamia.

Modern scholarly discussion of Mesopotamian religion emerges in the context of the debates over Semitic originary monotheism (Urmonotheismus), which developed following the decipherment of the Babylonian texts. The debate with Frantz Delitzsch as one of its main principals[72] focused on the potential dependency between biblical texts and ancient Near Eastern texts (the Bibel-Babel Debate). Another offshoot of that debate was the idea of an astral religion, explaining Mesopotamian mythology as a projection and allegory of the movement of the celestial bodies, first promulgated by Stucken in 1907 and subsequently promoted by Jeremias and Jensen.[73] While Sumero-Babylonian mythology cannot be reduced to the explanation of astral phenomena, the pan-Babylonist movement was important insofar as it brought the cultural interaction between the people of the ancient Near East to the fore. A short time prior to this, the German Assyriologist Jastrow had written a comprehensive study of Mesopotamian religion, in which he took an evolutionary approach from animism to more complex religious systems.[74] In the aftermath of Panbabylonism, Assyriologists for some decades shied away from the topic of religion, revisiting the subject only from 1945, when Dhorme published his study on the religions of the Babylonians and Assyrians.[75] This was followed some decades later by Jacobsen's pioneering and insightful study based primarily on the Sumerian evidence and Oppenheim's work focusing primarily on divination.[76] During this same period, Kramer impelled major advances in discussing and presenting both Mesopotamian mythology and Sumerian religion, followed by Bottéro.[77] Black initiated the important Electronic Text Corpus of Sumerian Literary Texts.[78] Black's collection of Sumerian myths and Dalley and Foster with their collections of Akkadian texts as well as Livingstone's collection of Neo-Assyrian court poetry and cultic commentaries similarly advanced the study and understanding of Assyro-Babylonian mythology and rationalization of religious thought.[79] The history of Mesopotamian religion overall was further advanced by Parpola, who initiated the Melammu Project,[80] which includes the edition of Neo-Assyrian texts published in the series "State Archives of Assyria and State Archives of Assyria Cuneiform Texts," a series of monographs several of which are dedicated to the study of religion, and the publication of the proceedings of the Melammu meetings. It is linked with a database and investigates the continuity and later reception of Mesopotamian culture and religion until Islamic times. The necessity of considering the local aspect of Mesopotamian religion showed in works such as the one by Beaulieu on the pantheon of Uruk.[81] The study of the weather god by Schwemer is representative for a diachronic and synchronic approach to a particular divinity.[82] In recent times, the relationship between polytheistic and monotheistic religious systems and the conceptualization of divinity has been tackled in collective volumes edited by Porter and Pongratz-Leisten, respectively.[83] The work of Glassner and Rochberg provides invaluable insight into the framework of cosmology and divination, and the relationship between science and religion.[84]

FURTHER READING

For a general introduction into the history of the ancient Near East see Van de Mieroop 2007. On aspects of history, society, and religion see Snell 2005 and Leick 2007. For the foundational character of myth and the mythical character of historiography see Liverani 2004. Jacobsen 1976 still represents an insightful study of Mesopotamian religion. For recent introductions see Foster 2007 and Snell 2011.

CHRONOLOGY

9500–6000	**PRECERAMIC NEOLITHIC PERIOD**
6500–3800	Ubaid
	ARCHAIC PERIOD
3800–3500	Uruk
3500–3200	Late Uruk (IV)
3200–2900	Uruk III (Jemdet Nasr)
2900–2350	Early Dynastic Period
	SARGONIC PERIOD
2350–2150	Akkad Dynasty
2150	Gutian Interregnum
2113–2017	**Ur III**

	OLD ASSYRIAN (1950–1750)	**ISIN-LARSA/ OLD BABYLONIAN** (2017–1600)
1900–1830	Kanesh/Kültepe, Anatolia	
1810–1760	Amorites, Shamshi-Adad	1595 Hittite sack of Babylon
	MIDDLE ASSYRIAN (1500–1000)	**MIDDLE BABYLONIAN** Kassite Dynasty (1600–1000)
	NEO-ASSYRIAN (1000–600)	**NEO-BABYLONIAN (1000–539)**
		LATE BABYLONIAN (539–Parthian)
	Arameans (1200–....)	

GLOSSARY

Akkadian: Oldest known Semitic language of the Eastern branch of the Semitic family.

Eblaite: A dialect or sub-branch of Akkadian and as such part of the Eastern branch of the Semitic languages. Only attested for some generations in the city of Ebla during the middle of the third millennium BCE, its historical development cannot be reconstructed.

hemerology: List of auspicious days.

hypostasis: Originally a Greek term used in Christian theology to denote the Father, the Son, and the Holy Spirit, "hypostasis" came to serve as a critical term in religious studies to denote a mode or facet of a particular deity.

menology: List of propitious months.

Notes

1   Van de Mieroop 1999 and 2007.
2   Renfrew and Morley 2009.
3   Schmidt 2006.
4   Rubio 2007:14.
5   Frankfort 1951 and Algaze 2008.
6   Jacobsen 1976, Bottéro 2001, and Lambert 1990.

7   Rochberg 1996, Selz 1997, Porter 2009, and Pongratz-Leisten 2011.
8   Bahrani 2008.
9   Bahrani 2003.
10 Pongratz-Leisten 2006.
11 Suter 2000.
12 Ellis 1968.
13 Wiggermann 2000.
14 Mander 1986, Krebernik 1986, Litke 1998, Richter 1999 and 2004, Peterson 2009, and Rubio 2011.
15 Rubio 2011.
16 Litke 1998.
17 Walker 1983.
18 Reiner 1958.
19 Wang 2011.
20 Prechel 1996.
21 Hawkins 1980–1983.
22 Such-Gutierrez 2003:366.
23 Porter 2009.
24 Winter 2007 and Pongratz-Leisten 2011.
25 Boyer 2001:85.
26 Foster 2005:III.17, 18b.
27 Livingstone 1989:81–105.
28 Schwemer 2001:11.
29 Abusch 1995.
30 Heinrich 1982:107.
31 Foster 2007:183.
32 Lambert 1997.
33 Schwartz and Falconer 1994:1.
34 Pongratz-Leisten 2001.
35 Foster 2005:II.36.
36 Ibid., III.17.
37 Flückiger-Hawker 1999.
38 Frayne 2001.
39 Horowitz 1998 and Rochberg 2005.
40 George 1986.
41 Pongratz-Leisten 1999 and Rochberg 2004.
42 Black 2004:163–186.
43 Foster 2005:III.23 and 17.
44 Ibid., III.19.
45 Feldman 2006:173.
46 Pongratz-Leisten 2009.
47 Sallaberger and Huber Vulliet 2005:§3.
48 Walker and Dick 2001:11.
49 Walker and Dick 2001.
50 Reiner 1958, Maul 1994, and Abusch and Schwemer 2008.
51 Schwemer 2007.
52 Parpola 2007.
53 Ambos 2004.

54   Edzard 1997.
55   Sallaberger 2004.
56   Tsukimoto 1985.
57   George 1992.
58   Pongratz-Leisten 2008.
59   Westenholz 2006.
60   Fleming 1992.
61   Harris 1975
62   *Gilgamesh Epic:* George 2003; *Tukulti-Ninurta Epic:* Foster 2005:III.1.
63   Smith 2003:101.
64   Pongratz-Leisten 1997 and Weissert 1997.
65   Pongratz-Leisten 2007.
66   Foster 2005:II.13.
67   Roth 1997.
68   Alster 2005.
69   Toorn 1985.
70   Eichler 2005.
71   Foster 2005:II.13, III.14, III.49d, IV.19.
72   Delitzsch 1903, 1905.
73   Stucken 1907, Jeremias 1911, and Jensen 1906.
74   Jastrow 1898.
75   Dhorme 1945.
76   Jacobsen 1976 and Oppenheim 1977.
77   Kramer/Maier 1989 and Bottéro 2001.
78   Electronic Text Corpus of Sumerian Literary Texts: http://www-etcsl.orient.
     ox.ac.uk.
79   Black 2004, Dalley 1989, and Foster 2005.
80   Melammu Project: http://www.aakkl.helsinki.fi/melammu/.
81   Beaulieu 2003.
82   Schwemer 2001.
83   Porter 2009 and Pongratz-Leisten 2011.
84   Glassner 2011 and Rochberg 2010.

Works Cited

Abusch, T. 1995. "Marduk." In *Dictionary of Deities and Demons.* Ed. K. van der
     Toorn et al., 1014–1026. Leiden.
Abusch, T. and D. Schwemer. 2008. "Das Abwehrzauber-Ritual Maqlû
     (>Verbrennung<)." In *Texte aus der Umwelt des Alten Testaments Neue
     Folge* 4. Ed. B. Janowski and G. Wilhelm, 128–186. Gütersloh.
Algaze, G. 2008. *Ancient Mesopotamia at the Dawn of Civilization: The
     Evolution of an Urban Landscape.* Chicago and London.
Alster, B. 2005. *Wisdom of Ancient Sumer.* Bethesda, MD.
Ambos, C. 2004. *Mesopotamische Baurituale aus dem 1. Jahrtausend v. Chr.*
     Dresden.
Bahrani, Z. 2003. *The Graven Image: Representation in Babylonia and Assyria.*
     Philadelphia.
———. 2008. *Rituals of War: The Body and Violence in Mesopotamia.* New York
     and Cambridge.

Beaulieu, P.-A. 2003. *The Pantheon of Uruk During the Neo-Babylonian Period*. Leiden and Boston.

Black, J. A. 2004. *Literature of Ancient Sumer*. Oxford and New York.

Bottéro, J. 2001. *Religion in Ancient Mesopotamia*. Trans. T. L. Fagan. Chicago.

Bottéro, J. and S. N. Kramer. 1989. *Lorsque les dieux faisaient l'homme*. Paris.

Boyer, P. 2001. *Religion Explained: The Evolutionary Origins of Religious Thought*. New York.

Dalley, S. 1989. *Myths from Mesopotamia*. Oxford.

Delitzsch, F. 1902. *Babel und Bibel*. Leipzig.

———. 1903. *Zweiter Vortrag über Babel und Bibel*. Stuttgart.

———. 1905. *Babel und Bibel*, dritter (Schluss-) Vortrag (Stuttgart 1905).

Dhorme, E. 1945. *Les religions de Babylonie et d'Assyrie*. Paris.

Edzard, D. O. 1997. *Gudea and His Dynasty*. Toronto.

Eichler, B. L. 2005. "Ethics and Law Codes. Mesopotamia." In *Religions of the Ancient World*. Ed. Sarah I. Johnston, 516–519. Cambridge, MA, and London.

Electronic Text Corpus of Sumerian Literature. http://www-etcsl.orient.ox.ac.uk.

Ellis, R. S. 1968. *Foundation Deposits in Ancient Mesopotamia*. New Haven, CT.

Feldman, M. H. 2006. *Diplomacy by Design: Luxury Arts and an "International Style" in the Ancient Near East, 1400–1200 BCE*. Chicago and London.

Fleming, D. H. 1992. *The Installation of Ba'al's High Priestess at Emar*. Atlanta.

Flückiger-Hawker, E. 1999. *Urnamma of Ur in Sumerian Literary Tradition*. Fribourg and Göttingen.

Foster, B. R. 2005. *Before the Muses*. Bethesda, MD.

———. 2007. "Mesopotamia." In *A Handbook of Ancient Religions*. Ed. John R. Hinnells, 161–213. Cambridge.

Frankfort, H. 1951. *The Birth of Civilization in the Near East*. Bloomington, IN.

Frayne, D. 2001. "The Sumerian Gilgamesh Poems." In *The Epic of Gilgamesh*. Ed. B. R. Foster, 129–143. New York and London.

George, A. R. 1986. "Sennacherib and the Tablet of Destinies." *Iraq* 48: 133–146.

———. 1992. *Babylonian Topographical Texts*. Leuven.

———. 2003. *The Babylonian Gilgamesh Epic*. Oxford and New York.

Glassner J.-J. 2011. "La fabrique des présages en Mésopotamie: la sémiologie des devins." In *La raison des signes. Présages, rites, destin*. Ed. S. Georgoudi, R. Koch Piettre, F. Schmidt et al. Leiden.

Harris, R. 1975. *Ancient Sippar: A Demographic Study of an Old Babylonian City*. Istanbul.

Hawkins, D. 1980–1983. *Kubaba. Reallexikon der Assyriologie*. Berlin and New York.

Heinrich, E. 1982. *Die Tempel und Heiligtümer im alten Mesopotamien*. Berlin.

Horowitz, W. 1998. *Mesopotamian Cosmic Geography*. Winona Lake, IN.

Jacobsen, T. 1976. *The Treasures of Darkness: A History of Mesopotamian Religion*. New Haven, CT, and London.

———. 1987. *The Harps that Once ...* New Haven, CT.

Jastrow, M. 1898. *Religion of Babylonia and Assyria*. Boston.

Jensen, P. 1906. *Das Gilgamesch-Epos in der Weltliteratur*. Strassbourg.

Jeremias, A. 1911. *The Old Testament in the Light of the Ancient Near East.* London and New York.

Kramer, S. N. 1961. *Sumerian Mythology.* New York.

———. 1969. *The Sacred Marriage Rite.* Bloomington and London.

——— & J. Maier. 1989. *Myths of Enki, the Crafty God.* New York.

Krebernik, M. 1986. "Die Götterlisten aus Fara." *Zeitschrift für Assyriologie* 76: 161–204.

Lambert, W. G. 1990. "Ancient Mesopotamian Gods: Superstition, Philosophy, Theology." *Revue de l'histoire des religions* 207(2): 115–130.

———. 1997. "The Assyrian Recension of Enūma Eliš." In *Assyrien im Wandel der Zeiten. XXXIXe Rencontre Assyriologique Internationale Heidelberg 6–10. Juli 1992.* Ed. H. Waetzoldt and H. Hauptmann, 77–79. Heidelberg.

Leick, G., ed. 2007. *The Babylonian World.* London and New York.

Litke, R. L. 1998. *A Reconstruction of the Babylonian God Lists.* New Haven, CT.

Liverani, M. 2004. *Myth and Politics in Ancient Near Eastern Historiography.* Ithaca, NY.

Livingstone, A. 1989. *Court Poetry and Literary Miscellanea.* Helsinki.

Mander, P. 1986. *Il pantheon di Abū Ṣalābīkh: contributo allo studio del pantheon sumerico-arcaico.* Napoli.

Maul, S. M. 1994. *Zukunftsbewältigung. Eine Untersuchung altorientalischen Denkens anhand der babylonisch-assyrischen Löserituale (Namburbi).* Mainz.

Melammu Project. http://www.aakkl.helsinki.fi/melammu/

Oppenheim, A. 1977. *Ancient Mesopotamia: Portrait of a Dead Civilization.* Chicago.

Parpola, S. 2007. *Letters from Assyrian Scholars to the Kings Esarhaddon and Assurbanipal.* Winona Lake, IN.

Peterson, J. 2009. *God Lists from Old Babylonian Nippur in the University Museum, Philadelphia.* Münster.

Pongratz-Leisten, B. 1997. "The Interplay of Military Strategy and Cultic Practice in Assyrian Politics." In *Assyria 1995.* Ed. S. Parpola and R. M. Whiting, 245–252. Helsinki.

———. 1999. *Herrschaftswissen in Mesopotamien: Formen der Kommunikation zwischen Gott und König im 2. Und 1. Jahrtausend v. Chr.* Helsinki.

———. 2001. "The Other and the Enemy in the Mesopotamian Conception of the World." In *Melammu Symposia* II. Ed. R. M. Whiting, 195–231. Helsinki.

———. 2006. "Prozession(sstrasse). A." *Reallexikon der Assyriologie* 11: 98–103.

———. 2007. "Rituelle Strategien zur Definition von Zentrum und Peripherie in der assyrischen Religion." *Saeculum* 58: 185–204.

———. 2008. "Sacred Marriage and the Transfer of Divine Knowledge: Alliances between the Gods and the King in Ancient Mesopotamia." In *Sacred Marriages.* Ed. M. Nissinen and R. Ur, 43–73. Winona Lake, IN.

———. 2009. "Reflections on the Translatability of the Notion of Holiness." In *Of God(s), Trees, Kings, and Scholars: Neo-Assyrian and Related Studies in Honour of Simo Parpola.* Ed. M. Luukko et al. Studia Orientalia 106: 409–427. Helsinki.

———. 2011. "Divine Agency and Astralization of the Gods in Ancient Mesopotamia." In *Reconsidering Revolutionary Monotheism*. Ed. B. Pongratz-Leisten. Winona Lake, IN.

Porter, P. N. 1997. "One God or Many? Concepts of Divinity in the Ancient World." *Transactions of the Casco Bay Assyriological Institute* 1.

———, ed. 2009. *"What is a God?" Transactions of the Casco Bay Assyriological Institute* 2.

Prechel, D. 1996. *Die Göttin Ishara*. Münster.

Reiner, E. 1958. *Šurpu. A Collection of Sumerian and Akkadian Incantations. Archiv für Orientforschung, Beiheft* 11. Graz.

Renfrew, C. and I. Morley. 2009. *Becoming Human: Innovation in Prehistoric Material and Spiritual Culture*. Cambridge.

Richter, Th. 1999 (2004, 2nd ed.). *Untersuchungen zu den lokalen Panthea Süd- und Mittelbabyloniens in altbabylonischer Zeit*. Münster.

Rochberg, F. 1996. "Personifications and Metaphors in Babylonian Celestial Omina." *Journal of the American Oriental Society* 116: 475–485.

———. 2004. *Heavenly Writing*. Cambridge.

———. 2005. "Mesopotamian Cosmology." In *A Companion to the Ancient Near East*. Ed. D. C. Snell, 316–329. Malden, MA, and Oxford.

———. 2010. *In the Path of the Moon. Babylonian Celestial Divination and its Legacy*. Leiden and Boston.

Roth, M. T. 1997. *Law Collections from Mesopotamia and Asia Minor*. Atlanta.

Rubio, G. 2007. In *Current Issues in the History of the Ancient Near East*. Ed. M. W. Chavalas, 7–51. Claremont.

———. 2011. "Mapping the Pantheon in Early Mesopotamia." In *Reconsidering Revolutionary Monotheism*. Ed. B. Pongratz-Leisten, 89–115. Winona Lake, IN.

Sallaberger, W. 2004. "Mesopotamia. Sacred Times." In *Religions of the Ancient World*. Ed. Sarah I. Johnston, 250–253. Cambridge, MA, and London.

———. 2007. "Ritual. A." In *Reallexikon der Assyriologie*, 421–30. Berlin and New York.

Sallaberger, W. and F. Huber Vulliet. 2005. "Priester. A. I." In *Reallexikon der Assyriologie* 10/7./8. Lief., 617–640. Berlin and New York.

Schmidt, K. 2006. *Sie bauten die ersten Tempel. Das rätselhafte Heiligtum der Steinzeitjäger*. München.

Schwartz, G. M. and S. E. Falconer, eds. 1994. *Archaeological Views from the Countryside. Village Communities in Complex Societies*. Washington and London.

Schwemer, D. 2001. *Wettergottgestalten. Die Wettergottgestalten Mesopotamiens und Nordsyriens im Zeitalter der Keilschriftkulturen*. Wiesbaden.

———. 2007. *Abwehrzauber und Behexung*. Wiesbaden.

Selz, G. J. 1997. "The Holy Drum, the Spear, and the Harp: Towards an Understanding of the Problems of Deification in Third Millennium Mesopotamia." In *Sumerian Gods and Their Representations*. Ed. I. L. Finkel and M. J. Geller, 167–209. Groningen.

Sjöberg, Å. W. 2002. "In the Beginning." In *Riches Hidden in Secret Places. Ancient Near Eastern Studies in Memory of Thorkild Jacobsen*. Ed. Tzvi Abusch, 229–247. Winona Lake, IN.

Smith, A. T. 2003. *The Political Landscape*. Berkeley et al.

Snell, D. C. 2005. *A Companion to the Ancient Near East. Blackwell Companions to the Ancient World*. Oxford.

———. 2011. *Religions of the Ancient Near East*. Cambridge and New York.

Stucken, E. 1907. *Astralmythen. Religionsgeschichtliche Untersuchungen*. Leipzig.

Such-Gutierrez, M. 2003. *Beiträge zum Pantheon von Nippur im 3. Jahrtausend*. Rome.

Suter, C. 2000. *Gudea's Temple Building: The Representation of an Early Mesopotamian Ruler in Text and Image*. Groningen.

Toorn, K. van der. 1985. *Sin and Sanction in Israel and Mesopotamia: A Comparative Study*. Aasen/Maastricht.

———. 1996. *Family Religion in Babylonia, Syria & Israel*. Leiden, New York, and Köln.

———. 2008. "Family Religion in Second Millennium West Asia (Mesopotamia, Emar, Nuzi)." In *Household and Family Religion in Antiquity*. Ed. John Bodel and Saul M. Olyan, 20–36. Malden, MA.

Tsukimoto, A. 1985. *Untersuchungen zur Totenpflege* (kispum) *im alten Mesopotamien*. Kevelaer and Neukirchen-Vluyn.

Van de Mieroop, M. 1999. *The Ancient Mesopotamian City*. Oxford.

———. 2007. *A History of the Ancient Near East ca. 3000–323 BC*. 2nd ed. Malden, MA, and Oxford.

Walker, Chr. 1983. "The Myth of Girra and Elamatum." *Anatolian Studies* 33: 151–154.

Walker, Chr. and M. Dick. 2001. *The Induction of the Cult Image in Ancient Mesopotamia*. Helsinki.

Wang, X. 2011. *The Metamorphosis of Enlil in Early Mesopotamia*. Münster.

Weissert, E. 1997. "Royal Hunt and Royal Triumph in a Prism Fragment of Ashurbanipal (82–5-22,2)." In *Assyria 1995*. Ed. S. Parpola and R. Whiting, 339–358. Helsinki.

Westenholz, J. Goodnick. 2006. "Women of Religion in Mesopotamia: The High Priestess in the Temple." *Canadian Society for Mesopotamian Studies Journal* 1: 31–44.

Wiggermann, F. A. M. 2000. "Lamashtu." In *Birth in Babylonia and the Bible*. Ed. M. Stol, 217–249. Groningen.

Winter, I. J. 2007. "Agency Marked, Agency Ascribed: The Affective Object in Ancient Mesopotamia." In *Art's Agency and Art History*. Ed. Robin Osborne and Jeremy Tanner. Malden, MA, and Oxford.

3 Syria-Canaan

SHAWNA DOLANSKY

Syria-Canaan is a geographically, economically, and politically diverse region, including pastoral nomadic populations, agricultural communities, large urban centers, and merchant port cities. The term "Syro-Canaanite" refers to a linguistic, cultural, and religious complex shared among population groups residing in the geographical region of modern Syria, Lebanon, Israel, and Jordan and extending into parts of Iraq and Turkey, from the third through the first millennia BCE. Residents of the various Syro-Canaanite polities not only lived millennia apart from each other but often went to great lengths to distinguish themselves ethnically from each other.[1] Despite this variety, scholars perceive a basic religious and cultural continuity founded on a shared West Semitic language base (although language alone does not explain the continuity; West Semitic Akkad is not considered part of Syria-Canaan) and extending beyond strict geographical boundaries; for example, Syro-Canaanite Ebla was a polity in Mesopotamia; Alalakh, Arslan Tash, and other Iron Age Syro-Canaanite city-states fell within the neo-Hittite complex of ancient Anatolia. Important Syro-Canaanite groups include the Arameans, Amorites, and Phoenicians.

I. HISTORICAL DEVELOPMENT

Paleolithic burials attest to religious thought long before the advent of civilization, and earlier than the development of agriculture in this area is evidence for a monumental community place of worship (Göbekli Tepe, c. 9000 BCE).[2] Permanent human settlement begins in the eighth millennium in Neolithic agricultural villages (e.g., Buqras, Ramad, and Jericho). Our exploration of Syro-Canaanite religion begins with the appearance of written sources in the third millennium, through an examination of iconography and other material remains alongside contemporary texts.

Ebla is the earliest Syro-Canaanite urban polity. Textual remains from 2500–2400 BCE demonstrate close ties to nearby Sumerian Ur and

Kish and evidence of trade with Egypt, and show some religious affinity with Mesopotamian cultures, but a greater continuity with later Syria-Canaan. After Ebla, there is very little in the way of religious texts until the mid-second millennium, although around 1800 BCE Amorite personal names with Eblaite theophoric elements appear. The Amorites traveled in pastoral groups from northwest of Mari along the middle Euphrates and lower Khabur Rivers, infiltrating and becoming powerful in various parts of Mesopotamia and Syria from the turn of the third millennium into the second.

Mari was another Syro-Canaanite power during the Middle Bronze period. Although established in the second millennium, it flourished under the Amorite Lim Dynasty in the nineteenth and eighteenth centuries, and thousands of royal documents have been recovered from this time.

The approximately 1,500 cuneiform tablets discovered at Tel Ras Shamra, the ancient city of Ugarit, are the most significant documents for understanding Syro-Canaanite religion. An Amorite port city, Ugarit was important in international trade between Mesopotamia and Egypt throughout the second millennium, peaking from 1450 to 1200 BCE. Most of the gods and basic religious concepts in the texts are familiar from Ebla, Mari, and attested Amorite names, and continuous with evidence from Emar, a polity on the western side of the Euphrates, from which about 400 texts dated 1340–1190 BCE have been retrieved. Other Late Bronze Age sites with important Syro-Canaanite material remains include Hazor, Lachish, Megiddo, Gezer, 'Ain Dara, Tell Tayinat, Zincirli/Samal, and Alalakh.

The economic and political shifts from the Late Bronze to the Iron Age resulted in the decline of many of these polities, some of which were rebuilt. An important Iron Age influence, Syrian Arameans are first mentioned in Assyrian literature in the late twelfth and eleventh centuries BCE in central and northern Mesopotamia, and groups of Arameans existed in southern Babylon from the beginning of the first millennium BCE. We have few written Aramean sources, mostly in the form of royal building or dedicatory inscriptions from the ninth and eighth centuries BCE.

The Phoenicians appear on the Lebanese coast in the second millennium BCE, but most Phoenician inscriptions come from the early first millennium and include dedicatory or building inscriptions from the port cities of Tyre, Sidon, and Byblos. Phoenician influence spread to the Punic colonies, and textual and iconographical remains pertaining to Phoenician religion and culture can be found as far away as Carthage and even Marseilles.

Other Iron Age cultures of Syria-Canaan include the kingdoms of Edom, Moab, and later Palmyra and Petra; other important sites from this period include Arslan Tash, Karatepe, Taanach, Tel Qasile, and Khirbet Qeiyafah. Despite the movement toward an aniconic monotheism, ancient Israelite biblical texts and archaeological remains demonstrate that this population also shared the basic names and characterizations of Syro-Canaanite deities, as well as associated beliefs and practices.

Syro-Canaanite religion manifested differently throughout the region. Those in sustained contact with Mesopotamia, Egypt, and the Hittites absorbed aspects of these religions and incorporated them into their own beliefs and practices, even as they in turn influenced those larger cultures.

The closest set of religious beliefs to Syria-Canaan both theologically and geographically were those of Mesopotamia. Like Mesopotamians, Syro-Canaanites believed in a pantheon of divine beings who met in a council, ruled by a chief deity or set of deities. Often the chief national god exemplified or represented the state itself. Gods were immanent as both manifestations of tangible phenomena as well as more abstract concepts (e.g., passion, war); their powers were known through nature in the form of crops, weather, natural disasters, disease, and illness, and also through human politics, as the rulers were understood to be the chosen representatives of the gods. Deities required propitiation through gifts and worship and would provide blessings in return. Divination and prophecy indicated a belief that the divine will was written into the very fabric of nature and could be revealed, interpreted, and manipulated by specialists. Illness and other bad fortune were signs of the disfavor of a god or gods, and gods and dead ancestors could be propitiated to avoid or deter such occurrences.

Outside of the Hebrew Bible and the Ugaritic texts – which differ from each other in significant ways – our extant Syro-Canaanite mythological corpus is quite meager relative to those of Mesopotamia and Egypt. However, among the texts we do have, influence from Mesopotamia is clearly discernible: for example, in the centrality of the combat myth. Although the characters differ, reflections of the main plots of Mesopotamian *Lugal-e*, *Anzu*, and *Enuma Elish* appear in both the Ugaritic Baal Cycle (thirteenth century BCE) and in the Hebrew Bible (e.g., Exodus 15; Psalm 89; both in the first millennium BCE[3]): forces of chaos, often the Sea in monstrous form, threaten the established order; the gods panic, empowering a previously lesser god or even an outsider – often the patron god of the ruling dynasty – to confront the forces of chaos on their behalf; he triumphs, is enthroned, and creates (or re-creates) the ordered world. Echoes of the combat motif find their way beyond the Hebrew Bible into Jewish and Christian apocalyptic literature from the second century BCE onward.[4]

Canaanites referred to in Egyptian literature as the Hyksos invaded and ruled Lower Egypt from roughly 1650 to 1550 BCE. Despite Egyptian antipathy toward these foreign rulers, the presence of Canaanite deities in the Egyptian pantheon is discernible thereafter. Baal, the warrior-god of Syria-Canaan, is identified iconographically with Egyptian Seth and further represented in a myth that has Seth pursuing Baal's Ugaritic consort Anat (Papyrus Chester Beatty VII). A Syro-Canaanite goddess, either Astarte or Asherah, is known in Egyptian iconography as Qudshu (West Semitic for "holy one") with her associated Syro-Canaanite artistic motifs of horses,[5] nudity,[6] as well as lions and trees (for which she may have been identified with Egyptian Hathor; in Egyptian-influenced parts of Syria-Canaan she comes to be represented with a Hathor hairstyle). Biblical wisdom literature suggests an absorption of Egyptian philosophy, both directly, as in the case of Proverbs 22–23, reflecting the sentiments (and much of the wording) of the Instruction of Amenemopet (British Museum 10474), and indirectly, for example, the ways in which Wisdom personified in Proverbs 8–9 closely resembles Egyptian portrayals of the goddess Maat.[7]

Hittite religion also shares much in common with Syro-Canaanite and Mesopotamian religions,[8] and influence can be seen in the Hittite preservation of a myth of the god "Elkunirsa" – a Hittite rendering of the West Semitic epithet of the god El, *qone'arts* "creator of the earth" (KAI A iii 18).[9] Hittite culture in turn influenced that of Syria-Canaan, most notably in the treaty format that served as a template for the Israelite conception of divine covenants.[10]

2. BELIEF

The Baal Cycle reflects the Ugaritic sense of dependence on the gods for order, prosperity, and fertility in an economy tied to shipping trade and agriculture. Baal Hadad is the strong, dynamic storm god who battles Yamm (Sea) and Mot (Death) for divine kingship. Anat, the goddess of war and Baal's sister and consort, saves Baal from Mot, El's favorite and ruler of the netherworld. Baal's death brings sterility to the land; his revival offers stability. The forces of Baal and Anat protect life and order by keeping death at bay, with the help of Shapshu, the sun-goddess, who represents divine order and justice.

The gods may have originated as manifestations of natural phenomena in rural and agricultural communities in which the fertility of plants and animals was a central concern. Later urban adaptations reflected in texts, inscriptions, and iconography organized the divine hierarchy along human familial and political social structures. In text and image, the gods are portrayed in human form, some with animal familiars: for example, El and Baal are often identified with a bull, and bovine horns became a symbol of divinity on anthropomorphic images.[11] The goddess Anat assumes the form of a cow to copulate with Baal (KTU 1.V.18–26[12]), and in some Egyptian texts Anat is called "the great cow of Seth."[13] Plants and animals frequently appear as imagery related to the goddesses Asherah and Astarte, and have been interpreted as symbols of their fertility aspects; in Iron Age iconography deities often come to be replaced by their animals and other symbols.[14]

Celestial imagery also abounded throughout Syria-Canaan, and there is evidence for astral religion, a belief that the planets were hypostases of gods, and worshiped as such. Sometimes this was accompanied by celestial divination, based on the notion that the movements of the planets were deliberate messages from gods to humans. While celestial divination assumes astral religion, it itself is not always present where celestial iconography is found; for example, in ancient Israel there is no evidence of celestial divination, but much evidence for astral religion.[15]

Although each polity had its own pantheon, the divine realm was always ordered hierarchically. Gods of minor importance in some pantheons assumed larger or even patronage roles in others. A variety of mythological texts describe a divine couple ruling in heaven, often El and Asherah. Asherah, mother of the gods, was understood to show favor among gods and humans, bestowing governing power on each. El was the father of the gods and humans, but not an active participant in the politics of the next tier of gods below him unless his intervention was necessary to maintain cosmic order. Although El is the head of the Ugaritic pantheon, Baal is representative of the next level in the divine hierarchy: active gods and goddesses striving for the favor of the divine pair and for power. Under these were specialized deities, propitiated for their patronage over certain specific areas (e.g., scribal activity, childbirth, weapons, and tools). At the bottom of the hierarchy were the messenger-gods.

There were about forty gods who received sacrifices at Ebla. One of the most frequently occurring gods from the earliest records through the latest in Syria-Canaan is Hadda/Hadad, known as Baal ("Lord") Hadad, the thunderer. One of Ebla's four gates was named for him; he later became the patron deity of Aram and Ugarit; and he is portrayed as Yahweh's chief rival for Israel's worship in the Hebrew Bible.[16] Dagan, the god of grain, was also widely worshiped throughout Syria-Canaan and became an important god among the Philistines on the Levantine coast in the first millennium. His consort Ishkhara was also popular at Ebla and attested in Mesopotamia and among the Hittites of Anatolia. Kamish, another important Eblaite deity, disappears from the Syro-Canaanite pantheon until resurfacing as the Moabite patron god Chemosh.

Ugaritic texts refer to more than 100 gods, but central were El (Il/Ilu), Dagan, Baal Hadad, Athirat (Asherah), Athtart (Astarte), Kothar, Sapsh, Yarikh, Anat, Rashp (Resheph), and Yamm.

Ur III Amorite names from the end of the third millennium include many with El and some with Hadda. Amorite names from eighteenth-century Mari reflect the importance of Hadda (who also appears as "Baal" in many names), El, Dagan, Anat, Samas (later Shamash, the sun-god), Rasap, and Ashtar.

The chief deity of the Arameans was Baal Hadad. Other gods mentioned in inscriptions include El, Shemesh, and Resheph. Phoenician cities each had their own pantheon, conceived as a council or assembly of the gods, led by a male and female pair: for example, Byblos revered Baal-Shamem, "lord of the heavens," who may be identified with Baal-Hadad (perhaps in combination with older conceptions of El), and Baalat, the "Lady of Byblos" – Asherah, Anat, or Astarte (or all in syncretistic combination) – to whom offerings for well-being were made as far away as Egypt. The chief gods of Sidon were Eshmun, a god of healing, and Astarte; the patron gods of Tyre were Melqart (a form of Baal; the name means "king of the city") and Astarte; and the Punic colony at Carthage revered Baal-Hammon and his consort Tanit, a goddess identified with Astarte in inscriptions whose shrine has been excavated at Sarepta. Inscriptions from Kuntillet 'Ajrud and Khirbet 'el Qom in Iron Age Judah indicate a similar pairing of Israelite Yahweh, identified with El, and Asherah.

Although few details of eschatological beliefs survive from this region, the Ugaritic story of Aqhat indicates that at death the spirit goes out from the nose like wind or smoke. It seems that, as in Mesopotamia, death was considered final and the afterlife dismal and empty. Ugaritic texts refer to the netherworld where the spirit descends as *'arts* (literally "earth"), muddy, putrid, and desolate; ruled by Mot, the deification of death and sterility entered beneath two mountains at the edge of the earth (KTU 1.5, 2.2–3). Later Phoenician mythology has the ruler of the netherworld as Muth (also called Thanatos and Pluto), a son of Cronus in Philo of Byblos. The dead seem to have been propitiated with offerings by their descendants at Ugarit, Ebla, and Emar. At Ugarit they were buried under homes and the royal palace in vaulted tombs reached by staircases under the floors, and pipes and gutters have been interpreted as functioning in the offering of libations.[17]

A funerary ritual text for Ugaritic King Niqmaddu III (KTU 1.161) calls for deceased kings to join the *rapi'uma* (cognate to Hebrew *repa'im* and Phoenician *rp'm*): in other Ugaritic texts, the *rapi'uma* are dead kings invited to feast as their power was invoked on behalf of a new king (KTU 1.20–22). It is possible that the *rapi'uma* were considered divine, and that therefore kings were thought to become gods upon death. Evidence in support of this is the use of a divine determinative on the names of dead kings in lists at both Ebla and Ugarit, and the fact that at Ebla these dead kings received sacrificial offerings. King Panammu of Samal (KAI 214, 750 BCE) enjoins his successor to offer sacrifices to the god Hadad with the words: "May the soul of Panammu eat with you [Hadad], and may the soul of Panammu drink with you! Let him always invoke the soul of Panammu alongside Hadad." The institution of the *marzeah* throughout Syria-Canaan may have also had a mortuary function and involved a communal meal thought by some to have been shared between the living and the dead. At Emar, dead ancestors were revered and propitiated with offerings, but there is no evidence that they were deified.

Although the extent to which the deceased were understood as gods by the living varied, Syro-Canaanite religion involved the propitiation of ancestral figures for blessings, and possibly as intercessors with the greater gods. In the Ugaritic story of Aqhat, one of the duties of a son is described as having to erect a stele for his *ilib*, often translated as "god of the father," but also possibly "divine ancestor."[18] The Eblaite offering lists include a "god of the father" or "divine ancestor" as well. An inscription from Tell Fekherye conveys a sense that the living brought gifts to the gods who shared them with the family ancestors; in Syrian family religion, the cult of the ancestors was combined with the veneration of family gods.[19]

Events in heaven among the gods were understood to have an impact on human life on Earth: in the Baal Cycle, when Mot conquers Baal, drought and famine ensue on Earth until Anat kills Mot and rescues Baal. Hymns, prayers, curses, and incantations recorded in liturgical texts, royal monuments, funerary inscriptions, votive offerings, and amulets from all over Syria-Canaan also demonstrate a basic belief that gods and demons could bring both good and bad fortune. Ugaritic KTU 1.19 records the prayer for Baal's protection that one should invoke "when a mighty one attacks your gates, a warrior your walls," assuring the reader that once pronounced, "then Baal will listen to your prayer, he will drive the mighty one from your gates, the warrior from your walls." Many Phoenician inscriptions survive on burial stelae and votive gifts; some ask for a long life or thank a god for answering a prayer; others are requests for material blessings or offspring. On the Karatepe Stele, King Azitiwada asks Baal for long life, good health, and power for himself, as well as fertility for his land and people. An inscription from Aramean King Zakkur states that Baal-Shamayn ("Lord of the Heavens") answered his prayer through seers and diviners with an oracle of salvation. Liturgical texts throughout Syria-Canaan detail prayers offered for protection and repulsion of enemies.

Gods, in turn, spoke to humans in dreams and through divination, performed by specialists on animal sacrifices, and in their analyses of birth abnormalities and planetary alignment. Gods were invoked in magical incantations against various evils including demons (KTU 1.169), the Evil Eye (KTU 1.96), and snakebites (KTU 1.100).[20] Demons were held responsible for ill fortune, disease, war, and plague, and had to be warded off in liminal situations such as childbirth and illness, as in some Akkadian texts found at Ugarit for warding off the female demon Lamashtu, who sought to eat unborn and newborn babies. Lamashtu amulets from elsewhere in Syro-Canaan are found throughout the first millennium. Phoenician plaques from Arslan Tash were used to ward off malevolent demons, one possibly against the Evil Eye. Gods were also invoked for demonic exorcisms, as in KTU 1.169 and KAI 27, precursors to the Aramaic amulets and magical bowls intended to ward off evil spirits, attested from the late first millennium BCE through the first millennium CE.

Often there is an inferred causal relationship between acting contrary to the will of a god, and becoming ill; for example, in the Ugaritic story, Kirta contracts an illness by the hand of Asherah because he failed to fulfill a vow to the goddess. El heals Kirta by creating the creature Shataqat (literally "the female who causes [illness] to pass"). El may have the epithet Rapiu ("healer") in KTU 1.101. The Sidonian god Eshmun was identified in various sources with the Greek healer-god Asclepius (e.g., KAI 66) and may therefore have been understood as a healing deity.

Ugaritic texts like Kirta and Aqhat also give examples of curses pronounced on towns and people in the name of gods, indicating a belief that gods would ensure that the curses were fulfilled in the same way that they answered worshipers' propitiations for blessings. Likewise, Kilamuwa of Zincirli sought to protect his inscription with the words: "And if anyone smashes this inscription, may Baal-Samad smash his head!" (KAI 24). Aramaic royal monuments, like the Tell Fekherye inscription, describe the curses at the hands of Hadad that would befall any future kings who might remove or alter their statues: "May his people scavenge barley from the garbage dumps to eat. May pestilence, the staff of Nergal, not cease from his land" (KAI 309). Similarly, Phoenician kings protected their graves with curses against those who would disturb their sarcophagi (e.g., KAI 14). Treaties also detailed the curses that the gods would enact on those who would break them, for example, KAI 222 from Sefire.

3. PRACTICE

A correlate of the Syro-Canaanite belief in the mutual dependence and influence of divine and human worlds is the abundance and elaboration of rituals of all types. Sacred space was defined both publically and privately, with elaborate official temples and priesthoods devoted to state gods coexisting with domestic shrines, family gods, and ancestor veneration.

Sacrifice was a central aspect of most public and private rituals, with cattle, sheep, textiles, and precious objects standard offerings for the gods. In texts from Ebla and Emar, sacrifices were denoted by words that signify "provision." The Ugaritic texts yield more detail, with parallels to the system of sacrifice elaborated in the Hebrew Bible: for example, a category of general offerings as well as specific types of sacrifices, with some terms cognate to biblical sacrificial categories. Later Phoenician texts also share cognate terms and concepts with Ugaritic and biblical sacrifices. More than 100 gods, as well as dead kings, were propitiated with sacrifices at Ugarit, at ritual banquets understood to be shared by gods and humans. We do not have any surviving details of the Aramean sacrificial system, but some inscriptions mention offerings of food and drink to the gods, and archaeology (e.g., at Palmyra) yields altars, various kinds of sacred vessels, and incense burners, and shows slaughter primarily of cattle and sheep, with other animals as well. In later Palmyra and Petra, there was a movement toward votive offerings instead of sacrificial, and archaeological finds include dedicated sacred objects as well as parts of buildings, statues, and other monuments.

Phoenician, Punic, and Israelite texts suggest that child sacrifice, known as a *mlk*-sacrifice, was practiced in various Syro-Canaanite polities.[21] Although the Hebrew Bible officially condemns it (Leviticus 18:21, 20:20–25; Deuteronomy 12:31, 18:10), certain biblical passages indicate its occurrence in Israel (2 Kings 17:16–17; Isaiah 30:27–33; Jeremiah 19:5,

32:35; Ezekiel 20:25–26). Sacred precincts for child sacrifices are known from excavations of Punic colonies at Carthage, as well as in Sicily, Sardinia, Spain, and possibly in the Phoenician city of Tyre.[22] A different form of human sacrifice was the devotional proscription, or *herem*, of war spoils – including all human and animal captives – to the god of the victors. The Mesha stele from Moab describes *herem* as the ritual slaughter of enemies in battle in dedication to the god Chemosh. The same concept occurs in the Hebrew Bible; for example, in Deuteronomy 20 *herem* is described as necessary in military encounters with Hittites, Amorites, Canaanites, Perizzites, Hivites, and Jebusites.

Other public rituals included those devoted to purity and atonement, although a dearth of textual evidence creates difficulty in drawing widespread conclusions for all Syria-Canaan in this regard. KTU 1.40 designates sacrifices for "justification" to be offered for the sins of all the people of Ugarit. Ugarit also had a purity system, evidenced by ritual prescriptions for festival participation by the king that include washing to become "pure," *brr* (KTU 1.41; 1.46; 1.87; 1.105; 1.106; 1.112). The requirement of purity in connection with holiness may be implied in the story of Kirta, who purifies himself by washing before making an offering to petition El and Baal (KTU 1.14; 3.52–54). In his description of the cult at Syrian Hierapolis, Lucian mentions purification rituals and the defilement caused by corpses and polluting foods. The most extensive Syro-Canaanite texts relating to pollution and purity are those of the Hebrew Bible, which, when regarded alongside some Mesopotamian ritual purity texts, suggests that the purpose of purity systems was to protect the sanctity of a deity's space from defilement.

Funerary rituals are not greatly detailed in archaeological remains, particularly outside of royal funerals and the texts relating to deceased kings noted earlier. They can, however, be inferred: for example, in the Baal Cycle, the gods mourn the death of Baal by weeping, sitting on the ground, throwing dust on their heads, wearing mourning clothes, lacerating their bodies, and sacrificing animals. It is likely that these actions reflect actual Ugaritic mourning rituals. Elsewhere, professional mourners were hired to gash their flesh and wail.

Vow taking and fulfillment was an important ritual for individuals. Many Aramean and Phoenician inscriptions have been found on objects devoted to gods in fulfillment of a vow (e.g., statues, weapons, altars, and buildings).

Ritual circumcision is also found among some Syro-Canaanites. Early-third-millennium male figures from the 'Amuq valley in North Syria show evidence for circumcision,[23] and according to Herodotus

2.104, some Phoenicians also practiced ritual circumcision. The Hebrew Bible requires ritual circumcision for ancient Israelite males.

From the scant surviving information, rituals surrounding betrothal, marriage, and divorce seem fairly standard. A bride price was presented by a potential groom or his father to the intended bride's father or brother(s), sometimes along with gifts to her, thereby transforming her status to betrothed. Inference from Mesopotamian parallels and biblical texts suggests that weddings involved some combination of feasting, ritualized movement of the bride from the father's house to the husband's house, and sexual intercourse.

Rituals for entry into the priesthood are documented in some texts, and KTU 1.111 and 1.113 from Ugarit describe funerary rituals for kings that served to transition a man from king to god.

In the Ugaritic tale of Aqhat, infertile King Danel offers sacrifices and participates in other rituals in order to have the god appear to him in a dream and grant his wish to be cured. Ugaritic texts attest to ritual specialists empowered to heal venomous snakebites with an incantation, and other incantation texts from Ugarit deal with birth and fertility. It is possible that healing rituals could be associated with public sanctuaries as well. Stager[24] argues that the 1,500 dogs buried at Ashkelon were associated with healing sanctuaries, as in the Hellenistic cult of Asclepius; dogs associated with healing were also found in Mesopotamian temples of Gula and at the Phoenician temple at Kition, Cyprus. Avalos[25] suggests that the metallic serpents in Canaanite sacred precincts (e.g., Megiddo, Hazor, Gezer, Timna, Tel Mevorakh) were also used for healing, as they were in Asclepius shrines; or possibly only for curing snakebites, as they were in Mesopotamia and in the example of Moses' bronze serpent *nehushtan* in the Hebrew Bible.

Divination rituals were important for understanding the will of the gods. The Idrimi Stele of Alalakh mentions divination by observing birds in flight and by examining the entrails (extispicy) of sacrificial sheep. Emar was influenced by similar Mesopotamian omen literature and traditions. At Ugarit, incubation rituals for divine appearances in dreams were practiced in temples, as in the Ugaritic Aqhat legend, and in Kirta, where a divine message is delivered by El to Kirta in a dream. Inscribed arrowheads may indicate divination by observing arrows in flight; liver models from Megiddo, Hazor, and Ugarit demonstrate the practice of Mesopotamian-influenced divinatory examination of the livers of sacrificed animals. There is possible evidence for astrology at Ugarit as well, but it is contentious.[26] Reflections of some of these divinatory practices appear in the Hebrew Bible.[27]

Under increasing political domination in the first millennium, Greco-Roman extispicy is attested as replacing older means of divination. Similarly, the zodiac became a common artistic feature (e.g., in the famous synagogue mosaic at Dura Europos), and classical authors (e.g., Lucian, Herodotus) refer to Syrians as consulting oracles as at Delphi.

Syro-Canaanite public rituals were held in sacred spaces. In the Syrian Middle Bronze Age a typical temple (e.g., at Amorite Ebla) was characterized by a large hall in which the sacrificial altar and other sacred furniture were placed, preceded by an atrium-type enclosure formed by the extended walls. These urban temples were dedicated to particular gods, while royal temples were part of the palace and royal cult, and built with a different structure. Ugarit had two large city temples dedicated to Dagan and Baal, with towers and terraces where the texts describe rites being conducted. Private sanctuaries may have been used for cultic activities under specialized priests and diviners.

An excavated Phoenician temple at Byblos was dedicated to the Lady of Byblos, but nothing remains of the sanctuaries of Tyre dedicated to Baal-Shamen and Melqart. Documents describe Aramean sanctuaries of Hadad at Aleppo and Damascus, but there are no remains; nor are there any of Atargatis' temple at Hierapolis. The temples of Nabu, Bel-Shamen, and Bel of Palmyra remain well preserved and show the influence of Hellenistic architectural style, as do the remains of Nabatean temples in Syria. Solomon's temple, as described in the Hebrew Bible, conforms to the many Syro-Canaanite temple standards attested archaeologically, as do the remains of the temple discovered at Arad in biblical Judah.[28]

Syro-Canaanite religion organized sacred time cyclically. Surviving calendars detail lunar months arranged in a solar cycle of twelve, with feast days established according to particular times in those months; days of the new and full moon had special significance. Lists of activities arranged according to months from Ugarit are the most explicit texts we have specifying sacred times and the ceremonies and offerings they entailed. The first month of the new year and the month of the dead seem to have been particularly important.

Texts from Emar provide four major festival documents. In one, a seven-day *zukru* rite for the year's first new moon (celebrated every seventh year over several months instead) was performed for their chief god Dagan, and included a procession in which the god was taken outside the city and passed between sacred stones anointed with oil and blood representing the council of the gods. An eight-day festival was for the installation of the priestess of Ashtart of Battle. Other texts discuss festivals to honor different gods. At Ebla, the ritual for the succession of a new ruler to the throne lasted several weeks, as the royal funeral ritual did at Ugarit. The Melqart festival at Tyre was a new year celebration mentioned in Greek sources of the Hellenistic period. Phoenician texts also mention offerings and festivals for the new moon and full moon (KAI 43).

The structural organization of Syro-Canaanite religion varied among the different polities and ethnic groups. The texts from Ebla describe a variety of priests and priestesses appointed to serve various functions. At Emar, the diviner was chief administrator of the cult and town, in charge of installing the different priests for each of the gods, and a high priestess as well as other priestesses oversaw the various festivals. Each temple had its own dynastic administration headed by a high priest. At Ugarit the king was the chief officiant of rituals, although there were a variety of other cultic and administrative functionaries with ritual and divinatory tasks. Priesthood was hereditary. Phoenician texts list a variety of cultic personnel, including sacred prostitutes. Kings and queens served as priests and priestesses, with other cultic personnel conducting the temple services in different roles under the leadership of a high priest and/or priestess. The Palmyra inscriptions describe temple personnel organized into groups presided over by a high priest, with the high priest of the temple of Bel as the chief of all clergy.

The *marzeah* attested from Ebla to Palmyra is mentioned in Emar and Ugarit as a religious organization that probably had a funerary function. A primary feature of the *marzeah* was a sacred meal. In the Ugaritic texts, El is described as having a *marzeah* to which he invited his sons and got drunk (KTU 1.114). Different deities were patrons of different *marzeah*, and the *rapi'uma* were also considered members. The Hebrew Bible attests to the existence of *marzeah* in Israel, and texts show it also functioned in Palmyra, among the Nabateans, and in the Phoenician lands.

The institution of prophecy was less formally organized. At Mari, as in Israel and Judah, prophets received messages or visions from gods ecstatically or by technically prescribed means akin to divination. In the Egyptian story of Wen-Amun, the author claims to have seen a court page at Byblos temporarily possessed by a god in order to deliver a message, which was then acted upon by the authorities. Professional seers and prophets were often present at court to indicate the will of the gods to the ruler, as evidenced in the Hamath inscription of King Zakkur. Prophets could also receive divine confirmation of royal succession, as in the case of Abiya in Aleppo, whose vision from Adad established Zimri-Lim as king. In the Hebrew Bible (1 Kings 19:16), Elijah similarly receives a message from the God of Israel directing him to anoint Hazael as king of the Arameans in Damascus. Many prophecies assure rulers of divine protection (e.g., Abiya, Hamiyatas, Zakkur, and Ammonite citadel prophecies). Prophets also functioned to warn the people about divine punishments. The Deir Alla inscription describes Balaam son of Beor (cf. Numbers 22–23) as a "seer" who receives a vision wherein the gods inform him that they will punish the land with darkness.[29]

4. SOCIAL CONTEXT

The social order of the polities of Syria-Canaan was both patrilineal and patrilocal, with households headed usually by the eldest son who has succeeded his father. The story of Aqhat (KTU 1.17, 1.26–33) details the duties of a son, including the obligations of the head of the family to take care of the ancestors and participate in the sacrificial meals in the local temples. The patriarch thus represented the family in the state religion and presided over the religion of the family household in the cults of the ancestors and family gods. Filial funerary duties are also seen on the Phoenician sarcophagus of Ahiram of Byblos, in the portrayal of the dead king seated on a throne receiving the offerings of mourners, with his son by his side running the proceedings.

Syro-Canaanite kings were the military, judicial, administrative, economic, and religious authorities, and kingship was divinely sanctioned: for example, Aramean King Zakkur attributed his kingship over Hamath and Luash to Baal-Shamem (KAI 202.3–4, 13), and King Yehaumilk of Byblos credited the Lady of Byblos. Kings built temples and monuments to the gods in thanksgiving and in the hope of a sustained dynasty, and dedicated battle spoils to their gods as well as other expensive gifts. Palaces and temples were often constructed in close proximity, as at Alalakh and Zincirli, visually illustrating the idea that the king was the divine representative on Earth, ruling on behalf of the gods and acting as intermediary between the gods and his people.

After the king, the queen mother was often the most important political figure. Phoenician King Eshmunazor II had his mother serve as regent until he came of age (KAI 14.14–20), and it has been argued that at Ugarit the queen mother served as regent whenever a king was away from the court.[30] Queen mothers at Ugarit could own property (other women could not) and played major roles in determining royal succession. Possibly, if the king (like Kirta in KTU 1.16.1.10) was understood as a "son" of El, then his mother could be identified metaphorically with Asherah.[31]

Ethics in Syria-Canaan reflected the basic theological belief that the gods were in control. In the Ugaritic stories, the human heroes accept divine authority and that human life proceeds under the direction of the gods. Kirta remains pious throughout his sufferings and tribulations, only inadvertently breaking a vow to Asherah. Danel also accepts his fate and the death of his sons as the will of the gods. The story of Ahiqar likewise urges acceptance of one's fate, and conformity to the status quo.

5. RESEARCH

Our primary literary sources for Syria-Canaan are the Bronze Age texts from Ugarit, Ebla, Emar, and Mari. Our only extensive literary source from the Iron Age is the Hebrew Bible, although a variety of Aramean and Phoenician inscriptions survive. Syro-Canaanite iconography from the Bronze and Iron Ages abounds, from stamps and cylinder seals to statues, reliefs, ivory carvings, cultic vessels and implements, plaques, pendants, amulets, and figurines, and since the landmark study of Keel and Uehlinger[32] it has been receiving more serious scholarly attention.

Syrian religion intrigued travelers from outside the area enough that writings from Egypt (the tales of Sinuhe and Wenamun[33]) document beliefs and practices that can be evaluated against the archaeological and literary evidence. Similarly in the Greco-Roman period, authors such as Philo of Byblos, Lucian, and Herodotus recorded their impressions and understandings of Syrian religion.

Scholarship of Syro-Canaanite religion began in the nineteenth century as a way of contextualizing Israelite religion, and thus practices of Israel's neighbors were evaluated negatively through the lens of biblical condemnations and prohibitions. By the mid- to late twentieth century, scholars had begun critically evaluating the Bible's historical and cultural reports of Israel's environment against an increasing body of evidence from Mesopotamia and Syria-Canaan. By the end of the twentieth century and into the twenty-first, mainstream biblical scholarship understands Israelite religion within its West Asian environment as but one manifestation (albeit a lasting one) of the myriad constellations of beliefs and practices that make up the religions and cultures of Syria-Canaan.

Scholarly evaluations of Syro-Canaanite religion now focus on the texts and archaeological remains of individual polities in more depth as independent entities, noting similarities and differences from the rest of Syria-Canaan, historical developments, and varying regional influences from Anatolia, Mesopotamia, and Egypt, as well as larger scale interactions with the Aegean via travel and trade.

FURTHER READING

Many helpful resources are available for the various sub-disciplines of ancient Near Eastern religions. On Israelite religion, Zevit 2003 provides a thorough multidisciplinary survey. For Israelite iconography in its Syro-Canaanite environment see Keel and Uehlinger 1998. Studies on biblical Asherah and other goddesses include Dever 2005, Hadley 2000, and Ackerman 1992. Sasson et al. 1995 is a multivolume collection concerning all aspects of ancient Near Eastern life. Dever and Gitin 2003 provide numerous articles on archaeology and society. For an overview of the gods of Syria-Canaan, see Smith 2010. Books focusing on specific Syro-Canaanite polities include Pardee 2002, Lete 1999, Heltzer 1982, and Parker 1997 for Ugarit; Chavalas 1996 and Fleming 2000 for Emar; Gordon and Rendsberg 1990 for Ebla; Dearman 1989 for Moab; Markoe 2000 on the Phoenicians; and Lipinski 2000 on the Arameans. Attridge and Oden 1981 produced the classic work on Philo of Byblos' *Phoenician History*.

CHRONOLOGY

Note: All dates are BCE

3500–2300	Fortified cities built across Syria-Canaan in trade network from Egypt to Mesopotamia. Writings from Ebla provide earliest textual witnesses to Syro-Canaanite religion; texts from Mari appear slightly later.
2000–1800	Nomadic populations, possibly Amorites, settle throughout northern region. Egyptian military incursions in Canaan; Semitic populations attested in Egypt.
1800–1600	Large-scale reurbanization from Ebla to Hazor.
1600–1200	International trade networks link Egypt, Syria-Canaan, Mesopotamia, and the Aegean. The Akkadian language dominates the Near East. Amarna archive provides detailed correspondence of Egyptian rulers with vassals in Syria, Canaan, Cyprus, Anatolia, Mitanni, and Mesopotamia.

[handwritten: → connect to polytheism]

1450–1200	Peak and decline of Ugarit.
1340–1190	A variety of texts from Emar document religion, culture, and society.
1200–1000	Regional upheaval brings Sea Peoples to the Levantine coast, migration of Arameans, and destruction of Late Bronze Age polities. Beginning of Iron Age.
1000–800	Phoenician inscriptions from Tyre, Sidon, and Byblos; also from Edom, Moab, and Israel/Judah. Punic colonies founded across the Mediterranean and in North Africa.
745–727	Assyria destroys and repopulates Syro-Canaanite polities, including Israel, resulting in the "ten lost tribes," as well as the spread of the Aramean language and alphabetic script throughout the region.
609	Assyria and its Egyptian allies are defeated by Babylon.
587/6	Jerusalem falls to Babylon. The people are exiled, and Solomon's Temple is destroyed.
539–525	Syria-Canaan comes under the control of Cyrus of Persia and the Achaemenid Empire, and exiled groups, including the Jews, are permitted to return to their lands.
334–323	Alexander the Great conquers the Persian Empire and brings the Greek language, political structures, and cultural influences throughout Syria-Canaan.
305–65	The eastern Mediterranean is contested by Alexander's successors, with the Seleucid Dynasty ruling Syria, Mesopotamia, and Iran, and the Ptolemies ruling Egypt. Greek colonies (e.g., Antioch) are established in Syria-Canaan.
64	Syria-Canaan is incorporated into the Roman state when Pompey deposes the last Seleucid king.

[handwritten: important figure]

[handwritten: → why? the mother]

GLOSSARY

Asherah: Mother of the gods, consort of El.

Anat: Warrior-goddess; sister/consort of Baal in Ugaritic myth.

Athtart/Astarte: Syro-Canaanite goddess; cognate to Mesopotamian Ishtar; goddess of battle at Emar, and Zincirli; wielder of the power of Baal's name at Ugarit, and often thought of as goddess of fertility and love because of her frequently nude depiction in art.

Dagan: Grain-god; worshiped widely in Syria-Canaan.

El (also Il/Ilu): West Semitic word for "god," and consort of Asherah in the Ugaritic myths; chief, patriarch, father of the gods.

Hadda: Thunderer, storm-god, also known as Baal – later Hadad, Baal Hadad; patron deity of Aram and Ugarit.

marzeah: Syro-Canaanite term for funerary cult and ritual feast with the dead.

Mot: God of the dead and ruler over the netherworld who battles with Baal in Ugaritic myth.

Rapi'uma/Rephaim: The (possibly divinized) dead kings and ancestors.

Rashp/Resheph: God associated with the desert, drought, destruction, disease, and death as guardian of the underworld; but also with healing in Egyptian texts, and worshiped as the god of metallurgy.

Shapsh(u): Female sun-goddess at Ugarit; known as the male Shemesh elsewhere in Syria-Canaan; overseer of divine justice.

Yamm(u): The divine Sea in Ugaritic myth.

Yarikh/Yareah: Moon-god; the lunar calendars of Syria-Canaan followed this god's movements, and he is frequently represented iconographically throughout Syria-Canaan.

Notes

1   Hackett 1997.
2   For Paleolithic and Neolithic Syria-Canaan see Levy 2001.
3   For strong arguments that some ancient poetry, like Exodus 15, originated in the late second millennium BCE, see Cross and Freedman 1975.
4   See Clifford 1998.
5   Gubel 2005.
6   Keel and Uehlinger 1998:66, n. 7; and 71–72; also Winter 1987:110–114. For further examples of Canaanite influence in Egypt, see Sparks 2004.
7   See Fontaine 2004.
8   See Wright 1987; also Smith 2010.
9   Smith 2010; note that here and elsewhere the abbreviation KAI refers to *Kanaanäische und aramäische Inschriften*, a standard reference for Northwest Semitic Inscriptions.
10   Weinfeld 1973.
11   Keel and Uehlinger 1998.
12   The abbreviation KTU stands for *Keilschrift Texte aus Ugarit*, the standard reference collection for the cuneiform texts from Ugarit.
13   Johnson 1999:121.
14   Keel and Uehlinger 1998.
15   See Cooley 2012.
16   See, e.g., 1 Kings 18–19.
17   See Lewis 1989.

18 See van der Toorn 1996, especially 153–77.
19 van der Toorn 1996.
20 Wyatt 2002.
21 See Heider 2009.
22 See Stager and Wolff 1984.
23 Sasson 1966.
24 Stager 1991.
25 Avalos 1995.
26 Cooley 2012.
27 Dolansky 2008.
28 See Faust 2010.
29 Hackett 1980.
30 Heltzer 1982.
31 Ackerman 1997.
32 Keel and Uehlinger 1998.
33 On dating Wenamun, see Sass 2002.

Works Cited

Ackerman, Susan. 1992. *Under Every Green Tree: Popular Religion in Sixth-Century Judah.* Atlanta.
———. 1997. "The Queen Mother and the Cult in the Ancient Near East." In *Women and Goddess Traditions: In Antiquity and Today.* Ed. K. L. King, 179–209. London.
Attridge, Harold W. and Robert A. Oden. 1981. *Philo of Byblos: The Phoenician History: Introduction, Critical Text, Translation, Notes.* Washington, DC.
Avalos, Hector. 1995. *Illness and Health Care in the Ancient Near East: The Role of the Temple in Greece, Mesopotamia, and Israel.* Atlanta.
Chavalas, Mark W. 1996. *Emar: The History, Religion, and Culture of a Syrian Town in the Late Bronze Age.* Bethesda, MD.
Clifford, Richard J. 1998. "The Roots of Apocalypticism in Near Eastern Myth." In *The Encyclopedia of Apocalypticism.* Ed. J. J. Collins, I.3–38. New York.
Cooley, Jeffrey. 2012. "Celestial Divination in Ugarit and Ancient Israel: A Reassessment." *Journal of Near East Studies* 71(1): 21–30.
Cross, Frank M. and David N. Freedman. 1975. *Studies in Ancient Yahwistic Poetry.* Atlanta.
Dearman, J. Andrew. 1989. *Studies in the Mesha Inscription and Moab.* Atlanta.
Dever, William G. 2005. *Did God Have a Wife? Archaeology and Religion in Ancient Israel.* Grand Rapids, MI.
Dever, William G. and Seymour Gitin. 2003. *Symbiosis, Symbolism, and the Power of the Past: Canaan, Ancient Israel, and Their Neighbors from the late Bronze Age through Roman Palaestina.* Winona Lake, IN.
Dolansky, Shawna. 2008. *Now You See It, Now You Don't: Biblical Perspectives on Religion and Magic in the Hebrew Bible.* Winona Lake, IN.
Faust, Avraham. 2010. "The Archaeology of the Israelite Cult: Questioning the Consensus." *Bulletin of the American Schools of Oriental Research* 360: 23–35.

Fleming, Daniel E. 2000. *Time at Emar: The Cultic Calendar and the Rituals from the Diviner's House*. Winona Lake, IN.

Fontaine, Carole. 2004. *Smooth Words: Women, Proverbs, and Performance in Biblical Wisdom*. London.

Gordon, Cyrus H. and Gary A. Rendsberg. 1990. *Eblaitica: Essays on the Ebla Archives and Eblaite Language*. Winona Lake, IN.

Gubel, Eric. 2005. "Phoenician and Aramaean Bridle-Harness Decoration: Examples of Cultural Contact and Innovation in the Eastern Mediterranean." In *Crafts and Images in Contact*. Ed. Claudia Suter and Christoph Uehlinger, 111–147. Fribourg.

Hackett, Jo Ann. 1980. *The Balaam Text from Deir 'Alla*. Chico, California.

———. 1997. "Canaanites." In *The Oxford Encyclopedia of Archaeology in the Near East*. Ed. E. M. Meyers, Vol. 1, 409–14. Oxford.

Hadley, Judith. 2000. *The Cult of Asherah in Ancient Israel and Judah: Evidence for a Hebrew Goddess*. Cambridge.

Heider, George C. 2009. *Cult of Molech: A Reassessment*. London.

Heltzer, Michael. 1982. *The Internal Organization of the Kingdom of Ugarit*. Wiesbaden.

Johnson, Paul. 1999. *The Civilization of Ancient Egypt*. New York.

Keel, Othmar and Christoph Uehlinger. 1998. *Gods, Goddesses, and Images of God in Ancient Israel*. Minneapolis.

Lete, Gregorio del Olmo. 1999. *Canaanite Religion according to the Liturgical Texts of Ugarit*. Bethesda, MD.

Levy, Thomas E. 2001. *The Archaeology of Society in the Holy Land*. Sheffield.

Lewis, Theodore J. 1989. *Cults of the Dead in Ancient Israel and Ugarit*. Atlanta.

———. 2011. "Athtartu's Incantations and the Use of Divine Names as Weapons." *JNES* 70(2): 207–227.

Lipinski, Eduard. 2000. *The Aramaeans: Their Ancient History, Culture, Religion*. Leuven.

Markoe, Glenn E. 2000. *Phoenicians*. Berkeley.

Parker, Simon B. 1997. *Ugaritic Narrative Poetry*. Atlanta.

Pardee, Dennis. 2002. *Ritual and Cult at Ugarit*. Atlanta.

Sass, Benjamin. 2002. "Wenamun and His Levant: 1075 BC or 925 BC?" *Ägypten und Levante* 12: 247–255.

Sasson, Jack M. 1966. "Circumcision in the Ancient Near East." *Journal of Biblical Literature* 85(4): 473–476.

———. 1995. *Civilizations of the Ancient Near East*. Peabody, MA.

Smith, Mark S. 2010. *God in Translation: Deities in Cross-Cultural Discourse in the Biblical World*. Grand Rapids, MI.

Sparks, Rachael. 2004. "Canaan in Egypt: Archaeological Evidence for a Social Phenomenon." In *Invention and Innovation. The Social Context of Technological Change 2: Egypt, the Aegean and the Near East, 1650–1150 B.C.* Ed. J. Bourriau and J. Phillips, 25–54. Oxford.

Stager, Lawrence. 1991. "Why Were Hundreds of Dogs Buried at Ashkelon?" *Biblical Archaeology Review* 17(3): 26–42.

Stager, Lawrence and S. R. Wolff. 1984. "Child Sacrifice at Carthage: Religious Rite or Population Control?" *Biblical Archaeology Review* 10(1): 30–51.

Van der Toorn, Karel. 1996. *Family Religion in Babylonia, Syria, and Israel: Continuity and Change in the Forms of Religious Life*. Leiden.

Weinfeld, Moshe. 1973. "The Covenant of Grant in the Old Testament and in the Ancient Near East." *Journal of Ancient Oriental Studies* 90(2): 184–203.

Winter, Urs. 1987. *Frau und Gottin: Exegetische und ikonographische Studien zum weiblichen Gottesbild im Alten Israel und in dessen Umwelt*. Fribourg.

Wright, David P. 1987. *The Disposal of Impurity: Elimination Rites in the Bible and in Hittite and Mesopotamian Literature*. Atlanta.

Wyatt, Nicolas. 2002. *Religious Texts from Ugarit*. Sheffield.

Zevit, Ziony. 2003. *The Religions of Israel: A Synthesis of Parallactic Approaches*. London.

4 Israel

MAYER I. GRUBER

Ancient Israel was an ethnic and faith community that appeared in the Southern Levant (the area corresponding to the modern political entities of Israel, Jordan, and Palestine) as early as the thirteenth century BCE. The earliest datable reference to Israel is the monument erected by Egyptian King Merneptah (c. 1224–1214 BCE), who claims to have annihilated Israel. In general, "Ancient Israel" is regarded as merging into "Judaism" in the sixth or fifth century BCE.

I. HISTORICAL DEVELOPMENT

Many ancient Israelite religious leaders held that the Israelites were bound from birth to worship only one deity. This deity is referred to by the name YHWH, which modern scholars believe should be pronounced Yahweh, and which means "He will bring into being." However, many biblical texts indicate that at various times many Israelites preferred to combine the worship of Yahweh with the worship of other deities or to abandon the worship of Yahweh altogether.

James Breasted argued that Moses adopted the belief in a single deity in Egypt, where a similar idea had been advocated in the fourteenth century BCE by King Akhenaten.[1] The biblical narrative assumes that reverencing only one God, who often bears the proper name Yahweh, is what distinguishes Israel from other peoples of the ancient Middle East. Biblical narrative likewise assumes that at various times many Israelites combined the worship of Yahweh with the worship of other deities. The Book of Judges declares repeatedly that the Israelites are punished for worshipping other deities and rewarded for returning to the exclusive worship of Yahweh.

The Books of 1–2 Kings declare that during the reign of King Ahab of Israel (873–852 BCE), the king's wife Jezebel persecuted the adherents of Yahweh and supported the adherents of Baal. It is reported that first Elijah and then King Jehu put an end to the dominance of the Baal-worshippers. Later it is reported that King Manasseh of Judah (698–642 BCE) promoted the worship of other deities.[2] During the reign of King Josiah (640–609 BCE) there was discovered in the Temple at Jerusalem a book of divine instruction, which modern scholars generally identify with the Book of Deuteronomy or at least the core of it (Chapters 12–26). The latter corpus prohibits the worship of Yahweh by sacrifice anywhere except "in the place which He shall choose," which King Josiah understood to mean the Temple at Jerusalem. According to 2 Kings, it was on the basis of this understanding of the prohibition that temples and altars devoted to the worship of Yahweh were, by royal decree, dismantled and desecrated all over the Kingdom of Judah. Since King Josiah did not create an alternative to temple worship for persons faithful to the single deity of Israel and Judah, Judeans apparently went in droves to worship other deities, whose temples and altars remained available while the Jerusalem temple remained largely inaccessible in an age when motor transportation had yet to be invented.[3] The complaint that Judeans worshipped other deities seems not to be heard again after the sixth century BCE.

The historical development of the worship of Yahweh was influenced by contact with other cultures and had its own influence on them. Many biblical narratives suggest that the Israelites were drawn to the worship of Canaanite deities. However, it is reported that Moses's father-in-law, Jethro (Exodus 18:11), and Rahab (Joshua 2), the innkeeper/prostitute at Jericho, were so impressed with the wonders that Yahweh had performed on behalf of Israel that they recognized Yahweh as the most powerful of all deities. Likewise, at the urging of an Israelite slave girl, Naaman, the Minister of Defense of the King of Aram (ninth century BCE) learned about Yahweh and worshipped Him and ceased worshipping other gods. According to the testimony of the later chapters of the Book of Isaiah (Isaiah 40–66), which reflect the period of Cyrus's conquest of Babylon (539 BCE), people who learned about Yahweh, the God of Israel, adopted the worship of Yahweh and observed the Sabbath rest at the end of the Jewish week. According to the Book of Zechariah, there were many non-Israelites in the post-539 BCE period who understood that the Jews possessed teachings about Yahweh, which other people wanted to learn. According to the Book of Ezra, persons of non-Israelite origin joined the Jews who returned from Babylonia (538 BCE and later) (Ezra 2:59–60; also Nehemiah 7:61–62) while other persons underwent a rite of purification from association with other gods and joined the community of Israel (Ezra 6:21). It has also been suggested that when Isaiah 45:7 declares that Yahweh creates both light and darkness, good and evil, the prophet may be countering the proto-Zoroastrian teaching that there is a god of light and goodness and another god of darkness and evil.[4]

2. BELIEF

The idea that Israelite religion venerated one specific deity, Yahweh, is shared by most of Hebrew Scripture. Nevertheless, Zevit argues that the personal names of Israelites and Judeans attested in Hebrew Scripture and place names and personal names recovered by archaeological research indicate that, "within Israel there was a minority ... that did not consider YHWH the deity whose name they wished to link to that of one of their children."[5] The conclusion that the names people bore or gave their children necessarily point to the religious affiliation of the parents is challenged by the fact that both in Hebrew Scripture and in later Judaism and Christianity persons who were zealous defenders of the faith such as Mordecai and Esther in the Book of Esther and the famous Archbishop Isidore of Seville (c. 560–636 CE) bore, respectively, names incorporating the names of Assyro-Babylonian Marduk, Assyro-Babylonian Ishtar, and Egyptian Isis. Similarly, the fifth-century BCE governor of Samaria named Sanballat (a form of Assyro-Babylonian Sin-uballit meaning "the Assyro-Babylonian moon god will give life/revive") gave his sons the names Delaiah and Shelemiah, both of which include the divine name Yah, a short form of Yahweh.

However, evidence that at least a minority of Israelites and Judeans in the first millennium BCE may have worshipped deities other than Yahweh either alongside of Yahweh or instead of Yahweh is claimed by Hebrew Scripture itself. According to 1 Kings 19:18, during Ahab's reign in Israel (873–852 BCE), "only 7,000 had not bowed down to Baal," that is, the Canaanite deity associated with rain. Zevit argues that those who remained loyal to Yahweh would have constituted less than 5 percent of the population.[6] The greater popularity of worship of Baal vis-à-vis the worship of Yahweh is attested in other texts that appear to reflect the situation in the northern Kingdom of Israel in the ninth century BCE, such as Hosea 1–3 and 2 Kings 10. The proliferation of the worship of other deities instead of or alongside of the worship of Yahweh in the time of King Manasseh (698–642 BCE) of Judah is described in 2 Kings 21:1–17 (cf. 33:1–20) and in the last years before the destruction of Jerusalem in 586 BCE in the diatribes of Jeremiah and Ezekiel.

Another divinity, this one female, may also have been worshipped by the ancient Israelites. In the latter half of the twentieth century it was frequently asserted that a few epigraphic finds point to Yahweh's having been believed to have a consort named Asherah. This interpretation of a small number of texts and illustrations from Kuntillet 'Ajrud and Khirbet el-Qom has been used to raise the question, *"Did God Have a Wife?"*[7] A number of scholars have responded that the inscriptions are simply graffiti and are of no consequence. Given (a) the large number of clay figurines of human females found by archaeologists in Israelite and Judean strata of the first millennium BCE and the widely held assumption that these figurines represent goddesses,[8] and (b) the very small number of pictorial illustrations that might possibly represent Yahweh, one might want to suggest the following: if the texts of Hebrew Scripture mostly concur in treating the worship of Yahweh alone as the only legitimate religion, and the archaeological record, on the other hand, attests primarily to an unnamed goddess or goddesses, perhaps one should distinguish between the religion of biblical texts and the religion recovered from archeology. The religion reflected in biblical texts refers mostly to Yahweh alone while the religion recovered from archaeology refers primarily to an unnamed goddess or goddesses. Consequently, with respect to the worship of the latter, an interesting research question might be, "Did God have a husband?" On the other hand, back in 1968, William Dever discovered in a tomb from the middle of the eighth century BCE at Khirbet el-Qom, west of Hebron, an inscription that contains in parallel clauses "Blessed is Uriyahu by Yahweh" and "By His Asherah." Dever argues that the latter clause refers to the goddess Asherah as the wife of Yahweh.[9] In addition, three inscriptions, commonly regarded as Israelite and dated to c. 800 BCE from Kuntillet 'Ajrud in the north of the Sinai Peninsula clearly refer to "Yahweh and his Asherah." While many scholars prefer to see "asherah" in this context as an object, specifically a stylized pole or tree employed in worship,[10] the inscriptions from Kuntillet 'Ajrud seem to treat Asherah as the wife of Yahweh.[11] More recently, however, in their treatment of inscriptions from this site, Shmuel Ahituv, Esther Eshel, and Ze'ev Meshel have argued that they have put an end to the scholarly myth that the God of Israel had a spouse named Asherah just as Gruber had put an end to the scholarly myth that held that sacred prostitution was a feature of religion in ancient Western Asia.[12]

If Yahweh were indeed perceived as male and were He not paired with a wife, one might conclude that Israelite religion, unlike the other religions of the ancient Middle East, placed less value on being female than did other religions of the ancient Middle East. In turn, this may account for the association of Judean women in particular with the worship of "the queen of heaven" as referred to in Jeremiah 44:17–19, 25. It has been suggested, therefore, that the unnamed prophet who appeared among the Jews at the end of the Babylonian Exile succeeded in virtually putting an end to the attraction of Jews to the worship of deities other than Yahweh because he chose to refer to Yahweh as both "father" and "mother" (Isaiah 42:13–14).[13] The divine name Anathyahu by whom some Jewish people swore in some documents from fifth-century BCE Elephantine may reflect a combination of the Canaanite goddess of war, Anath, and Yahweh. Possibly, the name Anathyahu, which combines the female Anath and the male Yahweh, reflects an attempt to deal with discomfort that some persons may have had (and certainly do now) with a single deity who is identified with only one of the two sexes. Our unnamed prophet who applies both masculine and feminine similes to Yahweh has supplied one solution to this dilemma. Iron Age persons who venerated "Yahweh and his Asherah" may have suggested another solution while the Elephantine Jews who swore by Anathyahu have offered an additional solution.

Despite these tantalizing hints of their worship of other gods, the ancient Israelites held as central to their belief system the idea that Yahweh was their one and only god. Indeed, the biblical texts consistently stress the importance of the Israelites adhering to this belief, and the consequences if they do not do so. The Books of Exodus–Leviticus–Numbers–Deuteronomy teach that Yahweh rescued the Israelites from enslavement in Egypt and promised that He would bring them into the Promised Land and allow them to abide there if they were loyal to Him and observed His rules. Loyalty to Yahweh is expressed primarily by not worshipping other deities. The prophet Jeremiah (Jeremiah 44) insists that it was disloyalty to Yahweh and worship of other deities that angered Yahweh so that he punished the Jews by allowing the Babylonian King Nebuchadrezzar to conquer Judah, burn the temple, and exile the Jews. Moreover, Jeremiah continues, the Jews in Egypt who continued to worship the Queen of Heaven (literal translation of Inanna, the Sumerian name of the Mesopotamian goddess Ishtar) continued in the bad behavior that resulted in the exile. Both Leviticus and Deuteronomy indicate that when and if the Israelites express remorse, Yahweh will allow them to return to the Promised Land. This idea that exile is punishment and redemption from exile is the reward of repentance is shared by the prophets Jeremiah and Ezekiel. The eighth-century BCE prophets Amos and Micah teach that exile is also an appropriate punishment for failure to maintain a just society in which all persons are given an equal share of the gross national product. Jeremiah and Ezekiel combine both the Leviticus–Deuteronomy view that exile is the just punishment for worship of other gods and the view that exile is the just punishment for a society that tolerates injustice. The Books of Proverbs, Job, and Ecclesiastes share with biblical narrative (primarily in Genesis and Judges–Samuel–Kings) the veneration of a single deity, but they are totally unconcerned with the past, present, and future of the people of Israel and Judah.

The centrality of Yahweh to the religion of ancient Israel is also seen in its cosmology and eschatology. The Books of Genesis, Proverbs, Psalms, and Job attest to diverse accounts concerning the manner in which the cosmos originated, but these books agree that one God created the cosmos. As for eschatology, Leviticus and Deuteronomy and the eighth-century BCE prophet Amos express the view that when the people of Israel will have repented of their erstwhile misbehavior, they will be allowed to return to the Promised Land. The Book of Amos adds the idea that the restoration of the dynasty of King David is an integral part of the hope for a better time yet to be. Amos's contemporary Micah (Chapter 4) looks forward (like Deuteronomy 4) to a world in which Israel will worship Yahweh while every other people will each worship her/his own deity. Contrary to this pluralistic view of the future, Isaiah (Chapter 2) expresses the idea that is afterwards taken up by Jeremiah 10:11, Isaiah 40–66, Zechariah, and some of the Psalms (e.g., 115 and 135, and so also 1 Chronicles 16:8–36) that ultimately all people will acknowledge only one God, who is Yahweh, and recognize that other deities are no more powerful than their images made of perishable materials. Isaiah (eighth century BCE) in particular stresses the idea (in Chapters 2 and 11 especially) that the recognition of the sovereignty over all the world of one God, Yahweh, will be associated with an age of universal harmony.

3. PRACTICE

Information about the practice of the religion of ancient Israel is provided in Hebrew Scripture, particularly in the legal corpora, but also scattered in the narratives. Hebrew Scripture contains more than nine distinct legal corpora, each with its own vocabulary. During the nineteenth and twentieth centuries it was widely accepted in the academic study of Hebrew Scripture that if these codes are arranged chronologically, they attest to stages in the development of the religions of ancient Israel. In our own time there is no longer a consensus among experts on ancient Israel as to the chronological sequence of these corpora. Consequently, the subtle debates on this point will be bypassed. The nine law corpora are the following: Exodus 20 (the Ten Commandments; with an alternative version contained in Deuteronomy 5); Exodus 21–24 (commonly called "the Covenant Code"); Exodus 34 (commonly called "the small Book of the Covenant"); Exodus 25–31 (elaborate prescriptions for the construction of a portable temple suitable for use during the travels of the people of Israel from Sinai to the Promised Land); Exodus 35–40 (either a variant of Exodus 25–31 or a description of how the provisions of Exodus 25–31 were carried out); Leviticus 1–16, 17–26, 27; Deuteronomy 11–26; and various legal corpora interspersed in the narratives contained in the Book of Numbers.

The only prescribed Israelite religious rite that is mentioned in the narratives of the three patriarchs is the circumcision of males, which is practiced upon Abraham, his son Ishmael, and all the slaves born in his house or acquired (Genesis 17) and later upon Isaac when he is eight days old (Genesis 21:4). The Genesis narratives occasionally mention prayers (Genesis 20:7, 17; 25:21, 22), never mention temples, and refer to the priesthood only as a non-Israelite office held by Melchizedek, the King of Salem (Genesis 14).

Sacrifice is also among the rites practiced by the early patriarchs. The Book of Genesis indicates that Noah built one altar, Abraham three, Isaac one, and Jacob three – not very impressive for a book that gives the superficial impression that the patriarchs went around establishing sanctuaries. Abraham is reported to have sacrificed a ram in place of the son he was willing to sacrifice. And Jacob is reported to have offered animal sacrifices on three occasions.

Sacred space for sacrificial worship later became limited to one particular site. The Books of Kings, Jeremiah, and Ezekiel reflect the idea that there is only one legitimate site of sacrificial worship, and that this is the temple on Mount Moriah in Jerusalem, traditionally said to have been built under King Solomon in the tenth century BCE. However, 2 Kings 18 (and parallel versions in Isaiah 36 and 2 Chronicles 32) indicate that as late as 701 BCE the idea that there is one legitimate site for sacrificial worship of Yahweh was a matter of controversy. On the other hand, 2 Kings 23 and 2 Chronicles 34 indicate that when a book of divine instruction was found in the temple at Jerusalem in 622 BCE it was taken for granted by the prophetess Huldah, King Josiah, and the king's officials that "the place He [God] will choose to cause his name to dwell there" is, indeed, Mount Moriah in Jerusalem. Consequently, other altars of Yahweh were summarily destroyed. Nevertheless, the Jews at Elephantine in Egypt in the fifth century BCE and the Jews at Heliopolis in Egypt in the first century CE maintained their own temples of sacrificial worship. Aside from the interdiction against sacrificial worship at places other than Mount Moriah, which is a recurring refrain in the

Book of Kings, there is testimony in the Books of Amos and Ezekiel to the view that lands other than the Land of Israel are inherently unclean and that therefore eating food of any kind outside the Land of Israel is tantamount to eating forbidden food.

Although sacred space, at least in the sense of sacrificial space, was thus highly restricted in the religion of ancient Israel, sacred time was open to all. All of the legal corpora of the Pentateuch emphasize the sanctity of the weekly Sabbath, a day on which all manner of physical exertion is prohibited. This institution is also reflected in biblical narrative in the Book of Kings and in the writings of the prophets from the eighth century and later. The Sabbath is also stressed in the memoirs of Nehemiah from the fifth century BCE. This revolutionary institution made leisure, heretofore the privilege only of royalty and nobility, accessible even to slaves.

Likewise, with the exception of the Ten Commandments, all the legal corpora of the Pentateuch recognize three annual festivals on which it is appropriate to go on pilgrimage to a temple or altar. These are the Festival of Unleavened Bread, the Festival of Weeks, and the Festival of Tabernacles. The Festival of Weeks was observed for only one day while the other two festivals were observed for seven days each. In addition, the Feast of Unleavened Bread was immediately preceded by the one-day Festival of Passover, on which the flesh of a slaughtered lamb was shared by God, priests, and laypersons – including men, women, and children. Just as Passover preceded Unleavened Bread by one day, so in two of the codes, Leviticus 23 and Numbers 28–29, Tabernacles was followed by another festival often called Conclusion. Thus, in the two most elaborate lists of festivals, in addition to the Sabbath occurring once every seven days and two seven-day festivals – Passover and Tabernacles – beginning at the full moon immediately after the spring and fall equinoxes, respectively – we have seven days on which work is prohibited. These are the New Year, the Day of Atonement, the first and last days of Passover, the Festival of Weeks, and the Feast of Conclusion following Tabernacles. The total number of seven festivals on which work is prohibited corresponds to the ordinal number of the day of the week when the Sabbath is to be observed and the number of days of each of the major festivals – Unleavened Bread and Tabernacles – celebrated at the full moon following the spring and fall equinoxes, respectively. The New Moon is sometimes juxtaposed with the Sabbath as a day of assembly in the temple (Isaiah 1:13; 66:23).

Information about the structural organization of the early religion of ancient Israel is limited. With the exceptions of (a) the account of King

Melchizedek of Salem, who was also priest of the Most High God in the time of the patriarch Abraham (Genesis 14); (b) the mention that Joseph married Asenath, the daughter of Potiphera the priest of On (Genesis 41:45, 50; 46:20); and (c) the report that Joseph acquired for the Egyptian state all the real estate in Egypt with the exception of the lands belonging to the priests (Genesis 47:22, 26), no religious officials are ever mentioned in the Book of Genesis. Obviously, since Salem may be another name for Jerusalem, the narrative of Melchizedek may be taken to convey the subtle message that the priesthood of Abiathar and Zadok at Jerusalem in the reigns of King David (1 Samuel 23; 30) and King Solomon (1 Kings 2:35), respectively, was adumbrated in the era of the patriarchs of Israel by the priesthood of Melchizedek. It is no less likely that both the account of Melchizedek and the references to Egyptian priests in the Joseph narrative convey the message that an official priesthood was, like kingship, an inherently non-Israelite institution.

Likewise, outside of the materials in Exodus 25–31 and Exodus 35–40, which modern biblical scholarship understands to be allied to the Book of Leviticus, and which, like the Book of Leviticus, is commonly assigned to priestly sources, the term "priest" is mentioned in the Book of Exodus only in connection with Moses's father-in-law, the priest of Midian (i.e., a Gentile priest like the father-in-law of Joseph (Exodus 3:1; 18:1 and 19)). In the latter chapter it is said that the entire people of Israel constitute a kingdom of priests and a holy nation (Exodus 19:6). However, at the end of a detailed series of instructions as to how the Israelite men and women are to purify themselves to prepare for the close public encounter of all Israel with their God at Mount Sinai, it is stated in Exodus19:24 that "The priests, also, who come near Yahweh must stay pure, lest the LORD break out against them." An obvious meaning of this warning is that priests are assumed by this text to constitute a self-important elite, who might not understand that purification before the close encounter with the deity also applies to them. Interestingly, anticipating the modern understanding that an organized Israelite priesthood seems to be peculiar to the priestly materials in Exodus 25–31 and Exodus 35–40 and foreign to the narratives that precede Exodus 25, ancient Jewish exegesis reflected in Babylonian Talmud (Zebahim 115b) suggests that the priests mentioned in Exodus 19:24 are not the organized priesthood of Aaron and his male descendants but rather the firstborn sons of every mother, who served as priests before the establishment of a hereditary priesthood of the Levites (Numbers 3:41, 45). The idea that Levites and priests are synonymous is reflected in most of the Book of Deuteronomy while Exodus 25–31 and 35–40 speak only of the priests who are the male descendants of Aaron. The Book of Numbers, on the other hand, dwells at length on the subdivision of the Levites into the priests, who are the sons of Aaron, and the assistant priests, who are the descendants of the other families among the Levites. A similar distinction between the priests and the Levites, who are, as it were, second-class priests, is reflected also in the Book of Chronicles. The Books of Judges and Malachi share with Deuteronomy the treatment of the terms "priest" and "Levite" as synonymous. In Exodus 38:8 and 1 Samuel 2:22 (although not in the Old Greek version or in a version from among the Dead Sea Scrolls) mention is also made of "the women who served at the entrance of the Tent of Meeting," who apparently constituted a group of persons who, like the Levites according to Numbers and Chronicles, supported the priests in carrying out their functions.

Priests and their attendants were not the only religious functionaries in the religion of ancient Israel. Jeremiah 18:18 and Ezekiel 7:26, both stemming from just before the destruction of Jerusalem by King Nebuchadrezzar II in 586 BCE, indicate that there were three types of personnel who transmitted God's will/word/instruction. These were the priest, the prophet, and the sage. The teaching of the priest is exemplified by the rules found in Leviticus while the teaching of the prophets is exemplified by the speeches of exhortation and consolation in the Books of Isaiah, Jeremiah, Ezekiel, and the Twelve Prophets. Likewise, the teachings of the sage or wise man or wise woman are exemplified by the Books of Proverbs, Ecclesiastes, and Job. Moreover, while aside from the aforementioned "women who served at the entrance of the Tent of Meeting," female priests seem not to have been known in the religion(s) of ancient Israel, but both women and men functioned as prophets of Israel. The named women prophets in Hebrew Scripture include Miriam (Exodus 15:20), Deborah (Judges 4:4), Huldah (2 Kings 22:14–20; 2 Chronicles 34:22–28), and Noadiah (Nehemiah 6:14). Unnamed prophetesses in Hebrew Scripture include the wife of the prophet Isaiah, son of Amoz, who refers to his wife as "the prophetess" in Isaiah 8:3 just as a modern-day spouse of a rabbi will refer to her/his spouse as "the rabbi." Recently, it was discovered that Micah 6–7 contains an unpleasant dialogue/diatribe between two prophetesses.[14] In ancient Israel both women and men functioned as "sages."[15] The principal function of the priest was to pour the blood of animal sacrifices on or near an altar and to present the deity with baked goods and offerings of wine and beer. The priests and their families (including in some cases wives and unmarried daughters) were privileged to consume portions of the food brought for offerings to God. Prophets – both male and female – and sages – both male and female – differed from the priests and Levites in that they had no special functions in communal worship. Nor were they granted portions of sacrifices. Prophets were expected not only to exhort people to exemplary behavior but also to intercede with God to rescind threatened punishments for misbehavior.[16] The eighth-century BCE prophets of Israel and Judah – Amos, Hosea (Chapters 4–14), Micah, and Isaiah – insisted that the highest form of worship is the practice of personal and public morality and the avoidance and eradication of personal and public immorality.

4. SOCIAL CONTEXT

The law codes of the Pentateuch mention no social classes other than free Israelites (both male and female) and slaves. The law codes bestow a day of leisure every seventh day (commonly called "the Sabbath") upon both free Israelites and their chattel slaves. Social class therefore seems not to have been an important distinction in the religion of ancient Israel.

Gender, however, was significant in the practice of ancient Israelite religion. The role of sage was open to members of both sexes, as was the prophetic vocation, while the priesthood seems to have been restricted to males. Both men and women could undertake vows, according to which they would adopt stringencies similar to those of an officiating priest in the temple (Numbers 6:1–21). Moreover, it is reported that both monetary contributions and the work involved in the production of the tabernacle, the priestly vestments, and the furniture were undertaken by both the women and the men of Israel. The office of prophet/ess was imposed upon a woman or man in an encounter initiated by the deity. The offices of Levite and priest, which were held only by males, were hereditary in the male line. We have no idea on what basis a woman or man determined that she/he was a sage.

In addition to gender, age was also an important discriminating factor for ancient Israelite religious practice. According to the Book of Numbers (4:3, 23, 30) the Levites could undertake their duties with respect to the care of the tabernacle and its appurtenances from the age of thirty until the age of fifty. Numbers 8:24 says that the Levites should begin their service from the age of twenty-five rather than from the age of thirty. However, Numbers 8:26 indicates that Levites over the age of fifty could help out with guard duty at the tabernacle. Contributions for the upkeep of the Temple and the providing of sacrifices on behalf of the public at large could be collected from males from age twenty and older. (Exodus 30:14, 38:26). Military service and being counted in the census (in Numbers 1 and again in Numbers 26) was required of males only from the age of twenty. In all of Hebrew Scripture the single admonition to honor elderly persons in Leviticus 19:32 may indicate that by and large adherents of the worship of Yahweh took for granted that deference was to be shown to elderly persons. However, the admonition itself indicates that it was not expected that all persons would honor their elders unless instructed to do so.

Other aspects of ancient Israelite society were intimately connected with the practice of religion. In addition to priests, prophets, and sages, Hebrew Scripture refers to leaders commonly called "judges" or "deliverers," some of whom God/Yahweh is said to have raised up when the people of Israel were under attack by their non-Israelite neighbors (Judges 2:9, 3:15). The narratives of Judges–Samuel and of 1 Chronicles give the impression that the prophet Samuel was the last of these non-royal leaders chosen by God to lead the people of Israel. Thus, from the time of Moses until the prophet Samuel's declining years, politics and religion were inseparable.

This intimate association between politics and religion is also indicated by the close connection of the kings of ancient Israel with its prophets. It is recorded in Samuel and Chronicles that Israel's first king, Saul (commonly dated to 1020–1000 BCE), was consecrated as king by the prophet Samuel acting as God's agent. Likewise, acting under divine orders, Samuel deposed Saul and replaced him with David. Nathan the prophet and Zadok the priest jointly consecrated King Solomon to succeed King David. The subsequent kings of Judah down to the destruction of Jerusalem by the forces of King Nebuchadrezzar in 586 BCE were believed to reign by virtue of a bond that had been established between God and the dynasty of David. Of Jehu son of Nimshi, King of Israel, it is also stated that he was consecrated by a prophet of Yahweh (1 Kings 19:16; 2 Kings 9:6) Thus, priesthood, prophecy, wisdom, and royalty were all sponsored by God.

Nevertheless, the prophet Nathan and King David established a precedent for recognizing the responsibility of government officials to accept prophetic critique and of the prophet to express necessary critiques of the moral failings of government officials. Just as the kings of Israel and Judah were subject to divine critique by the agency of prophets, so also, according to two narratives in 2 Samuel, were kings subject to divine critique by the agency of female sages (2 Samuel 14, 20).

The Book of Amos reports that in the eighth century BCE the prophet Amos challenged the power of both the priest (Amaziah) and the king (Jeroboam II), and he was not executed or exiled for so doing. Jeremiah

26:18–19 relates similarly that at the time of the Assyrian invasion of Judah in 701 BCE, when the prophet Micah declared that Jerusalem was going to be destroyed because of the sinfulness of the people of Judah, instead of ordering the execution of the prophet who was literally giving aid and comfort to the enemy, King Hezekiah asked Yahweh to renounce the punishment, and Yahweh acceded to the request of the God-fearing king. However, it is reported that Jeremiah suffered imprisonment at the hands of King Zedekiah (Jeremiah 37), that an earlier king Jehoiakim burnt the scroll of divine rebuke that had been written by Jeremiah's secretary Baruch, and that Jehoiakim would, indeed, have imprisoned Jeremiah had he not gone into hiding (Jeremiah 36). It appears that female sages and prophets of both sexes were charged with reviewing and critiquing the policies of kings just as in modern states executive orders of kings, presidents, and prime ministers and legislation approved by parliaments are reviewed and annulled by courts of justice.[17]

In addition to their connection with kings, the prophets were also associated with the encouragement of ethical behavior. Ethics was in fact intimately bound up with the religion of ancient Israel. With the major exceptions of Elijah the prophet's contest with the priests of Baal to determine who is the one true God, Yahweh or Baal, and the related material in Hosea 1–3 probably from the beginning of the reign of King Jehu, and the diatribes against Judean worship of "other gods" in Jeremiah and Ezekiel, prophetic literature is concerned primarily with encouraging ethical behavior and eschewing unethical behavior, in the name of Yahweh, among both Israelites/Judeans and human-kind at large. Likewise, biblical wisdom literature exemplified by the Books of Proverbs, Job, and Ecclesiastes gives the impression that ethical behavior and religion are synonymous. The law corpora contained in the Pentateuch – the Ten Commandments (Exodus 20; Deuteronomy 5), the Covenant Code (Exodus 21–24), the Holiness Code (Leviticus 17–26), and the Deuteronomic Code (Deuteronomy 11–26) – are concerned for the most part with ethical behavior. Indeed, they seem to concur with respect to a hierarchy of values, according to which the murder of a person is punishable by death and may not be compensated by a monetary payment. Likewise, in Hebrew Scripture, capital punishment is never contemplated as a just punishment for expropriation of property as it was elsewhere in the ancient Near East.[18] The one legal code that seems to have very little to say about ethics is the priestly code contained in Exodus 25–31, 35–40 and Leviticus 1–16. Israel Knohl explains this as follows: "According to the Priestly Torah, no new moral command is entrusted to the nation at Sinai, since the Sinai revelation [as it is expounded in Ex. 25–31, 35–40] focuses on the dimension of God that surpasses morality."[19]

In addition to ethical issues, certain philosophical questions were an important part of ancient Israelite religion. The literary legacy of ancient Israel deals, *inter alia*, with philosophical issues that include the existence of God, the reality of human suffering, and the debate as to whether human suffering is deserved. On one level the debate between Job and his friends in the Book of Job revolves around the question of whether Job in particular and people in general are the victims of undeserved suffering. His learned friends contend that there is no undeserved suffering, but Job is vindicated by Yahweh himself. Apparently some very smart and knowledgeable people (i.e., wise people) argued in Late Iron Age Israel that "there is no God." A psalmist whose words have been preserved in two slightly different versions in Psalm 14 and Psalm 53 responded to this atheist philosopher not by debating with her/his ideas but by attacking her/his credibility by saying, "The fool said in his heart, 'There is no God'," which is to say, "No truly educated person would say that."

Just as Job and his friends debate the question as to whether or not, in the long run, innocent people suffer and guilty people go unpunished, so also do they debate a theological question as to whether reliance on the words of angels in dreams is reasonable (Job and Elihu) or not (Job's friends). A recurring theme that runs through the wisdom literature of Hebrew Scriptures including the narrative of Joseph, the narrative of King Solomon in the Book of 1 Kings, the Book of Job (especially Chapter 28), the Book of Proverbs, Psalm 111, and the end of the Book of Ecclesiastes is that the highest wisdom is not that obtained by education and experience but that which is conferred as a divine gift. According to Deuteronomy 4, the highest manifestation of the highest wisdom is the code of laws contained in Deuteronomy 11–26, which ensure harmony at home and in the larger society, and which should cause all other peoples to admire the people whose God is Yahweh.

5. RESEARCH

What distinguishes the ancient literature referring to the religion(s) of the ancient states of Israel and Judah from the literature of the other peoples of the ancient Middle East is that some of the literary legacy of ancient Israel was cherished and copied and transmitted by the Samaritans, the Jews, and the Christians from antiquity to modern times. This literary legacy consists of the Five Books of Moses, which are still copied and revered and read by all of those faith communities, and the other thirty-four books of Hebrew Scripture, which are still copied, revered, and read by the Jews and the Christians. Each of these groups saw itself as the authentic continuation of the religion of ancient Israel. The religious literature of the other peoples of the ancient Middle East was not transmitted except for some brief quotations in the writings of ancient historians such as the Jew Josephus Flavius (37–100 CE) and Christian theologians such as Eusebius, the bishop of Caesarea (fourth century CE). While the religious and secular literature of the peoples of ancient Mesopotamia (Sumerians, Akkadians, Babylonians, and Assyrians) was not cherished, copied, and transmitted in late antiquity and the Middle Ages, original copies of a myriad of texts in the languages of ancient Mesopotamia came to light as a result of archaeological research since the middle of the nineteenth century CE. Since the Israelites did not write in cuneiform on clay tablets but rather on highly perishable organic materials such as papyrus and animal skins, very little of their literature has survived in ancient copies from the Iron Age. To date, no monumental inscriptions of any Israelite kings have been found. However, we have abundant references to the later kings of Israel and Judah in the inscriptions of the Assyrian kings who fought against Israel and Judah and in the annals of the Babylonians, who put an end to the State of Judah in 586 BCE. A stone inscription from the ninth-century BCE King Mesha of Moab corroborates the perception one would derive from most of the thirty-nine books of the Hebrew Bible or Old Testament, that the God of Israel is designated by the name YHWH just as the deity of Moab is called Chemosh.[20]

The scientific study of ancient Israelite religion, or, rather, the construct(s) of the beliefs and practices of adherents of the worship of one God commonly called Yahweh, has generally been pursued as part of biblical theology, which reflects primarily but no longer exclusively a Protestant belief that the Bible consisting of the Old Testament and the New Testament is the sole authoritative guidebook available to Christians in formulating their beliefs and governing their behavior. More recently, some Jewish biblical scholars have taken up the study of what they call "Jewish Biblical Theology" or "Hebrew Bible Theology." These scholars would like to understand the abiding value of the ideas of Hebrew Scripture independent of what has been read into them during the last two millennia. Since the nineteenth century CE, scholars have adopted an evolutionary model for understanding the religion(s) of Hebrew Scripture, especially the worship of a single deity, and they have widely assumed that it developed from polytheism, achieved its greatest heights in the sermons of Amos and Isaiah in the eighth century, and went into decline after the destruction of Jerusalem in 586 BCE.

Classic scholarship on the religion of ancient Israel is exemplified by Johannes Pedersen's *Israel: Its Life and Culture*, which deals with issues such as "the soul, its powers and capacity"; the power of blessing; salvation; sin and curse; and the world of life and death, as well as the various issues concerning religion raised in the present volume.[21] Since the discovery of inscriptions linking Yahweh to "his Asherah," there has been a proliferation of studies debating whether "many Israelites" or "most Israelites" actually venerated Yahweh alone, Yahweh with a consort, or Yahweh along with other deities. Typical are the studies by Mark Smith, Ziony Zevit, and Jeffrey Tigay.[22] Another major trend in the study of the religion(s) of ancient Israel is the debate as to whether there was an ancient Israel in the Early Iron Age or the Late Iron Age or at all.[23] Several recent works on Hebrew Bible Theology suggest that the sun may be rising on a new movement to reexamine the abiding truths about religious/spiritual issues in Hebrew Scripture.[24]

FURTHER READING

Especially recommended are *Israel* by Johannes Pedersen and *The Religions of Ancient Israel* by Ziony Zevit, listed under Works Cited.

CHRONOLOGY

1353–1336 BCE	King Ahkenaten of Egypt, possibly first monotheist in history
1224–1214 BCE	King Merneptah of Egypt (first datable mention of Israel in the first year of his reign, c. 1224 BCE)
1000 BCE	Saul, first king of Israel
1000–961 BCE	King David of Israel
961–922 BCE	King Solomon of Israel
873–852 BCE	King Ahab of Israel
722 BCE	Conquest of the Kingdom of Israel by Sargon II of Assyria
715–687 BCE	King Hezekiah of Judah
698–642 BCE	King Manasseh of Judah
640–609 BCE	King Josiah of Judah
609–598 BCE	King Jehoiakim of Judah
597–586 BCE	King Zedekiah of Judah

586 BCE	Conquest of the Kingdom of Judah by Nebuchadrezzar II of Babylonia (604–562 BCE)
539 BCE	Cyrus of Anshan conquers Babylonia, Isaiah 40–66 composed
522–486 BCE	Darius I of Persia Prophecies of Zechariah
445–425 BCE	Nehemiah the Persian Governor of Yehud (Judah)
Third century BCE	Dead Sea Scrolls, first century CE

GLOSSARY

Levites: The descendants of the third son of Jacob and Leah, from among whom, according to Numbers 3, the descendants of Aaron, brother of Moses, were selected to be "priests," while the other members of the tribe became assistants to the priests.

Samaritans: An Israelite sect, once found all over the Roman Empire, now confined to Holon, Israel, and Nablus, Palestine. They regard themselves as descendants of those Israelites who were not deported from Samaria in 722 BCE. The Jews regarded them as the persons whom the Assyrians deported *to* Samaria in 722 BCE. The content of their bible is limited to the Five Books of Moses.

Notes

1 Breasted 1933.
2 Cogan 1974 showed that there is no evidence that the Assyrians required their vassals to worship Assyrian deities.
3 Gruber 1999.
4 See the various standard commentaries on Isaiah 40–66 and the chapter on Iran in this volume.
5 Zevit 2001:608.
6 Ibid.
7 See Dever 2005.
8 See Kletter 1996 and Dever 2005:176–179.
9 See, in addition to Dever 2005:132, Niditch 1997:21 and Smith 2002, 2001:73; for dissenting views see Smith 2001:238, 55; Wiggins 1993; and Tigay 1986; for another interpretation see Hutton 2010.
10 See Ackerman 2006:1:298; for this meaning of *asherah* in Biblical Hebrew see, e.g., Deuteronomy 16:21; Judges 6:25, 26, 30; and Smith 2002:118–147.
11 Ackerman 2006:1:298 and Dever 2005:160–167; cf. Smith 2001:74.
12 Ahituv, Eshel, and Meshel 2012.
13 See Gruber 1992.
14 Ibid.
15 The speeches of unnamed female sages are found in 2 Samuel 14 and 2 Samuel 20, respectively. See Camp 1990.
16 See Muffs 1992.
17 Cf. Spiegel 1957.

18   Cf. Greenberg 1962.

19   Knohl 2003:33–34.

20   For this apt formulation, I am grateful to my colleague, Dr. Daniel Vainshtub.

21   Pedersen 1926–1940: soul (1:99–181); blessing (1:181–212); salvation (1:330–335); sin and curse (1:411–452); the world of life and death (1:453–496); for various other issues discussed in the current volume, see Vols. 3–4. A similar list of topics is discussed most succinctly in Niditch 1997.

22   Smith 2002, Zevit 2001, and Tigay 1986.

23   See Gruber 2001; key players in minimalizing ancient Israel are Thompson 1999 and Whitelam 1997. Key players in the backlash are reflected in Talshir 1999, Rainey 1995, Dever 2001, and Dever 2003.

24   Zevit 2005 and Kalimi 1997.

Works Cited

Ackerman, Susan. 2006–2009. *The New Interpreter's Dictionary of the Bible*, s.v. "Asherah." Nashville.

Ahituv, Shmuel, Esther Eshel, and Ze'ev Meshel. 2012. "The Inscriptions." In *Kuntillet, Ajrud (Horvat Teman: An Iron Age Religious Site on the Judah-Sinai Border)*. Ed. Ze'ev Meshel, 73–142. Jerusalem.

Breasted, James Henry. 1933. *The Dawn of Conscience*. New York and London.

Camp, Claudia V. 1990. "The Female Sage in Ancient Israel and in the Biblical Wisdom Literature." In *The Sage in Israel and the Ancient Near East*. Ed. John G. Gammie and Leo G. Perdue. Winona Lake, IN.

Cogan, Mordechai. 1974. *Imperialism and Religion*. Missoula, MT.

Dever, William G. 2001. *What Did the Biblical Writers Know and When Did They Know It?* Grand Rapids, MI.

———. 2003. *Who Were the Israelites and Where Did They Come From?* Grand Rapids, MI.

———. 2005. *Did God Have a Wife? Archaeology and Folk Religion in Ancient Israel*. Grand Rapids, MI.

Greenberg, Moshe. 1962. *Interpreter's Dictionary of the Bible*, s.v. "Crimes and Punishments." 1: 733–744.

Gruber, Mayer I. 1992. *The Motherhood of God and Other Studies*. University of South Florida Studies in the History of Judaism 57. Atlanta.

———. 1999. *Dictionary of Deities and Demons in the Bible*, s.v. "Gilulim." Ed. Karel van der Toorn, Bob Becking, and Pieter W. Van Der Horst, 2nd ed. Leiden and Grand Rapids, MI.

———. 2001. "The Ancient Israel Debate." *Ancient Near Eastern Studies* 18: 3–27.

———. 2008. "Is the Principal Human Speaker in Micah 6–7 a Woman?" (in Hebrew). *Shnaton Leheqer HaMiqra Ve-HaMizrah HaQadum* 18: 13–24.

Hutton, Jeremy M. 2010. "Local Manifestations of Yahweh and Worship in the Interstices: A Note on Kuntillet 'Ajrud." *Journal of Ancient Near Eastern Religions* 10: 177–210.

Kalimi, Isaac. 1997. "History of Israelite Religion or Old Testament Theology? Jewish Interest in Biblical Theology." *Scandinavian Journal of the Old Testament* 11(1): 100–123.

Kletter, Raz. 1996. *The Judean Pillar Figurines and the Archaeology of Asherah.* BAR International Series. Oxford.

Knohl, Israel. 2003. *The Divine Symphony.* Philadelphia.

Muffs, Yochanan. 1992. *Love and Joy: Law, Language and Religion in Ancient Israel.* 9–48. New York.

Niditch, Susan. 1997. *Ancient Israelite Religion.* New York and Oxford.

Pedersen, Johannes. 1926–1940. *Israel: Its Life and Culture.* 4 vols. London and Copenhagen.

Rainey, Anson F. 1995. "Uncritical Criticism." *Journal of the American Oriental Society* 115: 101–104.

Smith, Mark. 2001. *The Origins of Biblical Monotheism.* Oxford.

———. 2002. *The Early History of God: Yahweh and Other Deities in Ancient Israel.* 2nd ed. Grand Rapids, MI.

Spiegel, Shalom. 1957. *Amos Vs. Amaziah.* New York.

Talshir, Zipora. 1999. "Textual and Literary Criticism of the Bible in Post-Modern Times, the Untimely Demise of Classical Biblical Philology." *Henoch* 21: 235–252.

Thompson, Thomas L. 1999. *The Mythic Past: Biblical Archaeology and the Myth of Israel.* London.

Tigay, Jeffrey H. 1986. *You Shall Have No Other Gods: Israelite Religion in the Light of Hebrew Inscriptions.* Atlanta.

Whitelam, K. W. 1997. *The Invention of Ancient Israel: The Silencing of Palestinian History.* London.

Wiggins, Steve A. 1993. *A Reassessment of Asherah.* Kevelaer and Neukirchen-Vluyn.

Zevit, Ziony. 2001. *The Religions of Ancient Israel: A Synthesis of Parallactic Approaches.* London and New York

———. 2005. "Jewish Biblical Theology: Whence? Why? and Whither?" *Hebrew Union College Annual* 76: 289–340.

5 Anatolia

BILLIE JEAN COLLINS

Because Anatolia, the peninsula of land that is today the Republic of Turkey, was host in antiquity to a variety of peoples with distinct cultures and languages who were subject to shifting political forces over centuries and millennia, it is impossible to speak of Anatolian religion as a single, definable phenomenon. Here the discussion will be limited to the period of the Late Bronze Age, when Anatolia was largely under the control of the Hittite kingdom. Already in speaking of Hittite religion, we have to consider in tandem the religious beliefs and practices not only of the Hittites but of the Palaians, Hattians, and Luwians, and how they dovetail with Hurrian, Syrian, and Mesopotamian traditions.

I. HISTORICAL DEVELOPMENT

To what degree elements of prehistoric Anatolian religion can be seen in Hittite practices and beliefs is a matter of evolving debate as new information continues to come to light and new methodologies are employed to interpret the data. Already in the Neolithic period reverence for dead ancestors is unmistakable, a cult of stelae (the use of standing stones in worship) is in place, and the gods are conceived of in anthropomorphic form. Sometime in the Chalcolithic period these anthropomorphized deities are given material form and with it shrines served by a priesthood and a regular cult. The prevalence of bulls and stags in both cult and iconography from the Neolithic period on presage their prominence in the religions of Late Bronze Age Anatolia. The so-called standards in the form of deer, bulls, and solar disks from the Early Bronze Age "royal" tombs at Alaca Höyük have been interpreted by some as early representations of the tutelary, storm, and solar deities that dominate the pantheon of the Hittite period. Images on Anatolian seals from the trade emporium at Kanesh at the beginning of the second millennium (Middle Bronze Age) anticipate some of the themes visible in Hittite art, and deities named in Assyrian-language documents from this time are also attested in later Hittite sources.

Yet even as it retained at its core some very ancient elements, Anatolian religion in the second millennium BCE was dynamic and fluid.

Geographic and climatic considerations formed the basis for Hittite religious beliefs, but political developments on the plateau were primarily responsible for their evolution. What we refer to as "Hittite religion" is a blend of religious beliefs and practices emanating from the many distinct cultural traditions that fell within the range of Hittite political influence from the eighteenth to the early twelfth centuries BCE. These include the Indo-European Hittites who arrived in Anatolia sometime in the third millennium; the indigenous Hattians whom they encountered on their arrival on the plateau; the Hittites' close linguistic cousins, the Luwians, who settled in western and southern Anatolia; and the Hurrians, whose impact on Hittite religious and political life would escalate with the passing centuries, and through whom the Hittites were exposed to Syrian and Babylonian thoughts and concepts.

Whether one subscribes to the theory that a new Hurrian dynasty emerged out of Kizzuwatna with Tudhaliya II or assumes dynastic continuity, there is no question that Anatolia saw a profound shift in religious ideology from the beginning of the Empire period. Hurrian influence permeates the religion, with one of the main developments noticeable in the pantheon, whose final form is found beginning with the lists of divine witnesses in the state treaties of Suppiluliuma I and continues with only slight modifications until the end of Hittite history.[1] In addition, southern cults (both Luwian and Hurrian) were artificially introduced into northern towns where the deities of the Hattian pantheon were traditionally worshiped. The ideology of kingship that had taken shape already by the time of Hattusili I underwent a significant metamorphosis only at the end of the Empire, when its last two kings attempted to deify themselves as a means of shoring up their waning authority.[2] These and other developments indicate that throughout its history, Hittite religion was, in essence, a syncretistic system constructed for, and favored by, the state and thus has only a limited amount to tell us about Anatolian religion as it was practiced among the common people in the period of Hittite political domination.

Hittite religion as practiced and promoted by the state was shaped virtually entirely by contact with other cultures. In addition to the developments described previously, several instances of the appropriation of religious practices as a means of strengthening newly forged political alliances are a matter of historical record.[3] It was understood that deities introduced into the state cult for such reasons preferred to be worshiped according to their native customs, and thus their cult statues would have been accompanied by the necessary cultic personnel to ensure the proper conduct of their cult. Arguably the most significant example was Hattusili I's abduction of the Storm God of Aleppo during his campaigns in north Syria. At first worshiped as a foreign deity, he eventually became syncretized with the storm god Teshub, becoming fully integrated into the state pantheon by the early empire.

Less easily mapped but just as evident are the routes by which Hittite religion influenced its neighbors. At the forefront of this conversation have been contacts with the Greeks in western Anatolia. Anatolian deities with Greek equivalents include the Sun Goddess of the Earth and Demeter,[4] the Storm God who bears the epithet *pihassassi* and Pegasos,[5] and Telipinu and Dionysus.[6] Ritual practices have hinted at the depth and range of cultural exchange in Anatolia, in particular necromantic rites,[7] certain forms of pig sacrifice,[8] choral song,[9] and the scapegoat.[10] On the mythic level, the *kursa*, a hunting bag made of goatskin, has been connected with the Golden Fleece, Athena's aegis, and the "breasts" of the statue of Artemis of Ephesus;[11] the Illuyanka myth, involving a battle with a dragon, is also incorporated into the myth of the Golden Fleece;[12] and the Telipinu myth provides an antecedent for the Hesiodic Hymn to Demeter.[13] Finally, numerous correspondences between Hurro-Hittite poetry and Hittite prayer and Greek epic and prayer have been identified.[14]

On its southeastern border, the flexible organizational structure of the Hittite kingdom at the end of the Late Bronze Age facilitated the flow of goods and people, with the Syrian vassal states forming an effective bridge spanning the geographical distance between Hittite Anatolia and the Levant. Across this bridge many religious (as well as artistic and literary) ideas may have passed, most notably among them the scapegoat rite attested in Leviticus 16,[15] which is rooted in a common Anatolian ritual type, and the biblical covenant form, which draws on the structure of the Hittite vassal treaties.[16]

2. BELIEF

Their expansive pantheon was a point of pride for the Hittites, and they invoked the "thousand deities" collectively in blessings and as witnesses in their treaties. We may attribute the size of the pantheon to the absorption of foreign deities into the cult as a result of the growth of political control. Scribes brought a certain order to the pantheon by grouping together local deities who showed a common character. For example, they designated all bringers of rain and thunder with the same Mesopotamian ideogram (U) indicating a storm god. This system, though, renders it difficult to tell what deity is meant by the generic designation – the Mesopotamian sign for Tutelary Deity "LAMMA" could refer to any number of deities, including Zithariya, Hapantaliya, and Inara – and often the original names of the deities are entirely lost. So, to distinguish deities belonging to a particular "type," the scribes sometimes attached the name of the city that served as the deity's cult center. Thus are attested the storm gods of Nerik, Zippalanda, Aleppo, and Arinna.

In the Old Kingdom, the state pantheon was shaped by the traditions native to the new capital at Hattusa and the territories surrounding the fledgling state,[17] which included primarily Hattian and Palaian deities. The pantheon in this period was led by the Storm God of Hatti (Hattian Taru, Hittite Tarhuna) and the Sun Goddess of the city of Arinna (Hattian Wurunsemu). In the Empire, the pantheon was reorganized around the theological and administrative policies of the ruling house.[18] Thus, at least in court circles, the Storm God was worshiped in the guise of Hurrian Teshub and the Sun Goddess was identified with Hurrian Hebat. In addition, a complex set of circumstances that included a shift in focus to the southern reaches of the kingdom and the relocation of Luwian population groups to northern cities depopulated by plague resulted in the rise in prominence of deities from the Luwian-speaking territories of Anatolia, as well as from Hurrian Syria and Mesopotamia. These included, among others, the tutelary LAMMA deities and Sausga (Ishtar).

The myths and iconography indicate that the gods were conceived of in human terms. They required sustenance, exhibited a range of emotions, and were negatively affected by the acts of other gods – if one failed to perform his divine duties, all suffered. The gods were neither omniscient nor omnipotent, but made mistakes and were capable of being deceived. Still, they possessed a wisdom and power that was far above that of man. The level of wisdom and power varied widely depending on each deity's status within the pantheon, which itself often depended on the importance of the natural phenomenon that that deity represented.

Most important were the storm gods, who brought the rain and winds to fertilize the crops. Solar deities (Sun, Moon) of both genders were also prominent. Deities of grain, vineyards, and orchards were directly responsible for the prosperity of the crops. There were also deities of wildlife, of war and pestilence, and personal protective deities who often served as intermediaries to the other gods on behalf of their mortal charges. The mother goddesses were responsible for the creation of man and for birth in general, while the fate goddesses (Gulses) determined human destiny. Other groups of gods, some whose nature can hardly be determined, are attested, including the Heptad (the "Seven") and the twelve primordial (underworld) deities. Finally, the mountains, rivers, streams, heaven and earth, winds, and clouds are included in lists of divine witnesses to diplomatic treaties; we are not given their individual names in these contexts.

Hittite deities, particularly goddesses, were usually depicted in human form, that is, anthropomorphically, although divine representations could take a wide variety of forms. The Hittites endeavored to understand the cosmos through imagery drawn from the daily experiences of agrarian life. Hence the character of many deities was manifested through an association with some animal. They were frequently depicted standing on their associated animals and others were even represented by their associated animal. For example, a bull often stood in for the storm god. In other cases, inanimate objects or fetishes could stand in for the deity, so the cult image might be a stela (*huwasi*), a weapon (mountain gods), a rhyton in the shape of a fist (war gods), or a solar disk (sun gods).

The Hittites have left behind sparse evidence of an indigenous cosmogony or cosmology. Any ideas of a demiurge or a creation seem to be borrowings, either from Mesopotamia or from the Hurrians. A handful of allusions to cosmological ideas can be found in texts of various genres. In the Hurrian Song of Ullikummi, we find reference to the cutting apart of Heaven and Earth with a copper saw as the primary act of creation, a motif familiar from Sumerian myth. Somewhat closer to the Genesis tradition, a Hittite ritual fragment, again reflecting north Syrian tradition, contains this allusion to the creation: "The crescent moon rose, the darkness (bore) the Earth, the lightness bore the stars."[19]

Hittite art offers clues to a Hittite cosmology. The Hittite rock monument at Eflatun Pinar is comprised of monumental blocks of stone carved in a relief composition representing the cosmos, with the supreme deities of the land framed by symbols of the heavens (winged sun disks) and the earth (mountain gods). Interspersed on either side and in between the two seated deities are genii (mythic hybrid creatures) and bull men, poorly preserved today but whose arms are raised to support the winged disks above the deities as well as the larger one that caps the entire monument. This image of the cosmos is repeated in variant form elsewhere in Hittite iconography.

Prayers describe the Sun God crossing "the gate of heaven" and arising from the sea.[20] One Hattian ritual relates how the gods in primeval time constructed a palace and established the kingship.[21] The gods lived either in Heaven or in the Underworld, according to an incantation addressed to the divine river:[22]

> When they took heaven and earth, the gods divided (it) up for themselves. The upperworld deities took heaven for themselves, and the underworld deities took the land beneath the earth for themselves. So each took something for himself. But you, O River, have taken for yourself purification, the life of the progeny, and procreation(?).

As a conduit between the two spheres, the river was an appropriate locus for the performance of magic rituals connected with purification and fertility. Another incantation offers a possible eschatological reference: "When the ancient kings return and examine the lands and custom(s), only then shall this seal also be broken."[23] This sentence may be intended in the sense of "when hell freezes over," but it is also possible that it refers to an eschatological belief, similar to the Davidic tradition, in the return of an ancient line of kings.

How a person lived his life does not appear to have affected the quality of his afterlife, although an untimely death might be attributable to divine retribution for "sinful" behavior. When the Gulses, or fate deities, cut the thread of an individual's life on earth, and he arrived at the "day of his destiny," the body of the deceased was either inhumed or cremated according to the appropriate funerary rites, freeing his soul to embark on the journey along the road to the Underworld. The Sun Goddess of the Earth had the task of transporting souls to her realm, where, according to one text, the dead did not recognize their loved ones and their diet consisted of mud and waste water.[24] The souls of the fortunate apparently did not stay in this place for long, but rather, aided by the performance of the proper mortuary rites, ultimately reached the "meadow of the blessed." Thus, in Hittite theology, death was viewed as a kind of rebirth.

3. PRACTICE

The gods received the individual attentions of their human attendants on a daily basis. Offerings featured a variety of baked goods and libations of beer and wine, and depending on the time of year, first-fruits offerings. In the daily care of the gods, animals were also regularly sacrificed for their table. The blood sacrifice of a sheep or goat, or, less often, cattle was the high point of most offering rituals. The prospect of a feast attracted the deity to his temple, where the participants in the ritual (usually temple personnel) could join him or her in a communal meal.

The sacrificial ritual typically began with the consecration of the animal and the cleansing of the participants, the image of the deity, and the space in which the sacrifice would occur. A liturgy might be recited and incense burned. The animal, of top quality, was brought in, followed by a procession. The procession could include singers and musicians as well as other participants in the ritual, such as the cook. The animal was slaughtered and then butchered and the deity given the roasted heart and liver. The cook used the remainder of the animal to make a stew to be shared by the participants. The food was set out, libations poured, and the feasting began. At this point, the king might "drink the deity," that is, he toasted him.

Elaborate rituals of attraction, deriving primarily from Kizzuwatna, might be performed to draw the divinities to whatever festivities were being held in their honor. In addition to laying out honey, wine, milk, butter, and other offerings, ritual specialists drew paths with colorful textiles and branches to attract the gods and assist them in finding their way. These efforts were supplemented by incantations summoning the gods. On arrival at the festival, the deity took up residence in his or her statue, to which the offerings would be presented.

A less common form of sacrifice in Anatolia proper were burnt offerings, which were also introduced from Hurrian Kizzuwatna. Birds were the most frequent victim in such sacrifices, although lambs and kids might also be offered. Burnt offerings were often directed to the gods of the underworld.

Divination, the science of determining future events by means of signs sent by the gods, encompasses both oracles, or solicited portents, and omens, in which the deity took the initiative by sending a sign. The Hittites practiced several kinds of oracles, in each of which the professional diviner asked a question and the deity was expected to answer in the particular divinatory language chosen. The most common options included extispicy, entailing the examination of sheep entrails; "bed" (*sasta-*) oracles – so called because the "bed" plays an important part – in which the diviner observed the sheep's behavior on its way to slaughter; symbol oracles, involving the manipulation of tokens representing personages and concepts; augury, the observance of bird behavior; "snake" oracles, involving the movement of eels (or morays) in a basin of water; and the mysterious *ḪURRI*-bird (= partridge?) oracles, whose modus operandi remains unclear, but which were performed by diviners (not augurs).

Dreams as a means by which the gods communicated their will to humans were the most common form of omen in Hittite texts of the

Empire period. The deity could either speak to the dreamer directly or else send a messenger in the form of someone known to the dreamer. Dreams could also be oracles, if they were solicited by dream incubation, that is, by sleeping in the temple in the hopes of receiving a message from heaven. Prophets were also active in parts of Anatolia in the Late Bronze Age, but we know nothing about who they were or how and where they might have functioned.

Prayers offered an additional means of communicating with the divine realm. Royal prayers composed in the Empire period, and probably recited in cultic contexts as needed, were called *arkuwar*, "pleading, defense," and served as a justification to the gods, just as one would plead one's case in court. Prayers typically included an invocation to the deity, an argument or defense, and a plea or petition.

The worship of the gods was carried out in a variety of sacred spaces. Temples served not only to house the statue of the deity but also the priests and craftsmen who were in service to the deity. The Great Temple, dominating the northern part of Hattusa, had a large area set aside as offices and residences for temple dependents. The main temple quarter in Hattusa was located in the Upper City to the south. Here, sanctuaries of various sizes, but following a consistent architectural plan, were dedicated to the cults of the state gods. Every town and village of any size within the Hittite domain had at least one temple that was staffed with cult personnel. Excavations at Kuşaklı-Sarissa, considered to be a medium-sized Hittite town, have revealed a temple in the lower city whose plan resembles those of the temples in Hattusa's temple quarter. Another religious complex on the acropolis bears architectural similarities to the Great Temple in Hattusa and was dedicated to the local storm god. Hittite temples have also been excavated at the regional centers of Maşat-Tapikka and Ortaköy-Sapinuwa.

The image of the god was housed in the cella, or main shrine of the temple. Hattusa's Great Temple had two cellas, one for the Storm God and one for the Sun Goddess. Each temple contained many rooms surrounding a central courtyard. Crossing the courtyard from the temple entrance, those allowed access would have passed through a portico to reach the cella, which could have accommodated only priests and a small number of worshipers.

Worship of the Hittite gods was also frequently carried out in sacred precincts on rocks or mountains. Open-air sanctuaries were commonplace in Anatolia, particularly where some natural feature, such as a large rock outcropping or a spring, lent itself to the numinous. Such ceremonial complexes have been found at Yazılıkaya, Gavurkalesi,

Eflatun Pinar, Yalburt, Kuşaklı-Sarissa, Gölpinar near Alaca Höyük, and Ağilönü near Ortaköy-Sapinuwa, and it is possible that all Hittite towns of significance were equipped with such places. The texts often refer to rituals taking place on mountains, which were considered, from early Hittite times, to be the place where the presence of the celestial deities (especially the storm gods) could be felt, and where special ceremonies devoted to their worship were performed. A common element of open-air worship was the standing stone, called *huwasi*. Each stela belonged to a specific deity, for which it was a representation, functioning in this respect just as the god's statue functioned in his temple.

Festivals punctuated the cultic calendar at regular intervals throughout the year. The major yearly festivals, the festival of the crocus (AN.TAH.ŠUM), celebrated in the spring, and the festival of "haste" (*nuntarriyashas*), celebrated in the autumn, kept the king and his entourage on the road traveling from town to town visiting temples within the religious district of north-central Anatolia for weeks at a time. The *purulli*-festival was celebrated throughout Hittite times to mark the regeneration of life at the beginning of the agricultural year. The festival schedule included a recitation of the myth about the conflict between the storm god and a dragon, Illuyanka. The very ancient KI.LAM festival (Hittite *hilammar*) involved the hosting in Hattusa of delegations from various towns belonging to a kind of amphictyony,[25] or religious federation, who supplied produce for the festival. Among the many highlights of this festival was a lengthy parade before the king that included a troop of dancers and a display of images of wild animals in precious metal.

In addition to the major yearly festivals, there were also festivals commemorating other aspects of agrarian life. More than eighty Hittite festivals are known by name. Generally speaking, fall festivals celebrated the harvest in the filling of the storage vessels, while the spring festivals celebrated breaking open these stored goods.

The primary source of religious authority was the king. Under his auspices, an elaborate but largely anonymous priesthood maintained the state and local cults. Priests (the highest ranking were called *sankunni*) were responsible for the daily care of the gods, celebrating the festivals, and protecting the temple. Also serving the gods directly were the "anointed" priests (GUDU$_{12}$) and the "mother of the deity" (*siwanzanna*) and "lady of the deity" (EREŠ.DINGIR) priestesses. The reigning queen held the title *siwanzanna*. These, however, seem to be fairly generic designations masking what was a far more complex religious bureaucracy, as many more priestly titles are known from the texts. Beyond evidence of a rigid hierarchical structure, we know remarkably little about what specific responsibilities accompanied which title and where they fell within the temple hierarchy.

Towns within the core of Hittite political power participated in a kind of amphictyony manifested in the performance of festivals at the Hittite capital as well as within important towns. Civic participation in these festivals implies an awareness of (and desire to promote) distinct religious identities even as they publicly affirmed a collective one.[26] Whether individual towns operated local cults independent of the state is improbable, although it is likely that traditions associated with local shrines continued under state oversight and in juxtaposition with imposed state cults.

Outside of the royal family we have almost no information about personal piety. We may speculate that common people probably participated in festivals as musicians, singers, and dancers, and took part in whatever domestic rituals were customary in their household, including perhaps sacrificial meals, votive offerings, and the ancestor cult. The male head of the family would have been responsible for private sacrifices as well as for maintaining the cult of the ancestors. In addition, anyone might find him- or herself the client in a ritual performed by a specialist for a wide variety of reasons.

In the area of personal religion, numerous rituals were recorded that address a wide array of concerns, including illness, family discord, bad years, infertility of the fields, birth, death, sorcery and other criminal offences (e.g., perjury, physical injury, or murder), human fertility, and impotence. Rituals also addressed crises that affected the community as a whole, like plague, military defeat, bad omens, building rites, and cultic events, which included attracting absent deities, erecting divine images, and correcting offenses against the gods. The primary means of removing the affliction were analogic magic or sympathy, transference or contagion, and substitution. Analogic magic combines ritual action with an incantation that links that action to the desired outcome, as when the ritualist throws the wax and fat into a fire while reciting the incantation "Just as this wax melts and just as the sheep fat is rendered, who breaks the oath and takes deceptive action against the king of Hatti, may he melt like the wax and may he be rendered like the sheep fat."[27] Transference is particularly common in the Luwian milieu and might involve the waving of an animal over the patient or touching an animal to the parts of a patient's body. The rituals involving a scapegoat also fall into this category. Substitution of an object, animal, or human for the afflicted individual was practiced in response to inauspicious oracles.

4. SOCIAL CONTEXT

The relative anonymity under which priests and priestesses other than the king and queen – who sat at the top of the priestly hierarchy – operated is a reflection of the control exerted by the state over the religious structures of the kingdom. The priesthood was a state-sponsored profession, one to which certain privileges, such as exemption from taxes, were attached. While priests of temples in major cities were often of royal lineage, village priests may have been commoners occupying a relatively low rung in Hittite society. The existence of families of priests means that it is likely that in some cases the priesthood was a hereditary profession.[28] Besides the priests and priestesses, the personnel required to run the main temple at Hattusa included musicians, dancers, augurs, and diviners, as well as many occupations that were more "secular" in nature, including scribes, cooks, leather workers, potters and other artisans (goldsmiths, silversmiths, stonecutters, engravers, weavers), herders for the temple flocks, farmers who tilled the temple lands, and kitchen personnel, as well as the temple guards. In festivals belonging to the Hattian cultural layer, young girls (*zintuhis*) participated in choruses, as did groups of women or men belonging to specific towns. In the case of the latter, the choruses may have been attached to temples, either temporarily or permanently, or they may have been simply the citizens of towns sent as delegations to the festival.[29]

A variety of professional ritual practitioners of both genders were qualified to oversee the appropriate ritual performance on behalf of individuals. Physician-exorcists, augurs, and ritual experts called "wise women" are found. The exorcists and augurs were skilled (male) professionals, trained in ritual and divinatory techniques, while the wise women were repositories of folk knowledge. Rituals might also be performed by women of other professions, including midwives, hierodules, and priestesses. Women and men sometimes worked together in the performance of rituals, as in the case of the wise woman Anniwiyani and her son Armati, an augur. At least some of these practitioners were slaves, but through service to the royal family some did quite well for themselves. A systematic study dedicated to gender roles and the role of gender in Hittite ritual and religion has yet to be undertaken.[30]

Politics were central to the articulation of piety in the state-sponsored religion, and decisions regarding the cult were rarely made independently of political concerns. Tudhaliya II's adoption of the cult of the Goddess of the Night in Samuha as relations with her home territory of Kizzuwatna were intensifying, the promotion of the cult of the Storm God of Aleppo as Hatti's empire in Syria grew, Muwatalli II's move of the Hittite capital to Tarhuntassa in the Lower Land as part of a refocusing of the state religion on southern cults, and Tudhaliya IV's introduction of cults of deities connected with the kingship into Hurma are just a few examples of the interconnectedness of politics and religion. Conversely, political decisions were rarely made independently of religious concerns. Divination was a common tool of the kings for determining the optimum time for the inauguration of a monarch, or approving changes in a festival program, or deciding the best way to attack a city.

The interconnectedness of politics and religion is also apparent in royal ideology. In his role as military leader, the Hittite king was frequently depicted in the guise of a war god. Already in Hattusili I's annals, dating to the seventeenth century, the Sun Goddess was said to "run before" the king in battle, ensuring his victory, although in the Old Kingdom, the notion of divine guidance – of the intervention of the divine in human affairs – is not pronounced. Humans were accountable for their own actions and their own successes or failures. In Telipinu's Proclamation (c. 1500 BCE), divine judgment of Ammuna and other "failed" kings of the past was more implied than stated. By the Empire period, however, divine causality in historical events is much more in evidence; the gods are manifest in history, intervening to ensure victory or defeat. This is most in evidence in the Apology of Hattusili III, a document that credits the king's successes to the patronage of the goddess Sausga (Ishtar).

Theologically speaking, divine support (especially military) of the ruling house presupposed the correct performance of festivals.[31] At the same time, such state-sponsored festivals formed an important element in Hittite domestic policy. The festivals served for the participating towns and their representatives as an expression of allegiance to the king, and for the king as a means of forging a collective religious identity and unity among the subject peoples. Public officials, representatives of the amphictyony cities, and foreign diplomats attended the festivals. The farther away a participant was from the king physically during the performance, the lower was his or her status. Festivals were carried out not only in the capital but in other towns of cultic significance within the kingdom.

To what extent the temples participated in the state economy is unclear. The massive storerooms within the precinct of the Great Temple at Hattusa are witness to the redistributive role that temples played with the agricultural products harvested from temple-owned lands. Beyond this, evidence of an independent economic role for the temples is lacking. As the cult inventories suggest, individual temples, although administered by priests, were ultimately under the control of the king, and the extent of their resources depended on the degree of royal patronage that they enjoyed. To the extent then that the king presided over the state religion, we may say that it was intimately connected to the economic health of the kingdom even if the anatomy of its role cannot as yet fully be reconstructed.

Similarly, insofar as the king was identified with the Sun God of Heaven, the divine judge, and presided over the highest court in the land, the judicial system, too, was intimately tied to the state religion. As the representative of the deity on earth, the Hittite king was sometimes depicted in the priestly garb of the Sun God. The Sun's judicial role and his elevation in the pantheon may be due to the influx of Hurrian-mediated Mesopotamian ideas in the early Empire.[32]

The Hittite literati did not, so far as we know, engage in debate about the nature of things. Still, an ethical code was in place, although the term "ethics" in a Hittite context is out of place. The term *āra*, "right, acceptable, permitted," and its inverse *natta āra*, "wrong, unacceptable, not permitted," identified what was considered appropriate and civilized, that is, normative, behavior in Hittite society.[33] Because it was bestowed by the gods, *āra* has to do with divine law as distinguished from human law and, in religious contexts, with the sacred as opposed to the profane. This concept contributed to the regulation of moral behavior in Hittite society, as it helped to articulate the dangers of disorder and chaos.[34] Where *āra* circumscribed human behavior, *handandatar*, "divine providence," made possible the correct functioning of the world through the divine promise of order, justice, and balance.

When bad things happened, the inhabitants of ancient Anatolia sought the cause either in some transgression on the part of the afflicted individual or in the form of a sorcerer, demon, or angry deity. Whether committed willfully or accidentally, transgressions (sins) aroused the displeasure of the divine and could manifest themselves in pollution or impurity adhering to an individual. Social sins, such as murder or theft, brought on impurity and might be dealt with by ritual means in addition to whatever legal punishment awaited the guilty party. Inadvertent sins (stumbling upon an unclean object or location, or unknowingly transgressing a taboo) or ritual defilement stemming from a number of unavoidable sources had to be reckoned with. The burden for an offense ignored by the transgressor passed to the next generation, so once pollution had accrued to the individual it had to be dealt with by ritual means. Identifying the sin, acknowledging it, and correcting it were the necessary steps to reconciling man with his god and thus with society at large, particularly at the royal level. The purity of the king and his family was a major preoccupation of the state religion. His well-being was connected to that of the entire land and he of all humans operated in closest proximity to the gods.

5. RESEARCH

Religious documents constitute by far the largest percentage of the texts recovered from the archives and libraries of Hittite Anatolia. These religious compositions are official in nature, not canonical or theological, and were not written to aid in private devotion. Instead, the records were intended to aid the bureaucracy in the organization and maintenance of the religious responsibilities of the king, and as such are purely practical documents, including regulations to guide the temple personnel in the performance of their duties; records of cultic administration; prescriptions for the proper performance of festivals and rituals; reports of diviners; religious compositions, including mythological narratives, used in scribal education; and so on. Despite their limitations, these texts offer a wealth of information about religious life in Late Bronze Age Anatolia.

The material record also provides important clues to religious activities. Small figurines in precious metal and stone of divine beings and other cult objects, images carved into living rock, and scenes on seals reveal how the Hittites conceptualized the divine. Ground plans of temples allow us to imagine the daily activities of the priests and other temple personnel as they went about the business of maintaining the gods' cults. The remains of ancient waterworks (pools and wells, for example) and the religious structures built in and around natural water sources, such as springs and rivers, are vivid reminders of the role of water as a conduit to the world below the earth and to the beings that inhabited that world.

With these sources at our disposal, our understanding of Hittite religion in all its aspects continues to undergo constant revision as old assumptions are abandoned for a more nuanced interpretation of the motivations and mechanisms behind the textual sources. As our knowledge of Hittite geography improves, so does our grasp of local and regional permutations of the religion. Further, scholarship has become sensitive to the implications of the shifting political climate for the development of the religion. One subject currently undergoing close scrutiny is the large corpus of personal rituals and the relationship between the ritualists who performed them and the scribes who recorded them. Why were the rituals committed to writing? Who really used them? How did their textualization affect their practice? To what extent are the apparent geographic and ethnic signatures within the rituals blurred by scribal interference? Another line of inquiry is the ideology behind the religious texts. For example, were Hurrian myths about kingship in heaven connected to imperial royal ideology? And were they purely literary compositions or were they a part of a living festival tradition? A related question is the extent of Anatolia's role in the transmission of Near Eastern ideas to the West. One issue that has bedeviled scholars for some time is the problem of the beliefs of the common people, which can only be inferred from the textual sources. For example, did imported Hurrian concepts have an impact on the population of Anatolia at large? What role did court theologians play in propagating the royal cult among the rest of the population? Can we make meaningful distinctions between the state cult and local practices? And how long did native Hattian religious beliefs survive, and when and how did their concepts change? Finally, the degree of continuity between Hittite religion and the beliefs and practices of previous and subsequent periods of Anatolia's past continues to engage scholars.

FURTHER READING

Monographic works devoted to the topic of Anatolian religion are mercifully becoming more plentiful. These now include Haas 1994, 2003; Popko 1995; and Taracha 2009. Briefer overviews of Hittite religion may be found in Bryce 2002, Beckman 2005, and Collins 2007. Studies of specific cultural layers within Hittite religion include Klinger 1996, Miller 2004, Bawanypeck 2005, Christiansen 2006, Strauß 2006, and Hutter 2003. For studies of individual major festivals see Singer 1983–1984, Nakamura 2002, Wegner and Salvini 1991, and McMahon 1991. For divination see van den Hout 1998, 2003 and Beal 2002. For Hittite prayers see Singer 2002. For the priesthood see Taggar-Cohen 2006. For the cult inventories see Hazenbos 2003. Van Gessel's three-volume catalog of the Hittite pantheon (1998–2001) is accessible primarily to specialists. For the mythology see Hoffner 1998 and Pecchioli-Daddi and Polvani 1990. Important monographic studies of particular rituals are Glocker 1997 and Taracha 2000. Schuol's 2004 study of cult music is also worthwhile.

Works devoted to the study of specific ritual genres are Beckman 1983 (birth) and Kassian et al. 2002 (death). Specialized editions of individual religious compositions are too numerous to list here.

CHRONOLOGY

The following dates are all BCE. All dates are approximate.

9600–6000	Neolithic
6000–3100	Chalcolithic
3200–2000	Early Bronze Age
2000–1650	Middle Bronze Age
1690–	Huzziya I
1670–	Labarna
1650–1400	Old Kingdom
1650–	Hattusili I
1620–	Mursili I
1590–	Hantili I
1560–	Zidanta I
1550–	Ammuna
1530–	Huzziya II
1525–	Telipinu
1500–	Alluwamna
	Tahurwaili
	Hantili II
	Zidanta II
	Huzziya III
	Muwatalli I
1400–1180	Empire
1400–	Tudhaliya II
	Arnuwanda I
	Hattusili II?
	Tudhaliya III
1350–	Suppiluliuma I
1322–	Arnuwanda II
1321–	Mursili II
1295–	Muwattalli II
1272–	Mursili III
1267–	Hattusili III
1237–	Tudhaliya IV

1209–	Arnuwanda III
1207–	Suppiluliuma II
1180	Hattusa is abandoned

GLOSSARY

Assyrian: In the context of Middle Bronze Age Anatolia, the language of the merchants from the northern Mesopotamian city of Assur living in one of the trade emporia established in central Anatolia, most important among them Kanesh. The merchants left behind archives written in the Old Assyrian dialect of Akkadian.

Hurrians: A people who lived in northern Mesopotamia and Syria in the Bronze Age. The territories of the Hittite Empire in the south, especially Kizzuwatna, were largely populated by Hurrians.

Kizzuwatna: A politico-geographical territory in southeastern Anatolia, corresponding to Cilicia of the Classical period.

Palaian: The third Indo-European language spoken in Anatolia in the second millennium, spoken in the territory of Pala, corresponding geographically to the Roman province of Paphlagonia.

Sumerian: The language and people of southern Mesopotamia at the beginning of history. The language was a part of the scribal curriculum in the Hittite administration.

Lower Land: The territory of Hittite Anatolia incorporating the Konya Plain and eastern Pamphylia.

vassal states: Small kingdoms in Anatolia and Syria that were bound in vassalage to the Hittite authority by treaty.

Notes

1 Taracha 2009:86, 88.
2 van den Hout 1995:545–73 and Beckman 2002:37–43.
3 See, e.g., Bachvarova 2009:36–37.
4 Collins 2002.
5 Hutter 1995.
6 Tassignon 2001.
7 Steiner 1971.
8 Collins 2006.
9 Rutherford 2007.
10 Bremmer 2001.
11 Haas 1975, Watkins 1998, and Morris 2001; also Bremmer 2006.
12 Haas 1975, 1978 and Bremmer 2006.
13 Burkert 1979:123–42.

14   West 1997 and Bachvarova 2002, 2005, 2009.
15   For this rite, see, e.g., Janowski and Wilhelm 1993.
16   See most recently Berman 2006:79–113 and Collins 2007:109–11.
17   Taracha 2009:38.
18   Ibid, 82.
19   *KUB* 57.66 (*CTH* 670) iii 16.
20   Mursili II's Prayer to the Sun Goddess of Arinna (*CTH* 376.A §4, for which
     see Singer 2002:51) and Muwatalli's Prayer to the Assembly of Gods (*CTH*
     381 §66, for which see Singer 2002:91).
21   *KUB* 29.1 (*CTH* 414).
22   Bo 3617 (*CTH* 433) i 8'–14' with duplicates.
23   *CTH* 404, trans. Miller 2004:106.
24   *CTH* 457.6, §4, trans. Hoffner 1998:34 (no. 11).
25   Rutherford 2005.
26   Rutherford 2007:80.
27   *COS* 1.66:165, §5.
28   Taggar-Cohen 2006:441.
29   Rutherford 2007:78–79.
30   But see Beckman 1993.
31   Hutter 2008: 85.
32   Taracha 2009:89.
33   Cohen 2002:161–69.
34   Cohen 2002:167.

Works Cited

Bachvarova, M. 2002. "From Hittite to Homer: The Role of Anatolians in the
   Transmission of Epic and Prayer Motifs from the Ancient Near East to the
   Ancient Greeks." Ph.D. diss. University of Chicago.
———. 2005. "The Eastern Mediterranean Epic Tradition from Bilgames and
   Akka to the Song of Release to Homer's Iliad." *Greek, Roman and Byzantine
   Studies* 45: 131–54.
———. 2009. "Hittite and Greek Perspectives on Travelling Poets, Texts and
   Festivals." In *Wandering Poets in Ancient Greek Culture: Travel, Locality
   and Pan-Hellenism.* Ed. R. Hunter and I. Rutherford, 23–45. Cambridge.
Bawanypeck, Daliah. 2005. *Die Rituale der Auguren.* Theth 25. Heidelberg.
Beal, Richard H. 2002. "Hittite Oracles." In *Magic and Divination in the Ancient
   World.* Ed. Leda Ciralo and Jonathan Seidel, 57–81. Leiden.
Beckman, Gary. 1983. *Hittite Birth Rituals.* Studien zu den Bogazköy-Texten 29.
   Wiesbaden.
———. 1993. "From Cradle to Grave: Women's Role in Hittite Medicine and
   Magic." *Journal of Ancient Civilizations* 8: 25–39.
———. 2002. "'My Sun-God': Reflections of Mesopotamian Conceptions of
   Kingship among the Hittites." In *Ideologies as Intercultural Phenomena.*
   Ed. Antonio C. D. Panaino and Giovanni Pettinato, Melammu Symposia
   3. Milan.
———. 2005. "How Religion Was Done." In *Companion to the Ancient Near
   East.* Ed. D. Snell, 343–489. Oxford.

Berman, Joshua A. 2006. "God's Alliance with Man." *Azure* 25: 79–113. Online (by subscription): http://www.azure.org.il/article.php?id=131. Accessed Nov. 4, 2009.

Bremmer, Jan N. 2001. "The Scapegoat between Hittites, Greeks, Israelites and Christians." In *Kult, Konflikt und Versöhnung: Beiträge zur kultischen Sühne in religiösen, sozialen und politischen Auseinandersetzungen des antiken Mittelmeerraumes.* Ed. R. Albertz, 176–86. Alter Orient und Altes Testament 285. Münster.

———. 2006. "The Myth of the Golden Fleece." *Journal of Ancient Near Eastern Religion* 6: 9–38.

Bryce, Trevor. 2002. *Life and Society in the Hittite World.* Oxford.

Burkert, W. 1979. *Structure and History in Greek Mythology and Ritual.* Berkeley and Los Angeles.

Christiansen, B. 2006. *Die Ritualtradition der Ambazzi. Eine Philogoische und entstehungsgeschichtliche Analyse der Ritualtexte CTH 391, CTH 429 und CTH 463.* Studien zu den Bogazköy-Texten 48. Wiesbaden.

Cohen, Yoram. 2002. *Taboos and Prohibitions in Hittite Society.* Texte der Hethiter 24. Heidelberg.

Collins, Billie Jean. 2002. "Necromancy, Fertility and the Dark Earth: The Use of Ritual Pits in Hittite Cult." In *Magic and Ritual in the Ancient World.* Ed. Paul Mirecki and Marvin Meyer, 224–41. Leiden.

———. 2006. "Pigs at the Gate: Hittite Pig Sacrifice in Its Eastern Mediterranean Context." *Journal of Ancient Near Eastern Religion* 6: 155–88.

———. 2007. *The Hittites and Their World.* Atlanta.

COS = W. W. Hallo, ed., *The Context of Scripture,* vol. 1. Leiden 1997.

CTH = Emmanuel Laroche, *Catalogue des textes hittites* – Paris 1971 (mit Ergänzungen in RHA XXX, 1972, 94–133 = CTH Suppl., und RHA XXXIII, 1973, 68–71).

Gessel, Ben H. L. van. 1998–2001. *Onomasticon of the Hittite Pantheon.* 3 vols. Handbuch der Orientalistik 1/33. Leiden.

Glocker, Jürgen. 1997. *Das Ritual für den Wettergott von Kuliwišna. Textzeugnisse eines lokalen Kultfestes im Anatolien der Hethiterzeit.* Eothen 6. Florence.

Haas, Volkert. 1975. "Jasons Raub des Goldenen Vliesses im Lichte hethitischer Quellen." *Ugarit Forschungen* 7: 227–33.

———. 1978. "Medea und Jason im Lichte hethitischer Quellen." *Acta Antiqua* 26: 241–45.

———. 1994. *Geschichte der hethitischen Religion.* Handbuch der Orientalistik 1.15. Leiden.

———. 2003. *Materia Magica et Medica Hethitica. Ein Beitrag zur Heilkunde im Alten Orient.* 2 vols. Berlin.

Hazenbos, Joost. 2003. *The Organization of the Anatolian Local Cults during the Thirteenth Century B.C.* Cuneiform Monographs 21. Leiden.

Hoffner, Harry A. Jr. 1998. *Hittite Myths.* 2nd ed. Atlanta.

Hout, Theo van den. 1995. "Tuthalija IV. und die Ikonographie hethitischer Großkönige des 13. Jhs." *Bibliotheca Orientalis* 52: 545–73.

———. 1998. *The Purity of Kingship: An Edition of CTH 569 and Related Hittite Oracle Inquiries of Tuthaliya IV.* Documenta et monumenta Orientis Antiqui 25. Leiden.

———. 2003. "Orakel. B. Bei den Hethitern." *Reallexikon der Assyriologie* 10: 118–24.

Hutter, Manfred. 1995. "Der luwische Wettergott *piḫaššašši* und der griechische Pegasos." In *Studia onomastica et indogermanica: Festschrift für Fritz Lochner von Hüttenbach zum 65. Geburtstag*. Ed. M. Ofitsch and C. Zinko, 79–97. Graz.

———. 2003. "Aspects of Luwian Religion." In *The Luwians*. Ed. H. C. Melchert, 211–80. Handbuch der Orientalistik 1.68. Leiden.

———. 2008. "Die Interdependenz von Festen und Gesellschaft bei den Hethitern." In *Fest und Eid: Instrumente der Herrschaftssicherung im Alten Orient*. Ed. Doris Prechel, 73–87. Kulturelle und sprachliche Kontakte 3. Würzburg.

Janowski, Bernd and Wilhelm, Gernot. 1993. "Der Bock, der die Sünden hinausträgt: Zur Religionsgeschichte des Azazel-Ritus Lev 16,10.21f." In *Religionsgeschichtliche Beziehungen zwischen Kleinasien, Nordsyrien und dem Alten Testament*. Ed. Bernd Janowski, Klaus Koch, and Gernot Wilhelm, 109–69. Freiburg.

Kassian, Alexei, Andrej Korolëv, and Andrej Sidel'tsev. 2002. *Hittite Funerary Ritual: šalliš waštaiš*. Alter Orient und Altes Testament 288. Münster.

Klinger, Jörg. 1996. *Untersuchungen zur Rekonstruktion der hattischen Kultschicht*. Studien zu den Bogazköy-Texten 37. Wiesbaden.

KUB = Keilschrifturkunden aus Boghazköy – Berlin 1921ff.

McMahon, G. 1991. *The Hittite State Cult of the Tutelary Deities*. Assyriological Studies 25. Chicago.

Miller, Jared. 2004. *Studies in the Origins, Development and Interpretation of the Kizzuwatna Rituals*. Studien zu den Bogazköy-Texten 46. Wiesbaden.

Morris, Sarah. 2001. "The Prehistoric Background of Artemis Ephesia: A Solution to the Enigma of Her 'Breasts'?" In *Der Kosmos der Artemis von Ephesos*. Ed. U. Muss, 135–51. Österreichisches Archäologisches Institut Sonderschriften 37. Vienna.

Nakamura, M. 2002. *Das hethitische nuntarriyašha-Fest*. Publication de l'Institut Historique et Archéologique Néerlandais de Stamboul 94. Leiden.

Pecchioli Daddi, F. and A. M. Polvani. 1990. *La mitologia ittita*. Testi del Vicino Oriente Antico 4. Florence.

Popko, Maciej. 1995. *Religions of Asia Minor*. Warsaw.

Rutherford, Ian C. 2005. "The Dance of the Wolf-Men of Ankuwa. Networks, Amphictionies and Pilgrimage in Hittite Religion." In *Acts of the 5th International Congress of Hittitology*. Ed. Aygül Süel, 623–39. Ankara.

———. 2007. "The Songs of the Zintuhis: Chorus and Ritual in Anatolia and Greece." In *Anatolian Interfaces: Hittites, Greeks and Their Neighbours: Proceedings of an International Conference on Cross-Cultural Interaction, September 17–19, 2004, Emory University, Atlanta, GA*. Ed. B. J. Collins, M. R. Bachvarova, and I. C. Rutherford, 73–83. Oxford.

Schuol, Monika. 2004. *Hethitische Kultmusik: Eine Untersuchung der Instrumental- und Vokalmusik anhand hethitischer Ritualtexte und von archäologischen Zeugnissen*. Orient-Archäologie 14. Rahden/Westfalen.

Singer, Itamar. 1983–1984. *The Hittite KI.LAM. Parts One and Two*. Studien zu den Boğazköy-Texten 27 and 28. Wiesbaden.

———. 2002. *Hittite Prayers*. Atlanta.

Steiner, G. 1971. "Der Unterweltsbeschwörung des Odysseus im Lichte heth-itischer Texte." *Ugarit Forschungen* 3: 265–83.

Strauß, Rita. 2006. *Reinigungsrituale aus Kizzuwatna: Ein Beitrag zur Erforschung hethitischer Ritualtradition und Kulturgeschichte.* Berlin.

Taggar-Cohen, Ada. 2006. *Hittite Priesthood.* Texte der Hethiter 26. Heidelberg.

Taracha, Piotr. 2000. *Ersetzen und Entsühnen. Das mittelhethitische Ersatzritual für den Großkönig Tuthalija (CTH *448.4) und verwandte Texte.* Culture and History of the Ancient Near East 5. Leiden.

———. 2009. *Religions of Second Millennium Anatolia.* Dresdner Beiträge zur Hethitologie 27. Wiesbaden.

Tassignon, I. 2001. "Les éléments anatoliens du mythe et de la personnalité de Dionysos." *Revue de l'histoire des religions* 218: 307–37.

Watkins, Calvert. 1998. "Homer and Hittite Revisited." In *Style and Tradition: Studies in Honor of Wendell Clausen.* Ed. P. Knox and C. Foss, 201–11. Stuttgart.

Wegner, I. and M. Salvini. 1991. *Die hethitisch-hurritischen Ritualtafeln des (ḫ) išuwa-Festes.* Corpus der hurritischen Sprachdenkmäler I/4. Rome.

West, M. L. 1997. *The East Face of Helicon: West Asiatic Elements in Greek Poetry and Myth.* Oxford.

6 Iran

W. W. MALANDRA

Iran exercised considerable influence over peoples and cultures of the eastern Mediterranean, even though the Iranian plateau (including the modern states of Iran, Afghanistan, and parts of Iraq, Pakistan, and the old republics of the Soviet Union in the Caucasus and Central Asia) lies seemingly far to the east. Throughout this region people spoke various related languages and shared common religious beliefs and practices. This chapter deals with Iranian religion, and more specifically with Zoroastrianism, its traceable beginnings c. 1000 BCE to its eclipse by Islam (a process beginning 651 CE).

I. HISTORICAL DEVELOPMENT

During the third millennium a large group of loosely associated tribes calling themselves *Arya*, living somewhere in central Asia and speaking related dialects of what is now known as the Indo-Iranian group of Indo-European languages, differentiated itself into two major linguistic and cultural groups. By the middle of the second millennium the one group was migrating into the Punjab region of the Indian subcontinent and into Anatolia, while the other group was migrating over the Iranian plateau. The Indo-Aryans who found themselves in the ancient Near East played a brief role in political and military affairs, but they were soon absorbed by the dominant cultures. The Aryans who settled the Punjab and those who moved to Iran soon overwhelmed the respective indigenous populations politically, linguistically, and culturally. Once sharing common religious ideologies and cultic practices, as they settled down, the two groups began to develop their religious lives along separate lines. Nevertheless, when the religious texts of both are studied together they provide a basis for reconstructing common features and for identifying innovations. Central to both was the sacrificial worship of the gods in which an essential element was the preparation of the sacred drink (Avestan *haoma*, Old Indic *soma*). They worshiped deities some of whom bore the same or nearly identical names, for example, Mithra/Mitra, Wayu/Vayu (Wind), and Thvoreshtar/Tvashtar, some of whom represented common concepts of divine functions, for example, Werethraghna/Indra (warrior), Spenta Armaiti/Prithivi (Earth), and Atar/Agni (Fire). At the head of the ancient Iranian pantheon was the god Ahura Mazda. The concept of the cosmic force of truth and order *rta* (Avestan *asha*, Old Persian *arta*) was fundamental to both groups.

The ancient Iranian religion was transformed by the religious reformer Zarathushtra (Greek Zoroaster), who lived in northeastern Iran sometime during the first half of the first millennium, but before Cyrus. This man of profound religious insight reformed the inherited religion according to his "Vision" (*daena*) into a theological system of mostly abstractions that were seen as modalities of the great creator god Ahura Mazda, the Wise Lord (or Lord Wisdom). These modalities, called Entities, formed an interrelated group that came to be known as the Bounteous Immortals (Amesha Spentas). He also articulated an ethical dualism that pitted Ahura Mazda and the Entities as upholders of Truth and Order against the demonic forces of Lie and Disorder. He instituted certain cultic reforms having to do with sacrificial slaughter and with the *haoma* ritual. He and the community of believers who were his initial followers experienced strong opposition from traditionalists until he converted a local ruler, Wishtaspa, who became his protector and patron. In the absence of any historical record, we can only surmise that over time the religion of Zarathushtra spread in eastern Iran, and in the process made dramatic accommodations with traditional religion. In the Avesta, the sacred scriptures of Zoroastrianism, the Yashts, collections of verses dedicated to specific divinities, show the incorporation of the old pantheon into a new synthesis. It was this synthesis that eventually made its way into western Iran during the period of the Achaemenid Empire, where it assimilated some western Iranian ideas and practices and where its priesthood came to be dominated by the old Median priestly tribe of the Magi. Once it had become the religion of the empire, Zoroastrianism remained the official religion up to the Arab conquest.

Of particular interest in the history of this religion is the perplexing problem of whether Zoroastrianism exerted an influence on Judaism and Christianity, and if so, to what extent. It is well known that Cyrus is hailed in the Bible as a liberator and accorded the status of *mashiach* "(God's) anointed" (messiah) by Deutero–Isaiah. The return by Cyrus of the exiled elites from Babylon and the rebuilding of the temple and walls of Jerusalem are chronicled in Ezra–Nehemiah. To what extent, if any, were Judaism and later Christianity indebted to Zoroastrianism for ideas that surface beginning in the fifth century but persist well into the Parthian period, ideas such as a trans-historical *mashiach*, heaven and hell, and a day of judgment? Although Zarathushtra was the first in history to articulate these ideas, it is difficult to find any direct link, as such ideas may be *sui generis* among oppressed people.

2. BELIEF

Ancient Iranian religion identified two distinct classes of divine beings: *yazata* ("god," i.e., "one to be worshiped") and *daiwa* ("demon"). At the head of the pantheon stood Ahura Mazda. He was a creator in the sense that he exercised dominion over creation in establishing order and putting everything in its proper place. The actual crafting of the creation was the work of the demiurge, Thvoreshtar, "Craftsman." Ahura Mazda's consort was the Earth, known by the name Spenta Armaiti, though he seems to have had other wives, the Ahuranis, "Wives of Ahura." Ahura Mazda had a particular connection to the cosmic principle of order and truth called Rta, and, like the supreme Vedic god Varuna, was a source of insight into Truth for poets, the divinely inspired creators of sacred hymns. Two male deities were closely associated with Ahura Mazda. One was Rashnu, "Judge," who had a limited judicial function, analogous to that exercised by Varuna, in serving as the divine judge presiding over the oaths sworn by men. The other was Mithra. While Mithra was a complex deity, the essence of his being was that he was foremost the god "Covenant;" that is, he presided over all treaties between nations and covenants between people. The image of him as a mighty warrior riding in his chariot full of weapons reflects his ability to enforce the sanctity of covenants. As a warrior he shares much in common with another powerful deity, Werethraghna, "Victory," whose name etymologically means "the smashing of resistance." As such he embodied the ideal of the Iranian warrior who was capable of smashing the defenses of all enemies. Warriors invoked both Mithra and Werethraghna as they went into battle, yet when it came to the exercise of legitimate temporal power and the success of the ruler in wielding that power, two other forces came into play. The Iranians developed a unique concept of an impersonal force called Xᵂarenah, conceived as a fiery presence that attached itself to legitimate rulers but remained unseizable by illegitimate usurpers. Without this royal Glory one could not hope to hold power. Whereas Xᵂarenah was an impersonal power, victory to the legitimate ruler and righteous warrior was granted by the goddess Anahita. Like Athena and Ishtar, she dispensed success in arms. The ancient

Iranians also worshiped deities identified with natural phenomena, for example, the Wind, the Sun and Moon, as well as the rain-bringing star Tishtrya (Sirius) and the complex fluvial goddess Aredwi Sura.

The elements of Zarathushtra's belief system run through the history of Zoroastrianism, although its coherence as a system was never well articulated in the tradition. His system must be reconstructed out of the Gathas themselves. As already mentioned, Zarathushtra's theology needs to be understood against the background of his inherited religion. Although Ahura Mazda was a high-god in the ancient Iranian pantheon, Zarathushtra elevated him to a position that seems to have excluded most of the traditional deities. He was the Creator, and in this sense one might think of monotheism. However, neither Zarathushtra nor his followers ever expressed their belief in terms of the exclusivity of one God, as have Jews, Christians, and Muslims. In other words, "monotheism" was not a concept that Zarathushtra entertained. His Vision was that Ahura Mazda projected certain modalities of his nature that assumed a sort of quasi-independent existence. One begins with Good Mind, the modality of proper thought that leads to an understanding of Truth, the basis of the order of both nature and society that includes the individual. In order to bring the understanding of Truth into actual practice it is necessary to exercise Dominion or Power. Dominion mediated through Right-mindedness leads ultimately to the pair Wholeness and Life. Fundamental also to Zarathushtra's system of belief was his idea of a radical dualism of Truth and Lie. Transforming an ancient Indo-European mythic complex involving the existence of primal Twins, one of whom slaughters the other, and from the body parts constructs the world, Zarathushtra spoke of two primal twin Spirits. The one, the Most Bounteous Spirit, chose Truth, while the other, the Lying One, chose what is worst, and each created life and non-life. The choices made by the primordial Spirits are, accordingly, paradigms for human free will, whereby individuals will be judged by their actions.

Neither in Zarathushtra's Gathas ("Songs") nor in the Avesta as a whole do we get a clear exposition of the cosmology. The cosmos was basically three-tiered, consisting of earth, atmosphere, and heaven. The earth was divided into six concentric continents surrounding the central continent, where *aryana waejah*, "the Iranian Expanse," was located. At the center of the earth was the cosmic mountain, Hara Berezaiti, the Elburz, which acted as the *axis mundi*. At its southern flank was the sacred Wouru-kasha Sea, in the middle of which grew the Tree of Life. Over the earth and expanse of sky arched the stone vault of heaven beyond which was the realm of the Infinite Lights, and the heavenly abode called the Best Existence and the House of Song. Below the earth was the realm of Infinite Darkness. The entire earth rested upon and was surrounded by the waters of chaos. Fresh water flowed down Hara in the river goddess Aredwi Sura into the Wouru-kasha and from it the various rivers of the world flowed accumulating pollutants in their courses to the salt sea called Puitika, the Filterer, from which the hydrological cycle repeated itself.

As far as one can reconstruct on the basis of Pahlavi sources, thought concerning the temporal dimension of the cosmos was in terms of a system of three or four world ages, analogous to the *yuga* system of ancient India and the four metallic ages of Greece, with each lasting 3,000 years. One can guess that there was an idea of the degradation of the cosmos over the course of the ages and that a complete cycle would have ended with a cataclysm and subsequent creation that renewed the cycle, though in its present form the cycle has been thoroughly transformed into a myth of creation, a battle of good and evil, the final triumph of the good and the establishment of the eternal kingdom of God, Ohrmazd, the Pahlavi name for Ahura Mazda.

In the texts stemming from the Sassanid period we find a coherent cosmology, especially in the *Bundahishn*, in terms of an extensive myth that includes cosmogony and eschatology. Central to Zoroastrian cosmology is the belief that both Ohrmazd and Ahriman, the Evil Spirit, fashioned their respective creations first as non-material or spiritual, then as material. The "orthodox" or strict dualist version is as follows. From all eternity Ohrmazd was above in a realm of light, while below was Ahriman in a realm of darkness; and between them was the Void. At a certain moment Ohrmazd, through his omniscience, became aware that Ahriman, in his stupidity and aggression, would attack. He created his creation in the spiritual state. Meanwhile, rising to the Void, Ahriman became aware of the light-realm and of Ohrmazd and determined to attack. He also created a mis-creation in the spiritual state. Up to this point both Ohrmazd and Ahriman were infinite in time and space (though limited by the Void). Ohrmazd realized that in order to defeat Ahriman he would have to capture him in temporal finitude. At the close of the first 3,000-year period, Ahriman assaulted Ohrmazd's realm but was repulsed by the sacred *ahunwar* prayer and fell back stunned into the dark abyss. For the next 3,000 years both Ohrmazd and Ahriman created their material creations in preparation for battle. In terms of theology, it is important to understand that Ohrmazd's creation is neither an inexplicable nor capricious act. Creation has as its purpose the defeat of evil and at the head of creation is mankind as helpmate to God. In the year 6000 Ahriman and the demons invaded. Ohrmazd had created the world with its stone vault of heaven essentially as a trap. Once Ahriman broke through, his way was barred, and without means of retreat he and his evil creation were caught in finite space and time. In this dualistic system each creation of Ohrmazd was matched with an antagonistic creation of Ahriman. When Ahriman invaded, he and his demons set about to pollute and destroy the good creation. Especially grievous for man was that the Jeh (the Whore demoness) kissed Gayomard (the primal hermaphrodite Man), thereby polluting women and injecting corruption into human nature. In the year 8970 by Zoroastrian reckoning, Zardusht (Zarathushtra) was born in various miraculous circumstances. At age thirty he received the Religion from Ohrmazd, preached, and in 9012 converted Wishtaspa. Following Zardusht's death there began a gradual decline that has lasted even to the present. Then, in 9970, Ushedar, the first of three Saviors (soshyans) will be born from the miraculously preserved semen of Zardusht. His millennium will follow the pattern of Zardusht's. The pattern will again be repeated in 10970 with the birth of Ushedarmah. Then in 11943 will be born the true Soshyans. At the age of thirty he will inaugurate the Frashegird or Renovation of the World. Ahriman and the demons will be defeated in a final great battle and cast into outer darkness. The dead will be quickened, including those who had been condemned to hell for their misdeeds. There will be a last judgment and all will be cleansed in a bath of molten metal. History will end and the eternal kingdom of Ohrmazd will be established. There was also a Zurvanite variant of the myth in which Time was the father of Ohrmazd and Ahriman.

Beliefs about the soul, death, and an afterlife in Zoroastrianism were complex. A person possessed a number of what one might loosely call souls. In addition to animating forces, the *urwan* was the individual's soul that survived death and went to the other world; the *frawashi* was a guardian spirit, especially an ancestor spirit; the *daena* was a sort of spiritual double. At death, when the breath of life departed, the soul hovered near the corpse (immediately possessed by Nasu, the demon of putrefaction) for three days before journeying to a bridge crossing to the other world. This is the Cinwat-bridge mentioned already by Zarathushtra. It is not known what ethical concepts were originally applied to this perilous crossing, but with Zarathushtra and the rest of the Zoroastrian tradition the crossing meant the time of reckoning for one's good and evil deeds, with the righteous proceeding to heaven, the wicked to the abyss.

3. PRACTICE

Ancient Iranian cultic practices were quite similar to those referred to in the Vedic literature of India. Worship of the deities was ritually performed through the *yasna*. Originally this was a complex ritual that involved the offering of a victim (food) and the sacred *haoma* (drink). Modeled on rites of hospitality, the *yasna* was an elaborate festive meal to which a deity or deities were invited as honored guests. The deity was offered food and drink and was entertained through the recitation of poetry created for the occasion to magnify the divine guest. The Yashts of the Avesta are collections of such poetry. Over the passage of time the *yasna* became increasingly formalized. Avestan texts specify eight priests necessary to perform the various functions of the *yasna*, but over time this was reduced to just two who subsumed the older separate functions. As in all religions, the cycles of life were observed through rites of passage. Two such rites merit special attention: initiation and death. The initiation rite marked the passage for both boys and girls from childhood to the beginnings of adulthood. Investiture with the sacred girdle is an ancient tradition that probably has the same origin as the sacred thread of twice-born Hindus. This had to be worn at all times. In addition there was a sacred shirt to be worn. Death posed a great problem for Zoroastrian society owing, on the one hand, to the fate of the soul, and on the other, to the threat of ritual contagion to society by the corpse, which upon death becomes possessed by the Corpse Demon, the Nasu Druj. Three days of wake were required for the soul to leave the body and journey to the Bridge of Judgment, after which the corpse was placed in a precinct called *daxma* where it was exposed to the elements and the ravages of scavenger birds and beasts. The *daxma* was constructed in such a way that the sacred elements of earth and water were isolated from pollution. Cremation was not an option, since the corpse would pollute the sacred element of fire. Moreover, since pollution from demonic creation threatened people at all times, there were elaborate purification ceremonies to render people clean who had come into contact with polluting agents, especially carrion and menstrual blood.

In the material world in which Iranians lived and practiced their religion, one must consider sacred time according to the calendar and sacred space according to places of cultic practice. The basic organization of the Zoroastrian calendar was established probably during the fourth century BCE and is still in use to this day. The day was divided into five watches during which prescribed religious activities could be performed. Each month was thirty days long with no division into weeks, though 1, 8, 15 and 23 are each dedicated to Ahura Mazda and the rest are dedicated to the six Amesha Spentas and other deities of the pantheon. Each of the twelve months is also dedicated to a deity. Thus, the year was a solar year of 360 days, with five intercalary days observed between the last and first months. Further, there was (and is) a series of seasonal festivals, all harkening back to pre-Zoroastrian times. No Roz (New Day) is the New Year festival, still a major holiday in Muslim Iran. Marking the Spring Equinox, it is followed by Mid-Spring, Mid-Summer, Bringing-in-Grain, Homecoming (of the herds from summer pasture), Mid-Winter, and All-Souls. The latter was the five-day period marking year's end, a liminal time when the souls of the ancestors return to dwell among the living. Cultic rituals were located in fire temples. There the sacred fires were tended and kept perpetually burning by priests and the daily *haoma* sacrifice (*yasna*) was performed. Only initiated males were permitted in the general precincts of the temple and only duly consecrated priests could enter the holy of holies to enact the *yasna*.

As for the organization of cultic practice, for the earliest stages of Iranian religion there appears to have been no ecclesiastical structure beyond hereditary priests who served their communities. The presiding priest was the *zaotar*, "the one who offers libations," who was attended by various functionaries. Another functional title, *athaurwan*, became the name for the sacerdotal caste, though originally it may have designated those priests charged with the care of the sacred fire, *atar*, both the element and a deity. For the Achaemenid and Arsacid periods there is little information beyond references to the priestly caste of the Magi. Herodotus described the Magi as a Median tribe who officiated at all religious ceremonies where they recited theogonies (*Histories* 1.132). Though ignored by the eastern Iranian Avesta, they were certainly a powerful priestly caste in western Iran. Although the Magi must have been formally organized, our sources give no real details. The controversial role of the Magi in the politics of the Achaemenid period is discussed later. It is only with the Sassanids that we begin to learn of a priestly hierarchy and a complex network of fire temples situated throughout the empire supported by taxation.

4. SOCIAL CONTEXT

Ancient Iranian society had structures that were close in conception to the caste system of ancient India. The nomenclature for the classes shows a basic dichotomy between elites and commoners. The former also embraced a dichotomy between priests and nobles. Commoners were called "herdsman-husbandman," originally a pastoralist designation that came to be a blanket term for those engaged in menial occupations. There was also a fourth class of artisans. Rulers were from the nobility. Across the classes society was patriarchal, with women playing a subordinate role to men. Women were excluded, as in most traditional religions, from participation in the cult. This was especially true for Zoroastrians due to the great fear they had of pollution issuing from demonic forces. After carrion, menstrual blood was most dangerous. The Pahlavi books exhibit ambivalence toward women, with a strong misogynistic current flowing from the pollution of the Jeh, the Whore demoness. Since the purpose of human existence is that we participate in the struggle with and ultimate victory over evil, the Lie, both boys and girls needed to be initiated into Zoroastrian society. Although the ideal age at which men and women reached the height of physical power was fifteen, elders were accorded respect.

As among pre-modern peoples generally, religion and government were closely related in Achaemenid and later Iran. The well-known passage from Deutero–Isaiah (45:1–4) concerning God's anointing of Cyrus is not only a bold theological statement about the role of Israel's god in history, but also an indirect comment on the religio-political policy of the Achaemenids toward conquered peoples within their vast empire. As the architect of the new empire's administration, Cyrus adopted an overt policy of embracing the deities of these peoples. The return of the Israelite exiles under Cyrus and the rebuilding of Jerusalem's walls and of the temple under Darius, Xerxes, and Artaxerxes, chronicled especially in the biblical books of Nehemiah and Ezra, show a continuation of Cyrus' policies, although we know little about his personal theology. In sharp contrast, Darius the Great and his son Xerxes published their personal theologies throughout the empire. Scholars continue to debate the question of whether the early Achaemenid kings were Zoroastrians and, if so, whether this begins with Cyrus or a later ruler. While the relationship of Zoroastrianism to the power of the state is crucial for the Sassanid Empire, it goes unnoticed in Achaemenid sources. What is important is that Darius and his successors were fervent Mazdeans, that is, worshipers of Ahura Mazda. After Darius had seized power, he needed an ideological framework in which to legitimize his rule. Through his long inscription at Behistun and in subsequent inscriptions, he promoted in nearly monotheistic language the supremacy of Ahura Mazda, "the great god who created this earth and yonder heaven, who created man, who created the happiness of man" (Darius Naqsh-e Rustam a 1–5). Relying on ancient Indo-Iranian ideas of a social and natural dichotomy between Truth and the Lie (or order and chaos), Darius expounded a religio-political theology that placed him as Ahura Mazda's appointee to overcome chaos (= rebellion) and to establish order in the world. The inscriptions of Xerxes follow closely the formulas of his father. However, an element of intolerance toward the worship of the *daiwa*s (evil deities) may signal a departure from the policies of his predecessors, as in his Daiwadana inscription (Xerxes Persepolis h 35–56), where he proscribes the worship of the *daiwa*s and describes the destruction of their sanctuary (*daiwadana*) while advocating the correct worship of Ahura Mazda. Unfortunately, we do not know where this sanctuary was or whether the encouragement to worship Ahura Mazda was directed at Iranians only or at all peoples. Noteworthy is the promotion by Artaxerxes II of the cult of Anahita, the goddess of royal power in the Avesta and in Sassanid ideology.

A matter of some uncertainty is the role played by the priestly order of the Magi in the power structure of Achaemenid Iran. In the initial struggle for power, Darius put to death a pretender whom he calls Gaumata the Magu. This is all he has to say about the Magi. However, Herodotus (3.80) describes in detail a Magian conspiracy that so outraged the Persians that when it was exposed there was a wholesale slaughter of Magi. Thereafter there was an annual festival named the Magophonia (killing of Magi) during which Magi were obliged to remain in seclusion or risk death. Herodotus' story may reflect a festival of social inversion, but owing to the general awe the Magi inspired throughout the ancient world and in consideration of their prominence in the priestly nomenclature of Sassanid Iran, we can only assume power had to be negotiated with this priesthood. A Manichaean Sogdian ascription of magophonia to Alexander shows that subsequent to the downfall of the Achaemenid dynasty, the Magi were successful in rewriting the history of this embarrassment.

Very little is known about religion and politics in the Parthian Empire. Both their art and notices by classical authors point to a high level of eclecticism. In the east, coinage of the Kushan Empire during the first two centuries of the common era preserves elements of Greek, Hindu, Buddhist, and Iranian iconography, indicating a policy of religious accommodation consistent with Achaemenid traditions. However, all that changes with the rise of the Sassanid state.

When Ardashir established the Sassanid dynasty c. 224 CE, he followed a deliberate ideological program that, emphasizing his revival of the Achaemenid heritage, promoted the distinctively Iranian nature of the state and the civilization that it embraced. Symbolic of the disavowal of non-Iranian influences was the demonization of Alexander "the Roman," who was blamed especially for the disorganization of the Zoroastrian religion. Concrete was the enfranchisement of the Zoroastrian, that is, Magian, priesthood and the establishment of the Zoroastrian church as the authority in all religious matters. Under his chief-priest, Tosar, a major attempt was made to compile an orthodox canon. But, it was not until the reign of his son Shabuhr that the power of the Zoroastrian clergy truly asserted itself. The chief-priest Kirder, who had begun his career under Ardashir, became engaged in a power struggle for the loyalty of the emperor with the charismatic prophet Mani, the founder of Manichaeanism. In the end, the priest was triumphant over the prophet; and, even though Manichaeanism exercised a wide influence in late antiquity from Rome to China, it was never allowed to prosper in the Iranian heartland. Kirder's unprecedented power is heralded in a series of his inscriptions, unprecedented since inscriptions were otherwise the prerogative of rulers. In the inscriptions, Kirder established his authority in religious matters by recounting a marvelous journey to the other world in which reports are brought to him of Paradise and Hell. His ascendance and tenure as supreme ecclesiastical authority "at court ... in all the land" are chronicled through the reigns of four emperors, culminating in the reign of Bahram II (276–293 CE) under whom Jews, Buddhists, Hindus, Nazareans, Christians, Baptists, and Manichaeans were being persecuted. At the end of the fifth century a religio-social(ist) movement among the oppressed classes was founded by a certain Mazdak. After some initial success it was ruthlessly suppressed by Kawad (488–531 CE).

The Sassanids always insisted on the inseparability of religion and the state. Whereas the Achaemenids only wished to publicize their divine mandate to rule, the Sassanids claimed some sort of divine lineage by using the expression "from the seed of the gods." Monumental sculptural scenes show the investiture of several emperors by the deities Ohrmazd and Anahid. In keeping with the general Zoroastrian theology of a cosmic dualistic struggle between Truth and the Lie, the king was held up as the one locus of the religio-political power necessary to accomplish the defeat of Ahriman. As the ninth-century encyclopedia *Denkard* puts it: "The thing against which the Destructive Spirit struggles most violently is the coming together in full force of the glory of kingship and the Good Religion in one person, because such a conjunction must destroy him" (Denkard edit. Madan 1911:129). While there are many reasons for the rapid eclipse of Zoroastrianism by Islam, this conception of power residing in the fusion of religion and kingship in the concrete person of the king resulted in a theological vacuum that could not be filled after the death of Yazdagird III (631–651 CE), the last "king of kings."

Another aspect of the social context of ancient Iranian religion was its relationship to philosophy, theology, and ethics. Philosophy as we might understand it in Greek or in Indian Buddhist and Hindu forms did not exist in Zoroastrianism in any meaningful way. Zarathushtra had a coherent theological system that was imbedded in his Gathas in the form of ecstatic dialogues between him and Ahura Mazda. But these are in no way either discursive or didactic. Rather, the arena of theological discourse was primarily myth. Only in the ninth-century Pahlavi books do we find samples of apologetics, with Zoroastrians defending their religion against Jews and Christians, and obliquely against Muslims. The best examples of mytho-theological discourse are the competing myths of creation promulgated by strict dualists and Zurvanists. Also, many of Zarathushtra's revolutionary abstractions are transformations of old myths and conceptions of deity. Zoroastrian theology, as articulated by the ninth-century apologist Mardan Farrox in his *Shikand-gumani-wizar*, presented a cogent defense of dualism against monotheism. Whereas we have theology expressed in the language of myth in the *Bundahisn*, he articulated that theology in rational discourse. The fundamental issue is theodicy. How, it is argued, can a sole omnipotent, omniscient, and benevolent God allow evil to run rampant in His world? Job's anguish is senseless. Clearly God cannot in any way be the author of evil either by design or by acquiescence. The dualist position is that the authors of good and evil are primordially separate in every respect.

Although philosophy, as distinct from theology, did not play an important role in Zoroastrianism, ethics certainly did. From the time when Zarathushtra established the theology of an ethical dualism of Truth and Lie, the primary concern of Zoroastrianism was ethics, that is, a system of beliefs and practices that would allow members of society to live righteously. Already in the ancient Yasna Haptanghaiti the opening verse proclaims the triad of good thought, good speech, and good action, which is the basis of Zoroastrian ethics. In his inscriptions Darius I singles out the Lie as the source of rebellion and chaos both social and political. Even Herodotus (1.138) mentions that truthfulness was a supreme virtue among the Persians. It is important to realize that because of its understanding of the very motivation of creation as a defense against the Lie, Zoroastrianism has always been life-affirming and has shunned all forms of asceticism. This led to the doctrine, fully articulated in the Pahlavi books, of the "Mean." Somewhat similar to Aristotle's Golden

Mean or Buddhism's Middle Way, the concept of the Mean is that the good life is one to be lived in avoidance of the extremes of hedonism and asceticism. Within the bounds of ethical behavior one is enjoined to rejoice in life's pleasures.

5. RESEARCH

Sources for our knowledge of ancient Iranian religion are of two sorts: 1) textual and epigraphical and 2) material. Textual sources are both indigenous and foreign. For the early period the latter are primarily Greek, though, for purposes of historical reconstruction, the ancient Indian Vedic literature is indispensable. This literature, which contains the earliest religious texts of the closely related Indo-Aryans, is indispensable for making historical reconstructions of the development of Iranian religion. The Rig Veda, a collection of more than 1,000 hymns to various deities, can be dated to approximately 1300–900 BCE. The main problem with the Greek sources, the most important of which is Herodotus, is that the information passed on is not always very reliable, either because it is outright erroneous or because it is based on misunderstandings. The main indigenous sources are the Achaemenid royal inscriptions in the Old Persian language (with Akkadian, Elamite, and Aramaic translations) and the Avesta, the sacred scriptures of Zoroastrianism, in Avestan. The royal inscriptions, especially those of Darius (522–486 BCE) and his son Xerxes (486–465 BCE), for the most part eloquent pieces of propaganda, are rich in references to religion. In addition to the information they contain, they have the great advantage of being fixed in time and place. Matters are quite otherwise in the case of the Avesta, which is the main source of knowledge of ancient Iranian religion. Like the Bible, the Avesta is a collection of a variety of texts composed over a considerable span of time by different authors, and it has endured editing and redaction at several points during the history of its development. The text we now possess represents only a fragment of what remained in the ninth century CE of the late Sassanid Avesta. Summaries of the contents of the Sassanid Avesta in the *Denkard*, a ninth-century encyclopedia of Zoroastrianism, show that it was an enormous collection containing texts in Avestan as well as in, and predominantly in, Pahlavi, the language of Sassanid Zoroastrianism. In spite of the relatively recent date of the existing Avesta, it contains matter of great antiquity, of which the Gathas or "Songs" of Zarathushtra (Zoroaster) and much of the Yashts are among the oldest. Apart from the Achaemenid inscriptions, there is no secure evidence that religious compositions were reduced to writing until the late Arsacid or early Sassanid periods; that is, unlike the other religions of the Middle East, the Iranian religions had no written texts in the ancient period. All religious "literature" was oral both in composition and transmission. That began to change toward the end of the first millennium. With the establishment of the Sassanid dynasty, literacy gained ground. Inscriptions of Shapur I and of the chief cleric, Kirder, contain much relating to religion. As alluded to previously, there developed a large body of written texts in Pahlavi during this period, and even after the Arab conquest, especially in the ninth century, many works were composed. For the later period, there are Roman, Byzantine, and Arab sources.

The Gathas contain poetic expressions of Zarathushtra's religious Vision that, in many ways, is a very complicated reinterpretation of inherited Iranian religious ideas. The Yashts are collections of verses dedicated to the various deities. Most of the Yashts, though touched up with Zoroastrian terminology and ideas, have little to do with anything specifically Zoroastrian. The gods invoked are essentially the gods of pre-Zoroastrian Iran. Unfortunately, there is little agreement as to when Zarathushtra lived, though most scholars agree that he lived sometime between c. 600 and c. 1200 BCE! It does not seem possible to date the Yashts much more precisely, except to believe that their redaction (not necessarily composition) may have first taken place in the fifth century BCE. Two other important parts of the Avesta are the Vendidad and the Yasna. The former is mostly concerned with questions of purity and pollution; the latter is a heterogeneous collection of texts, which includes the Gathas, to accompany the performance of the *yasna* ritual.

Material sources for ancient Iranian religion are much more limited and are, for the most part, restricted to western Iran. The remains of Achaemenid architecture and art, by far the most important, provide abundant evidence of imperial articulation of religious symbols and show a thorough dependence on Middle Eastern precedents. The coinage of the Kushan dynasty of eastern Iran is a valuable source for knowledge of the pantheon since named deities appear on the coins. Among the syncretistic cultures of the Middle East from Seleucid times onward, visual images on a variety of materials display Iranian influence. Especially important from the Sassanid period are monumental friezes depicting royal investitures.

Although, as we have seen, some scattered knowledge of Persian religion was found in classical writers beginning with Herodotus, it was not until the beginning of the nineteenth century that serious Western scholarship could commence after the publication in 1771 of Anquetil-Duperron's *Zend-Avesta*, based on manuscripts and their interpretation by Zoroastrian-Parsi priests in Bombay. With the deciphering of the Achaemenid inscriptions written in Old Persian and the further gathering of manuscripts in Avestan and Pahlavi that took place in the first half of the nineteenth century, a sufficient body of textual material was available to philologists for comparison with the ancient Vedic texts of India. By the end of the century, the science of comparative historical linguistics provided a generally accurate understanding of the languages of the indigenous texts. After the fashion of nineteenth-century ideas about the origins and development of religion, "nature religion" was an accepted label attached to the obviously polytheistic portions of the Avesta. In contrast, there was a fascination with the figure of Zoroaster/Zarathushtra as a rational enlightened prophet and reformer. By the third decade of the twentieth century two novel theories, primarily about Zoroaster, were advanced. The most interesting and influential was that of H. S. Nyberg.[1] Influenced by contemporary Scandinavian anthropologists, he held that there were a number of religions in ancient Iran defined by religio-social communities devoted to a particular deity and that Zoroaster was to be understood in the mold of the northern Asian shaman. The other theory, advanced by E. Herzfeld,[2] held that Zoroaster was no more than a clever politician at the Achaemenid court. Both theories were subjected to devastating criticism by W. B. Henning,[3] who advocated a return to the view of a rational prophet. Following the Second World War, G. Dumézil published a series of monographs detailing the "tripartite ideology of the Indo-Europeans."[4] A new trend in scholarship that took inspiration from Vedic studies was begun by H. Humbach in his translation of the Gathas,[5] in which he attempted to show ritual concerns behind nearly every verse. Although he has backed away substantially from his original position, it was carried *in extremis* by M. Molé and more recently by J. Kellens and E. Pirart.[6] The hot topic in contemporary scholarship concerns the argument made by Kellens that Zarathushtra never existed at all, or at least not as the author of the Gathas. Rather, the Gathas were composed by a committee of poets commissioned to compose some verses to accompany the ritual (see my critique in www.iranicaonline.org under "Zoroaster II: General Survey"). An ongoing problem since the beginnings of Iranian studies has been how to use the materials contained in the late Sassanid writings as sources for reconstructing ancient forms of religion. The late M. Boyce, perhaps the greatest authority on Zoroastrianism, relied heavily on the absolute fidelity of late writings to earlier traditions.[7]

FURTHER READING

There is a vast bibliography for pre-Islamic Zoroastrianism. For the most part references cited here are in English. There are several comprehensive works: Boyce 1975, 1982 and Grenet 1991. These volumes of the *History of Zoroastrianism* (the entire work remains incomplete) present a comprehensive, detailed, and richly documented account of Zoroastrianism's beginnings and its development during the Achaemenid period and during a long period extending from the Macedonian conquest into the fourth century CE in the Greco-Roman cultural and political spheres. Boyce 1975 must be used with some caution where later Pahlavi sources are used uncritically to provide a reconstruction of Zarathushtra's religion. Boyce also seeks to establish a very early date for Zarathushtra and to demonstrate the great continuity of belief and practice. Intended for the general reader is Boyce 1979. Following the contours of Boyce 1975, with both the strengths and weaknesses of the latter, it presents a summary history of Zoroastrianism from its beginnings to the present. An invaluable resource for all matters pertaining to ancient Iran is the monumental *Encyclopaedia Iranica* (*EIr*), available both in print and online. Although it remains incomplete, articles under all alphabetical headings are being added regularly to the online version. Its articles, written by leading scholars, contain in-depth discussions of the topics as well as detailed bibliographies. It is easily accessed at www.iranicaonline.org. Though in German, Stausberg 2002 provides an excellent history of pre-Islamic Zoroastrianism that is rich in detail, though not as comprehensive as Boyce. In contrast to Boyce, Stausberg 2002 provides much useful and necessary discussion of methodological problems. The bibliography is rich and the most up-to-date works are cited here. Zaehner 1961 remains useful, though as its title suggests, this history of Zoroastrianism basically ignores the Greco-Roman and Arsacid periods. Although somewhat idiosyncratic and dogmatic, Zaehner's approach provides a balance to the weight of Dumézil's and Nyberg's theories so prevalent in the mid-twentieth century. The book also contains an annotated bibliography. A valuable reference work for Zoroastrian ritual is Modi 1937. Still the best comprehensive source for pre-Islamic Iranian history and civilization is Frye 1963. Unfortunately, the only comprehensive translation of the Avesta is the outdated and often inaccurate *The Zend-Avesta* by J. Darmesteter. First published in English in 1880–1883 exclusive of the *Yasna*, a revised and comprehensive translation was published in three volumes in French in Darmsteter 1892–1893. A sound German translation of the texts in K. F. Geldner's (1896) critical edition is Wolff 1910.

An anthology of Avestan texts and Achaemenid inscriptions relevant to religion is Malandra 1983. As a companion to Boyce 1992, Boyce 1984 contains materials from the Gathas through the twentieth century. Many of the most important of the Pahlavi books are translated by West 1880–1897. While still useful, West's translations should be read with care owing to the great advances in knowledge of Middle Iranian languages since his day. In addition to Boyce's anthology, a very readable selection of Pahlavi texts is Zaehner 1956/1975.

CHRONOLOGY

Dates	Persons	Events
1200–600 BCE		Zarathushtra active in eastern Iran at some point within this time frame. Composition of the Gathas; establishment of community of followers
c. 614–550 BCE		Median Empire in western Iran and the Near East
550–330 BCE		Persian (Achaemenid) Empire
550–530 BCE	Cyrus the Great	Gradual spread of Zoroastrianism throughout the empire; compilation of Avestan texts; ascendancy of the Magi
522–486 BCE	Darius the Great	Inscriptions extolling Ahura Mazda as creator of the world and guarantor of Darius' legitimacy
486–465 BCE	Xerxes	Daiwadana inscription; establishment of the Zoroastrian calendar in 441
404–358 BCE	Artaxerxes II	Included Mithra and Anahita besides Ahura Mazda in his inscriptions. Statues of Anahita
336–330 BCE	Darius III	Last Achaemenid king, remembered as Dara in later tradition
330–326 BCE	Alexander the Great	Conquest of the Achaemenid Empire. Remembered in later Zoroastrian traditions as ushering in a long period of chaos and degradation of the Den, with loss and dispersion of the oral texts

Dates	Persons	Events
323–c. 141 BCE	Successors to Alexander	Seleucid Empire in the Near East Gradual development of scripts for Iranian languages.
c. 141 BCE– c. 224 CE		Parthian Arsacid Empire
c. 51–80 CE	Vologases I	Convocation of priests to rescue the dispersed texts; probable initial attempts to transcribe oral texts into writing, using the Aramaic script
c. 224–651 CE		Sassanid Empire
c. 224–240 CE	Ardashir	Founder of Sassanid Empire
	Tosar (Tansar)	Chief priest during reign of Ardashir; established an official canon
240–c.272 CE	Shapur	
	Kirder	Chief priest from the reign of Shapur to that of Narseh (293–302); firmly established the Zoroastrian "church" authority throughout the empire; persecuted followers of other religions
309–379 CE	Shapur II	
	Adurbad Mahrspandan	Chief priest who upheld orthodoxy against heresy. Revised official canon
488–531 CE	Kawad	Suppressed Mazdakite movement
531–579 CE	Xusro	"Golden Age," perhaps invention of Avestan script and establishment of the 21 Nasks
636 CE >		Arab conquest and gradual Islamization of Iran; death of Yazdagird III, last Sassanid king, 651.
Ninth century CE		Intense literary activity in Pahlavi; writing or final redaction of most Pahlavi books, including the *Bundahisn* and *Denkard*

GLOSSARY

Note: The names of deities are given in their Avestan, Old Persian, or Pahlavi spellings.

Achaemenid: The Persian dynasty and empire 559–330 BCE.

Ahriman: The Pahlavi form of Ahra Manyu (Av. *aŋra mainyu*), the Evil Spirit.

Arsacid: The Parthian empire c. 247 BCE–224 CE.

Avestan: The Old Iranian language of the oldest Zoroastrian scriptures known as the Avesta.

Bundahishn: A digest of Pahlavi sources composed in the ninth century CE dealing with the creation of the world, geography, zoology, dynasties, and last days.

Daena: In the Gathas "Vision" and to be read as *dayanā. This became the name for the Zoroastrian religion.

Den: The Pahlavi term for the religion revealed to Zarathushtra by Ohrmazd/Ahura Mazda, Avestan *daena.*

Denkard: An encyclopedia of Zoroastrianism composed in the ninth century CE.

Kushan: An eastern Iranian dynasty of Central Asian origin that flourished between the first century BCE and the second century CE.

Manichaeanism: The gnostic religion founded by Mani (assassinated c. 274 CE) that enjoyed a brief acceptance in Iran under Shapur I. It became widespread in Central Asia and in the Roman Empire, its most famous adherent being St. Augustine.

Pahlavi: The Middle Persian language of the Sassanid and later writings.

Ohrmazd: The Pahlavi form of Ahura Mazda.

Sassanid: The Persian dynasty and empire 224–651 CE.

Seleucid: The Near Eastern dynasty and empire founded by one of Alexander's generals, Seleucus I Nicator (c. 321 BCE).

Sogdia: A Central Asian region of greater Iran, whose language became the *lingua franca* of trade routes to China and which preserved texts of the Manichaean, Buddhist, and Christian communities.

Zoroaster/Zarathushtra/Zardusht: Zoroaster is the Greek rendering; Zarathushtra is the form found in the Avesta; Zardusht is the Pahlavi form.

Zurvanism: A heterodox theology within Zoroastrianism that held Zurwan "Time" to be the original deity, whose two sons Ohrmazd and Ahriman played out the dualistic combat common to orthodox theology.

Notes

1   Nyberg 1938 (reprint 1966).
2   Herzfeld 1947.
3   Henning 1951.
4   Dumézil 1958.

5   Humbach 1959 (English translation: Humbach 1991).
6   Molé 1963, and Kellens and Pirart 1988/1990/1991.
7   Boyce 1992.

Works Cited

Anquetil-Duperron. 1771. *Zend-Avesta*. 3 vols. Paris.

Boyce, M. 1975. *A History of Zoroastrianism. Vol 1*. Leiden.

———. 1979. *Zoroastrians*. London.

———. 1982. *A History of Zoroastrianism. Vol 2*. Leiden.

———. 1984. *Textual Sources for the Study of Zoroastrianism*. Chicago.

———. 1992. *Zoroastrianism, its Antiquity and Constant Vigour*. Costa Mesa, CA.

Darmesteter, J. 1880–1883. *The Zend-Avesta*. In *Sacred Books of the East. Pt. I and Pt II*. Oxford.

———. 1892–1893. *Le Zend-Avesta*. Paris.

Dumézil, G. 1958. *L'idéologie tripartie des indo-européens*. Bruxelles.

Encyclopaedia Iranica Online. <iranicaonline.com> 1996–2010. (EIr)

Frye, R. N. 1963. *The Heritage of Persia*. Cleveland, OH.

Geldner, K. F., ed. 1896. *Avesta, the Sacred Books of the Parsis*. 3 vols. Stuttgart.

Grenet, F. 1991. *A History of Zoroastrianism*. Vol. 3. Leiden.

Henning, W. B. 1951. *Zoroaster, Politician or Witch-Doctor*. Oxford.

Herzfeld, E. 1947. *Zoroaster*. Princeton, NJ.

Humbach, H. 1959. *Die Gathas des Zarathushtra*. 2 Bde. Heidelberg.

———. 1991. *The Gathas of Zarathushtra and the other Old Avestan Texts*. 2 vols. Heidelberg.

Kellens, J. and E. Pirart. 1988/1990/1991. *Les textes vieil-avestiques*. 3 vols. Wiesbaden.

Madan, D. M., ed. 1911. *The Complete Text of the Pahlavi Dinkard*, Bombay. (DkM)

Malandra, W. W. 1983. *An Introduction to Ancient Iranian Religion*. Minneapolis, MN.

Modi, J. J. 1937. *The Religious Ceremonies and Customs of the Parsees*. 2nd ed. Bombay.

Molé, M. 1963. *Culte, mythe et cosmologie dans l'Iran ancien*. Paris.

Nyberg, H. S. 1938 (reprint 1966). *Die Religionen des alten Iran*. Leipzig.

Stausberg, M. 2002. *Die Religion Zarathushtras. Bd. 1*. Stuttgart.

West, E. W. 1880–1897. *Sacred Books of the East*. 5 vols. Oxford.

Wolff, F. 1910. *Avesta, die heiligen Bücher der Parsen*.

Zaehner, R. C. 1956 /1975. *The Teachings of the Magi*. London. (selections from *Bundahišn* and *Shikand-gumānī-wizār*).

———. 1961. *The Dawn and Twilight of Zoroastrianism*. London.

7 Greece

JENNIFER LARSON

Although application of the modern concept of "religion" to ancient cultures has been questioned as anachronistic, for our purposes religion can be defined simply as the actions and beliefs pertaining to relations with supernatural agencies (gods, heroes, demons, etc.) that are characteristic of a culture.[1] In this case, the culture we are studying is that of the ancient Greeks, the people who spoke Greek as their native tongue and occupied mainland Greece, the Aegean, and a host of colonies on the Mediterranean and Black Sea coasts from the Bronze Age through the Roman period. We also take account of the fact that the Greek culture and language, along with Greek religion, were conveyed to other peoples in the region through trade, war, and colonization.

I. HISTORICAL DEVELOPMENT

The origins of what we recognize as "Greek religion" lie in the religious thought and practices of the non-Hellenic peoples of Greece, the Aegean islands, Anatolia, and Crete, as well as those of the Indo-European–speaking peoples who entered Greece during the Bronze Age and brought with them the Greek tongue.[2] Greek religion was the synthetic result of the blending of these cultures in all their variety, and it continued to evolve until its suppression by Christians in the fourth and fifth centuries CE. There was no centralization of authority over Greek religious practices and beliefs; change was regulated only at the civic level. Thus, the phenomenon we are studying is not in fact an organized "religion." Instead we might think of the beliefs and practices of Greeks in relation to the gods as a group of closely related "religious dialects" that resembled each other far more than they did those of non-Greeks. Like the dialects of a language, they were mutually intelligible (for the most part) and they shared basic features but could grow increasingly diverse in isolation.

During the Bronze Age, gods such as Zeus, Hera, and Poseidon were already being worshiped, but major changes to the pantheon occurred with the collapse of the Mycenaean civilization. Some deities (like the Mycenaean Drimios) were forgotten, while others were gradually absorbed into the personae of major Olympian gods such as Apollo (as with Hyakinthos at Sparta) and Athena (as with Alea at Tegea and Aphaia at Aigina). Although the trend of Panhellenization apparent in the epic poetry of the Early Iron Age resulted in a widely recognized core group of gods, new deities continued to achieve Panhellenic recognition after the eighth century (e.g., Kybele in the sixth century and Asklepios in the fourth).[3]

From the tenth to the eighth centuries, the period before alphabetic literacy, sanctuaries begin to appear in the archaeological record and to attract the investment of resources from local rulers and aristocratic families. It has often been noted that the eighth century is a time of shifting priorities, so that wealth (especially in the form of metal objects) begins to be displayed in sanctuaries as votives rather than buried in tombs.[4] This development is related to the rise of the city-state, which provided an arena for competition among citizens who shared civic patron gods. The construction of Greek temples, which housed the cult statue of the deity and his or her ritual equipment, became widespread during the eighth century. Temples and sanctuaries functioned as important vehicles for competition between city-states, though the first temples were built of wood and mudbrick and were extremely small by later standards. Limestone or marble "hundred-footers" (*hekatompeda*) became the fashion during the early Archaic period, and were quickly followed in the sixth century by colossal structures such as the Temple of Artemis at Ephesos, which exceeded 100 meters in length and had 127 columns, each a stunning 18 meters tall.[5]

The tendency of Greeks to emphasize the maintenance of "ancestral customs" may suggest an erroneous view of Greek religion as a fairly static and conservative system. In fact, it varied substantially by time and especially by place with respect to ritual details and pantheons. On the other hand, the underlying suppositions and the worldview of its practitioners – that the gods expected to be recognized through sacrifices or other offerings, and would reward the regular observance of their rites while punishing those who spurned them – remained surprisingly constant over several centuries. The periods of the most rapid change are coincident with the rise and fall of the *polis* system, which, while it lasted, provided a relatively stable framework for Greek polytheism. The replacement of *polis* government with the rule of the Hellenistic monarchs accelerated the rate of change and ushered in new developments, including the divine worship of rulers and their families, a more cosmopolitan pantheon with deities (Isis, Sarapis) from the regions of Alexander's conquests, and the weakening of institutionalized civic worship in favor of more elective and private religious activities.[6]

One of the most important factors affecting the historical development of Greek religion was contact with other cultures. From its beginnings in the Bronze Age, "Greek" religion was a synthesis. The strong influence of Minoan ideas and aesthetics is clearly discernable in the material culture of Mycenaean religion, while the far-flung trade networks of the Mycenaeans exposed them to Egyptian, Hittite, and Syro-Phoenician deities. Periods of intense cultural exchanges took place during the tenth century, as illustrated by the finds from the elaborate "heroön" at Lefkandi in Euboia, and again during the eighth and seventh centuries, when commercial contacts with Anatolia, the Near East, and Egypt again proved the vectors for religious ideas and art to enter Greece.[7] Cyprus, settled by both Greeks and Phoenicians, repeatedly served as an intermediary for both goods and ideas traveling west. The best example of such a transfer is the arrival from Cyprus of a major goddess resembling Babylonian Ishtar and Phoenician Astarte. Like these Near Eastern goddesses, Aphrodite was closely concerned with sexuality, had a cult title referring to the heavens (Ourania), received offerings of incense and doves, and had a doomed consort (Adonis) who was ritually mourned by women devotees.[8]

Specific foreign cults, complete with characteristic ritual practices, were regularly adopted by Greek cities, sometimes at the request of resident foreigners. In the late fifth century, the Athenians officially recognized the worship of the Thracian goddess Bendis, probably for diplomatic reasons (Plato, *Republic* 354a); the Spartans maintained close relations with the oracle of "Zeus" Ammon at Siwa and established the worship of Zeus Ammon in Lakonia (Pausanias 3.18.3). Less easily recognized but more profound are the divergences of Greek colonies from the religion of their mother cities in response to indigenous belief and practice. The famous "many breasted" statue of Artemis at Ephesos reflects the impact of the Anatolian goddess whose cult preceded that of Artemis on the site.

Greek religion, like other aspects of Greek culture, was carried to other peoples through trade, colonization, and conquest. One of the best examples of the reception of Greek religion in the Mediterranean is the great popularity of the hero-god Herakles among non-Greeks. The Phoenician god Melqart was syncretized with Herakles in Cyprus, Sicily, and Spain.[9] Among the Etruscans he became Hercle; among the Romans, Hercules. On the other hand, we should be cautious about overapplying the *interpretatio Graeca* to the religions of other Mediterranean cultures. Greek authors like Herodotus regularly refer to the gods and heroes of other peoples using the names of their Greek equivalents, conveying an erroneous impression that the peoples in question had adopted Greek deities. Still, we know that the Etruscans and later the Romans absorbed and refashioned for their own tastes a great quantity of Greek traditions. Ultimately Greek religion had a substantial impact on Christianity through the use of Apollo and Dionysos as iconographic and conceptual models for understanding Christ.[10]

2. BELIEF

The Greeks worshiped a large number of anthropomorphic gods with overlapping yet roughly distinct functions. Under the *polis* system, each city-state boasted a distinctive pantheon, and the particular gods one worshiped depended on one's ethnicity, ancestry, civic affiliations, neighborhood, and (to a lesser extent) personal preferences. The major Greek divinities were synthetic figures who had absorbed the characteristics and titles of earlier gods. These deities developed not in isolation but in relation to one another, so that they share a plethora of interlocking sympathies, oppositions, and complementarities. Most Greek gods had spheres of interest encompassing both natural processes and human culture. Zeus, for example, was the god of rain, clouds, and the thunderbolt, but he also enforced the laws of hospitality; Aphrodite governed both sexual and political persuasion. The gods also represented various aspects of the human psyche. In the persona of Athena, reason, self-restraint, and the arts of civilization were dominant, while Dionysos was connected with license, transgressions, and alternate states of consciousness.

Inhabiting the land and waters were a plethora of minor local deities. The nymphs of the springs, trees, and caves appeared as alluring young women, while the river gods were usually man–bull hybrids. From at least the eighth century, the Greeks also worshiped heroes and heroines, who were unique to each city and whose influence was generally limited to the district in which their tombs lay (although a minority of heroic figures, like Herakles and Helen, were far more widely worshiped). This type of cult arose partly as a response to the faded glories of the Bronze Age, which was viewed in retrospect as a time when the progeny of deities performed great deeds beyond the capabilities of later men. As the Greek city-state emerged, rituals honoring the ancestral dead of the nobles were gradually transferred to the heroes and heroines, who functioned as communal ancestors for the city. Heroic cults eventually were broadened to include the occasional worship of those recent dead who had distinguished themselves through athletic, political, or literary achievements. By the Hellenistic period, the common man and woman could themselves expect to receive "heroic" honors in private cults established by their families.

The cosmology and eschatology of Greek religion were shaped primarily by the poets, who refined and transmitted a great body of traditions about death, destiny, and the role of the gods in shaping human affairs. The Archaic Greek conception of the cosmos is best known to us from Hesiod's *Theogony*, which describes how the primordial beings, including Earth and Desire (Eros), came into existence spontaneously, and how the process of creation was thereafter primarily a matter of sexual reproduction. Hesiod envisioned earth as a flat disk penetrated by the sea and surrounded by a great river (Okeanos), beneath which lay the pit of the dead and above which stretched the dome of the sky. Each level of the tripartite cosmos of heaven, earth, and underworld was inhabited by its proper gods: the celestial Olympians, the earthbound and marine deities such as nymphs, and the Chthonians who dwelt beneath the earth with the dead. In an alternative tradition represented by Odysseus' *katabasis* in Book 11 of the *Odyssey*, the land of the dead is thought to exist at the ends of the earth rather than beneath it, usually in the far west where the sun sets. Other poets were free to devise their own theogonic systems, but they appear not to have strayed far from Hesiod's concept of a series of ages in which successive generations of gods ruled, punctuated by periods of cosmic battle, until equilibrium was established under the permanent rule of Zeus.[11] As the Greeks grew more knowledgeable about geography and astronomy, the educated developed far more sophisticated concepts of the cosmos, its arrangement, and origins. Yet the worldview set forth in the Hesiodic and Homeric poems long retained its cultural resonance.

The eschatological beliefs of the Greeks were diverse and often contradictory. Characteristic of Archaic and Classical Greek thought is the idea that each individual's ineluctable fate is determined in advance; this fate is conceived of as one's portion or allotment (*moira*) and is distributed through the personified trio of Moirai (Fates), who spin, allot, and cut the thread of life. A different concept of fate, derived from Egypt, is represented by the weighing of souls; gods including Zeus and Hermes are sometimes represented weighing souls to determine whether an individual must die. At the moment of death, a mortal's soul (*psychê*) leaves its body and proceeds to the land of the dead, where it leads a pitiable existence, scarcely aware of its own identity, in an otherworld of shadows ruled by Hades and Persephone.[12]

Means of securing a more pleasant afterlife (to be distinguished from the Christian concept of "salvation" from the torments of Hell) were available through membership in various initiatory cults and sects. From the seventh century at the latest, initiates of the mystery cult at Eleusis expected a better afterlife as a result of their participation in the mysteries of Demeter and Persephone; similar cults abounded, especially during the late Classical and Hellenistic periods. The most influential of these were the Bacchic or Orphic mysteries, propagated by traveling holy men who worked with individuals or small groups and claimed to have secret knowledge handed down from the poet Orpheus. Through the observation of various purifications and rites while they lived, initiates sought to win the favor of Dionysos and/or Persephone in order to retain their self-awareness in the afterlife and gain positions of privilege among the dead. Membership in such a Bacchic or Orphic group involved burial with a thin gold tablet, often inscribed with instructions for the afterlife journey.[13]

3. PRACTICE

Gods and men participated in a reciprocal relationship: gods provided mortals with health, progeny, victory, and material abundance, while mortals acknowledged the gods through ritual performances and gifts. A central ritual in Greek religion was alimentary sacrifice, which resulted in a meat meal for the participants and a burnt offering for the god. Unblemished animals were preferred for this purpose. Typically they were adorned with garlands or ribbons and led to the altar in a procession; after the animal was dispatched, some combination of bones and fat was burned on the altar, while the organ meats and muscle were cooked and divided among the participants. In literary sources, failure to sacrifice to a deity is often equated with impiety and considered reason for divine anger. Except in the case of game animals, virtually all meat consumption occurred as the result of sacrifice and was a highly social activity by which group identity was defined and the relative status of group members was mapped through their access to desirable cuts of meat. Thus, meat avoidance, as practiced for different reasons by sects such as the Pythagoreans or Christians, implied a voluntary self-exclusion from normative social and religious activity.

Holocaust sacrifice, a far less common procedure performed for deities of the underworld, was the total destruction of the animal's body through burning. In sacrifice to heroes and heroines, consumption of the meat remained the norm, although the slaughtered animal's blood was often collected and poured into a pit, or otherwise handled in order to maintain a distinction between sacrifice to heroes and to Olympian gods.[14] Other types of ritual slaughter served different functions; for example, piglets' blood was used to purify ritual spaces.

Non-animal offerings to the gods and heroes included breads, porridge, legumes, fruits, cheese, and a number of liquids poured as libations (oil, wine, honey, milk, and water). Each cult and deity had specific requirements with respect to the type of sacrificial animal to be used (if any) and the appropriate vegetable, dairy, and liquid offerings. More permanent gifts were also common, especially in fulfillment of vows. During the early Archaic period, these "votive gifts" were usually personal possessions of the giver, such as jewelry, vessels, textiles, and armor. Later, many types of objects were manufactured specifically for dedication to the gods; these included miniature and full-size vases; figurines cast from bronze, molded of terracotta or cut from lead sheets; and relief sculptures on inscribed marble or limestone slabs. Such gifts were deposited in sanctuaries and could not be removed without offense to the deity; when their number became excessive, they were buried.

The gods delighted in ritual performance, which took many forms. Processions were integral to most rituals and helped participants and spectators to define the transition into sacred space and time. With the exception of sacrifice and procession, most Greek rituals involved competition among rivals whose performances pleased both divine and human spectators. The Olympic Games, which featured athletic and equestrian events, are the most familiar manifestation of this agonistic spirit, but there were also competitions involving dance, musical performance, and recitation of Homer's epics. Comic and tragic poets competed at dramatic festivals such as the Great Dionysia of Athens.[15] Certain rituals, in particular those for Dionysos, Demeter, and Kybele, involved transgressive behaviors (bantering insults, sex-talk) or ecstatic states (maenadism).

Divination was available from prestigious sanctuary-based oracles, but also from wandering prophets and seers practicing a hereditary craft. City-states and individuals consulted oracles and seers to determine whether the gods approved their endeavors and how best to mend their fortunes. At Delphi, Apollo spoke through the medium of his priestess, the Pythia, and often advised on the best ritual actions by which to appease gods and the angry dead. At Dodona, one of the oldest Greek oracles, Zeus with his consort Dione spoke through the rustling of oak leaves and the cooing of doves, or responded to queries scratched on strips of lead and tightly folded; the exact mechanisms of this oracle are unknown. Other methods of divination were many, from the observation of omens in the behavior of animals and humans, to the examination of entrails from sacrificial animals, to the casting of lots.[16]

The ritual practices of Greek religion were carried out within prescribed spatial and temporal boundaries. Sacred space was defined primarily through the sanctuary or *temenos*, a parcel of land set aside and marked with boundary stones or walls. Those entering a sanctuary were expected to be ritually pure (as defined by general observance and any local rules) and to follow a set of behavioral taboos intended to maintain the sanctity of the space (e.g., those who had recently come in contact with the dead or engaged in sexual intercourse were normally excluded). Entry was restricted to one well-defined gate equipped with water basins for purification, which helped to emphasize that the worshiper was passing into a sacred space. Within the sanctuary, access to certain spaces might be restricted in ways that advertised their sacredness. The cella of a temple, with its precious cult image, was often opened only on festival days, while other rooms might be completely off-limits except to the priest or priestess.

Besides space set aside for a god, the only essential element of the sanctuary was an altar, but even this could be as simple as a pile of stones in a rustic sanctuary. In practice, most sanctuaries had more elaborate furnishings. The altar was normally positioned in front of the temple, allowing a line of sight from the cult image to the sacrificial activities. *Hestiatoria* or dining rooms were common additions to sanctuaries, while large, Panhellenic sanctuaries also possessed athletic facilities, theaters, and treasuries. Major gods hosted subsidiary shrines of other deities in their sanctuaries, as well as the tombs of heroes or heroines. The sanctuaries of oracular and healing deities often included natural or artificial caves and subterranean chambers, baths, and special sleeping areas.

The location of a given sanctuary was not random, but resulted from the interaction of many factors such as the nature of the deity (Archaic Zeus sanctuaries were often situated on mountain tops, while Artemis was associated with marshy areas), the availability of fresh water for purification and sacrificial activities, and the belief that certain types of places (caves, springs, groves, and mountaintops) were inherently sacred. Sanctuaries are sometimes categorized as urban, suburban (i.e., outside the city walls), rural, and extraurban.[17] An extraurban sanctuary was situated on the borders of the city-state and helped to define its territory. The relationship between an extraurban sanctuary and its corresponding city was often reinforced through processions on festival occasions. Other types of sanctuaries were federal or regional and served people from a number of cities (the Argive Heraion) or a region with many smaller towns that lacked a centralized urban space (Apollo at Thermon).

Sacred time was organized according to a series of annual festivals tied to months of the year, a system that dates to the Mycenaean period or earlier. All the Greeks used a lunar calendar but the names and order of the months varied by city, with strong correlations between cities of the same ethnic background. For example, the kinship of the Athenians with the Ionians, who colonized Asia Minor in the tenth century, is demonstrated by the shared months and festivals in their calendars (e.g., the Dionysiac festival of Anthesteria) while many Dorian cities shared festivals and associated months (e.g., the Karneia for Apollo). The agricultural year underlay the system (the New Year normally began after the harvest in July/August), but the correlation between festivals and agricultural tasks was relatively weak by the historical period. More complex festival schedules also existed: Dionysos is especially associated with biennial festivals, while the great Panhellenic sanctuary of Olympia organized its athletic festivals on a quadrennial basis. The association of deities with fixed days of the month, first attested in Hesiod's *Works and Days*, was a Panhellenic practice. These days fell primarily in the auspicious first half of the month when the moon was waxing.[18]

Greek ritual practices were generally organized and supervised by priests and priestesses. Yet Greek religion lacked a well-defined priestly hierarchy, and it is characterized by the parallel evolution of cults associated with the household, the lineage (*genos*), the village, the "tribe" (*phylê*), the *polis*, the ethnic group (Dorian, Ionian, etc.), and so on. Thus the religious system was a mirror image of societal organization. The primary source of religious authority was the state, which undertook the sponsorship of cults within its territorial boundaries. Subdivisions of the state, such as the demes in Attica, reflected the same system in miniature as they regulated the local cults. Many "religious" officials had responsibilities that we would consider more administrative than priestly, such as the financial and physical organization of large festivals with major processions, public games or performances, and the sacrifice of hundreds of animals. Others were deputized to keep accounts and inventories of sanctuary holdings, expenditures, and income from leased properties. Large, Panhellenic sanctuaries often possessed their own officials and a priestly hierarchy, and functioned on a partially or completely independent basis. On the other end of the scale were domestic worship, in which the male head of the family took the leading role, and those cults that were communally maintained by the residents of a neighborhood or village. These included local shrines of heroes or heroines as well as minor deities, often sponsored by private associations whose members met monthly to perform sacrifices and share dinners.[19]

4. SOCIAL CONTEXT

In Archaic Greek religion, worship was typically organized and led by members of aristocratic families who inherited their priesthoods. With the social changes accompanying the rise of the *polis*, this aristocratic monopoly was broken and the variety of cults became broader. New modes of worship were imported to and spread within Greece in response to popular interest, while priesthoods were awarded by lottery or auctioned off. Some of the more prestigious positions, such as the priesthood of Athena in Athens or the priesthoods of the Eleusinian Mysteries, remained hereditary. Because religious and social organization were to a great extent parallel, many cults were associated with a particular ethnic or professional status. In Lakonia, the relationship between the Spartan helots and Poseidon of Tainaron dated to the period before their enslavement, while Athenian artisans were particularly devoted to Hephaistos, and Corinthian prostitutes to the city patroness Aphrodite.

Some types of participation were determined by age group and/or gender. Male deities were usually served by priests and female deities by priestesses, though there are many exceptions to this rule. Unmarried girls carried a *kanoun* (basket with ritual implements) in processions, but females were usually barred from wielding the sacrificial knife.[20] Choruses, who danced and sang for the gods, were typically homogeneous with respect to age, gender, and social class. Sanctuaries sometimes barred entry to a given group (thus Dorians were prohibited from entering the Athenian Acropolis: Herodotus 5.72) and certain celebrations were segregated by gender. Women, for example, were not permitted to be participants in, or spectators at, the Olympic Games, while men were barred from many celebrations for Demeter and Kore.

As we have noted, the role of the state was instrumental in shaping the social contexts for worship. This meant that it was the state's concern to ensure that the proper sacrifices and festivals were observed for all the gods, on the one hand, and on the other that the gods were not outraged by violations of the accepted rules concerning purity and pollution. Murderers, for example, were to be expelled from the city lest they bring divine retribution onto their neighbors. Especially during the Archaic period, Greek states consulted oracles whenever a change to the status quo (such as plague, war, or famine) left them uncertain how to proceed. They also used divination in order to secure evidence of divine approval for undertakings already planned. For example, Athens (Pausanias. 10.10.1) asked the Delphic oracle to select (or more likely to confirm) ten heroes to serve as patrons for the ten new tribes established in its democratic constitution. Greek states regularly invoked religion and mythology in the service of political goals. The Thebans and Aiginetans, for example, framed their political alliance (Herodotus 5.80) as a reference to the relationship between the mythical sisters Thebe and Aigina, both daughters of the river Asopos. As a sign of hostility against Argos (Herodotus 5.67), Kleisthenes, the tyrant of Sikyon, cast out the Argive hero Adrastos from the market-place shrine where he was housed and replaced him with his mythical enemy, Melanippos.

Greek religion was inextricably tied to the economic lives of the Greeks. The markets for livestock were dominated by the sacrificial animals purchased for consumption during the many civic festivals throughout the year. The same festivals created markets for other types of goods and services, such as wood, clay, and bronze votive objects; the costuming of players in dramas; or the training of elite athletes. The hallmark of the *polis* was the monumental stone temple, which required vast resources to design, construct, and ornament. The gods of a city were major property owners whose lands were often leased out at a profit; the dedications and furnishings in sanctuaries represented a vast collective investment. According to Thucydides (2.13), Perikles viewed the contents of Athens' temples, up to and including the gold plates on the statue of Athena in the Parthenon, as state resources that could be used if necessary to finance the Peloponnesian war, though in order to avoid impiety, such moneys had to be paid back in full.

With respect to the development of Greek ethical thought as it related to the gods, the poets and philosophers had a substantial role to play. Hesiod is greatly concerned with the question of theodicy, and takes pains to emphasize that Zeus will exercise justice in smiting evildoers, even though the necessity to punish the wicked often results in the suffering of the innocent (Hesiod, *Works and Days* 240–1, 330–4). Hesiod's Zeus is represented as guaranteeing the stability of the cosmos, and he is the source of legitimacy for the rule of kings. This concept of the "Justice of Zeus" was explored by Aeschylus in his plays about Prometheus. He portrayed a Zeus who evolved from an insecure tyrant imposing his rule by force to a seasoned and wise king. The Archaic Greek ethical system was enforced by divine sanctions and focused on basic obligations and prohibitions, such as the sanctity of oaths, hospitality, and guest-friendship; the behavior of suppliants and the supplicated; and the need to give proper respect to the gods. An oft-cited dictum (e.g., Xenophon, *Memorabilia* 4.5.10) was that one should help one's friends and harm one's enemies, which is how the gods themselves were perceived to operate.

From the Archaic period onward, traditional Greek religion had its critics among Greek thinkers. The Presocratic philosopher Xenophanes ridiculed the anthropomorphism of the Greek gods. Plato strongly disapproved of the poor moral example set by the gods in traditional poetry, going so far as to banish imaginative poetry from his ideal state (e.g., *Republic* 386a, 595a). Although the philosophers were only a few in number, and most people never had access to their writings, their ideas were indirectly disseminated to the people through tragedy and comedy. Euripides' plays, for example, echo critiques of traditional religion that were current in philosophic circles. He highlights the cruelty and selfishness of the gods, who share the faults of mortals but have far more power than they to do harm.[21]

Plato and his predecessors championed a different conception of the divine, not personal but flawless and eternal. During the Classical period, the development of monumental cult statues reflected an analogous shift in beliefs about the divine. Formerly, worship was conducted with life-size or smaller statues that could be bathed, dressed, and carried in procession; the gods were treated like honored guests who had needs like those of mortals. This Archaic mode gave way to a fashion for colossal stone or chryselephantine images, whose massive and awe-inspiring presence suited less localized and more august, universal powers. During the late Classical and Hellenistic periods, philosophical schools including Epicureanism and Stoicism grew more important as a substitute for, or complement to, traditional public worship. The popularity of the philosophical schools, which acknowledged the existence of the divine but drew the focus away from traditional gods and cult practices, coincided with the development of Greek astronomy and other empirical disciplines.

5. RESEARCH

The sources for the study of Greek religion include almost every type of evidence from antiquity, because religious ideas and practices were embedded in daily life and pervasive in literature. There is no sacred text or canon comparable to the Hebrew scriptures, New Testament, or Koran, but the works attributed to Homer and Hesiod possessed special authority from the Classical period on because of their antiquity and broad appeal. Using information from Homer and Hesiod alone, we can reconstruct a pantheon of the major Greek deities as well as the basic operations of sacrifice, votive activity, purification, and divination. Such a reconstruction will, however, reflect the tendency of epic poetry toward Panhellenism, which implies the omission of local peculiarities in favor of a synthetic and, to some degree, artificial portrait of religion. Tragedies, comedies, history, and oratory, nearly all Athenian productions of Classical date, are often used as source material for the study of Greek religion, although each genre presents its own methodological challenges. Extant lyric poetry is more geographically diverse, while hymns from all periods are well represented in the preserved corpus of Greek literature and provide much additional material on the personalities, cult centers, and attributes of the gods.[22]

Epigraphic sources encompass a wide variety of inscribed texts as diverse as clay Linear B tablets of Mycenaean date, Archaic votive inscriptions on bronze objects, cult decrees and temple inventories on stone, and thin gold leaves incised with funerary texts. These inscriptions are indispensable to the study of Greek religion, for contemporary documents are by their very nature specific to a given time and place, so they provide a better gauge of geographical and diachronic variation. Among the most fruitful epigraphic sources are the sacrificial calendars of cities, towns, and private groups that record annual offerings to deities, heroes, and heroines, often including the type of victim and its price.[23]

The interpretation of archaeological evidence vis-à-vis religion presents its own methodological difficulties. Vase paintings, coins, and sculptures depict gods and rituals, but they must be interpreted in terms of their own geographical and chronological contexts; they do not necessarily benefit from being forced into relation with textual sources.[24] Archaeological excavation provides a wealth of information about the spatial organization of sanctuaries, temples, and other sacred structures; votive practices; and domestic cults, but it often raises as many questions as it answers. Archaeozoological analysis tells us what animal species were sacrificed as well as their age and sex, and how their bones were processed and deposited after sacrificial meals.[25]

In spite of all the contemporary sources of information, we still depend on numerous authors of the Hellenistic and Roman periods who interpret and describe religious practices and beliefs. Two examples will suffice here. Pausanias' *Description of Greece* is a lengthy travel guide recording the author's journeys through Greece during the second century CE. Everywhere he visited, Pausanias took pains to see sanctuaries, temples, cult statues, and relics, almost always focusing on works long predating the arrival of the Romans. The accuracy of his descriptions has often been affirmed by archaeological finds, yet his book is not free of errors, and it represents only the information available to a scholarly but casual traveler. In particular, his descriptions of rituals such as the great holocaust of live animals in the celebration of Artemis Laphria at Patrai (Pausanias 7.18.8–13) reflect the customs of his own day, not necessarily those of the Classical Greeks.[26] More difficult to gauge is the accuracy of works by hostile Christian fathers such as Clement of Alexandria (c. 150–211 CE), whose books contain much information about Greek mystery cults and sacrificial practices (e.g., *Exhortation to the Greeks*, Ch. 2) that is unavailable elsewhere.

Over the past century, the scholarship on these sources and their interpretation has seen major advances in methodology. Early-twentieth-century scholarship on Greek religion was dominated by two ideas: first, that the purpose of most Greek religious activity was to promote human, animal, and agricultural fertility; and, second, that there was a direct, one-to-one relationship between Greek myths and Greek rituals. The fertility model of religion gained great popularity as a result of J. G. Frazer's monumental work, *The Golden Bough*, which collected cross-cultural examples of "fertility rites" and related customs.[27] The so-called Cambridge Ritualists, led by Gilbert Murray and Jane Ellen Harrison, viewed myths as narratives inextricably tied to rituals. These movements were reactions against the Enlightenment idealization of the Greeks as the first fully rational society, an idea that has lingered in Classical scholarship. As late as 1951, E. R. Dodds' work demonstrating the affinity of the Greeks for ecstatic experiences was groundbreaking, though Harrison had long before explicated the "primitive" aspects of Greek belief and practice.[28]

During the mid-twentieth century, the debate moved away from questions of fertility and primitivism, which were deemed to have been overly influenced by Christian and colonialist patterns of thought, and toward models drawn from contemporary sociology, psychology, and anthropology. The focus for the study of Greek religion, as expressed through ritual, was now its function in society and its role as a non-verbal system of communication. Using different approaches, both Walter Burkert and Jean-Pierre Vernant described how individual rituals (especially animal sacrifice) both possess a structure themselves and form elements in larger systems.[29] This period was characterized by a strong emphasis on functionalism; ritual activity was thought to promote the stability of social groups through the release of tensions that would otherwise be destructive, to enhance the creation of group identity and cohesiveness, and to function as a communicative tool through which people were able to name and define themselves and their history in relation to others. The late twentieth century also saw much new work on the material culture of Greek religion, especially with respect to the relationship between sanctuaries and city-states.[30]

Currently the primacy of ritual (especially animal sacrifice) is coming more and more into question; whereas twentieth-century models of Greek religion stressed group experience, civic religion, and orthopraxy, holding that "belief" was irrelevant, there are signs of new efforts to focus on the experience of the individual, particularly as interpreted through the lens of cognitive psychology. "Belief," understood as intellectual assent to the proposition that the gods exist and take an interest in human affairs, was taken for granted as part of the worldview, just as we today take for granted that people know the world is not flat. The affective and emotional impact of such a worldview is also becoming the subject of study.[31]

FURTHER READING

The bibliography on Greek religion has been growing in recent years and the field has become better recognized as a sub-discipline within Classics. For reasons of space, I will focus here on newer scholarship and give priority to works in English, which are now plentiful. The works of Vernant and Burkert, which draw in different ways on anthropological theory, provided the foundation on which the current conceptual framework of the discipline has been constructed. Many of their seminal writings, mostly produced in the 1970s, are available in English translation; see especially Burkert 1983, 1985. With Marcel Detienne, Nicole Loraux, and Pierre Vidal-Naquet, Vernant established the "Paris school" of comparative research in ancient societies. Vernant 1991 and Detienne and Vernant 1989 are good introductions to the thought of this group. Nilsson 1955 remains an indispensable handbook of Greek religion; Farnell 1896–1909 should be used with caution, yet still contains valuable insights. Among newer introductions to the subject in English see Mikalson 2005 and Ogden 2007. For the Hellenistic period see Mikalson 1998 and Arnaoutoglou 2003. For individual gods, consult the bibliographies in Larson 2007. For festivals see Simon 1983; for temples and sanctuaries see Pedley 2005 and Spawforth 2006. For heroes and heroines see Brelich [1958], Kearns 1989, and Larson 1995. For oral communication with the gods see Pulleyn 1997 (on prayer) and Furley and Bremer 2001 (on hymns). For sacrifice see the volume by Vernant and Detienne mentioned previously and Ekroth 2002 (on hero cult). For divination, the works of H. W. Parke are indispensable; consult the bibliography in Johnston 2008. For priests and priestesses see Connelly 2007 and Dignas and Trampedach 2008. For eschatology and mysteries see the classic work of Rohde 1925 as well as Cosmopoulos 2003 and Graf and Johnston 2007. For pollution and purification, Parker 1983 is still essential; for magic one should begin by consulting Faraone 1999 and Collins 2008. Despite a growing awareness of the geographical diversity of Greek religion, Athens is still the focus of much research because the evidence for Athenian religion is relatively abundant. Parker 1996, 2005 are the key works in this area. Robin Hägg has made an important contribution in a long-running series of edited and co-edited volumes of papers from international symposia and seminars, e.g., Hägg 1988, 1996. Classic papers, including two seminal works on *polis* religion by Christiane Sourvinou-Inwood, are collected in Buxton 2000. Primary sources are gathered in Meyer 1987, Warrior 2009, and Stears and Stafford 2010. The single most important reference work in Greek religion is the series of volumes entitled *Thesaurus cultus et rituum antiquorum* (Los Angeles 2004–). These provide detailed articles, including copious images and references to primary sources, on all aspects of Greek cult and religious ritual.

CHRONOLOGY

All dates are BCE, unless otherwise noted.

1400–1100	Late Bronze Age
c. 1200	Linear B tablets from Mycenaean Pylos list gods including Zeus, Hera, and Poseidon
1100–800	Early Iron Age
1050	Greeks colonize coast of Asia Minor; encounter Anatolian deities
c. 950	First signs of ritual activity at Olympia
c. 800	Earliest Greek temples built of mud, brick, and wood
800–500	Archaic period
776	Traditional date for founding of Olympic games
c. 700	Hesiod's *Theogony* composed
c. 625	Earliest hundred-foot stone temples constructed

500–323	Classical period
500s	Cults of Cybele and Adonis imported to Greek world
534	First performance of tragedies at festival of Dionysos in Athens
508	Eponymous heroes of the ten tribes installed under Athens' democratic constitution
500s	Tradition of Herakles' apotheosis as an Olympian god spreads among Greeks
432	Parthenon at Athens completed
323–30	Hellenistic period
300s	Healing cult of Asklepios and mystery cult of Isis spread over Greek world
332	Alexander declared "son of Zeus" by the oracle of Zeus Ammon at Siwa in Egypt
c. 300	Epicurean and Stoic philosophical schools founded; provide alternatives to traditional Greek religion
150–50	Construction of new monumental Greek temples slows, then ceases
30 BCE on	Roman period
CE 340–350	Decrees by Constantine's successors outlaw all pagan worship
CE 393/2	Delphic oracle and Eleusinian Mysteries shut down by Christian Emperor Theodosius

GLOSSARY

cella: The central chamber of a Greek or Roman temple.

helots: Slaves of the Spartan city-state.

heroön: Shrine of a hero or heroine.

interpretatio Graeca: Latin term denoting the tendency to equate foreign gods with Greek gods.

katabasis: A journey to the underworld where the dead reside.

maenadism: "Madness" experienced by female worshipers of Dionysos in Greek myth and cult.

mystery cult: A cult offering secret knowledge to members, who must undergo an initiation ritual.

Panhellenic: Pertaining to "all the Greeks" rather than an individual city-state or ethnic group.

polis: A Greek city-state such as Athens or Sparta.

Notes

1   For "religion" as a modern construct see Humphreys 2004:42, 218.
2   Laffineur and Hägg 2001 (Aegean) and West 1997, 2007 (Near East, Indo-Europeans).
3   For new gods at Athens see Garland 1992.
4   E.g., Snodgrass 1980:52–56.
5   Spawforth 2006:198–200.
6   Mikalson 1998.
7   Popham, Touloupa, and Sackett 1982 and Morris 1992:73–211.
8   Pirenne-Delforge 1994:309–69.
9   Melqart: Bonnet 1988:219–20.
10 Jensen 2000:125.
11 For an alternative cosmogony see Betegh 2004.
12 Bremmer 2002:1–26.
13 Cosmopoulos 2003 (mysteries) and Graf and Johnston 2007 (Orphism).
14 Ekroth 2002.
15 Kowalzig 2007 (choruses) and Sourvinou-Inwood 2002:67–120 (Dionysia).
16 Johnston 2008.
17 De Polignac 1995.
18 Hannah 2005:16–82.
19 Jones 1999:221–67.
20 Connelly 2007:180–81.
21 Sourvinou-Inwood 2002:409 and Parker 2005:146–47.
22 Nagy 1990:70–81 (Panhellenism), Sourvinou-Inwood 2002:1–14 (tragedy and religion), and Furley and Bremer 2001 (hymns).
23 Whitehead 1986:176–212 (deme calendars), Chadwick 1985 (Linear B), and Graf and Johnston 2007 (gold tablets).
24 Sourvinou-Inwood 1991:7–12.
25 Pedley 2005 (sanctuaries) and Kotjabopolou and Hamilakis 2003 (bones).
26 Habicht 1998 and Pretzler 2007 (Pausanias).
27 Frazer 1912–1916.
28 Harrison 1922 and Dodds 1951.
29 Burkert 1983, Detienne and Vernant 1989, and Vernant 1990.
30 Alcock and Osborne 1994 and De Polignac 1995.
31 Humphreys 2004:195–96 (belief) and Chaniotis 2010 (emotion).

Works Cited

Alcock, Susan E. and Robin Osborne, eds. 1994. *Placing the Gods: Sanctuaries and Sacred Space in Ancient Greece.* New York and Oxford.

Arnaoutoglou, Ilias N. 2003. *Thusias heneka kai sunousias. Private Religious Associations in Hellenistic Athens.* Athens.

Betegh, Gábor. 2004. *The Derveni Papyrus. Cosmology, Theology and Interpretation.* Cambridge.

Bonnet, Corinne. 1988. *Melqart: cultes et mythes de l'Héraclès tyrien en Méditerranée.* Leuven.

Brelich, Angelo. [1958]. *Gli eroi greci; un problema storico-religioso.* Rome.

Bremmer, Jan N. 2002. *The Rise and Fall of the Afterlife: The 1995 Read-Tuckwell Lectures at the University of Bristol.* London and New York.

Burkert, Walter. 1983. *Homo Necans: The Anthropology of Ancient Greek Sacrificial Ritual and Myth.* Trans. Peter Bing. Berkeley.

———. 1985. *Greek Religion.* Trans. John Raffan. Cambridge, MA.

Buxton, Richard, ed. 2000. *Oxford Readings in Greek Religion.* Oxford and New York.

Chadwick, John. 1985. "What Do We Know about Mycenaean Religion?" In *Linear B, a 1984 Survey.* Ed. Anna Morpurgo Davies and Yves Duhoux, 191–202. Louvain-la-Neuve.

Chaniotis, Angelos. 2010. "Dynamic of Emotions and Dynamic of Rituals. Do Emotions Change Ritual Norms?" In *Ritual Matters. Dynamic Dimensions in Practice.* Ed. Christiane Brosius and Ute Hüsken, 210–235. London and New Delhi.

Collins, Derek. 2008. *Magic in the Ancient Greek World.* Malden, MA.

Connelly, Joan Breton. 2007. *Portrait of a Priestess: Women and Ritual in Ancient Greece.* Princeton, NJ.

Cosmopoulos, Michael, ed. 2003. *Greek Mysteries: The Archaeology and Ritual of Ancient Greek Secret Cults.* London and New York.

De Polignac, François. 1995. [French original 1984.] *Cults, Territory, and the Origins of the Greek City-State.* Trans. J. Lloyd. Chicago.

Detienne, Marcel and Jean-Pierre Vernant. 1989. *The Cuisine of Sacrifice among the Greeks.* Trans. Paula Wissig. Chicago.

Dignas, Beate and Kai Trampedach, eds. 2008. *Practitioners of the Divine: Greek Priests and Religious Officials from Homer to Heliodorus.* Cambridge.

Dodds, Eric R. 1951. *The Greeks and the Irrational.* Berkeley.

Ekroth, Gunnel. 2002. *The Sacrificial Rituals of Greek Hero-Cults in the Archaic to the Early Hellenistic Periods.* Liège.

Faraone, Christopher. 1999. *Ancient Greek Love Magic.* Cambridge, MA.

Farnell, Lewis Richard. 1896–1909. *The Cults of the Greek States.* 5 vols. Oxford.

Frazer, James George. 1912–1916. *The Golden Bough. A Study in Magic and Religion.* 3rd ed. 12 vols. New York.

Furley, William D. and Jan M. Bremer. 2001. *Greek Hymns: Selected Cult Songs from the Archaic to the Hellenistic Period.* Tübingen.

Garland, Robert. 1992. *Introducing New Gods: The Politics of Athenian Religion.* London.

Graf, Fritz and Sarah Iles Johnston. 2007. *Ritual Texts for the Afterlife: Orpheus and the Bacchic Gold Tablets.* London and New York.

Habicht, Christian. 1998. *Pausanias' Guide to Ancient Greece.* 2nd ed. Berkeley.

Hägg, Robin, ed. 1988. *Early Greek Cult Practice.* Stockholm.

———, ed. 1996. *The Role of Religion in the Early Greek Polis.* Stockholm.

Hannah, Robert. 2005. *Greek and Roman Calendars. Constructions of Time in the Classical World.* London.

Harrison, Jane Ellen. 1922. *Prolegomena to the Study of Greek Religion.* 3rd ed. Cambridge.

Humphreys, Sarah C. 2004. *The Strangeness of Gods: Historical Perspectives on the Interpretation of Athenian Religion.* Oxford.

Jensen, Robin Margaret. 2000. *Understanding Early Christian Art.* London and New York.

Johnston, Sarah Iles. 2008. *Ancient Greek Divination.* Malden, MA.

Jones, Nicholas F. 1999. *The Associations of Classical Athens: The Response to Democracy.* New York.

Kearns, Emily. 1989. *The Heroes of Attica.* London.

Kotjabopolou, Eleni and Yannis Hamilakis et al., eds. 2003. *Zooarcheology in Greece: Recent Advances.* London.

Kowalzig, Barbara. 2007. *Singing for the Gods: Performances of Myth and Ritual in Archaic and Classical Greece.* Oxford and New York.

Laffineur, Robert and Robin Hägg, eds. 2001. *Potnia: Deities and Religion in the Aegean Bronze Age.* Liège.

Larson, Jennifer. 1995. *Greek Heroine Cults.* Madison, WI.

———. 2007. *Ancient Greek Cults: A Guide.* London and New York.

Meyer, Marvin. 1987. *The Ancient Mysteries: A Sourcebook.* San Francisco.

Mikalson, Jon. 1998. *Religion in Hellenistic Athens.* Berkeley.

———. 2005. *Ancient Greek Religion.* Malden, MA.

Morris, Sarah P. 1992. *Daidalos and the Origins of Greek Art.* Princeton, NJ.

Nagy, Gregory. 1990. *Pindar's Homer: The Lyric Possession of an Epic Past.* Baltimore and London.

Nilsson, Martin Persson. 1955. *Geschichte der griechischen Religion.* Handbuch der Altertumswissenschaft 5. 2 vols. Munich.

Odgen, Daniel, ed. 2007. *A Companion to Greek Religion.* Malden, MA.

Parker, Robert. 1983. *Miasma: Pollution and Purification in Early Greek Religion.* Oxford.

———. 1996. *Athenian Religion: A History.* Oxford and New York.

———. 2005. *Polytheism and Society at Athens.* Oxford and New York.

Pedley, John. 2005. *Sanctuaries and the Sacred in the Ancient Greek World.* New York.

Pirenne-Delforge, Vincianne. 1994. *L'Aphrodite grecque: contribution à l'étude de ses cultes et de sa personnalité dans le panthéon archaïque et classique.* Athens.

Popham, Mervin R., Evi Touloupa, and L. H. Sackett. 1982. "The Hero of Lefkandi." *Antiquity* 56: 169–74.

Pretzler, Maria. 2007. *Pausanias: Travel Writing in Ancient Greece.* London.

Pulleyn, Simon. 1997. *Prayer in Greek Religion.* Oxford.

Rohde, Erwin. 1925. *Psyche; the Cult of Souls and Belief in Immortality among the Greeks.* New York.

Simon, Erika. 1983. *Festivals of Attica: An Archaeological Commentary.* Madison, WI.

Snodgrass, Anthony M. 1980. *Archaic Greece: The Age of Experiment.* London.

Sourvinou-Inwood, Christiane. 1991. *"Reading" Greek Culture: Texts and Images, Rituals and Myths.* Oxford.

———. 2002. *Tragedy and Athenian Religion.* Lanham, MD.

Spawforth, Anthony. 2006. *The Complete Greek Temples.* London.

Stears, Karen and Emma Stafford. 2010. *Greek Religion: A Sourcebook*. London and New York.

Vernant, Jean-Pierre. 1991. *Mortals and Immortals: Collected Essays*. Princeton, NJ.

Warrior, Valerie. 2009. *Greek Religion: A Sourcebook*. Newburyport, MA.

West, Martin L. 1997. *The East Face of Helicon. West Asiatic Elements in Greek Poetry and Myth*. Oxford.

———. 2007. *Indo-European Poetry and Myth*. Oxford.

Whitehead, David. 1986. *The Demes of Attica, 508/7–ca. 250 B.C.: A Political and Social Study*. Princeton, NJ.

8 Rome

CELIA E. SCHULTZ

At the core of Roman religion are the gods and cults of the city of Rome and its neighbors in west-central Italy worshipped over several centuries of the Roman Republic (late sixth to mid-first centuries BCE, a period preceded by 250 years of monarchy) and then the Roman Empire (roughly from the fall of the Republic until the end of the fourth century CE). Worship of many of these deities spread to new areas as Roman dominion expanded, first across the Italian peninsula and then to include the entire Mediterranean basin, reaching as far north as Britain, as far south as North Africa, and stretching from Spain to the westernmost edge of China. In addition, the Romans took on the worship of many of the new gods with which their empire building brought them into contact.

I. HISTORICAL BACKGROUND

Ancient writers were intensely interested in the origin of Roman religion. Descriptions of early Rome by Vergil, Livy, Dionysius of Halicarnassus, and others present some religious practices tied to the site of the city (e.g., sacrifice to Hercules at the Ara Maxima) and priesthoods (augurs, Vestal Virgins) as predating Rome's founding by Romulus in the mid-eighth century BCE. Other practices and organizational structures central to Roman religion were attributed to the second king of Rome, Numa Pompilius. The Romans believed they had shared from the earliest times some rituals observed outside the sacred limits of Rome with other, distinct Latin communities, such as the worship of Diana at Aricia and of Jupiter Latiaris on the Alban Mount.

The ancients were also profoundly aware of foreign elements in Roman religious life, and this has been borne out in much recent research. The Romans were never free from the influence of other groups. The Etruscans and other Italic peoples were active in Italy long before the Romans were worthy of notice, and the Greeks established themselves in Italy at about the same time as Romulus was supposed to have founded Rome. Roman religion seems to have shared much with that observed by other Latin communities, to have taken on some practices of the Etruscans (most notably haruspicy, divination through entrails), and to have been open to successive waves of Greek influence over the centuries. The integration of archaeological evidence with literary sources and advances in linguistic analysis have gone a long way to setting the origins of Roman religion in an Italic, multiethnic context.

Roman religion remained open to foreign influences, including accepting and naturalizing gods whose homes were not originally at Rome. The Romans often persisted in identifying foreign elements as such long after those elements had been absorbed into Roman religious life. For example, the Romans never lost sight of the fact that, long before the historical period, they had taken over from the Etruscans the particulars of haruspicy, which the Romans called not only *haruspicina*, but also the *Etrusca disciplina*, the Etruscan science. The Roman Senate passed a law sometime prior to the mid-first century BCE, long after Etruria had been absorbed into the Roman state, that made provisions for Etruscan (not Roman) youths to be schooled in it (Cicero, *De Divinatione* 1.92; Valerius Maximus 1.1.1). Juno Sospita, who was co-opted by the Romans after they defeated her hometown of Lanuvium in the Latin War that ended in 338 BCE, could still be identified by Cicero almost 300 years later as the Lanuvian Juno (*De Natura Deorum* 1.82). A particular way of wearing a toga at certain religious ceremonies was called the *cinctus Gabinus*, a name that identified it with its origin at the Latin town of Gabii (Livy 5.46.2); the cults founded by Romulus were observed *ritu Albano*, that is, in the manner particular to Alba Longa, where Romulus had been born (Livy 1.7.3).

The most important foreign influences came from further afield: Greece and Greek-speaking Asia Minor, Egypt, and Persia. The Greek element in Roman religion seems to have been present from very early on (e.g., cults of Hercules, Apollo, and Castor and Pollux), though in some cases it is difficult to discern if the Romans were introduced to a Greek god directly by the Greeks themselves (those living in southern Italy and Sicily) or at secondhand by the Etruscans. Other gods entered Rome later on. Aesculapius, who could heal the sick, was installed on the Tiber Island in 291 BCE, and Cybele (also known as *Magna Mater*, the Great Mother) was brought to Rome from Pergamum with much fanfare in 204 BCE. New gods continued to arrive during the late Republic and throughout the Imperial period. The Persian deity Mithras may have arrived in Rome as early as the mid-first century BCE (Plutarch, *Pompey* 24.5), but certainly by the late first century CE. Worship of other gods from the east, including Isis and Serapis, Sol Invictus, Artemis of Ephesus, and the Dea Syria, flourished under the emperors. Of course, Judaism and Christianity also flourished in the Empire, the latter eventually replacing the old gods altogether by the end of the fourth century CE.

Foreign elements were not always warmly welcomed. Astrologers (often identified as Chaldeans) were periodically banned from Rome, though the fact that such interdictions were repeated over time indicates that astrologers moved back into the city not long after they were thrown out of it. The eunuch priests of Cybele caused a good deal of discomfort among Roman senators, who curbed their activities in the city and banned any Roman citizen from joining their numbers (Dionysius of Halicarnassus 2.19.5). Some emperors endorsed attacks on the Christians (most famously Nero in 64 CE), though there was no sustained, universal anti-Christian stance among pagan emperors. The most aggressive response by the government in the thousand years of Rome's history was directed against the cult of Dionysus (Bacchus), which was brutally suppressed in 186 BCE. Our main source for this event, Livy 39.8.1–19.7, reports that the Senate ordered the legions be brought out to destroy the cult in Italy. Some 7,000 people were implicated in the affair, and far more were put to death than were imprisoned. The exact reason for the extreme nature of the Roman response is contested.

The expansion of Roman political control also had an effect on the religious lives of the peoples incorporated into the Roman state. In keeping with Roman religion's general openness to other people's gods, the Romans did not usually restrict the worship of local deities when they took control of an area, nor was there any sort of systematic imposition of Roman cults on provincial populations. The result is that the impact of Roman religion varies greatly from region to region within the Empire, but some basic trends are universal. For instance, there is ample evidence for gods indigenous to Rome being worshipped at the far edges of the Empire: Roman governors, soldiers, businessmen, and settlers brought their gods with them. In many cases Roman deities merged over time with local gods and were worshipped as single entities with composite names (e.g., Sul Minerva in Britain).

Roman officials also ensured that people in the provinces made sacrifices to the gods on behalf of the emperor and the Empire. This is one aspect of a complex phenomenon called "imperial cult," that is, the performance of rituals on behalf of, or offered to, the emperor and members of his family. The health and well-being of the living emperor became a concern for all residents of the Empire, whether citizen or not: the emperor was under the special protection of the gods. Although it never took root in Rome and Italy, in the provinces the living emperor could even be worshipped as a god himself (Dio 51.20.8). Some communities voluntarily established such cults; on others it was imposed from the capital. Throughout the Empire, including Rome and Italy, we also find cults of deceased emperors and, sometimes, members of their families. This shared reverence for the emperor and the imperial family served as a unifying factor for the Empire as a whole.[1]

2. BELIEF

The Romans had a polytheistic system of anthropomorphic male and female gods, some of whom can be identified in artistic representations by their distinctive attributes (e.g., Hercules by his lion skin and club, Juno Sospita by her goatskin and pointy-toed shoes). Others, however, are hard to distinguish, as in the case of the goddess on the Ara Pacis of Augustus (Fig. 8.1) whose identity is famously contested (Italia? Ceres? Tellus? Fortuna?). One reason for this difficulty is that Roman divinities, unlike the gods of Greece, were not endowed with a rich native mythology that detailed their exploits, loves, and familial relationships. The ancient literature preserves only a few sketchy tales about some of the gods worshipped at Rome. Over time, some Roman deities came to be identified with Greek counterparts (Jupiter/Zeus, Juno/Hera, Minerva/Athena), but the identifications were never perfect and were not always very close.

While Roman gods come across to us as less distinct personalities than those of the Greeks, they were not interchangeable with one another. Each Roman deity had multiple spheres of influence, with some being stronger than others. Jupiter was primarily interested in the political realm, but he was also asked by individuals to ensure the health of family members and livestock. Hercules could cure the sick and make a worshipper's business profitable, but was also worshipped on behalf of the state by Roman magistrates. Vesta preserved the state, but also the family. Mars, invoked in war, could also be enlisted to protect crops and animals.

Roman religion did not have at its core an authoritative text, or group of texts, that laid out central beliefs, explained the order of the universe and the origins of the world, or described what happened to people after death. Where Roman authors do talk about the formation of the world or the development of mankind, these accounts come from relatively late sources and owe a clear debt to Greek thought and mythology. When Romans talk about the origins of the Roman people, they are

Figure 8.1. So-called Tellus Relief of the Ara Pacis Augustae, 13–9 BCE. Ara Pacis Museum, Rome. Photo: German Archaeological Institute, Rome (D-DAI-ROM-86.1449).

consistent in their presentation of themselves as relative latecomers to a populated, if rustic, Italy and of themselves and their gods as a mix of foreign (Trojan) and indigenous (Latin) elements.

It is clear that ritual, not dogma, was of central importance to the Romans. Our literary sources focus on what the Romans did, rather than what they thought. This should not, however, be taken as a sign that we cannot recover anything about Roman beliefs or that Roman religion was simply empty ritual, the meaningfulness of which no one (or at least no one among the educated classes) truly believed.[2] We can get some idea of what the Romans, both as individuals and as a society, believed about their gods, but we must do so mostly by looking at their actions, both as they are described by ancient authors and through the physical record they left (i.e., inscriptions and votive offerings).

Beginning with our earliest material, votive offerings, it is quite clear that Romans, like their neighbors, believed that the gods were interested in the health and well-being of individual worshippers. The large numbers of anatomical votives (representations of parts of the human body generally made of terracotta) found at every sanctuary indicates that all deities (not just those labeled "healing gods" in modern scholarship) were thought to be able to effect a cure for a physical malady. The presence at many sites of votive uteri, phalluses, breasts, and infant figurines make clear that the gods could help with fertility as well. The belief continued on into later centuries, though the evidence for it shifts from inarticulate votives to dedicatory inscriptions that thank a god(dess) for a cure or ask for the continued good health of loved ones. Inscriptional evidence also makes clear that the gods took an interest in business affairs, travel plans, and some matters of the heart.

The Romans had at least a vague notion of existence after death. The deceased became in some sense divine, though exact details of this are lost to us. The May festival of the Lemuria included offerings intended to appease hostile spirits of dead ancestors. Sacrifices and libations were also offered to the dead on the anniversary of their death. Numerous altars were dedicated to the *di manes*, chthonic deities who may have been the shades of the ancestors, though this, too, is not certain. Literary presentations of an underworld, such as that in Book VI of Vergil's *Aeneid*, and artistic representations, like those on imperial sarcophagi, are heavily dependent on Greek models and, therefore, should not be taken as uncomplicated evidence for a widespread Roman notion of a place where souls go after death.

The gods took an intense interest in state affairs. One of the fundamental principles of the Roman view of the world was that their continued success as a society was owed to the gods' favor (e.g., Cicero, *De Natura Deorum* 3.5); military defeat, natural disasters, and civil strife were signs that the gods were not pleased. Accordingly, the Romans sought divine approval before embarking on any public matter, whether a meeting of the Senate, a military campaign, or a political election. Magistrates and generals, with the assistance of skilled priests, assessed the state of Rome's relationship with the gods, called the *pax deorum* ("the peace with the gods"), by observing the flight and cry of birds, watching the heavens, or inspecting the entrails of a sacrificed animal. If the gods endorsed the action, that is, if the signs were positive, then all proceeded as planned. If not, plans were put on hold until the next day, when the gods were asked once again for their opinion or until later, after expiatory actions could be taken (sacrifices, presentation of gifts at temples, etc.). Sometimes the gods sent signs (such as natural disasters or prodigies, i.e., aberrations in the natural order, such as talking cows or bleeding statues) without being asked to do so. Though these were occasionally indicative of good things to come, far more often they indicated significant ruptures in the *pax deorum* and impending doom.

3. PRACTICE

It is through ritual that the Romans communicated with the gods and the gods communicated with them; hence the proper performance of ritual was of the utmost importance to Roman religious life. As a people and as individuals, the Romans demonstrated their reverence for the gods through prayers, by making blood sacrifice and other offerings, and through the presentation of votives (statues, figurines, anatomical representations, etc.). Throughout the Empire, foundations of all sorts (cities, colonies, temples) had a ritual component. Lustrations, or purification ceremonies, in various forms, were performed throughout the year for fields, cities, the people, and the army. No act of public business was undertaken without the proper ritual preliminaries being observed first.

The gods, especially Jupiter, sent signs of their (dis)approval through regular elements in the natural world (e.g., celestial phenomena), through prodigies, or by invisibly guiding the random selection of a written text (such as the casting of lots or the choosing of a verse from a revered text). While some signs were so clear that anyone could interpret them, the majority required detailed knowledge of the appropriate divinatory science (e.g., augury for birds, haruspicy for celestial phenomena and entrails) that, at the state level, was the province of public priests. At the private level this knowledge was held by specialists available for hire. Though in modern parlance divination refers to predicting the future, for the Romans it was primarily aimed at clarifying the present and at ascertaining the state of the *pax deorum*.

Ad hoc observances were sometimes arranged in response to prodigies or other signs of divine displeasure. For the most part the origins of, and technical distinctions among, different types of rituals (such as *supplicatio, obsecratio,* and *lectisternium*) cannot be recovered. Most seem to have required the participation of adult men and women, with occasional special roles set aside for young people. Multiple forms of ritual were brought together in the festivals that punctuated the Roman year. Many festivals lasted for several days and included sacrifices, prayers, votive offerings, and the pouring of libations. Some large festivals celebrated publicly also included theatrical performances, athletic competitions, and horse races.

The most important location for the practice of Roman religion was the city of Rome itself, defined as a sacred space by a ritual boundary called the *pomerium*, which was purportedly marked out with a plow by Romulus in a ritual manner inherited from the Etruscans (Cato, frag. 18 Peter = Servius, on *Aeneid* 7.755; Varro, *De Lingua Latina* 5.143). As it marked off the city from the profane landscape, the *pomerium* also divided civil and military affairs. Magistrates could only take up their full military power (*imperium*) once outside the *pomerium*, and had to lay it down before crossing back inside. Some voting assemblies could meet within the *pomerium*, but the most important of these, the *comitia centuriata*, which elected the highest ranking magistrates, could not because in this assembly the citizens voted in their military groupings. Only the most exceptional individuals could be buried within the *pomerium* (Vestal Virgins and emperors [Servius, on *Aeneid* 11.206]). Foreign gods accepted at Rome were generally given temples outside it.

A more temporary demarcation of sacred space was the *templum*, used in taking the auspices (i.e., reading signs sent by Jupiter). Critical to the interpretation of divine signs was where they originated in relationship to the magistrate or augur who was seeking the god's opinion. A *templum* was a rectangular space that the asker defined in the heavens, marking front, back, right, and left. This way he could track where the bird (or lightning or other phenomenon) first appeared and to where it traveled. Some *templa* had permanent equivalents marked out on the ground and, despite the similarity to the English word, these terrestrial *templa* were rarely temples in the modern sense. For example, the meetinghouse of the Roman Senate, the Curia, was itself a *templum*.

Monumentalized sacred space for the Romans consisted primarily of sanctuaries, complexes in both urban and rural settings (often on the top of hills or along travel routes) that comprised at least a temple housing a statue of the god worshipped there and an altar for sacrifice. Sometimes a single sanctuary contained more than one temple and/or more than one altar; in many instances statues of more than one god were set up in a single temple, as in the Capitoline temple of Jupiter Optimus Maximus, which had three *cellae* (inner chambers) to house his statue and those of Juno and Minerva. It is clear from the remains of some sanctuaries that temples also held many of the votive offerings brought by worshippers. Excess, broken, or otherwise damaged votives, leftover sacrificial material (e.g., bones), and damaged architectural items were buried within the precinct: such items still belonged to the gods and could not be disposed of as regular refuse.[3] Collections of these items are called "votive deposits."

The physical remains of some sanctuaries give an idea of the human activity that took place there. For example, the sanctuary of Fortuna Primigenia at Praeneste has yielded numerous dedications indicating that many professional groups, as well as individuals, came to worship there. The sanctuary itself was built into a very steep mountainside and consisted of many terraces connected by stairs and ramps with the temple itself sitting at the summit. The presence of both stairs and ramps suggests the ritual movement of people and animals. At some other sites, archaeologists have been able to identify kitchens for the preparation of the ritual meal that usually followed sacrifice among the Romans and evidence for shops that sold offerings or other ritual paraphernalia to worshippers.

Sacred time in Roman religious practice was organized by a regular twelve-month lunar calendar maintained by Roman priests. We have approximately forty copies of the calendar from ancient Italy, nearly all of which date to the reign of Augustus (27 BCE–13 CE) or later. The calendars are not identical to each other, but they do show general agreement on the most important annual festivals, games, and celebrations to mark major events in the lives of the imperial family. Certain days were consecrated to particular gods: the first day of each month was dedicated to Juno and the ides (either the thirteenth or fifteenth day of the month) was sacred to Jupiter (Ovid, *Fasti* 1.55–7; Macrobius, *Saturnalia* 1.15.16).

For the most part, Roman religion does not fit the profile of a modern, organized religion. In addition to having no central text, it functioned without a central authority, had no sects or congregations to join, and no specific requirements for being allowed to take part in the worship of the gods beyond the observance of certain ritual restrictions (e.g., dietary restrictions, sexual abstinence) in some cases. That said, there are some elements of religious life, particularly at the public level, that seem to have functioned in an organized way.

The closest thing the Romans had to a central religious authority was the Senate, which also served as the ultimate political authority in the Republic and bowed only to the emperor during the Imperial period. The Senate was the body that decided what foreign religious elements might be invited to Rome officially (e.g., Apollo, Cybele), what foreign elements to exclude (e.g., astrologers), and when to rob an enemy of its chief protective deity (such as Juno Regina from Veii in 396 BCE or Juno/Astarte from Carthage in 146 BCE). The Senate also determined which reported prodigies were to be accepted as legitimate and, therefore, expiated at state expense. The precise form of expiation, however, was determined by the Senate only in consultation with one of the main groups (colleges) of public priests – all of whom were also members of the Senate.

Each college of public priests, religious specialists who were permitted to perform rituals *pro populo* (on behalf of the people), had an area of expertise. Augurs specialized in the interpretation of signs sent by Jupiter through the flight of birds and celestial phenomenon; the areas of public life most affected by their rulings were elections and other civic affairs. The *quindecemviri sacris faciundis* (Board of Fifteen for Performing Rites) originally only had two members (*duoviri*), but expanded to ten (*decemviri*) in 367 BCE, and eventually to fifteen (*quindecemviri*) and finally sixteen, yet retaining the designation *quindecemviri*, by the Late Republic. These priests generally oversaw matters arising from the importation of foreign cults. They also had exclusive access to the Sibylline Books, a collection of prophecies written in Greek hexameters purportedly given to the last king of Rome by the Sibyl herself, a female Greek prophet at Cumae. The *pontifices*, headed by the *pontifex maximus*, controlled the calendar and were authorities on sacred law, including matters of state as well as more private issues affecting the constitution of a Roman family (inheritance, adoption, burial, etc.). These three main colleges were thought to go back to the days of Numa Pompilius, the second king of Rome. The *epulones*, the last of the major priestly colleges, was established in 196 BCE (Livy 33.42.1). Their duties were tied primarily to two sets of public games (the Roman and the Plebeian Games) and included arranging the *epulum Iovis* (the feast of Jupiter) that was a prominent part of those celebrations. Official declarations of war were made by a group of less well known priests, the *fetiales* (Livy 1.24.1–9 and 1.32.4–14; Dionysius of Halicarnassus 2.72.1–9). The *fetiales* ensured that any war the Romans entered was a just war (*bellum iustum*) by giving the offending party time to rectify the situation before war was declared, and they enforced treaties by invoking curses upon the Romans should they be the party to break the agreement.

None of the public priests discussed thus far was truly attached to the cult of a particular deity. In contrast, each of the fifteen public priests called *flamines* was assigned to a single god. The three most important were the *flamen Dialis*, who was Jupiter's priest; the *flamen Martialis*, priest of Mars; and the *flamen Quirinalis*, priest of Quirinus, a little-known god thought to be the deified Romulus. The remaining *flamines* were all attached to old Italic deities, not all of whom can be identified. In the Empire, deified emperors were also given a *flamen*. It is certain the *flamen Dialis* shared his priesthood with his wife (the *flaminica Dialis*): she was subject to all the same religious restrictions he was, and he had to resign his position if she died (Aulus Gellius 10.15.22). The *flaminica Dialis* also had her own ritual obligations that she did not share with her husband. It is not certain if all the other *flamines* were required to have a spouse to share their duties, but given the Roman penchant for balance and similitude, this seems likely.

Another public priesthood at Rome that was shared by a married pair was that of the *rex* and *regina sacrorum* ("the king and queen of rites"), who were thought to have inherited much of the religious duties of the kings who had ruled Rome until the establishment of the Republic in 509 BCE, though in the historical period the *pontifex maximus* was a far more powerful figure. Not much is known about the specific ritual duties of the *rex* and *regina sacrorum* except that the *rex* announced the festivals for each month and performed sacrifices on fixed days in March and May. The *rex* (accompanied by a *pontifex*) and the *regina sacrorum* each made sacrifices to Juno on the Kalends (first day) of each month (Macrobius, *Saturnalia* 1.15.19).

There were a few public priesthoods at Rome open only to women, all tied to particular cults. Most famous are the Vestal Virgins, six priestesses of the goddess Vesta who were required to maintain their virginal chastity for the thirty-year tenure of their service. They lived apart from their natal families in a special house next to the goddess' small temple in the Roman Forum. Their main duties were to keep the flame in the temple's hearth going at all times and to prepare certain items needed for other observances throughout the year. Another female public priesthood was that of Ceres (Cicero, *Pro Balbo* 55). Inscriptional evidence raises the possibility that the older women who were priestesses of Liber were public priestesses as well.[4]

Below this most visible, public level, Roman religion involved numerous religious officials, not just priests and priestesses but many others who worked alongside them. Record of these officials – both male and female, of every status (free, freed, and slave) – is preserved almost exclusively in inscriptions. We cannot recover what were the responsibilities of a *magister* or a *magistra*, a *minister* or *ministra*, titles common to many different cults, or how these differed from the duties given to a *sacerdos* (priest). Many more titles are specific to a particular cult. Rüpke's comprehensive gathering of the evidence for all religious officials known to have lived in Rome over a span of 800 years makes clear the huge scope of formal religious participation beyond public rites.[5]

Within a Roman household, worship of the domestic deities and the ancestors was led primarily by the *paterfamilias* (the male head of house). The Roman state had no interest in monitoring or directing these activities. Every family worshipped the household gods (*dii familiares*), three groups of deities: the Lares, who were responsible for protecting the household; the Penates and Vesta, who protected the family's storeroom; and the *genius*, best understood as the procreative force of the family, especially of the *paterfamilias*. Numerous *lararia*, small decorated shrines where images of the gods were kept and offerings were made, have been found set into the walls of homes uncovered in the excavations at Pompeii and Herculaneum. The letters of Cicero and of the younger Pliny indicate that wealthy estate owners could maintain, at their own discretion, large shrines on their property that could be visited by neighboring folk.

4. SOCIAL CONTEXT

As in many other nations, religion helped to unify the Roman state while at the same time reinforcing social divisions among its people. An early division that was thought to have gone back to the time of the kings (754–509 BCE) was that between patrician and plebeian *gentes*, extended family groups similar to clans. The basis for, and meaning of, this distinction among families is not entirely clear. In archaic Rome, the patrician/plebeian division mapped rather neatly onto other divisions, such as rich/poor and patron/client. Until the fourth century BCE, religious and political control rested firmly in the hands of a closed patrician aristocracy. In religious terms, patrician status seems to have entailed the right to take the public auspices. Over time the patrician/plebeian divide became less important to Roman society as the barrier between the two groups broke down and a mixed patrician-plebeian aristocracy developed through intermarriage. The right to public auspices may have been the original, fundamental distinction: if so, it would explain in part the fact that plebeians were admitted to political office long before they were admitted to Rome's public priesthoods.[6]

Another basic division in Roman religion was between men and women. There were relatively few rites and cults from which women were explicitly interdicted (e.g., the worship of Hercules at some cult sites). More numerous were the rituals open only to them, such as the December ritual of the Bona Dea (the Good Goddess) and the paired springtime observances in honor of Fortuna Virilis and Venus Verticordia (Manly Fortune and Venus, the Changer of Hearts). Further distinctions were sometimes made within an exclusively female group, with special roles marked out for matrons (*matronae*) and unmarried girls (*virgines*). Prostitutes had a prominent role in the festival of the Floralia. A female slave was ritually beaten and then driven out of the temple of Mater Matuta at the June festival of the Matralia. When the Senate ordered the people of Rome to undertake expiatory observances to remedy a rupture in the *pax deorum*, that body sometimes decreed special roles for freeborn matrons, freedwomen, and *virgines*. Ritual roles for men were divided along fewer lines, with distinctions mostly between adult men and boys. Some roles in the cult of deified emperors were reserved for freedmen.

High social status was an unofficial prerequisite for membership in any of the public priesthoods. In all periods, the same groups of families that provided senators and magistrates also provided members of all the public priesthoods. The overlap went even further than this, however. A prosopographical study of male priests in the period of the Republic demonstrates that the majority of male public priests had also reached the highest echelons of political power, the praetorship and the consulship.[7]

Roman religion was an "embedded" religion that permeated not only political life, but also affected every aspect of day-to-day existence, a situation reflected in the fact that the Romans never had a single word that maps onto English's "religion." Even Latin *religio*, from which our word descends, was used in a more narrow sense to refer to scrupulousness in religious practice. As we have already seen, no major military or governmental action was taken and no public assembly or meeting of the Senate convened without first taking the auspices to see if the gods approved. The gods were honored and consulted at less weighty events as well, such as public entertainments, and in private affairs like the daily conduct of business and personal travel. Our sources make clear that the gods (though not necessarily which gods specifically) always took an interest in the rites of passage that punctuated a Roman's life.

At a basic level, the gods enforced proper behavior among the Romans. Gods were invoked in the swearing of oaths and the striking of treaties by both individuals and the state. Taking of the auspices ensured that the gods endorsed elections and approved of military campaigns. Despite all this, philosophy, not religion, was the primary venue for discussion of ethics, values, and proper behavior in Rome. The Romans never developed a philosophical system of their own, but over the course of the second and first centuries BCE the major schools of Hellenistic Greek philosophy that developed in the century following the death of Plato (Epicureanism, Academicism, and especially Stoicism) gained followings among the upper classes in Rome. Most notable among the philosophical works produced by Roman intellectuals during the Late Republic are Lucretius' *De Rerum Natura* (*On the Nature of the Universe*), an epic poem in six books that lays out the tenets of Epicureanism, and the extensive philosophical oeuvre of the great orator M. Tullius Cicero that touches on everything from the ideal state, law, the nature of friendship and of old age, to the validity of fate and divination. Although he stops short of acceptance, Cicero is sympathetic to the Stoic position, which endorsed the notion that the gods were interested in the well-being of mortals and that they communicated that concern through signs in the natural world. While Epicureanism, which argued for gods that enjoyed perfect bliss at a complete remove from human affairs, and Academicism, which argued for the impossibility of true knowledge, including about the existence of gods and fate, did not enjoy long-lived success in Rome, the Stoic school flourished under the Empire, with major works produced by the younger Seneca and the Emperor Marcus Aurelius.

The majority of Roman philosophical works focus on the practical application of philosophy to the workings of the state and to the definition of the proper role of the citizen (the aristocratic citizen, that is) within society. In general, theology does not receive much attention. The great exception to this is a group of three religious works written by Cicero in 45–44 BCE: *De Natura Deorum (On the Nature of the Gods)*, *De Divinatione (On Divination)*, and *De Fato (On Fate)*. But even here, Cicero is ultimately interested in how these topics affect the functioning of the state rather than in how they might alter an individual's conduct.

5. RESEARCH

The types of evidence for Roman religion are literary, epigraphic (inscriptional), and archaeological, each of which offers insight into different aspects of religious life in the Roman Empire. No one type of evidence is equally well preserved across all of the more than 1,000 years that the Roman gods were worshipped, and the result is that we can only ever have an incomplete and uneven picture of what Roman religion was like, especially for its earliest period (from the eighth through the third centuries BCE). That said, there is much that is preserved, and the picture of Roman religion becomes richer and more detailed when different types of sources are brought into concert with each other.

Scholarship on Roman religion has long relied primarily on literary sources – poetry, histories, speeches, personal letters, technical treatises, biographies, and philosophical works – written by the Romans themselves or by the Greeks who observed them. Our authors were almost exclusively elite (or at least reasonably wealthy) men who were interested in religion as it affected public life. Thus literary sources have preserved detailed descriptions of a range of public rituals, philosophical discussions, and political debates on religious issues. Very little record remains of private and domestic religious life. Few extant ancient works have religion as their main focus, yet religious themes are ubiquitous in all genres: a reflection of the fact that religion permeated every aspect of life in the Roman world. Private life, commerce, governance, and warfare all required the involvement of the gods.

One of the fundamental difficulties for a history of Roman religion is that the texts we have are rarely contemporary with the events they record, often distant by several centuries. Although we can identify a form of worship we can reasonably call "Roman religion" as early as the eighth century BCE, the Romans did not start producing literature until almost 500 years later, and even then not much survives today that was written before the first century BCE. Literary accounts of early events must always remain suspect, but while due caution is necessary, these later accounts should not be dismissed out of hand. Our sources had access to earlier works and archives, now lost to us, and Roman religion was, by nature, conservative in its ritual performance over many centuries.

Epigraphic material presents a much wider swath of Roman society, including slaves, women, and children, and provides a great deal of information about religious life that is not noted by literary sources. There are more than 300,000 Latin inscriptions carved into stone and metal, or painted onto walls and household objects, from all over the Roman world. Many inscriptions record the dedication of objects (mostly now lost) to a god or gods, many of whom are not mentioned in extant literary texts. Another major group of inscriptions is found on tombstones that sometimes proudly announce that the deceased held a priesthood or some other official position in a cult. *Leges sacrae* ("sacred laws") preserve the rules for proper conduct at certain temples.

The most visible type of evidence for Roman religion is archaeological. It comes in myriad forms: the remains of sanctuaries and temples, altars, household shrines, statues and figurines of gods and worshippers, paintings and reliefs depicting public and private rituals, coins bearing religious images, ritual implements like libation cups (called *pocula*), and votive offerings.

The study of Roman religion in its own right was only established among modern scholars in the mid-nineteenth century. Much early work followed the ancient sources' preoccupation with separating out what elements were Greek (or Etruscan or eastern) importations and what were "purely" Roman in order to recover the original form of Roman religion. The influence of this trend can be seen in the foundational handbook of G. Wissowa, which has separate chapters devoted to *di indigetes* (native gods) and those of Italic and of Greek extraction.[8]

In the first half of the twentieth century, some who sought the origins of Roman religion looked to the fields of cultural anthropology and comparative religion for a way to reconstruct its prehistoric period.[9] The "primitivist" school (the most prominent members of which are the British scholars W. Warde Fowler, Sir James Frazer, and H. J. Rose) compared certain Roman rituals that they identified as archaic with the religious practices of modern "primitive" societies.[10] The result was a reconstruction of Roman religion in which magic, *mana*, and *taboo* were prominent. Another group of scholars, referred to as the Frankfurt School, whose most famous member, F. Altheim, taught at the Universität Frankfurt in the 1920s and 1930s,[11] reacted against the primitivists' emphasis on ritual and focused instead on myth, tracing tales told by later authors back to an earlier period.

The comparative method was also employed, though on a much grander scale, by the structuralists, most significantly G. Dumézil, whose *Archaic Roman Religion* set out to highlight the elements of their religion that the Romans shared with other Indo-European peoples.[12] His overarching argument, based in large part on linguistic analysis and comparative mythology, is that Roman religious thought was Indo-European in its basic organization: a tripartite system where the roles of king, warrior, and producer serve as structuring principles. Work in this vein suffers from the insurmountable problems of a lack of evidence datable to the Archaic period and a necessary reliance on uncertain linguistic reconstructions. For these reasons Dumézil's methods have largely been set aside in the last few decades.[13]

The focus of more recent work on Roman religion has shifted from the question of origins and the nature of "pure" Roman religion to recovering what the Romans did, not just among the elites but at all levels. Archaeological excavation has been a particularly fruitful avenue for research into the activities of less affluent Romans. The technicalities of Roman religious praxis (augury, prayer, sacrifice, the functioning of priesthoods) have also received renewed attention.

Contemporary studies of Roman religion very often look at aspects of the relationship between religion and other areas of day-to-day existence. For example, the role of gender in shaping religious experience has received considerable attention, as has the relationship between religion and politics, and the role of religion in forming Roman identity and in unifying the Empire.[14] Some very good work has been done by literary specialists on the handling of religious matters in ancient literature,[15] which has pushed for more sensitive treatment of texts like Ovid's *Fasti*, a poem whose six surviving books detail the Roman festival calendar from January through June. There is also now considerable interest among both classicists and biblical scholars in expanding the dialogue between their disciplines.[16]

FURTHER READING

There is no dearth of good introductions to Roman religion. Beard, North, and Price 1998 was quickly followed by English translations of works by Turcan 2000, Scheid 2003, and Rüpke 2007a, as well as other original English-language works such as Warrior 2006 and Rives 2007. Each of these studies has much to offer but, as suggested by the number of them that has appeared in recent years, the definitive volume has yet to be written. The great German handbooks, Wissowa 1912 and Latte 1960, remain indispensable repositories of information even if the interpretations they offer are now dated. The articles (in English, German, Italian, and French) in Haas 1986, and those in Rüpke 2007b, are useful summaries of the state of our understanding of individual aspects of religious life and provide helpful bibliographies. Translations of most ancient sources, both Greek and Latin, are readily available in the volumes of the Loeb Classical Library from Harvard University Press. These also provide the original text on facing pages.

CHRONOLOGY

c. 1170 BCE	Aeneas and his Trojan followers arrive in Italy
754 BCE	Rome founded by Romulus, monarchy established
509 BCE	Last of the kings thrown out of Rome; Republic established
367 BCE	Plebeians allowed to serve as *decemviri sacris faciundis*
300 BCE	*Lex Ogulnia* allows plebeians entrance to colleges of pontiffs and augurs
186 BCE	Suppression of Bacchic cult throughout Italy
44 BCE	Assassination of C. Julius Caesar
27 BCE	Augustus becomes first emperor of Rome; empire established
64 CE	Persecution of Christians under Nero
312 CE	Constantine the Great becomes the first Christian emperor
394 CE	Emperor Theodosius bans pagan cult

GLOSSARY

auspicia: Signs sent by Jupiter through the flight and cry of birds, the behavior of other animals, celestial phenomena, and unusual occurrences in the natural world.

augury: The science of interpreting the will of the gods through the taking of the auspices (*auspicia*). It was practiced in its public form by priests called augurs.

freedperson (-man, -woman): An individual who has been emancipated from slavery.

gens: An extended kinship group or clan. The term is often somewhat imperfectly translated as "clan."

haruspicy: Also known as the *Etrusca disciplina* (the Etruscan science). Practitioners of this form of divination, called *haruspices* (sing. *haruspex*), were expert in interpreting thunderbolts (*fulgora*), some types of prodigies, and especially *exta*, the entrails of a slaughtered animal (cow, sheep, or pig).

Latin: A linguistic and ethnic designation. Until the middle of the fourth century, Rome was just one of the Latin towns, united by a common language (also called Latin) and shared culture, in Latium (the name given to west-central Italy between the Tiber River and the Circeian promontory).

mana: An impersonal supernatural power that can be associated with people or objects.

patricians: Members of a privileged class of Romans, a status that in the Republic could be attained only by birth to patrician parents. In the early Republic, patricians had a lock on all magistracies and priesthoods, although over time access to these prestigious offices was granted to those of plebeian (non-patrician) status.

pax deorum: Literally, "peace with the gods." Rome's relationship with the gods, the state of which could be assessed through divination. In some instances a rupture of the *pax deorum* could be made clear by the gods through prodigies or natural disasters.

plebeian: Originally Rome's poorer citizens who were dependent on their patrician patrons for financial aid and legal representation. Over time, as leading members of this group came to be wealthy and powerful in their own right, the term ceased to have strong connotations of poverty and exclusion.

pomerium: The ritual boundary of the city of Rome that marked it off from the profane landscape.

prodigy: An event that could be viewed as violating the natural order, such as meat falling from the sky or the birth of a two-headed cow.

taboo: Prohibition or interdiction.

templum: A rectangular space marked off in the sky for augural purposes to assist in determining from which quadrant of the sky a sign originated. Occasionally the celestial *templum* had a terrestrial counterpart.

votive deposit: Properly a collection of votive offerings such as statues, figurines, and anatomical representations, intentionally buried within the precinct of a sanctuary. The term has come to be used more loosely for any collection of votive offerings from a single site regardless of whether they represent a purposeful grouping and whether they were deliberately buried.

Notes

1 See Hopkins 1978:197–242.
2 For a forceful statement of this now outdated view see Taylor 1949:76–97.
3 Glinister 2000.
4 See Schultz 2006:79.
5 Rüpke 2008.
6 Linderski 1990.
7 Szemler 1972.
8 Wissowa 1912.
9 A concise summary can be found in Michels 1955.
10 See Fowler 1899, Frazer 1911–1915, and Rose 1948.
11 See Altheim 1938.
12 Dumézil 1970.
13 Woodard 2006 remains a significant exception.
14 Such as Schultz 2006, Ando 2008, and Ando and Rüpke 2006.
15 E.g., Feeney 1998.
16 Works like Ando and Rüpke 2006 and Ando 2008 that aim at both constituencies help to bridge the gap.

Works Cited

Altheim, Franz. 1938. *A History of Roman Religion*. Trans. H. Mattingly. London.

Ando, Clifford. 2008. *The Matter of the Gods*. Berkeley.

Ando, Clifford and Jörg Rüpke, eds. 2006. *Religion and Law in Classical and Christian Rome*. Stuttgart.

Beard, Mary, John North, and Simon Price. 1998. *Religions of Rome*. 2 vols. Cambridge.

Dumézil, Georges. 1970. *Archaic Roman Religion*. Trans. P. Krapp. 2 vols. Chicago.

Feeney, Denis. 1998. *Literature and Religion at Rome: Cultures, Contexts, and Beliefs*. Cambridge.

Fowler, W. Warde. 1899. *The Roman Festivals of the Period of the Republic*. London.

Frazer, James G. 1911–1915. *The Golden Bough*. 3rd ed. 12 vols. London.

Glinister, Fay. 2000. "Sacred Rubbish." In *Religion in Archaic and Republican Rome and Italy*. Ed. E. Bispham and C. Smith, 54–70. Edinburgh.

Haas, Wolfgang, ed. 1986. *Aufstieg und Niedergang der römischen Welt*. Vol. 2.16.3. Berlin and New York.

Hopkins, Keith. 1978. *Conquerors and Slaves*. Cambridge.

Latte, Kurt. 1960. *Römische Religionsgeschichte*. Munich.

Linderski, Jerzy. 1986. "The Augural Law." *Aufstieg und Niedergang der römischen Welt* 2(16.3): 2146–312.

————. 1990. "The Auspices and the Struggle of the Orders." In *Staat und Staatlichkeit in der frühen römischen Republik.* Ed. W. Eder, 34–48. Stuttgart.

Michels, Agnes Kirsopp. 1955. "Early Roman Religion, 1945–52." *Classical World* 48: 25–35, 41–5.

Rives, James B. 2007. *Religion in the Roman Empire.* Oxford.

Rose, H. J. 1948. *Ancient Roman Religion.* London.

Rüpke, Jörg. 2007a. *Religion of the Romans.* Cambridge.

————. 2007b. *A Companion to Roman Religion.* Oxford.

————. 2008. *Fasti Sacerdotum.* Trans. D. M. B. Richardson. Oxford.

Scheid, John. 2003. *An Introduction to Roman Religion.* Edinburgh.

Schultz, Celia. 2006. *Women's Religious Activity in the Roman Republic.* Chapel Hill, NC.

Szemler, G. J. 1972. *The Priests of the Roman Republic.* Collection Latomus 127. Brussels.

Taylor, Lily Ross. 1949. *Party Politics in the Age of Caesar.* Berkeley.

Turcan, Robert. 2000. *The Gods of Ancient Rome.* Edinburgh.

Warrior, Valerie M. 2006. *Roman Religion.* Cambridge.

Wissowa, Georg. 1912. *Religion und Kultus der Römer.* 2nd ed. Munich.

Woodard, Roger D. 2006. *Indo-European Sacred Space: Vedic and Roman Cult.* Urbana, IL.

9 Early Christianity

H. GREGORY SNYDER

Even before the end of the second century, the tiny movement inspired by Jesus of Nazareth had touched nearly every country around the Mediterranean Sea, from Spain all the way to northern India. Scholars debate whether a univocal term like "Christianity" does justice to the diversity that existed in such a far-flung movement, and some would prefer to speak of early "Christianities" as a way of acknowledging such diversity. In addition to this geographical diversity, the changes and struggles endured by the movement over time are also quite well documented compared to many other religious movements. Given the constraints of space, the present essay will focus on developments during the first two centuries of Christianity, occasionally up to and rarely beyond the legalization of Christianity by Constantine in 313 CE. Diversity across geographical boundaries and ethnic groups should be assumed even if it cannot be discussed. Some attention will be devoted to the changes experienced by the movement as it moved from its Jewish milieu into the wider Greco-Roman world.

I. HISTORICAL DEVELOPMENT

Christianity began as a millenarian sect within Judaism. It gathered around Jesus of Nazareth, a charismatic teacher and healer who announced the imminent arrival of God's judgment. Having begun as a follower of the apocalyptic preacher John the Baptist, Jesus separated from his teacher and gathered a following in the towns and villages of Galilee, in the Roman province of Judaea. The men and women stirred by his preaching anticipated the coming of the Kingdom of God "with power" (Mark 9:1, 13:30), believing that Jesus' activity as a healer and exorcist gave a foretaste of the righting of wrongs and the rearrangement of social structures that would accompany that Kingdom. With respect to this lively apocalyptic expectation, they were not unlike their contemporaries the

Essenes, another sect within Judaism that nourished apocalyptic hopes in their community by the shores of the Dead Sea.

After a short period of activity in Galilee, Jesus traveled to Jerusalem for Passover. There, following a demonstration in the Temple, he was arrested and executed by Roman soldiers on the orders of Pontius Pilate, the Roman governor of Judaea. As the official responsible for preventing outbreaks of violence, Pilate would have been remiss in the eyes of his superiors had he not acted swiftly to extinguish even the hint of a disturbance during such a politically flammable occasion as Passover. It may well be that some members of the Jewish religious bureaucracy participated in his demise, but Christian retellings of the incident such as survive in Matthew 27:25 – "then the people as a whole cried out, 'his blood be on us and on our children!'" – are the later fabrications of Jesus' followers who sought to blame Jews for the crucifixion of their beloved teacher.

While the resurrection of Jesus was supremely important for the future of his movement, it is a moment that is in principle inaccessible to historians. From the historical point of view, one can only say that Jesus' followers came to believe that he had truly died but that God honored his righteous death and raised him bodily from the grave to an exalted status in heaven, whence he would soon come to claim those who believed in him. This, at least, is the formulation that Paul, one of Christianity's foundational figures, uses some fifteen to twenty years later, around 50 CE, when he commends members of his church in the Greek city of Thessalonica for "turning from idols to serve a living and true God, and to await his son from heaven, whom he raised from the dead, Jesus, the one preserving us from the coming wrath" (1 Thessalonians 1:9).

In the wake of Jesus' death, his circle of followers was led by Jesus' brother James, not one of his twelve disciples. While Simon Peter was no doubt highly respected, and in fact took the news about Jesus to cities as far afield as Antioch, James seems to have had the last word in debates about policy (Acts 15), and he exerted considerable authority through traveling emissaries (Galatians 2:11–12). In the multicultural environment of cities like Damascus and Antioch, the preaching about Jesus began to attract interest from Gentiles, or non-Jews.

The apostle Paul was also a crucial figure in the growth of the Jesus Movement. Scholars are divided over whether Paul's reorientation to the new group should be called a "conversion."[1] While it did involve an abrupt change of sympathies, it was certainly not a conversion to a different religion opposed to Judaism but rather a continuation and an extension of Judaism. Paul never uses the term "Christian." However this change is to be conceived, Paul started by being a persecutor of the movement and ended as a passionate advocate for it. He believed that in Jesus, membership in God's covenant – hitherto restricted only to Jews – was being extended to Gentiles, and that the terms of the covenant had changed: circumcision and the observance of Jewish food and purity laws were no longer required. Belief in Christ as God's messenger, symbolic participation in Jesus' death through baptism, and membership in a local assembly of fellow believers sufficed for Gentiles who wished to join the Jesus Movement. Paul and his co-workers crisscrossed the eastern Mediterranean, founding small groups of believers in Asia Minor and in Greece, and he corresponded actively with these groups when he was not present. During a stop in Jerusalem, he was caught up in an incident that led to his arrest and imprisonment. According to Acts, Paul made an appeal to Caesar based on his Roman citizenship and was thereupon dispatched to Rome, where he seems to have died. But other followers of Jesus arrived in Rome well before Paul. In traveling merchants and craftspeople such as Prisca and Aquila, we glimpse the sorts of individuals who took the message about Jesus to the city of Rome before Paul ever arrived there (1 Corinthians 16:19; Romans 16:3).

One important group in the broadening of the Jesus Movement to non-Jews was the "God-fearers," non-Jews who patronized Jewish synagogues, adopting some Jewish practices but stopping short of the act of circumcision. For this group, Paul's message would have been attractive, grounded as it was in the Hebrew scriptures and reflecting its ethical teaching, while baptism, its rite of admission, was open to both sexes and somewhat easier to undergo than circumcision. It is quite possible that competition over this group of sympathizers may have led to conflict between Paul and members of local synagogues.[2]

While the Jesus Movement was gaining a foothold among Gentiles in cities around the Mediterranean, it was staggered by two catastrophes in Judaea. The Jewish revolt from 66 to 70 CE, which culminated in the sack of the city and the destruction of the Temple, was preceded by significant social unrest. James, the brother of Jesus, was killed by a mob around the year 61 CE.[3] According to Eusebius, followers of Jesus decamped from Jerusalem before the siege, moving to the city of Pella in nearby Transjordan (*Historia Ecclesiastica* 3.5). If there is any truth to this report, this migration would have marked an important moment in the separation of personnel within the Jesus Movement from the major institutions of Judaism. Given the degree of separation in Judaea after the first Jewish revolt, and the increasing spread of the Jesus Movement among Greeks and Romans around the Mediterranean, we may with confidence begin to speak of "Christianity" as a religion discernibly separate from Judaism around the beginning of the second century. In fact, the first attested use of the term "Christianity" (*Christianismos*) occurs around the year 110 CE, in Ignatius' *Letter to the Magnesians* (§10). The Bar Kochba revolt in 132–35 CE drove a further wedge between the two groups, as many Jews with messianic hopes supported the guerrilla leader Simon bar Kochba; followers of Jesus did not rally around this banner and in some cases were persecuted when they did not (Justin Martyr, *1 Apologia* 31.6).

Even while Judaea was vexed by these misfortunes, the Jesus Movement continued to spread rapidly around the Mediterranean and beyond. The Book of Acts, written around 90–100 CE, records how the Apostle Phillip converted and baptized a court official from Ethiopia, who, the narrative would have us believe, returned to his native country along with his new religion (Acts 8). The letters of Paul, the Book of Revelation, and the Letters of Ignatius document the spread of Christianity in Asia Minor in the latter part of the first and the early part of the second century. Basilides, Valentinus, and their students were active in Alexandria during the early decades of the second century, and their writings came to the attention of Irenaeus, bishop of Lyon, on the far side of the Mediterranean basin. The Acts of Thomas, dating from the first decades of the third century, suggest that Christianity had spread east and south as far as India. The speed of this expansion is one of early Christianity's most remarkable features.

While Christians and their small communities were widely diffused around the Mediterranean, their cultural impact was most often negligible: the number of people in question and their modest social class meant they were mostly invisible among the general hubbub of religious activity in major cities. There are notable exceptions, however. Tacitus records that Christians were scapegoated by the Emperor Nero for the great fires in 64 CE that destroyed a large portion of Rome (*Annals* 15.44). The Book of Acts describes a violent altercation between Christians in Ephesus and patrons of Ephesian Artemis. Acts portrays the event as motivated by commercial, rather than religious, scruples: local merchants producing images of Artemis for the tourist trade feared that Christians would bring Artemis – and their trade in her images – into disrepute (Acts 19:21–41). Similar concerns are preserved in one of the first non-Christian sources that mentions Christians: a letter from Pliny, the Roman governor of Bithynia on the coast of the Black Sea, to the Emperor Trajan written in 112 CE. Having suppressed the "depraved superstition" of the Christians, Pliny observes a resurgence in traditional religious rites: temples are frequented, and sacrificial animals are once again on sale in the marketplace (Pliny, *Epistulae* 10.96). So in some instances, Christians found themselves in conflict with local religious and commercial interests.

Finally, given the cultural importance of the Christian Bible in the modern world, a word about the historical growth of Christian literature is in order. Compared with many of the religions discussed in this volume, Christianity has an extraordinarily rich spectrum of surviving literature, dating from its earliest periods. This fact may be traced to its origins within the scripture-centered religion of Judaism, to the connections that were forged between groups in different locations and the ensuing communication among them, and to the subsequent success of Christianity, which allowed for the preservation of evidence from its early stages.

The genuine letters of Paul (1 Thessalonians, Galatians, 1, 2 Corinthians, Romans, Philippians, and Philemon) are the earliest documents in the New Testament, dating between 50 and 65 CE. The Gospel of Mark is generally regarded as the earliest gospel, dating to around 70–75 CE. The Gospels of Matthew, Luke, and John were probably intact before the end of the first century. The non-canonical *Gospel of Thomas*, composed of 114 sayings of Jesus, was discovered in the Egyptian desert in 1945. Some of these sayings reflect early traditions contemporaneous with the sources behind the canonical gospels, even if the final form of this Gospel dates to the second century. The non-Pauline letters that make up the rest of the New Testament may date as early as 70 or as late as 120 CE, as in the case of 2 Peter, which mentions that Paul's letters have been circulating in a collection. The Pastoral Epistles (1, 2 Timothy; Titus), purportedly by Paul, are widely regarded as having been written long after his death by a Christian anxious to adapt Paul's theology to issues arising at the beginning of the second century.

The origins of gospel literature and the degree to which it reliably preserves the sayings and deeds of Jesus are often misunderstood. Scholars agree that the gospels were not written by eyewitnesses to Jesus' life. They contain reminiscences of such material, transmitted orally, shaped and changed by the tides of memory and developing beliefs about Jesus, fitfully and partially written down at first, attaining their final form forty to sixty years after the events they describe. Even when it was roughly complete, this gospel literature circulated anonymously. While early second-century writers such as Ignatius and the author of a short treatise on liturgical practice known as *The Didache* quote material that derives from the canonical gospels, none of them do so by name. When Justin Martyr, writing in the middle of the second century, quotes from New Testament gospel literature, he cites it as deriving from the "memoirs of the apostles." Irenaeus (c. 180 CE) is the first Christian writer to refer to the canonical gospels by the names they now bear.

2. BELIEF

In 1 Thessalonians 1:9, cited previously, we have a brief statement that captures at least three aspects of early Christian belief. The first involves a turn from image-centered polytheism to monotheism: "You turned to God from idols, to serve a living and true God." The phrase could be uttered by a Jewish missionary, and in fact *is* uttered by a Jewish missionary: by origin and continuing commitment, Paul is simply Jewish in his theological orientation. The God of Israel alone was to be worshipped, "the creator of the world, who shaped the beginning of humankind and devised the origin of all things" (2 Maccabees 7.23). These sentiments from a Jewish author of the second century BCE would have been entirely acceptable to Paul. To faithful Jews, the deities recognized by Greeks, Romans, and others simply did not exist, or were inferior, even malevolent semi-divine powers.

Second, by describing Jesus as God's "son," Paul alludes to beliefs about the special standing Jesus has with respect to God. For Paul, Jesus is God's chosen heir and agent. This special standing is chiefly a matter of relationship, not of metaphysical identity. In Romans 1:3–4, Paul affirms that Jesus is "descended from David according to the flesh," but that in light of his resurrection from the dead, was "declared to be the Son of God." If asked, Paul would not have asserted that "Jesus is God," after the manner of later creedal formulations.

Third, members of Paul's group in Thessalonica believed that Jesus had a role to play in God's coming judgment and that he would soon return from heaven to save them from that apocalyptic event. They remained unsure, however, of what would happen to members of their community who had died before the return of Jesus. Paul assured them that those who had died would not be left behind: when the Lord returns, says Paul, the dead will be raised and taken up with the living to "meet the Lord in the air" (1 Thessalonians 4:17). This belief, known as "The Rapture" in Christian parlance, does not appear elsewhere in Paul's correspondence nor in other New Testament literature, though it is a point of ardent belief among some modern Christians.

Such realistic apocalyptic beliefs were held by some gospel writers (see Mark 9:1, 13:1–36), though not by all. Certain passages in John's gospel, for instance, suggest that some early Christians thought of resurrection as a present reality. At the tomb of Lazarus, when Martha confesses her belief that her brother Lazarus will rise again at the Day of Judgment, Jesus responds, "I am the resurrection and the life; whoever believes in me, even though he dies, he will live." By de-emphasizing the future resurrection and emphasizing the present reality of resurrection, John's gospel gives voice to lines of thought also found in the Gospel of Thomas. When asked by his disciples about the resurrection of the dead and the advent of the Kingdom, Jesus replied, "That which you look for has already come, but you do not recognize it" (Gospel of Thomas 51; see also 3, 113).

Other statements of early Christian belief about the nature of Jesus and his relationship to God surface in Paul's letters where he transmits early Christian creedal slogans, for example, at 1 Corinthians 15:3–5 ("Christ died for our sins according to the scriptures, he was buried, and raised on the third day in accordance with the scriptures ..."). In Philippians 2:6–11, Paul preserves an early Christian hymn that recounts the descent into human form of the savior, his shameful death, resurrection, and exaltation. Colossians 2:9, written by an early follower of Paul, states, "in him [Christ] the whole fullness of deity dwells bodily" (also Colossians 1:19).

The notion that Jesus was not simply a prophet, divinely adopted son, or messianic figure but something still more divine arises in the Gospel of John, where the "word" (*logos*) that became flesh in Jesus is not only in the presence of God but is equated with God (John 1:1). Like the feminine principle of Wisdom in the Hebrew Bible, this *logos* was the principal agent in the process of creation: nothing was created apart from it. In the mid-second century, Justin Martyr speaks of the *logos* as "another god also called Lord, different than the creator, also called an angel" (*Dialogue with Trypho* 56). On these foundations were laid the subsequent debates about the relationship between divine and human natures in Jesus that culminated in the Council of Nicaea (325 CE), which produced the famous phrase "of one substance with the Father."

While "trinitarian" language of Father, Son, and Holy Spirit can be found in the New Testament, as in Matthew 28:20, it contains no doctrine of the Trinity properly speaking. Irenaeus, writing around 180 CE, assigns different and complementary functions to these three entities, but he does not engage in philosophical speculation about metaphysical relationships among them. The original Nicene Creed of 325 is primarily concerned with the relationship between the Father and the Son; belief in the "Holy Spirit" is added on later in the creed, almost as an afterthought. The revised creed of 381 shows greater attention to the relationship between the Father, Son, and Holy Spirit, foreshadowing developments among theologians such as Gregory of Nyssa in the East and Augustine in the West.

Orthodox Christianity – sanctioned by Constantine and captured in the Nicene Creed – came to overshadow many diverse theological currents in early Christianity that died out or were actively suppressed. In the mid-second century, a ship-owner named Marcion left his home in Bithynia and came to Rome, where he founded a movement that rejected the Hebrew Bible, finding in the teaching of Jesus evidence of a higher, more compassionate deity than the imperious and arbitrary Jehovah of the Hebrew Bible. Forty years later, he was attacked as a "mutilator of the Gospel" by Tertullian, one of the founding fathers of early Christian polemic. Shortly afterwards, Tertullian himself was drawn to a charismatic movement known as the New Prophecy, founded in Asia Minor by Montanus and two female prophetesses named Priscilla and Maximilla. The documents in the Nag Hammadi library, discovered in Egypt in 1945, capture a rich cross section of Christian groups who practiced innovative interpretation of scripture inspired by Platonic philosophy and who staged their own distinctive rituals. The overall picture of Christianity in the second century resembles a field of competing saplings more than a central tree (orthodoxy) surrounded by deviant offshoots (heresies).

And even this mercilessly truncated version of "Christianities" on offer in the second and third centuries misrepresents the state of affairs by approaching it in terms of competing positions promoted by literate intellectuals. It is unlikely that a majority of Christians would have been troubled by subtle theological distinctions. For many people, the pattern of abasement and exaltation evident in Jesus' life captured their social predicament and satisfied their aspirations; the precise details could be left at the level of generality.[4] For others, Jesus' death and resurrection created the hope that they too would regain their fleshly bodies after death.[5] For still others, Jesus was a wonder-worker and divine advocate who promised benefits not only in the next life but in the present one as well, a patron in whose movement they found a social network offering refuge, support, or social advantage.[6] We should expect that the reasons for which a person might join such a movement would be quite diverse.

3. PRACTICE

Two ritual practices became especially prominent within the Jesus Movement: baptism and the Lord's Supper, also known as the Eucharist. Both grew out of liturgies prevalent among Jews: ritual purification by immersion and the Passover meal. The Jewish practice of animal sacrifice in the Jerusalem temple would have remained central to Jesus' first followers, and it was important to the writer of Luke–Acts to demonstrate continuity between the new movement and traditional temple worship (Luke 24:53; Acts 3:1, 21:26). This overlap between traditional Jewish worship and the ritual practices of Jesus' followers was severed with the destruction of the Temple in 70 CE, an event that increased separation between the two groups.

Ritual washing had long been established in Judaism when John the Baptist tailored the rite to his own apocalyptic message. The rite was ubiquitous at Qumran, based on remarks in the texts (e.g., *Manual of Discipline* 3:8–10) and on the presence of stepped pools (*mikvot*) and water sources to provide for them. Unlike the practice at Qumran, John's baptism seems to have been a one-time affair, marking repentance and preparation for the coming judgment of God (Mark 1:1–8). While it would be reasonable to suppose that Jesus also baptized based on the example of John, the sources give ambiguous evidence. Whatever Jesus' practice might have been, Matthew 28:19 and Acts 2:38 imply that baptism was widely practiced among early Christians.

The ritual acquired a new set of connotations in Paul's communities. There, it functioned as a ritual initiation into a group, understood by Paul as the body of Christ. The cycle of descent, immersion, and emergence from water was imagined as a kind of ritual death: "All of us who were baptized into Christ Jesus were baptized into his death" (Romans 6:3). In addition to this symbolic joining in the death of Jesus, the rite may also have had the effect of muting or erasing social distinctions. In Galatians 3:28, the phrase, "no longer Jew or Greek, no longer slave or free, no longer male or female" probably captures part of a baptismal liturgy.[7] In Paul's communities, then, the ritual acquired a complex set of associations. Surprisingly, notions of repentance and forgiveness of sins are not foremost among them, though they are found in the later literature. 1 Peter 3:21 mentions baptism, "which now saves you," and in one of his evangelical sermons, Peter appeals to his hearers, "Repent and be baptized every one of you in the name of Jesus Christ so that your sins may be forgiven" (Acts 2:38). The emphasis on baptism as a requirement for the forgiveness of sins continues in Justin, Tertullian, and other

Christian writers of the second and third centuries. In fact, baptism was often deferred until the moment of death, in order that the baptized person might die in a sinless state.

The Lord's Supper, or Eucharist, commemorates the Passover meal that Jesus shared with his disciples immediately before his arrest and execution. Once again, Paul provides the earliest record of the practice, the language of which he reproduces in 1 Corinthians 11:23–34 ("This is my body …"). In its earliest stages, the Eucharist was celebrated as part of a community meal; only later did it become a stand-alone ritual. As to its significance, Paul calls Christ "our Passover lamb" (1 Corinthians 5:7) and thinks of the Eucharist as a remembrance and a restaging of Christ's death "until he comes" (1 Corinthians 11:26), thereby making a connection between the Jewish Passover sacrifice, the death of Jesus, and the Eucharistic meal. Other early Christian communities, such as that represented by *The Didache*, label the rite the "Thanksgiving Meal" and use different celebratory language. *The Didache* also makes baptism a requirement for participation in the Lord's Supper.

For most religions in the ancient Mediterranean, temples were the loci of worship. But for a long time, Christians did not require such intentionally designed spaces: houses of group members sufficed for Paul's group in Corinth. According to Acts 19:9–10, Paul argued for two years in the guild hall of Tyrannus; Justin Martyr's students met in his apartment over a neighborhood bathhouse in Rome. The first space known to have been specifically dedicated to Christian worship is the church at Dura Europos, in modern Syria, dating to the middle of the third century.[8] Christians also gathered in cemeteries above ground and in catacombs underground for worship, to commune with deceased relatives in funerary meals and to venerate the bodies of martyrs. Indeed, the presence of a martyr's remains served as a powerful nucleus for the creation of sacred space, as Christians sought to bury their dead as closely as possible to these heroes of the faith.

The loose attitude of Christians toward sacred space seems to have extended also to the liturgical calendar: The writer of Colossians condemns those who observe "festivals, new moons, and Sabbaths" (2:16). Christians did from a very early stage begin to gather on the first day of the week in commemoration of Jesus' resurrection. Easter was the first and most important date on the Christian calendar, and consequently the first about which there was bitter disagreement. It had been early Christian practice to celebrate Easter on the same day as Jewish Passover, 14 Nisan, though the practice was not universal: it arrived in Rome only during the mid-second century, and when it did, it was celebrated on

Sunday, the day after Jewish Passover. Around the year 190, however, Bishop Victor of Rome declared that Roman practice should henceforth become standard and that those Christians who preferred to celebrate Easter on Passover – so-called Quartodecimans – were deviating from accepted practice. By the fourth century, the period of fasting before Easter laid the foundations for Holy Week; the forty-day period of Lent appears in 337 CE.[9]

Christmas looms large on modern Christian calendars, but early Christians showed little interest in marking the day. Clement of Alexandria, writing around the year 200, thought the birthday of Jesus fell in May, as did the chronographer Julius Africanus. Only in the fourth century, in the Codex Calendar of 354, do we find mention of Jesus' birthday as falling on December 25, the same day as that of Sol Invictus, the Unconquered Sun, whose worship and temple were established in Rome by Emperor Aurelian c. 275. As an avid patron of both deities, Constantine may be responsible for the conflation of dates.

The structure of authority in Christian churches may be described under three heads: genealogical connections to authoritative figures, charismatic prowess, and offices in emerging religious institutions. Later, special authority was granted to the martyrs and their memory.

With respect to emerging authority structures in early Christian communities, one of the most fateful utterances of Jesus would seem to be Matthew 16:18: "You are Peter, and on this rock I will build my church, and the gates of Hell will not prevail against it." Modern scholars, dubious as to whether an apocalyptic prophet who expected the imminent arrival of God's Kingdom intended to found an institutional church, see here the later editorial hand of the gospel writer. Mark, the earliest Gospel, contains no such remark, and according to Mark, neither Peter nor any of the twelve disciples are granted a post-resurrection viewing of Jesus or gifted with the spiritual authority that such a vision would confer.

Even so, connections with these and other founder figures were often played up in later debates among Christians. Irenaeus, writing at the end of the second century, traces a twelve-step succession of bishops down to his own day, and takes pride in the fact that he himself is a mere two degrees of separation away from Jesus: as a young boy in Asia Minor, Irenaeus heard Polycarp, who was in turn supposedly a disciple of John the Apostle (*Against Heresies* 3.3). But others made similar claims: Valentinus, against whom Irenaeus directed his polemic, supposedly inherited his teaching from a certain Theudas who was in turn a disciple of Paul.

Authority was also granted to charismatic figures who demonstrated the gift of powerful utterance, spirit-inspired experiences, and in some cases, intellectual prowess. In 2 Corinthians, Paul derides certain opponents, whom he terms "super-apostles." They have apparently made a strong impression as public speakers, disparaging Paul's own speaking as "weak and contemptible." The Book of Acts records that Apollos, a native of Alexandria, was especially articulate and persuasive as a speaker (18:24). As for spiritual experiences, Paul attempts to trump the "super-apostles" in 2 Corinthians with a coy allusion to his own visionary ascent to the third heaven. As noted previously, the ecstatic movement known as the "New Prophecy" marked a charismatic outbreak in Asia Minor toward the end of the second century. The movement became very popular and eventually encountered sharp opposition from Christian bishops unwilling to tolerate unpredictable and uncontrollable outbreaks of the Holy Spirit.

Defined roles in church offices are barely present in Paul's authentic correspondence. Paul mentions the role of bishop (episkopos) and deacon in Philippians 1:2, and he gives the latter title to a woman named Phoebe (Romans 16:1). These designations are probably casual and temporary: they do not imply the existence of a developed institution. In the Pastoral Epistles (1, 2 Timothy; Titus), written perhaps by second- or third-generation followers of Paul, these offices rose to a more defined level, complete with entrance requirements. Ignatius of Antioch, writing around the year 112, boosts the authority of bishops even further: one must "respect the bishop as being an image of the Father" (Epistle to the Trallians 2.2; 3.2). In some cases, special authority began to accrue to bishops holding office in major cities. As noted previously, Victor, the Bishop of Rome, issued an opinion about the date for the celebration of Easter that he felt should be binding on the churches of Asia Minor. But the crown of martyrdom conferred the highest authority: bishops might petition the favor and counsel of those willing to undergo martyrdom, such as the woman Perpetua (Martyrdom of Perpetua 13). Perpetua's leverage extends even higher: by her willingness to undergo martyrdom, she is able to win release for her deceased brother Dinocrates from hell itself.

4. SOCIAL CONTEXT

Jesus came from a humble background. His father Joseph was a tradesman, a tektôn, often translated as "carpenter," though the term is better understood in the broader sense of "builder." His hometown of Nazareth was only four miles from Sepphoris, the largest city in Galilee, so it is possible that Joseph and his sons would have found work in that city, especially during the aggressive building campaign of Herod Antipas. And yet the Gospels say nothing at all about any visits to Sepphoris by Jesus or his followers. Rather, Jesus seems to have worked in the countryside fringing on the Sea of Galilee and in small towns such as Capernaum. Given that his parables invoked images of agriculture and life in rural villages, his audience was largely drawn from the ranks of farmers, fishermen, and day laborers.

Jesus' work as a teacher and healer attracted both men and women. The canonical gospels record the names of twelve male disciples, but apart from Simon Peter, very little can be said about any of these figures. Women were among his first and most loyal followers. In the Gospel of Mark, women, more than men, demonstrate conspicuous faith, from the woman with the hemorrhage (Mark 5:25–34), the Syro-Phoenician woman (Mark 7:24–30), to the anonymous woman who anoints Jesus with ointment (Mark 14:3–9). In all four gospels, women are the only disciples of Jesus who witness the crucifixion, and all four gospels report that women were the first to visit his tomb and to witness his resurrection. Developments in the new movement influenced memories and the way stories were recounted later, but it is safe to assume, as Luke 8:2–3 asserts, that women were both patrons and members of his entourage. In particular, Mary Magdalene had a special place in Christian memory, no doubt based on a close association with Jesus.

When it came to crossing ethnic boundaries, there may have been some initial resistance to extending the movement to non-Jews: even Jesus seems to hesitate when his message threatens to go beyond the line dividing Israel from the Gentiles (Mark 7:27). Paul appears to transcend the social divisions of race, gender, and class when he says, "There is no longer Jew or Greek, there is no longer slave or free; there is no longer male and female" (Galatians 3:28). In the wake of baptism, these distinctions no longer matter, and in fact, Paul's groups also afforded unusual opportunities for women: women were allowed to pray and prophesy, as long as they did so with covered hair, presumably in order to distinguish themselves from female members of Dionysian groups with their free-flowing hair (1 Corinthians 11:2–17).

And yet, the divisions supposedly transcended in Galatians 3:28 proved more entrenched than Paul might have hoped. Members of his group in Corinth tended to segregate into traditional class groups when sharing the Lord's Supper, and this threatened Paul's vision for group cohesion. He warned that those who approached the rite without "discerning the body" – probably his way of censoring higher status members of the community who were disregarding the needs of lower status members – were liable to suffer physical consequences: "This is why some of you are sick and some of you have died" (1 Corinthians 11:30). Opportunities for female speaking were rolled back in later Pauline groups (1 Timothy 2:8–15). Slaves were simply told to be submissive and not to steal (Titus 2:9–10); no corresponding advice is given to masters about how slaves are to be treated, as in Colossians 4:1: "Masters, treat your slaves fairly, since you too have a master in heaven."

Not all Christian groups, however, fell back into traditional patterns. The *Acts of Paul*, a second-century text, records the heroic exploits of a woman named Thecla, who, having heard the preaching of Paul, fled from the constraints of marriage, cut her hair short, donned male garments, and became an itinerant follower of Paul.[10] Women appear to have enjoyed exceptional opportunities in certain gnostic groups. According to Tertullian, the "wanton women" of the heretics make bold to teach, dispute with men, exorcise demons, perform healings, and "perhaps even to baptize!" (*De praescriptione haereticorum* 41). The precise identity of the "heretics" to which he alludes is not entirely clear, though followers of both Marcion and Valentinus may be in view. Mary Magdalene was held in high regard among certain gnostic groups, as may be inferred from the *Gospel of Mary Magdalene*, and Priscilla and Maximilla were founding figures in the New Prophecy Movement.[11]

Given Jesus' execution as a political criminal, the movement that grew up in his wake enjoyed a mixed relationship with Roman authorities. It is surely the case that Jesus' preaching of the coming reign of God had political ramifications, though it seems that Jesus did not actively seek to start a social movement that would overthrow existing political structures. If he had, the Roman officials who crucified him might have gone a step further and hunted down his associates, as they did thirty years earlier with the followers of Judas and Matthias, two other politically inclined rabbis known to us from Josephus (*Jewish Antiquities* 17.149–67). Paul, too, seems to have enjoyed relative freedom of action: he came to the attention of authorities only when his activities led to social disturbances. In some texts, early Christians seem positively bourgeois: in Romans 13, Paul recommends that "every person be subject to the governing authorities," and the writer of 1 Peter advises believers to accept the authority of the governing authorities without complaint, and to "honor the emperor" (2:17).

But in spite of all this, Christians did encounter difficulties with the authorities. The author of 1 Peter, writing from the city of Rome, speaks of sufferings that Christians are undergoing, and of the "fiery ordeal that is taking place among you" (1 Peter 4:12); he may be alluding to the persecutions inflicted on Christians by Nero (Tacitus, *Annals* 15.44). The writer of Revelation refers to those "slaughtered for the word of God" (6:9) and of a certain Antipas, a member of the church in Smyrna who was slain (2:13). For this author, Rome is the Great Whore, drunk on abominations and the blood of the saints. Some twenty years later, the Roman governor Pliny encounters Christians in Bithynia and while he finds nothing objectionable in their actions or beliefs, executes some of them for their stubborn refusal to pay homage to the emperor with a pinch of incense. Justin Martyr earned his surname in the middle of the second century in Rome under the relatively enlightened reign of Marcus Aurelius. The diary of Perpetua, a first-hand account of a young woman and her companions martyred in Carthage at the beginning of the third century, is one of the most affecting pieces of early Christian literature.

In some quarters, however, the zeal for martyrdom reached a disturbing pitch. Ignatius approached the arena with alarming relish: "Let there come fire and cross, crowds of wild beasts, tearing, mangling, dislocations, amputations, shattering of the body; only let me attain to Jesus Christ!" (*Epistle to the Romans* 5). Should the beasts hesitate, Ignatius planned to goad them on to greater efforts. In the latter part of the second century, a group of Christians presented themselves to C. Arrius Antoninus, a provincial governor in Asia Minor, demanding that he punish them for their beliefs. After a few such executions, Antoninus drove them off, advising them to throw themselves over cliffs or hang themselves if they wished.[12] In fact, the movement was divided within itself on the value of martyrdom. The recently discovered *Gospel According to Judas* criticizes Christian authorities who glorified martyrdom. But for all its excesses, the fearlessness of Christians like Perpetua may have earned the movement a measure of respect. Even if the reasons Christians gave for dying were incomprehensible, their courage in the face of death was not: as the second-century physician Galen observed, "Their contempt of death is evident to us every day."[13]

As for the role of ethics and philosophy in early Christianity, the record is mixed. Jesus' ethical teachings were grounded in the Hebrew scriptures that informed his vision of the Kingdom of God. Had a letter from Paul fallen into the hands of a Roman reader, it might have looked vaguely like a piece of philosophical writing, mostly because it urged its readers to adopt certain patterns of behavior. An informed reader might have sensed a resemblance to the teaching of moralists such as Musonius

Rufus or Epictetus. But inside the movement, Christians would have mostly rejected the label of "philosophy," as early Christians oriented themselves toward the imminent apocalypse rather than to philosophical questions. Ethical teachings in earliest Christianity provided guidance to communities waiting for the coming judgment and accordingly had a provisional character.

Even so, writings that presume some knowledge of and respect for philosophical discourse can be found within the pages of early Christian literature. The writer of John's Gospel is thinking in a philosophical vein when he describes Jesus as the *logos*, or expressed rationality of God (John 1:1). In this regard, he shares an affinity with Philo, the Alexandrian Jewish philosopher who spoke of God's *logos* as a "second god" (*Quaestiones in Genesim* 2.62). The writer of Acts hopes to impress his readers by having Peter and John mimic Socrates' bold speech before a tyrant (Acts 4:19–20) and by ascribing a philosophically inspired homily to Paul (Acts 17:22–31). While Justin Martyr, writing in the mid-second century, is often credited as the first Christian to integrate Greco-Roman philosophy and Christian belief, credit for that development should probably go to Basilides, an older contemporary of Justin's who was active in Alexandria.[14]

Paul's methods of working might also have led some observers to compare him to philosophers known as Cynics, itinerant teachers who questioned social conventions, and it may even be that some of his ascetical advice shares points with Cynic doctrine.[15] Galen afforded the Christians a measure of respect for their moral character: some of them, "in self-discipline and self-control in matters of food and drink, and in their keen pursuit of justice, have attained a pitch not inferior to that of genuine philosophers."[16] However, when it came to philosophical argument, "members of the schools of Moses and Christ" were impervious to reason, being dogmatically attached to the doctrines of their founders – no better than physicians, in Galen's estimation.[17] Tertullian would have celebrated Galen's low opinion of Christian skill in philosophy, given his memorable formulation: "What has Athens to do with Jerusalem? What concord is there between the Academy and the Church?" (*De praescriptione haereticorum* 7).

5. RESEARCH

The subsequent history and cultural influence of Christianity tends to distort our understanding of its humble origins. Looking back to the roots of the movement, it has often proven difficult for scholars, especially those who are insiders to the Christian tradition, to avoid thinking of its development as inevitable, and to understand early historical data as trending toward what Christianity eventually became, rather like commenting after the fact on a race in which the winner is already known. Students of early Christianity must beware, therefore, of simply assuming that the terminology, agendas, and emphases of modern scholars give an accurate picture of what the field of play looked like to the first Christians.

There has also been a significant shift in the demographics of scholarship on early Christianity. When the vast majority of scholars in the field were found in divinity schools and seminaries, theological and doctrinal agendas took precedence. As an increasing number of scholars of early Christianity are found in religious studies departments in colleges and universities, the range of questions asked and the methodologies employed have broadened considerably to include sociology, anthropology, and economics. With this broadening has come increasing skepticism about certain value-laden categories, for example, "heresy" and "orthodoxy." Other categories within the study of early Christianity that have been deeply intertwined with this restrictive typology, for example "Gnosticism," are undergoing a healthy revision.[18] The textual focus of scholarship in the field has also given way to an increased interest in archaeology and material culture, which opens a window on the large mass of Christians who were not represented in or addressed by the writings of the literate classes.

FURTHER READING

For biblical literature and related topics, consult *The Anchor Bible Dictionary* 1992. Up-to-date essays on topics in early Christianity by prominent scholars may be found in Mitchell and Young 2004. Sanders 1996 treats the historical Jesus; Meeks 1983 was groundbreaking for its use of sociological and anthropological theory applied to Paul's letters. Reed 2003 raises important issues for the relation between texts and archaeology.

For new translations of non-canonical Christian literature of the late first and early second centuries, see Ehrman 2003. On the canonization of New Testament literature see Gamble 1985. An authoritative history of Christianity is Frend 1986; a shorter work, focusing on doctrinal developments, is Chadwick 1993. For collections of Gnostic literature consult Layton 1995 and Robinson 2004; for a highly readable account of gnostic currents in early Christianity see Pagels 1989; for reassessment of the term "Gnosticism" see Brakke 2011 and King 2005. For Christianity in the Late Antique period see Bowersock et al. 1999; also see any book or essay by Peter Brown, in particular, his life of Augustine (Brown 2000) and, on the important topic of asceticism in early Christianity, Brown 2008.

On Christian architecture see White 1990 and MacMullen 2009; on art see Finney 1997 and Jensen 2000; and on Christian material remains in the pre-Nicene period see Snyder 2003.

CHRONOLOGY

Note: All dates are CE.

c. 30	Death of Jesus
c. 37	Paul joins the Jesus Movement
50–65	Genuine Pauline letters written
66–70	First Jewish Revolt; destruction of Jewish Temple; death of Paul in Rome
70–75	First Gospel (Mark) written
85–100	Gospels of Matthew, Luke, and John written
112	Pliny encounters Christians in Bithynia
132–5	Bar Kochba Revolt
130–65	Marcion, Valentinus, and Justin active in Rome
163–7	Martyrdom of Justin
180–95	Irenaeus writes *Adversus haereses*
203	Martyrdom of Perpetua and her companions
249	Decian Persecution
313	Edict of Milan: official toleration of Christianity
325	Council of Nicaea

GLOSSARY

Gnostics: Philosophically inclined Christians who subscribed to an elaborate myth of origins inspired by Plato's *Timaeus*, and who practiced distinctive rituals beyond baptism and Eucharist.
Jesus Movement: The group of early followers of Jesus, who were still considered Jews, not yet members of a new religion, Christianity.

Notes

1   Eisenbaum 2010.
2   Crossan and Reed 2005.

3 Josephus, *Jewish Antiquities* 20.200; Hegesippus, as quoted by Eusebius, *Historia Ecclesiastica* 2.23.
4 Meeks 1983:164–92.
5 Bynum 1995.
6 MacMullen 1984.
7 On this "baptismal reunification formula" see Meeks 1974.
8 MacMullen 2009:1–10.
9 Chadwick 1993:259.
10 Davis 2001.
11 King 2003.
12 Tertullian, *ad Scapulam* 5, quoted by Bowersock 1995:1.
13 Walzer 1949:15.
14 Layton 1989.
15 Downing 1998.
16 Walzer 1949:15.
17 Ibid., 14.
18 King 2005.

Works Cited

The Anchor Bible Dictionary. 1992. David Noel Freedman, ed. New York.

Bowersock, G. 1995. *Martyrdom and Rome.* Cambridge.

Bowersock, G., P. Brown, and O. Grabar, eds. 1999. *Late Antiquity: A Guide to the Postclassical World.* Cambridge, MA.

Brakke, David. 2011. *The Gnostics: Myth, Ritual, and Diversity in Early Christianity.* Cambridge, MA.

Brown, Peter. 2000. *Augustine of Hippo: a Biography.* 2nd rev. ed. Berkeley.

———. 2008. *The Body and Society: Men, Women and Sexual Renunciation in Early Christianity.* 2nd ed. New York.

Bynum, C. W. 1995. *The Resurrection of the Body in Western Christianity, 200–1336.* New York.

Chadwick, Henry. 1993. *The Early Church.* London.

Crossan, John Dominic and Jonathan Reed. 2005. *In Search of Paul.* San Francisco.

Davis, Stephen. 2001. *The Cult of St. Thecla: A Tradition of Women's Piety in Late Antiquity.* Oxford.

Downing, Gerald. 1998. *Cynics, Paul, and the Pauline Churches.* London.

Ehrman, Bart. 2003. *The Apostolic Fathers.* 2 volumes. Cambridge, MA.

Eisenbaum, Pamela. 2010. *Paul Was Not a Christian: The Original Message of a Misunderstood Apostle.* San Francisco.

Finney, Paul Corby. 1997. *The Invisible God: The Earliest Christians on Art.* Oxford.

Frend, W. H. C. 1986. *The Rise of Christianity.* Minneapolis.

Gamble, Harry. 1985. *The New Testament Canon: Its Making and Meaning.* Philadelphia.

Jensen, Robin M. 2000. *Understanding Early Christian Art.* London.

King, Karen. 2003. *The Gospel of Mary of Magdala.* Salem, OR.

———. 2005. *What is Gnosticism?* Cambridge, MA.

Layton, Bentley. 1989. "The Significance of Basilides in Ancient Christian Thought." *Representations* 28: 135–51.

———. 1995. *The Gnostic Scriptures*. Garden City, NY.

MacMullen, Ramsay. 1984. *Christianizing the Roman Empire*. New Haven, CT.

———. 2009. *The Second Church. Popular Christianity A.D. 200–400*. Atlanta.

Meeks, Wayne. 1974. "The Image of the Androgyne: Some Uses of a Symbol in Earliest Christianity." *History of Religions* 13: 165–208.

———. 1983. *The First Urban Christians: The Social World of the Apostle*. New Haven, CT.

Mitchell, M. and F. Young, eds. 2004. *The Cambridge History of Christianity: Origins to Constantine*. Cambridge.

Pagels, Elaine. 1989. *The Gnostic Gospels*. New York.

Reed, Jonathan. 2003. *Archaeology and the Galilean Jesus*. Harrisburg, PA.

Robinson, James. 2004. *The Nag Hammadi Library in English*. 2nd rev. ed. San Francisco.

Sanders, E.P. 1996. *The Historical Figure of Jesus*. London.

Snyder, Graydon. 2003. *Ante Pacem: Archaeological Evidence of Church Life Before Constantine*. 2nd rev. ed. Macon, GA.

Walzer, R. 1949. *Galen on Jews and Christians*. London.

White, Michael. 1990. *Building God's House in the Roman World: Architectural Adaptation among Pagans, Jews, and Christians*. Baltimore and London.

Part II

10 Violence

BRUCE LINCOLN

I

In the pages that follow, I will attempt three approaches to the topic of religious violence in the ancient Mediterranean. First, I consider the nature of violence and its relation to domination. Second, I sketch four relatively common ways that acts, campaigns, and systems of violence were invested with specifically religious significance. Sometimes this attempt to sacralize the bloody acts was carried out by the authors of violence and their apologists and sometimes by its victims and those loyal to them, but in either case, this was usually done within the context of empire. Third, I provide a somewhat more thorough (but still too brief) analysis of one phenomenon that holds particular theoretic interest and historic importance.

Initially, then, let me take my lead from three classic texts: Simone Weil's anguished meditation on the *Iliad* as "*le poème de la force*," which was written in 1940, just after the Nazi occupation of France;[1] Alexandre Kojève's highly politicized lectures on Hegel's master-slave dialectic, delivered in 1933–1939, as the Third Republic descended into terminal crisis and the Second World War became inevitable;[2] and Orlando Patterson's treatment of slavery as a form of social death.[3] Consistent with the lines of argument developed in these works, I would suggest we can best theorize violence as the deployment of physical force in a manner that tends to convert subjects – individual or collective, but in either case fully human actors – into depersonalized objects. Murder, for instance, transforms a previously living subject into a corpse, that is, an inanimate *thing*. Equally instructive examples include rape, where force is used to make some other person an instrument of the aggressor's sexual pleasure; enslavement, where it reduces human subjects to their labor power, stripped of rights and dignity; and conquest and punitive discipline, where overlords of whatever sort (rulers, jailers, bosses, etc.) attempt to render their charges submissive and compliant.

Comparison between murder and surgery may also be instructive, insofar as it shows that violence is not simply a type of action – for example, the rending of another person's flesh – but more importantly, a type of effect and a type of intention. Thus, where the killer transforms what was once a fully human subject into a dead object, the surgeon's actions (ideally) restore a patient (i.e., one whose physical personhood is compromised in some fashion) to health. Notwithstanding bloody, greedy, and arrogant aspects of their practice, surgeons are expected to respect their patients' essential humanity, which they endeavor to preserve and repair. That killers and surgeons both achieve their results (and reap their profits) in similar bloody fashion is a coincidence that obscures their much more important difference: one practices violence, destroying the subjectivity of others, while the other attempts to repair it.

At the analytic core of violence, then, are not just rough acts, but the way such acts mediate relations between an actor (individual or collective) whose power, status, pride, sense of well-being, and control over situations and over others are all enhanced in the process and one for whom these same qualities are diminished, deformed, or extinguished. Such negative effects exist on a cline of increasing intensity, as does violence itself, and one should observe that only the most extreme type of violence – that is, lethal force – physically accomplishes that toward which all other forms gesture, but from which they ultimately retreat: the irreversible transformation of a living subject into an inert object.

Although this formulation is heuristically useful, it ignores some crucial points. Most important of these is the need to distinguish between the immediate victims of lethal violence – those whom it converts into corpses – and others for whose eyes this spectacle may be intended, with the expectation that they will be intimidated by it and thereafter submit more readily to those who have shown themselves willing and able to kill. The immediate victims are fully objectified by lethal violence; the others – who may be designated mediated victims, victims at a second remove, or spectator-victims – are only partially so. One can also theorize this distinction in other ways, contrasting the physical and discursive effects of lethal violence, for example, or its use-value and its sign-value.

Similar points can also be made concerning non-lethal violence and the credible threat of force, both of which gesture toward the same end as lethal force but stop short of the ultimate act of converting live people into dead things. What is more, they hesitate by design. For whatever damage these lesser forms of violence may inflict (both physical and psychic), they are concerned to leave their victims alive and with some measure of personhood, agency, and interiority intact. This is because victors are typically concerned that the vanquished retain vital energy in the form of labor-power, even when they have been forced to surrender the bulk of their autonomy, for it is at this point that they become useful. All victims thus do not become corpses; in many cases, the intent is to make them into something rather like zombies, that is, less than human creatures, situated somewhere between life and death, stripped of most but not *all* subjectivity, and retaining their power to labor.

The situation of those who have survived violence is also complex and often contradictory. Thus, to the extent that survivors remain intimidated by the (implicit, explicit, or imagined) threat that violence against them may be renewed, they are likely to participate in their own partial and superficial objectification by *performing* a radically diminished subjectivity. Not zombies, but cautious (and skilled) actors who restrict themselves to a zombified public existence, suppressing most signs of autonomous will or desire, for fear that these signs of life might be read as a threat, provocation, or excuse for their enemies to turn violent again.

Having provisionally defined violence as the use of force to objectify the other, we are thus led to theorize domination in corollary terms as the cultivation of fear through the threat of violence, thereby producing – and perpetuating – a docile, compliant, and semi-objectified state among the community of the fearful. One can describe that community as having been intimidated: not just bullied, but literally *made timid*. Alternatively, one may speak of them as "cowed," a metaphor that signals the loss (or surrender) of certain human qualities and properties – autonomy, spontaneity, physical confidence, social pride, virility, aggressivity, legal rights and safeguards, territory, patrimony, the products of one's labor, and so on – as the result of fear and a cultivated belief that resistance is futile.

Domination also produces contradictory attitudes in the dominated as regards their own inclination and capacity for violence. Surely fear and memories of past suffering work together to inhibit the defeated from taking arms against their oppressor. But the same memories also stimulate lasting resentment, fantasies of revenge, and hopes for liberation, all of which can inspire bloody acts, should such people overcome their fear.

In its incipient moments, insurrectionary violence holds the promise of reversing the subject–object relations in the existing system of domination, with liberatory intention and effects. It is a sad fact of history, however, that all too often those who have waged such campaigns

subsequently establish structures of domination that are formally identical to those they overthrew, changing only the identity of who holds
the whip and who lives in fear. This is not to say that such victories are
sterile, ironic, or inconsequential, but violence that actually ends domination, instead of just inverting it, is regrettably rare.

II

The preceding discussion helps us understand why violence is regularly
condemned on aesthetic and ethical grounds as something both ugly and
inhumane. One can also imagine good religious reasons for its condemnation, since it is possible to describe the objectifying effects of violence
(in a vocabulary that differs only slightly from that we have adopted)
as something akin to the sacrilegious degradation of human subjects,
whereby beings who are properly recognized as compounds of matter
and spirit are reduced to matter alone.

Commentators of many sorts (e.g., politicians, clergy, journalists)
often voice the opinion that religion stands categorically opposed to violence and necessarily condemns it, but several problems undermine this
bromide. First, the straightforward empirical question – How often do
religions actually condemn violence, and how often do they adopt other
stances? – proves surprisingly difficult to answer, since no representative body of data has been assembled or analyzed, and it is hard to imagine just how this might be done. (Ought one distinguish, for instance,
between statements of general principle ["*Thou shalt not kill*": Genesis
20:13] and casuistic injunctions or judgments ["*And the Lord said to
him, 'I will be with you, and you shall smite the Midianites'*": Judges
6:16]? Statements of the latter sort seem to be more numerous in most
religious traditions, while the former are decidedly more weighty and
emphatic.)

Beyond the strictly empirical issues, one also has to ask what is
meant by the term "religion." The problem is particularly acute in any
sentence where this abstract noun appears to govern a transitive verb,
since properly speaking it is only human subjects who possess agency.
Thus, to pursue the example, in order to make sense of the claim that
"religion" "opposes" or "condemns" something, one must replace the
vague and global abstraction with specific animate actors, for example,
the official representatives of religious institutions, the authors of canonical texts, or persons who represent and experience their views not as
idiosyncratic opinions but as founded on sacred truths and transcendent
principles to which they have either direct or mediated access. Once this

is done, counterexamples are all too readily available, for – as everyone knows – religious authorities, texts, and communities have frequently reacted to incidents, campaigns, and systems of violence not just with condemnation, but also by ignoring, condoning, mitigating, and even encouraging and rewarding them, according to circumstances.

Of course, it is possible to dismiss such episodes as embarrassing aberrations: moments when flawed people misinterpreted what "true religion" *really* had to say. As a historian and a realist, I am inclined to dismiss such a view as naïve, for history contains only flawed human actors and no true religion. But those considerably more pious than I also reject attempts to constitute the religious as categorically opposed to the violent, as witness, for example, St. Augustine's theory of Just War,[4] or Kierkegaard's characterization of the most profound faith (typified by Abraham's willingness to sacrifice Isaac) as requiring a *"religious suspension of the ethical."*[5]

In the face of these difficulties, let me advance three propositions that, I hope, all but the most doctrinaire can accept. First, the relation between "religion" and violence takes many forms, being contingent and variable, rather than categorical, fixed, and absolute. Second, it is the norm for "religion" to condemn acts of violence, so much so that this is often taken for granted and need not be rendered explicit. Third, there are countless cases in which interested actors seek – and find – reasons for investing specific violent episodes with religious value, adopting attitudes that can range from sorrowful, world-weary acceptance to eager incitement and celebration.

The question thus arises: under what kinds of circumstances might acts of violence, which by definition dehumanize and objectify their victims, be positively valorized *on religious grounds*? I can think of five general patterns that recur with some frequency in late antiquity, but the list is by no means exhaustive.[6] Let me treat four of them briefly, holding the fifth for somewhat fuller discussion when other pieces of the argument are in place.

1. Conquest as divinely sanctioned. Here, a group that enjoys certain material and sociopolitical advantages (superior numbers, wealth, weaponry, organization, etc.) sheds whatever moral inhibitions previously kept it from using force against neighbors and rivals by defining itself as more righteous, pure, or divinely favored than those who, in that moment, begin to become its prey. Insofar as incipient aggressors persuade themselves that their victims are morally and spiritually defective, the use of violence against them becomes more acceptable since it only dehumanizes that which was already somewhat less than fully human. Such a perspective also permits victors to narrate their campaigns of conquest as a form of religious generosity and noblesse-oblige, through which they bear priceless gifts – non-material goods like law, order, morality, enlightenment, and even salvation – to the conquered: gifts that promise to raise the benighted closer to the conqueror's higher, more blessed level. (Material goods flow in the opposite direction, of course, bringing wealth, glory, and compensation that can be construed as confirmation of divine favor.) Recently, I have studied the way ideas of this sort animated the Achaemenian kings of Persia, who represented themselves as God's chosen instruments to establish paradisal perfection throughout the world,[7] but similar themes also attend the Hellenizing mission of Alexander's Macedonian Empire and its successor states,[8] Roman imperialism as theorized in pagan terms under Augustus,[9] in Christian terms under Constantine,[10] and Zoroastrian imperialism in Sassanian Iran.[11]

2. Defeat as humiliation. If conquerors can justify aggression by demeaning their enemies and arguing, in effect, *"They deserved what they got and in the long run they were better for it,"* the same logic permits victims to make sense of the violence they suffer by a simple substitution of *"We"* for *"They."* Such a construction avoids dwelling on the superiority of the enemy's armies and steadfastly refuses to entertain the superiority of their gods. Instead, it locates responsibility for historic trauma in one's own cultic and moral failings or, more often perhaps, on the failings of one's wayward countrymen, whom earlier polemics and cleavages had identified as somehow inadequate in their observances, devotion, loyalty, or commitment.[12]

In a theodicy of great daring and originality, these offenses are construed as having prompted chastisement by one's own god, who is thus permitted to retain all his power and benevolence as the sole causal agent of importance. From this perspective, conquest and domination are represented, and also experienced, as salutary humiliations: harsh reminders that prompt a wayward people to restore their proper relation to a god from whom they had become estranged. Such an analysis posits five distinct stages to a process simultaneously historic and religious: a) an initial ideal; b) a state of gradual fall, during which the people in question lose their proper piety and humanity, while becoming rich, lazy, deluded, and decadent; c) the disillusioning experience of defeat and foreign domination, which forces them to realize their failings; d) a process of repentance, through which they gradually recover their moral and religious bearing; and e) escape from bondage, restoration of political independence, moral righteousness, and proper relation to god: a step normally set in the future. The scenario I have sketched most closely follows the interpretation that Israel's exilic prophets gave to military defeat by Assyria and Babylon,[13] but similar (if less elaborate) strains of self-chastising discourse are attested in Babylonian responses to defeat by Persians,[14] Persian responses to defeat by Greeks,[15] and certain Roman responses to sufferings of the civil wars.[16]

3. Millennarian revolt. When defeat is construed as divine humiliation, what happens when the cathartic process of repentance has been completed? Or, to put the problem in its most acute form, when a conquered people feels it has recovered its proper moral and religious status, its full measure of humanity, subjectivity, and agency, also its ideal relation with the divine, but still remains oppressed and exploited, what then is to be done? Foreign conquerors are not easily persuaded to depart, nor is it easy to drive them out. Straightforward calculations of a military and political sort would lead one to judge most attempts at insurrection against more powerful overlords ill advised, even suicidal. And yet, such insurrections do occur, and sometimes even succeed, fueled by a conviction that supernatural assistance is available, either by virtue of the completion of some cosmic cycle (typically, a period of 1,000 years) or through the miraculous appearance of a charismatic hero (in both the theological and the sociological sense of the term). Such salvific figures take many forms: angelic beings, sons of a god, inspired prophets or their descendants, revivified mythic heroes, and pretenders in royal lines dethroned by imperial conquest. In all cases, however, messianic figures of this sort embody the conviction that there are forms of power superior to those of brute force, through which the Evil Empire can – and will – be defeated. Whether such heroes reside in popular fantasy alone or if they come to be more actively instantiated in the human actors who claim these roles for themselves, they can inspire a dominated people to rise up in the belief that divine favor and superior moral/religious status (as embodied in such figures) will ensure victory over oppressors and a salvation simultaneously this- and other-worldly. Further, rebels' portrayal of their overlords as more corrupt, more debased, more impious – indeed, less fully human – than themselves helps justify violence against them. Such situations are well attested in Israel under the Seleucids,[17] then again under Roman rule,[18] and in Iran after the defeat of the Achaemenians,[19] and one can also perceive similar dynamics in the rebellions of Spartacus, Vercingetorix, Civilis, and others.[20]

The three types we have considered strike me as particularly characteristic of late antiquity, where most collective violence – and most attempts to provide religious valorization for violence – occurs in the context of empire. Thus, a divinely sanctioned conquest is the mode

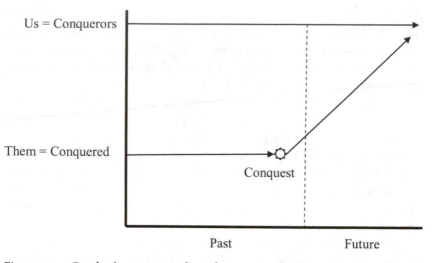

Figure 10.1. Graph of conquest as divinely sanctioned. The aggressor justifies his violence, first by believing it falls on victims of deficient religious and human status, and second by suggesting that the long-term result will be the elevation of the other.

that best serves those who would pursue imperial projects, imbuing them with the requisite moral confidence. Conversely, defeat as humiliation is the theme best suited to provide solace for the empire's victims, as they struggle to endure. Finally, millennarian revolt is the type that emerges when endurance gives way to anti-imperial activism and movements of national liberation. These three types can be conveniently (if a bit roughly) schematized in the form of graphs, where the vertical or Y-axis represents the religious and human status attributed to the people concerned, while the horizontal or X-axis represents time and historic process (Figs. 10.1–10.3). The dotted lines represent the present moment (which divides the past and the future), while the sun-shaped symbols represent dramatic episodes of violence.

III

In addition to these three types, religious valorization was also available for certain kinds of violence less directly connected to sociopolitical considerations. I would note one such form here, before moving to the last and most complex type of all.

4. Mortification of the flesh. Second only to lethal violence, ascetic rigors offer the clearest example of violent practices that reduce a human subject to an inert object. The chief difference, however, is that

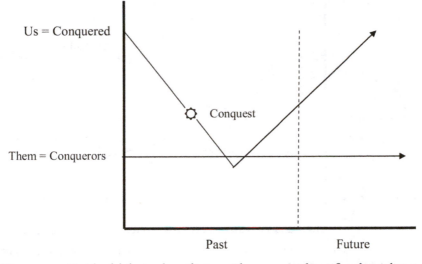

Figure 10.2. Graph of defeat as humiliation. The conquered justifies the violence he has suffered by interpreting it as the result of his own prior failings. The experience of captivity and domination then spurs repentance and recovery of proper religious and human status.

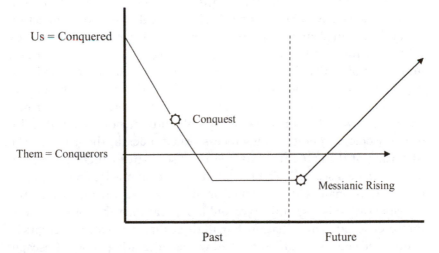

Figure 10.3. Graph of millennarian revolt. The conquered experiences himself as trapped in a demeaning domination. To recover proper human and religious status requires not only violent action, but also divine assistance and sanction, which take the form of a salvific hero.

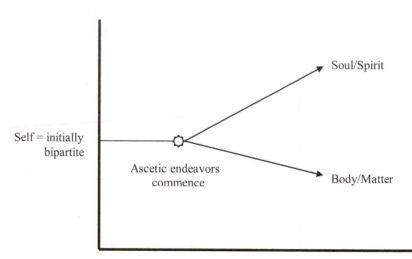

Figure 10.4. Graph of mortification of the flesh. Understanding the person to be a compound of base matter and divine spirit, the agentive will, which associates itself with spirit, uses violence to separate itself from the body, construing this as an act of liberation.

two actors are involved in lethal violence, one of whom is left standing when the deed is done. In mortification, by contrast, the same person performs violence on him- (or her-) self, although the actor in question is hardly a unified subject. Rather, ascetics work across a division they take to be internal to themselves, construing subjectivity proper as a dimension of spiritual being while regarding the body as degraded (and degrading) matter. Consistent with this view, that part of the person associated with will and spirit uses physical force against his (or her) flesh, while withdrawing as far as possible into the non-material realm of the sacred. Implicitly, this process leads to death, theorized as the liberation of the spirit from its bodily prison, after which the corpse-object can be discarded. The liberation in question is less political and this-worldly than is that pursued in millennarian revolt, just as the self-abnegation is less collective and historical than that of those who interpret defeat as humiliation, but all three types represent attempts to endure the pains of a difficult world while cultivating hopes of escape. The process of mortification can be graphed, as in Fig. 10.4. Examples include not only Christian ascetics,[21] but Manichaeans,[22] Gnostics,[23] the Phrygian Galli,[24] certain strains of Rabbinic Judaism,[25] and also the Stoics, who pursued the less radical goal of disciplining, rather than mortifying, the body.[26]

IV

In the preceding discussion, we have considered four styles of providing religious valorization for violent acts. Of these, two were used by aggressors to justify what they did to their enemies (conquest as divinely sanctioned and millennarian revolt); one by victims, to justify what was done to them (defeat as humiliation); and one by people who were simultaneously aggressors and victims, to justify the violence one part of a divided self practiced against the other (mortification of the flesh). There is, however, one last type that has certain continuities with all the others, while differing sharply from them. This is martyrdom, a phenomenon that occurs when groups who suffer imperial violence respond, not with self-blame or acts of insurrectionary violence, but by embracing the violence done to them in a way that discredits and delegitimates their adversaries while elevating their own moral, religious, and ontological status above that of all other humans.

Make no mistake: These are jujitsu tactics of paramount skill, whereby the intended victim captures his enemy's violence and then redirects it to fall back on the original aggressor with potentially devastating effect. I will not attempt to summarize or amplify what authors as varied and distinguished as Elizabeth A. Castelli, Daniel Boyarin, Glenn Bowersock, and G. E. M. de Ste. Croix have written concerning the history of martyrdom, or the way Jewish, Roman, and Christian traditions influenced each other.[27] Rather, let me limit myself to some more general observations consistent with the broader lines of analysis explored in this essay.

First, however, one must say a few things about imperial religious policies and episodes of persecution. Although there are some noteworthy partial exceptions (Sassanian Iran and Christian Rome, chief among them), few empires aspire to achieve religious unity or to convert the peoples they conquer. These tasks are simply too daunting and the benefits are normally considered too slim to justify the effort. Rather, rulers usually understand that in an imperial context, stability is secured by political and military control; economic integration; maintenance of extractive taxation at tolerable levels; impressive public works; and reasonable tolerance of the multiple languages, cultures, and religions that flourish in the provinces. Accordingly, the goal toward which most empires labor is not assimilation, homogeneity, or orthodoxy (i.e., the production of religious uniformity in one fashion or another), but encompassment. That is to say, conquered peoples are permitted to keep their own gods, cults, temples, and the like, so long as they make certain requisite gestures of deference to those of the imperial power. From the ruler's perspective, such gestures acknowledge his hierarchic supremacy and that of his gods, but it may look and feel different to others. In practice, all sorts of compromises get struck (via syncretism, deliberate ambiguity, and the like) that preserve the dignity of all who cooperate in the bargain, as becomes clear from the many creative ways local elites managed to implement emperor worship and turn it to their advantage.[28]

Only when subordinate populations bluntly refused such intentionally modest demands did the authorities become exercised. Normally, they would settle for select symbolic concessions from elite strata of provincial populations (even if these were disingenuous, bribed, or coerced). And normally that is what they got. Occasionally, however, certain groups were so exclusive as regards the object and nature of their devotion that they adamantly refused to compromise, viewing such accommodation as anathema and apostasy.

In a stable imperial order, credible threats are normally enough to produce compliance, but in the face of sustained defiance, rulers may (feel forced to) employ violence itself. When they do so in public, however – even more so, when they do this in spectacular ways – one should distinguish the immediate use-value of the violence employed (i.e., physical elimination of intransigents) and its much more diffuse, but much more important sign-value (i.e., an object lesson designed to discourage others of like persuasion).[29]

All signs being reversible, however, Christian martyrs managed to turn the drama in the arena upside down.[30] Where the Romans meant to cast them as incorrigible fanatics who had brought just punishment on their own heads, martyrs constituted themselves as the most devoted servants of the one true God: as such, they were figures deserving veneration and emulation. The extraordinary courage and calm they displayed *in extremis* was meant – and understood – to testify on behalf of their faith and its saving power (such is the literal meaning of Greek *martus* = "*one who bears witness*"). More broadly, they disarticulated might and right, and asked their immediate audience (also that which would later hear of their deeds at second hand) to judge who really was the victor in these encounters between an impious, violent state and its righteous, unflinching victims.

The practice of martyrdom thus redefined what the imperial state understood as exemplary punishment, transforming this into a contest between adversaries of radically different natures (might vs. right), the outcome of which hung in the balance. Martyrological discourse went further still, crafting narratives in which the victory won by the martyrs

Table 10.1. Martyrological inversion of imperial narratives. A spectacle in which the state understands itself to be using just punishment on those who defy its rightful authority and enlightened policies is transformed into a narrative that shows worldly power to be inferior in every way to power of a spiritual nature.

	Subjects of Violent Acts	*Objects of Violent Acts*	*Victor*
Imperial spectacle of exemplary punishment	Hero of story: Legitimate rulers + Might + Right	Villain of story: Intransigent fanatics – Might – Right	State Authorities
Practice of martyrdom	Villain of story: Tyrants + Might – Right	Hero of story: The faithful – Might + Right	Open to interpretation of spectators
Discourse of martyrology	Villain of story: Tyrants and Devils – True Might (≠Physical Force) – Right	Hero of story: Sainted martyrs + True Might (= Spiritual Force) + Right	Martyrs, their church, and their god

was unmistakable and unambiguous.[31] In these stories, imperial violence did not reduce living persons to inert objects, but had quite the opposite effect. As in the case of mortification, a martyr's death served to liberate an immortal spirit from its base matter, winning sainthood and heavenly reward for the soul thus freed while creating a name and reputation that would endure forever and provide inspiration to others. Such stories not only cast agents of the empire as villains, sometimes they went so far as to treat them as demonically inspired. In this and other ways, they radically questioned the nature of power, arguing that the physical might of the state, being exclusively material in nature, was inferior to the spiritual power of the martyrs (and the discursive power of those who told their story). Lacking sacred sanction, the "power" in which rulers naively put their trust is a lesser form of power, and a self-deluded one at that, marked by arrogance and brutality. It is not the martyr whose humanity is diminished by the encounter in the arena, but the emperor, whose callous use of violence reveals him to be no better than the lion. The extraordinary inversions accomplished by the practice of martyrdom and the discourse of martyrology are not easily graphed, but they may be summarized, as in Table 10.1.

V

As a general principle, scholarly discourse ought not uncritically reproduce the self-representations and self-perceptions of those it purports
to study. In the case of martyrs and martyrology, it is easy enough to
introduce other explanatory frameworks – for example, masochism, self-
righteousness, *ressentiment*, passive aggression – and to note the unfor-
tunate tendency of those who have suffered violence, persecution, and
domination to turn violent, dominating, and vengeful, when given the
opportunity.[32]

Even granting the validity of these revisionist critiques, as one
must, it is hard not to harbor some admiration for the martyrs, and this
for two reasons. First is the way martyrdom responds to the objectifying effects of violence. For when rulers use force to make inert things
of those who dare resist, and stage this as a spectacle of intimidating
power, martyrs fight with the only weapons at their disposal. These
consist chiefly of language and a dignified bodily comportment: subjective qualities, through which they assert their ineradicable humanity,
even *in extremis*.

Second, I am struck by the way martyrdom responds to intimida-
tion. For if violence is the use of force so as to objectify the other, and
domination is the cultivation of fear (through the threat of violence) so
as to keep that other in a docile, compliant, and semi-objectified state,
then the reversal of domination begins with the victory of fearlessness
over fear. Or, to put it differently, it begins with the discovery of an
alternative form of power with which to challenge those whose power
is based on violence and threats. This alternative form of power can be
theorized – and experienced – as something spiritual, moral, religious,
psychological, discursive, rhetorical, or semiotic in nature, and it may
be all the above. Regardless of how one conceives it, martyrs (and the
martyrologists who tell their tales) provide one of the clearest and most
extreme examples of just how potent this power can be.

FURTHER READING

The literature treating religious violence in antiquity is large and varied,
especially if one considers works that deal with one type, style, or episode only. Noteworthy for their breadth are MacMullen 1966, Vernant
1969, Sordi 1990, Cantarella 1991, Gaddis 2005, and Sizgorich 2009.
Among the more useful and/or challenging specialized studies, one
might note Burkert 1983, Horsley 1988, Futrell 1997, Horowitz 2006,

and Lincoln 2007. The question of martyrdom has produced a particularly rich literature, including Boyarin 1999, Castelli 2004, Ste. Croix 2006, and Middleton 2006.

Notes

1 Holoka 2003.
2 Kojève 1969.
3 Patterson 1982.
4 The literature on this topic grows whenever a state that defines itself as Christian finds itself making war. For example, see Mattox 2006.
5 Kierkegaard 1983.
6 Concerning an even more extreme pattern, which involves defining one's enemies as demonic beings whose bodies must be destroyed in order to purify the world, see Frankfurter 2006 and Davis 1975.
7 Lincoln 2007 and Lincoln 2009.
8 See, *inter alia*, Bilde et al. 1990, Billows 1995, Hazzard 2000, Worthington 2004, and Pfeiffer 2008.
9 Adler 2003, Lucrezi 1996:1–14, and Zanker 1988. Here, as in other notes of this sort, I have pointed to only a few items in an enormous bibliography.
10 Girardet 2006, Odahl 2004, and Drake 2000.
11 Tafazzoli 2000, Shaked 1994, and Mosiq-Walburg 1982.
12 I have treated this pattern in a very different historical context. See Lincoln 2005:33–50.
13 Lipschitz 2005, Kiefer 2005, Albertz 2004, Seitz 1989, and Smith 1989.
14 This is evident in texts that depict Babylon's last king, Nabonidus, as having so offended the god Marduk that he shifted his favor to the Persians, which are most easily available in Pritchard 1969:305–16. For discussion see Kuhrt 1990:119–55, Beaulieu 1989, and Soden 1983: 61–68.
15 The classic work is Eddy 1961. More recently, see Boyce and Grenet 1991.
16 Note, for instance, the description of omens, divine displeasure, and human guilt in the context of civil war that is found in Dio Cass. 47.40. Jal 1963, 1962a:170–200, 1962b:395–414.
17 Bickerman 1947, Bickerman 1979, Harrington 1988, and Firpo 1999.
18 Collins 1998, Horsley 1988, Schäfer 1981, and Brandon 1967.
19 Hultgård 1988, Boyce 1984:57–75, and Hinnells 1973.
20 Spartacus was said to bear signs of divine election according to Plutarch (*Vit. Crass.* 8–11), the importance of which was noted by Grottanelli 1985:18–19; Tacitus's description of Civilis as one-eyed (*Hist.* 4.13) suggests that his countrymen associated him with the god Woðanaz, and several authors report that he was the beneficiary of prophecies made by a sibylline figure (Tac. *Hist.* 4.61 and 65, *Germ.* 8, and Stat., *Silv.* 1.4.90). Caesar scrupulously avoids reporting anything that would indicate the charismatic basis of Vercingetorix's claims, but the last element in the rebel's name (Gallic -*rix* = Latin *rex*) makes clear that he was regarded as the rightful heir to royal status among the Arverni, and more broadly among the Gauls. See further Martin 2000, Goudineau 2001, Markale 1995, or Jullian 1903.

21 Clark 1999, Petersen-Szemeredy 1993, Brown 1988, and Gager 1982.
22 BeDuhn 2000.
23 Thomassen 2006, Turner 2001, and Lancellotti 2000.
24 Grottanelli 1985:22–24, Vermaseren 1977, Näsström 1989, and Södergård 1993.
25 Diamond 2004.
26 Bénatouli 2006, Sellars 2006, Reydams-Schils 2005, Sherman 2005, and Brennan 2005.
27 The topic has received a great deal of attention in recent years. *Inter alia*, see Ste. Croix 2006, Middleton 2006, Castelli 2004, Cormack 2001, Boyarin 1999, Shaw 1996, Bowersock 1995, Barton 1994, Potter 1993:53–88, Droge and Tabor 1992, Bremmer 1991, and Février 1990:265–73. Although my discussion focuses on the early Christian martyrs, one ought also attend to the ideology of martyrs in other traditions. See, *inter alia*, Scholten 1987; Henten 1989, 1997, 2002; and Sordi 1990.
28 Gradel 2002, Friesen 2001, and Warmind 1993:211–20.
29 Futrell 1997, Gundarson 1996:113–51, Visnara 1990, Baltrusch 1988:324–37, and MacMullen 1986:81–96.
30 Given the public nature, familiarity, and high drama of Christian martyrdom, I have chosen to highlight this case. In its broad outlines, this sketch is still applicable to the cases of the Maccabean martyrs and the suicides of noble Roman stoics and others who opposed imperial power on philosophical grounds (see further the classic discussion of MacMullen 1966:46–94, although some modifications would be necessary). The case of Socrates also holds interest, particularly as it stands in the context of a recently defeated imperial power. *Inter alia*, see Stone 1988, Hansen 1995, Mossé 1996, Green 2001, and Brockhouse and Smith 2002.
31 Castelli 2004 is quite useful on this point. See also Mühlenberg 1997 and Heim 1987.
32 The struggle of Donatists and Catholics in Roman North Africa is particularly instructive but much too complex to pursue here. The classic account is Frend 1965, but more recently see Gaddis 2005, Tilley 1997, Tilley 1996, and Atkinson 1992:488–99.

Works Cited

Adler, Eve. 2003. *Vergil's Empire: Political Thought in the Aeneid*. Lanham, MD.

Albertz, Rainer. 2004. *Israel in Exile: The History and Literature of the Sixth Century B.C.E.* Leiden.

Atkinson, J. E. 1992. "Out of Order: The Circumcellions and *Codex Theodosianus* 16.5.52." *Historia* 61: 488–99.

Baltrusch, Ernst. 1988. "Die Verstaatlichung der Gladiatorenspiele." *Hermes* 116: 324–37.

Barton, Carlin. 1994. "Savage Miracles: The Redemption of Lost Honor in Roman Society and the Sacrament of the Gladiator and the Martyr." *Representations* 45: 41–71.

Beaulieu, Paul-Alain. 1989. *The Reign of Nabonidus, King of Babylon 556–539 B.C.* New Haven, CT.

BeDuhn, Jason. 2000. *The Manichaean Body in Discipline and Ritual.* Baltimore, MD.

Bénatouil, Thomas. 2006. *Faire usage: la pratique du stoïcisme.* Paris.

Bickerman, E. J. 1947. *The Maccabees.* New York.

———. 1979. *The God of the Maccabees. Studies on the Meaning and Origin of the Maccabean Revolt.* Leiden.

Bilde, Per, et al. 1990. *Religion and Religious Practice in the Seleucid Kingdom.* Aarhus.

Billows, Richard. 1995. *Kings and Colonists: Aspects of Macedonian Imperialism.* Leiden.

Bowersock, G. W. 1995. *Martyrdom and Rome.* Cambridge.

Boyarin, Daniel. 1999. *Dying for God: Martyrdom and the Making of Christianity and Judaism.* Stanford, CA.

Boyce, Mary. 1984. "On the Antiquity of Zoroastrian Apocalyptic." *Bulletin of the School of Oriental and African Studies* 47: 57–75.

Boyce, Mary and Frantz Grenet. 1991. *A History of Zoroastrianism.* Vol. 3. *Zoroastrianism under Macedonian and Roman Rule.* Leiden.

Brandon, S. G. F. 1967. *Jesus and the Zealots: A Study of the Political Factor in Primitive Christianity.* Manchester.

Bremmer, Jan. 1991. "'Christianus sum': The Early Christian Martyrs and Christ." In *Eulogia: Mélanges offerts à Antoon A.R. Bastiansen.* Ed. G. J. M. Bartelink et al., 11–20. The Hague.

Brennan, Ted. 2005. *The Stoic Life: Emotions, Duties, and Fate.* Oxford.

Brockhouse, Thomas and Nicholas Smith. 2002. *The Trial and Execution of Socrates: Sources and Controversies.* New York.

Brown, Peter. 1988. *The Body and Society: Men, Women, and Sexual Renunciation in Early Christianity.* New York.

Burkert, Walter. 1983 (German original 1972). *Homo Necans. The Anthropology of Ancient Greek Sacrificial Ritual and Myth.* Berkeley.

Cantarella, Eva. 1991. *I supplizi capitali in Grecia e a Roma.* Milan.

Castelli, Elizabeth. 2004. *Martyrdom and Memory: Early Christian Culture Making.* New York.

Clark, Elizabeth. 1999. *Reading Renunciation: Asceticism and Scripture in Early Christianity.* Princeton, NJ.

Collins, John J., ed. 1998. *The Encyclopedia of Apocalypticism.* Vol. 1. *The Origins of Apocalypticism.* New York.

Cormack, Margaret, ed. 2001. *Sacrificing the Self: Perspectives on Martyrdom and Religion.* New York.

Davis, Natalie Zemon. 1975. "The Rites of Violence." In *Society and Culture in Early Modern France.* Ed. Natalie Zemon Davis, 152–87. Stanford, CA.

Diamond, Eliezer. 2004. *Holy Men and Hunger Artists: Fasting and Asceticism in Rabbinic Culture.* Oxford.

Drake, H. A. 2000. *Constantine and the Bishops: The Politics of Intolerance.* Baltimore, MD.

Droge, Arthur and James Tabor. 1992. *A Noble Death: Suicide and Martyrdom among Christians and Jews in Antiquity.* San Francisco.

Eddy, Samuel K. 1961. *The King is Dead. Studies in the Near Eastern Resistance to Hellenism, 334–31 B.C.* Lincoln, NE.

Février, Paul-Albert. 1990. "Les chrétiens dans l'arène." In *Spectacula I: Gladiateurs et amphitheatres*. Ed. Claude Domerge et al., 265–73. Lattes.

Firpo, Giulio. 1999. *Le revolte giudaiche*. Rome.

Frankfurter, David. 2006. *Evil Incarnate: Rumors of Demonic Conspiracy and Ritual Abuse in History*. Princeton, NJ.

Frend, W. H. C. 1965. *Martyrdom and Persecution in the Early Church: A Study of a Conflict from the Maccabees to Donatus*. Oxford.

Friesen, Steven J. 2001. *Imperial Cults and the Apocalypse of John*. Oxford.

Futrell, Alison. 1997. *Blood in the Arena: The Spectacle of Roman Power*. Austin.

Gaddis, Michael. 2005. *There is No Crime for Those Who Have Christ: Religious Violence in the Christian Roman Empire*. Berkeley.

Gager, John. 1982. "Body-Symbols and Social Reality: Resurrection, Incarnation, and Asceticism in Early Christianity." *Religion* 12: 345–64.

Girardet, Klaus Martin. 2006. *Die konstantinische Wende: Voraussetzungen und geistige Grundlägen der Religionspolitik Konstantins des Grossen*. Darmstadt.

Goudineau, Christian. 2001. *Le dossier Vercingétorix*. Paris.

Gradel, Ittai. 2002. *Emperor Worship and Roman Religion*. Oxford.

Green, Ricky. 2001. *Democratic Virtue in the Trial and Death of Socrates. Resistance to Imperialism in Classical Athens*. New York.

Grottanelli, Cristiano. 1985. "Archaic Forms of Rebellion and their Religious Background." In *Religion, Rebellion, Revolution*. Ed. Bruce Lincoln, 18–24. New York.

Gundarson, Erik. 1996. "The Ideology of the Arena." *Classical Antiquity* 15: 113–51.

Hansen, Mogens Herman. 1995. *The Trial of Sokrates from the Athenian Point of View*. Copenhagen.

Harrington, Daniel. 1988. *The Maccabean Revolt: Anatomy of a Biblical Revolution*. Wilmington, DE.

Hazzard, R. A. 2000. *Imagination of a Monarchy: Studies in Ptolemaic Propaganda*. Toronto.

Heim, François. "Les panegyriques des martyrs ou l'impossible conversion d'un genre littéraire." *Revue des Sciences Religieuses* 61 (1987): 105–28.

Henten, J. W. van, ed. 1989. *Die Entstehung der jüdischen Martyrologie*. Leiden.

———. 1997. *The Maccabean Martyrs as Saviours of the Jewish People*. Leiden.

———. 2002. *Martyrdom and Noble Death: Selected Texts from Graeco-Roman, Jewish, and Christian Antiquity*. New York.

Hinnells, John. 1973. "The Zoroastrian Doctrine of Salvation in the Roman World: A Study of the Oracles of Hystaspes." In *Man and His Salvation: Studies in Honor of S. G. F. Brandon*. Ed. E. J. Sharpe and J. R. Hinnells, 125–48. Manchester.

Holoka, James P., ed. 2003. *Simone Weil's The Iliad, or, The Poem of Force: A Critical Edition*. New York.

Horowitz, Elliott S. 2006. *Reckless Rites: Purim and the Legacy of Jewish Violence*. Princeton, NJ.

Horsley, Richard A. 1988. *Bandits, Prophets, and Messiahs: Popular Movements in the Time of Jesus*. San Francisco.

Hultgård, Anders. 1988. "Persian Apocalypticism." In *Encyclopedia of Apocalypticism*, Vol. 1. *The Origins of Apocalypticism*. Ed. John J. Collins, 39–83. New York.

Jal, Paul. 1962a. "Les dieux et les guerres civiles dans la Rome de la fin de la république." *Revue des études latines* 40 (1962a): 170–200.

———. 1962b. "La propagande réligieuse à Rome au cours des guerres civiles de la fin de la république." *L'Antiquité classique* 30: 396–414.

———. 1963. *La guerre civile à Rome. Étude littéraire et morale*. Paris.

Jullian, Camille. 1903. *Vercingétorix*. Paris.

Kiefer, Jom. 2005. *Exil und Diaspora: Begrifflichkeit und Deutungen im antiken Judentum und in der Hebräischen Bibel*. Leipzig.

Kierkegaard, Søren. 1983 (Danish original 1843). *Fear and Trembling*. Ed. and Trans. Howard V. Hong and Edna H. Hong. Princeton, NJ.

Kojève, Alexandre. 1969 (French original 1947). *Introduction to the Reading of Hegel: Lectures on The Phenomenology of Spirit*. Trans. James H. Nichols. New York.

Kuhrt, Amélie. 1990. "Nabonidus and the Babylonian Priesthood." In *Pagan Priests: Religion and Power in the Ancient World*. Ed. Mary Beard and John North, 119–55. Ithaca, NY.

Lancellotti, Maria Grazia. 2000. *The Naasssenes: A Gnostic Identity among Judaism, Christianity, Classical and Ancient Near Eastern Traditions*. Münster.

Lincoln, Bruce. 2005. *Holy Terrors: Thinking about Religion after September 11*. Chicago.

———. 2007. *Religion, Empire, and Torture: The Case of Achaemenian Persia*. Chicago.

Lipschitz, Oded. 2005. *The Fall and Rise of Jerusalem: Judah under Babylonian Rule*. Winona Lake, IN.

Lucrezi, Francesco. 1996. *Messianismo, Regalità, Impero: Idee religiose e idea imperiale nel mondo romano*. Florence.

MacMullen, Ramsay. 1966 (reprint ed. 1992). *Enemies of the Roman Order: Treason, Unrest, and Alienation in the Empire*. New York.

———. 1986. "Judicial Savagery in the Roman Empire." *Chiron* 16: 147–66.

Markale, Jean. 1995. *Vercingétorix*. Monaco.

Martin, Paul M. 2000. *Vercingétorix: le politique, le stratège*. Paris.

Mattox, John Mark. 2006. *Saint Augustine and the Theory of Just War*. London.

Middleton, Paul. 2006. *Radical Martyrdom and Cosmic Conflict in Early Christianity*. London.

Mosiq-Walburg, Karin. 1982. *Die frühen sasanidischen Könige als Bertreter und Förderer der zarathustrischen Religion: eine Untersuchung der zeitgenössischen Quellen*. Frankfurt am Main.

Mossé, Claude. 1996. *Le procès de Socrate*. Paris.

Mühlenberg, Ekkehard. 1997. "The Martyr's Death and its Literary Presentation." *Studia Patristica* 29: 85–93.

Näsström, Britt-Mari. 1989. *The Abhorrence of Love. Studies in Rituals and Mystic Aspects in Catullus' Poem of Attis*. Stockholm.

Odahl, Charles Matson. 2004. *Constantine and the Christian Empire.* New York.

Patterson, Orlando. 1982. *Slavery and Social Death: A Comparative Study.* Cambridge, MA.

Petersen-Szemeredy, Griet. 1993. *Zwischen Wentstadt und Wüste: Römische Asketinnen in der Spätantike.* Göttingen.

Pfeiffer, Stefan. 2008. *Herrscher- und Dynastiekulte im Ptolemäerreich: Systematik und Einordnung der Kultformen.* Munich.

Potter, David S. 1993. "Martyrdom as Spectacle." In *Theater and Society in the Classical World.* Ed. Ruth Scodel, 53–88. Ann Arbor, MI.

Pritchard, James B. 1969. *Ancient Near Eastern Texts Relating to the Old Testament.* 3rd ed. Princeton, NJ.

Reydams-Schils, Gretchen. 2005. *The Roman Stoics: Self, Responsibility, and Affection.* Chicago.

Ste. Croix, G. E. M. de. 2006. *Christian Persecution, Martyrdom, and Orthodoxy.* New York.

Schäfer, Peter. 1981. *Der Bar Kokhba-Aufstand: Studien zum zweiten jüdischen Krieg gegen Rom.* Tübingen.

Scholten, Clemens. 1987. *Martyrium und Sophiamythos im Gnostizismus nach den Texten von Nag Hammadi.* Münster.

Seitz, Christopher. 1989. *Theology in Conflict: Reactions to the Exile in the Book of Jeremiah.* Berlin.

Sellars, John. 2006. *Stoicism.* Berkeley, CA.

Shaked, Shaul. 1994. *Dualism in Transformation: Varieties of Religion in Sassanian Iran.* London.

Shaw, Brent. 1996. "Body/Power/Identity: Passions of the Martyrs." *Journal of Early Christian Studies* 4: 269–312.

Sherman, Nancy. 2005. *Stoic Warriors: The Ancient Philosophy behind the Military Mind.* New York.

Sizgorich, Thomas. 2009. *Violence and Belief in Late Antiquity: Militant Devotion in Christianity and Islam.* Philadelphia.

Smith, Daniel. 1989. *The Religion of the Landless: The Social Context of the Babylonian Exile.* Bloomington, IN.

Soden, Wolfram von. 1983. "Kyros und Nabonid. Propaganda und Gegenpropaganda." In *Kunst, Kultur und Geschichte der Achamenidenzeit und ihr Fortleben.* Ed. Heidemarie Koch and D. N. MacKenzie, 61–68. Berlin.

Södergård, J. Peter. 1993. "The Ritualized Bodies of Cybele's Galli and the Methodological Problem of the Plurality of Explanations." In *The Problem of Ritual: Based on papers read at the symposium on religious rites held at Åbo, Finland on the 13th–16th of August, 1991.* Ed. Tore Ahlbäck, 169–93. Scripta Instituti Donneriani Aboensis 15. Åbo, Finland.

Sordi, Marta, ed. 1990. *Dulce et decorum est pro patria mori: La morte in combattimento nell' antichità.* Milan.

Stone, I. F. 1988. *The Trial of Socrates.* New York.

Tafazzoli, A. 2000. *Sassanian Society.*

Thomassen, Einar. 2006. *The Spiritual Seed: The Church of the "Valentinians."* Leiden.

Tilley, Maureen. 1996. *Donatist Martyr Stories: The Church in Conflict in Roman North Africa*. Liverpool.

———. 1997. *The Bible in Christian North Africa: The Donatist World*. Minneapolis, MN.

Turner, John Douglas. 2001. *Sethian Gnosticism and the Platonic Tradition*. Louvain.

Vermaseren, M. J. 1977. *Cybele and Attis. The Myth and the Cult*. London.

Vernant, Jean-Pierre. 1969 (reprint ed. 1999). *Problèmes de la guerre en Grèce ancienne*. The Hague.

Visnara, Cinzia. 1990. *Il supplizio come spettacolo*. Rome.

Warmind, Morten Lund. 1993. "The Cult of the Roman Emperor before and after Christianity." In *The Problem of Ritual: Based on papers read at the symposium on religious rites held at Åbo, Finland on the 13th–16th of August, 1991*. Ed. Tore Ahlbäck, 211–20. Scripta Instituti Donneriani Aboensis 15. Åbo, Finland.

Worthington, Ian. 2004. *Alexander the Great: Man and God*. New York.

Zanker, Paul. 1988. *The Power of Images in the Age of Augustus*. Ann Arbor, MI.

11 Identity

KIMBERLY B. STRATTON

Those areas of ancient life recognized as religious coincide often with areas of life where identity was being negotiated, contested, and constructed. In cosmopolitan centers, where people from different regions of the ancient Mediterranean crowded urban neighborhoods and market squares, identity might hinge on variables such as the choice of gods to worship, whether one revered a particular sacred place, the holidays and festivals one chose to celebrate, as well as daily practices governed by divine prescription, such as prayer, eating, and sexual relations. Finally, one often proclaimed one's identity in death through mortuary inscriptions, decorations on tombs, or in catacomb art; while people might choose to emphasize their social rank or trade on an epitaph, we also frequently find indicators of religious affiliation such as depicting the deceased as a priestess of Ceres or Isis, or the inclusion of symbols such as a menorah or fish.[1]

Whether we identify the origin of religion as a discrete category of human existence with the emergence of Christianity, as Daniel Boyarin does,[2] or with the Protestant Reformation as Talal Asad and others have done,[3] or claim that it has always existed as part of human societies, it is clear that beliefs and practices coterminous with what we now call "religion" comprised an important element of ancient identities. "Identity" itself, however, as a unified and stable entity, has been questioned. Freudian analysis first revealed the disturbing presence of multiple levels of consciousness and fragmented selves within the minds of rational self-controlled Europeans, allowing for the emergence of post-modern and deconstructionist theories that underscore the mutability and complexity of modern identities. Post-colonial theory has also contributed to a more nuanced understanding of modern identity by highlighting the complicated and ambivalent relationships that develop in colonial contexts between natives and occupiers, who both resist and imitate each other.[4]

These insights into identity from post-modern and post-colonial theory have been applied recently to understand the ancient

220

Mediterranean, which was similarly characterized by war, dislocation, migration, and colonial occupation. Scholars of antiquity have been able to illuminate strategies of resistance to colonial domination as well as the hybrid identities that emerged with multiple social roles and competing ethnic and civic allegiances in various diaspora communities. These theoretical approaches highlight how the spread of Hellenism in the form of Greek aesthetics and education (*paideia*), as well as the granting of Roman citizenship, created multiple identities that routinely needed to be negotiated by individuals in different contexts. This chapter explores some of the ways that religion intersected with the construction, negotiation, and representation of identity in the ancient Mediterranean. The investigation ranges across cultures and societies, concentrating on two fundamental modes by which religious identity was expressed, inculcated, and maintained: 1) narrative – myths about one's group or others that are understood to be defining; and 2) performance – religious acts, observances, and ways of locating a community in space and time that differentiate its members from outsiders.

NARRATIVE

In his book *Narrative and the Self*, Anthony Paul Kerby argues that "the self is given content, is delineated and embodied, primarily in narrative constructions or stories," which situate an individual within a larger history.[5] Stories about one's family, city, and country, as well as about appropriate roles for gendered members of these communities, shape self-conceptions, actions, and aspirations of individuals. This insight into the close relationship between narrative and identity is amply born out in the research of numerous scholars working on religions of the ancient Mediterranean. Jonathan Hall's seminal book on ethnicity in ancient Greece, for example, argues that ethnic identity is discursive, constructed through mythic lineages, stories of origin, and descent from eponymous ancestors.[6] Although not explicitly concerned with religion as a separate component of ethnicity, the origin myths Hall discusses often link directly to religious practices; they provide the mythic basis for local cults and rituals that served to orient denizens of Greek cities in a sacred history and located them on a cosmic map. Similarly, most of the Hebrew Bible constitutes a myth of common descent, outlining the shared political history of a group of people who identified themselves as descendants of a single ancient family, whose story forms the basis of Judaism, Christianity, and Islam.

Common Descent

Myths of shared descent unite communities and construct collective identities through (real or imagined) kinship bonds. Athens, for example, is famous for its myth of autochthony: Athenians claimed to have sprung from the land as descendants of Erechtheus, who, according to mythic tradition, was born of the earth and raised by Athena, with whom he was worshipped on the Athenian Acropolis (Homer, *Iliad* 2.546–9, 2.550–1; Herodotus 5.82.3).[7] By making all Athenians in essence cousins, sharing the same ancestry and blood, the myth (and cult to which it was related) fostered a unique Athenian identity that intersected with the emergence of democracy as a political system – no one could claim special privileges based on nobility of birth. Furthermore, the narrative functioned patriotically to unite all Athenians, no matter how humble, against other Greeks and foreigners and could be called upon to mobilize heroic defense of the city or provide a grand mythic explanation for past acts of heroism and self-sacrifice. In Pericles' famous funeral oration, for example, which he delivered as an encomium for soldiers who died in the Peloponnesian War (431–404 BCE), he identifies Athenian freedom and democracy explicitly with ancestors who inhabited the land from time immemorial and passed it down unfettered to their descendants (Thucydides 2.36). While the antiquity of this mythic narrative is debated, it was frequently mobilized during the fifth century as Athens vied for control over its empire against other venerable Greek city-states, such as Sparta and Thebes.[8] In this context the myth of autochthony and cult of Erechtheus bolstered Athens's new democratic identity, which lay at the heart of Athenian claims to political dominance.[9]

Israelites also relied on a myth of shared descent to define themselves as a people. According to the Hebrew Bible, Israelites are descended from a Mesopotamian patriarch, Abraham, his son Isaac, and grandson Jacob. Following a divine command, Abraham immigrated to the land of Canaan, which God pledged to Abraham's descendants. His great-grandchildren, however, moved to Egypt during a famine and eventually became a nation of slaves there. Under the leadership of Moses they escaped slavery, wandered in the desert for forty years, and finally conquered the land of Canaan (Genesis 11:27–50:26; Exodus 1:1–19:25; Joshua 1:1–19:51). Contrary to the Bible's story of outside origins and conquest, archaeology has made it abundantly clear that Israel's origins are to be found indigenously, in the collapse of the Canaanite city-states of the Late Bronze Age (thirteenth century BCE).[10] Over centuries, a collection of scattered agricultural hamlets in the central highlands formed a distinct culture and religious identity based around a shared story of divine liberation from bondage in Egypt and the worship of Yahweh (among other gods).[11]

Peter Machinist points out that references to Israel's origins in the Exodus and desert wanderings appear in every stratum of the Bible from archaic poetry to post-exilic prophecy.[12] The persistence of this story throughout the biblical period and across many different genres of biblical writings indicates its centrality for ancient Israel's self-conception. Without regarding this narrative as historically factual, against the weight of material evidence,[13] Machinist investigates why a story of foreign origins, which emphasizes Israel as an outsider to its territory, would have gained such importance. He notes two discursive functions such a tale plays: first, it emphasizes Israel's separateness from its neighbors, which is underscored by a fear of contamination through intermarriage (most pronounced in the Deuteronomic corpus); second, it reveals Israel's independence from the land.[14] Unlike autochthonous peoples, whose identity is tied to the land, a story of outside origins emphasizes the integrity and solidarity of the community irrespective of the land; just as they are said to have survived during forty years in the desert, they can survive political exile in Babylonia. While Machinist proposes that the story of outsider origins reflects the cultural dislocation of the twelfth century BCE and the emergence of new communities following the collapse of the great city-states at the end of the Bronze Age, Finkelstein and Silberman rely on archaeology to date the existing version of the Exodus story to the late monarchic period (seventh century BCE), when Judah was straining under the oppressive yoke of Egyptian vassalage. Later, in the exilic and post-exilic periods (587–c. 400 BCE), they argue, the story was re-edited to reflect the needs and concerns of exiles returning from Babylonia to rebuild their nation and temple in their former homeland.[15] According to both theories, biblical stories of outsider origin served as boundary markers, affirming the existence of an "us" over a "them." Yet, "the more sharply they affirm the boundary, the more we can be certain that the reality was muddier and more fragile."[16]

Mixed Descent and Fictitious Kinship

Indeed, such are the conclusions of Erich Gruen, in his recent book, *Rethinking the Other in Antiquity.*[17] Contrary to much recent scholarship that has emphasized boundary drawing, "othering" strategies, and the construction of separate identities, Gruen attempts to reveal the many ways that those same discourses were undermined by others that describe ethnic mixing and shared origins. Thus, in contrast to legends that emphasize real or imagined separateness and cultural purity, Gruen examines competing narratives that emphasize foreign roots and establish fictitious genealogies that link disparate communities together. For example, according to mythic tradition, Cadmus, the legendary founder of Greek Thebes, hailed from Phoenicia in the Near East; when Zeus kidnapped and raped Cadmus' sister Europa, Cadmus went in search of her. Forbidden by his father to return home without her, Cadmus settled in Boeotia and founded the famous city of Thebes (Apollodorus, *Bibliotheca* 3.1.1; Ovid, *Metamorphoses* 3.1–137).[18] The foreign origin of Thebes' founder never appears to have caused any shame for the Thebans.[19] Similarly, the Greek city of Argos connected its dynastic founder with Egypt: Danaus, a descendent of Io, who was turned into a heifer by Zeus and fled to Egypt to escape Hera's jealous fury, returned from Egypt with his fifty daughters and settled among the Argives, eventually attaining the throne (Apollodorus, *Bibliotheca* 2.1.4; Pausanias 2.16.1, 2.19.3–4). This legend, linking Argos and Egypt through the blood of its founding hero, was embraced by the Argives as part of their "venerated tradition," demonstrating the willingness of some Greeks to identify their origins with foreign people and lands.[20]

These fictitious genealogies established "sentiments of affinity"[21] between different groups of people and could be invoked for religious or political purposes. In addition to the well-known mythic kinship that unites the twelve tribes of Israel as descendants of the eponymous patriarch, Jacob/Israel (Genesis 29:31–30:22), two ancient writers assert a less well known kinship between Judeans and Spartans. According to 1 Maccabees (12:20–23) and Josephus's *Antiquitates Judaicae* (12.225–227), the High Priest Onias received a letter from the Spartan king Areus, asserting their shared descent from Abraham (through his second wife, Keturah) and offering to share goods and cattle. This correspondence and the kinship link it purports is clearly manufactured, but it reveals an attempt by certain Judeans to ally themselves with a noble Greek nation that was respected for bravery, loyalty, and adherence to ancient customs and laws.[22] By claiming Abraham as the progenitor of both peoples, this myth attributes the rugged, heroic qualities of the Lacedaemonians to the biblical patriarch and, consequently, to the Judeans.[23]

The importance of fictitious kinship, thus, lay not only in the friendly relations it could foster between distinct cultural and political communities, but also in the symbolic value of stories to promote particular collective identities, which were further reinforced by religion. Rome, for example, traced its lineage to Phrygian Troy through Aeneas, who escaped the burning city as it fell to the Greek armies. By linking Rome to Troy, this foundation myth conferred antiquity and venerability on Rome's otherwise humble origins. The story of Aeneas served other ideological purposes as well; he is praised as a paradigm of filial piety for risking his own life to save his aging father.[24] He is also credited with rescuing the sacred fire of Vesta and statue of Athena (the Palladium), transferring them to Italy where they eventually found their way to Rome.[25] These sacred items were regarded as essential to Rome's security and prosperity, placing them at the center of Roman religion (Dionysius of Halicarnassus, *Antiquitates Romanae*, 2.65–66). Aeneas thus represented for Romans not only an august heritage, but one that was associated with filial and religious piety. Augustus, the first emperor, capitalized on these associations with Aeneas, whom he counted as a direct ancestor, by decorating the Augustan Forum with a statue of Aeneas, carrying his aged father, and son. Augustus thus used this image of the three Trojans to identify himself with Aeneas's piety and courage. The statue was frequently copied onto oil lamps for use in private homes, indicating the popularity of the story and its edifying message among common Romans.[26] Karl Galinsky argues, that by the second century CE the identification of Rome with piety as a characteristic inherited from the Trojans "had become the common property of the entire Roman people."[27]

Collective Memory

In addition to origin myths, which relate stories about the distant past beyond the historical record, pivotal events that occurred in historical memory – such as war, conquest, victory, and subjugation – also figure prominently in identity formation; they create powerful collective memories based on shared experiences that define the group's self-understanding for generations to come. These memories can become highly mythologized and integrated into a people's religious practices, thereby being transmitted to successive generations. In Bruce Lincoln's terminology, they are elevated from being "history" – which is regarded as true – to having the status of "myth," which is regarded as both true and authoritative.[28] Lincoln characterizes myths as paradigmatic; they shape the self-understanding and behavior of a community in a way that history does not. For example, the Deuteronomic corpus of the Hebrew Bible (comprising Deuteronomy and the books Joshua through 2 Kings) recounts the story of the Israelite people from their first entry into the land of Canaan, their struggles against local enemies and distant empires, culminating in the destruction of Jerusalem and exile of the ruling class to Babylonia. It is largely agreed that the first layer of the text dates to the reign of Josiah (641–609 BCE) and reflects the ideology of his religious reforms. This text was subsequently redacted during the Babylonian exile (597–538 BCE) to preserve national identity for the community forced to reside outside the land.[29] It frames events in terms of a covenantal relationship with Israel's god that both explains the cataclysm of the destruction and offers a model for future redemption and national restoration.

The Judeans' experience of conquest, subjugation, and exile thus defined their self-understanding as a separate people, chosen by God, and punished for apostasy. This conception of history became central to their collective identity and framed an understanding of all subsequent catastrophes that befell the nation as well as shaped their religious expression.[30] The Jewish historian Josephus (b. 37/8 CE), for example, iterates the Deuteronomistic perception of the Babylonian conquest in his account of the Roman destruction of the Second Temple (70 CE), which had been built to replace Solomon's Temple that was destroyed in 587 BCE by the Babylonians. In both cases, Josephus affirms, the temples had been desecrated and were consigned to the flames by God, as demonstrated by the fact they were destroyed on the same day centuries apart (*Bellum Iudaicum* 6.4.5).

Defining Characteristics

Collective memory distils and transmits ideas about a people's character, often shaping their sense of identity. The Persian Wars (499–449 BCE), for instance, defined Athenian self-understanding for centuries. In 490 BCE a numerically inferior army comprised of Athens and Plataea, the sole ally to send support troops, succeeded in routing a large Persian invasion in the Battle of Marathon (Herodotus 6.102–117). The victory created a new breed of heroes and an enduring sense of Athenian superiority.[31] In the collective memory of Athens, victory against the Persians constituted a triumph of democracy over tyranny, freedom over oppression, and proof of divine providence.[32] Very quickly, Athenians shaped their nascent democratic identity around this event, which was memorialized in public veneration of the dead and cults dedicated to the gods and heroes responsible for that success.[33] The collective memory of Athenian fortitude and suffering during the Persian Wars forged a powerful sense of civic unity and purpose, which was perpetuated through cults well into the Hellenistic period (Herodotus 6.105; Plutarch, *De Herodote malignitate* 26).[34]

Some Christians similarly formulated a collective identity out of their shared experience of suffering and resistance. The Roman Empire enforced compliance among its subjects through demonstrations of violence.[35] Accused of treason and subjected to a humiliating form of execution, Jesus of Nazareth should have served as a witness to Rome's unmitigated authority and as a warning to others to accede to Rome's power. Instead, many early followers of Jesus remembered his death in ways that upended the discourse of violence employed by Rome; they regarded his suffering and denigrating death as soteriological and worthy of emulation. One of the earliest writings of the Jesus Movement captures this subversive character of Christianito: Paul of Tarsus describes his soteriological understanding of Jesus's death as "a stumbling block to Jews and folly to Gentiles" (1 Corinthians 1:23). In a social context where salvation was expected to come through warrior heroes who liberated their people from subordination and occupation, it was unfathomable and foolish to proclaim a crucified criminal the savior. But this was the claim that many early Christians made about Jesus. These Christians regarded his crucifixion to be the most significant of his actions and the very purpose and fulfillment of his life mission (Revelation 5:6–14). They also sacrificed their own lives to witness this belief and to imitate Jesus, whom they revered. This understanding of Jesus' death gradually became the collective memory for Christianity and drastically shaped Christian behavior and identity.[36]

Collective memories and the identities they engender, however, are not monolithic and can be contested even within a single group. Often, if the disagreement is strong enough and concerns fundamental aspects of the community's shared narrative, schism results. The Dead Sea Scrolls reveal this sort of split in Second Temple Judean belief and practice. A close study of the scrolls reveals that the community that produced these documents splintered off from the Jerusalem Temple during the early Hasmonean Dynasty (140–37 BCE) over differences related to purity, temple practices, and beliefs about who could legitimately be High Priest. It is largely agreed that the schism occurred during the reign of either Simon or Jonathan Maccabee, most likely in response to a self-appointment to the position of High Priest.[37] The collective memory of the group's exile from Jerusalem (self-imposed or otherwise) forged a sectarian and dualistic identity that divided the world into two religious groups: the Sons of Light and the Sons of Darkness. This opposition was further reinforced by an ascetic lifestyle focused on rigorous ritual purity that separated the Sons of Light from outsiders (including other Judeans) (*War Scroll* 1.1–17).

Discourses of Alterity

As this brief discussion of the Dead Sea Scrolls indicates, separate religious identity is often expressed through labeling and, sometimes, name calling. By projecting onto the proverbial "other" those characteristics one does not desire to possess, a sense of identity emerges by way of contrast. And so, in the decades following the Persian Wars, Persians served as a foil for Athenian artists, politicians, and playwrights to reflect upon and theorize a distinct Athenian identity that was esteemed to be more pious, rational, self-controlled, and courageous. In her seminal book, *Inventing the Barbarian*, Edith Hall documents the emergence of a discourse of barbarism that emerged in the wake of the Persian invasions and reified an idealized Athenian identity. Less than a decade after the Battles of Salamis and Plataea (480 and 479 BCE), Aeschylus produced his tragedy *The Persians*, which presented the aftermath of King Xerxes' invasion from the Persian point of view but reflected a distinctly Hellenic perspective. In that production, Aeschylus depicts the Persians as excessively emotional and accustomed to luxury.[38] They are consequently identified as morally soft and lacking self-restraint (*sophrosyne*), the cardinal virtue esteemed by Athenians. Throughout the fifth century, Hall demonstrates, ancient myths were reworked to present foreigners as monstrous and bestial agents of social disorder. This distrust of barbarians was reinforced by Greek ethnography, which discovered "lawlessness, incest, cannibalism, and other deviations from the socially authorized way of life" and religion not in faraway mythic lands but "amongst known barbarian communities."[39] Euripides, for example, emphasizes the barbarian origins of Medea,[40] the infamous sorceress of Greek mythology, thereby helping to cement an association between magic and outsiders, which influenced Roman and, later, Christian thought.[41]

The Hebrew Bible also employed narrative to construct powerful images of otherness that reinforced Judean self-understanding as God's chosen people at a time when their political fortunes did not reflect their expectations. Ronald Hendel offers an interesting discussion of the literary role of Mesopotamia in the book of Genesis. He notes that the biblical writers needed to acknowledge Mesopotamian temporal priority as well as political dominance in their myth of national origins. Yet, they did it in such a way that Mesopotamia was deprecated. In the flood story, Hendel notes, there are linguistic hints that suggest Mesopotamia as the site of Noah's Ark. Indeed, in light of the discovery of an earlier Mesopotamian version of this story embedded in the Epic of Gilgamesh, it is clear that the biblical authors appropriated the story for themselves.[42] By linking the flood to rebellion and violence, however, the Bible associates these characteristics with Mesopotamia, even while subtly acknowledging Mesopotamia as the older nation and source of Israelite tradition.[43] Similarly the Garden of Eden and Tower of Babel stories both link Mesopotamia with acts of rebellion; it is a place of sin and punishment that has been superseded by the new covenant in a new land.[44] The Bible, thus, distances itself from and denigrates Mesopotamia by mapping acts of violence, deceit, and rebellion against God onto it, which clears a narrative path for the emergence of Yahwistic monotheism (singular devotion to the god Yahweh) with Abraham and his descendants, and the formulation of a distinct Israelite identity predicated on it.[45]

A similar ambivalence that we see in the attitude of biblical authors toward Mesopotamia appears among Roman writers toward Greece. Responding to the influx of Greek art, ideas, and religion following Rome's conquest of Corinth in 146 BCE, certain Roman authors dismissed all things Greek as extravagant luxuries that weaken the morale and virtue of the Roman people. Rustic Roman tradition was modeled against an imagined Greek depravity. Juvenal, for example, castigates noble women's unchastity, which he attributes to modern luxuries and Greek influence (*Satires* 6). The Roman censor, Cato, in a speech attributed to him by Livy, denounces the insidious effects of excessive luxury, which he attributes to Roman expansion into Greece and Asia and predicts will lead to the overthrow of social order by women (*Ab Urbe Condita* 34.4.1–4). Dionysius of Halicarnassus takes special aim at the ecstatic and irrational excesses of Greek religion, which he contrasts with the temperance and piety of Roman religion as established, according to legend, by the city's founder, Romulus (*Antiquitates Romanae* 2.18). There is no tradition among the Romans, he argues, for such immoral acts as fathers devouring children or sons castrating their fathers, which occur in Greek mythology (2.19). Thus the chaotic and immoral world of Greek mythology serves as an analogy for the disorder and impiety of Greek cultural influences on Roman society.

Not surprisingly, Rome operated as the paradigmatic "other" in the literature and traditions of its military opponents and subjugated peoples. Josef Wiesehöfer discusses the varied and complex ways that Rome (Rūm) operated in Persian literature and legend over the course of their combative history. One of the more interesting features of this tradition is the cultural appropriation of Alexander the Great, known in Middle Persian traditions as Alexander of Rūm, demonstrating an amalgamation of Greeks and Romans in the Persian imagination. In these stories, he is portrayed as "evil incarnate" and "the devil's henchman," who is responsible for killing many members of the royal family, as well as priests and scholars.[46] He also waged a war against cultural and religious institutions by destroying temples and cities and burning sacred scriptures. In these narratives, Rūm is identified with evil, tyranny, and chaos. This representation resonates with the portrait of Rome in much Christian and rabbinic literature. Rome, for example, figures as Edom in rabbinic literature, where it is coded as the biblical enemy in predictions of eschatological vindication (*Pesikta de Rav Kahana* 7.11; *Mechilta deshira* 2). The Apocalypse of John presents Rome as a rapacious whore, drunk on the blood of martyrs (Revelation 17:6). Her sexual depravity, insatiable greed, and violence stand starkly in opposition to the purity of the Christian martyrs in their white robes, and function as a call to martyrdom. At a time when cultural accommodation with Roman civic traditions and customs was advocated or at least tolerated by notable Christians, including Paul, the portrait of Rome in Revelation served as a potent counterstrategy, driving a wedge between Christians, the state, and their pagan neighbors and families.

Often the most vituperative othering language occurs in internecine struggles between groups contesting over a shared identity. Early Christian literature is replete with examples of charged language, accusing one group or another of sexual misconduct, sorcery, or just plain stupidity. These accusations did not originate among Christians but constituted well-known invective strategies in Greece and Rome for centuries before Christianity emerged. Laura Nasrallah, for example, examines how epistemological debates in antiquity participated in larger contests over authority; accusations of folly, stupidity, or being "out of one's mind" served to discredit competing claims to prophetic knowledge.[47] Jennifer Wright Knust similarly demonstrates the way ancient rhetoric leveraged accusations of sexual deviance in contests over religious authority and legitimacy; charges of sexual misconduct not only undercut an opponent's political authority but served to unify a community around claims to being especially pure and moral, thus serving as a focal point for the construction of a shared religious identity.[48]

Accusations of magic often combined with one or both of the previous two strategies in contests over legitimate belief and practice. For example, an early Christian leader named Marcus, who included women in his celebration of the Eucharist, was accused of using magic to seduce his female followers and to deceive his church into believing he could perform miracles (Irenaeus, *Contra Haereses*, 7.4.1–6, 13.1). The charges against him combine elements of sexual slander with the rhetoric of foolishness to delegitimize not only Marcus's claims to spiritual authority but the intelligence and good judgment of his church members as well.[49] Invective, in this case, not only seeks to forge a legitimate

Christian community by way of contrast with an illegitimate one, but casts the allegations in cosmic dualistic terms – charges of using magic were equivalent to charges of being allied with Satan.

PERFORMANCE

In addition to narrative constructions of identity that either create an idealized past around which a social group can rally or construct an "other" as a foil for projecting unwanted characteristics, much recent scholarship has examined how identity is performed. In this respect the work of theorists, such as Judith Butler, Pierre Bourdieu, and Catherine Bell, who examine how ideas of self and community are constructed through actions that move the individual body through space and place in socially meaningful ways, has been especially influential.[50] The following section will examine how religious identity was performed in the ancient Mediterranean.

Which God?

In a fundamental way, which gods one worshipped defined to a significant extent one's identity in the ancient world. This is because the basic acts involved in reverence, respect, and worship of the gods played central roles in constructing and maintaining identity. Ancient Greeks, for example, presented their newborn infants, brides, and newly purchased slaves to the household gods, represented by the deified hearth (Hestia), in order to signal their entrance into the family; adoption of these deities effected membership in the new household (*oikos*).[51] Ensuring continued worship of the ancestral gods was important for the welfare of the city-state (*polis*); Plato stipulates that the head of each *oikos* must designate (or adopt) one son to be "the inheritor of his dwelling, to be his successor in worshipping the deified ancestors both of family and of State, whether living or already dead" (*Leges* 740b–c).[52] Thus, at the most basic social level, that of the family, identity was intimately bound up with worship of the gods. Transfer to another *oikos*, through marriage or adoption, involved the transfer of religious loyalty. Identity as a member of a particular family was something performed both privately in the home and, more significantly, publicly at festivals celebrated by *phratries* (kinship groups) and other special occasions when the ancestral deities were revered through sacrifice and feasting.[53] In cases of disputed heredity, one ancient witness asserts that being included in sacrifices to a particular household's gods could establish heredity since it demonstrated intimacy and affinity (Isaeus 1.31, 8.15).[54] Although women were excluded from these events, their social status and identity were also effectuated cultically; as they passed from virgins to wives they transferred worship from gods of their natal home and city to those of their husband.[55]

On a broader scale, festivals of a city brought together and unified its residents, fostering a collective identity around the *polis* and its divine protectors. Non-citizen residents (*metics*), for example, processed alongside citizens in the Panathenaia of Athens, celebrating the city's patron deity, Athena. Other Athenian festivals most likely restricted formal participation to citizens but allowed non-citizens to share in the festive atmosphere as spectators, thus articulating a formal distinction between citizens and non-citizens while fostering social bonds as residents who share a common fate living in the same *polis*.[56] Greeks from different cities also cultivated a pan-Hellenic identity through participation in international festivals that honored shared deities such as Zeus at Olympia and Apollo at Delphi. Attendance at these festivals drew Greeks from across the Aegean and was protected by an armistice during the holiday, allowing safe passage to pilgrims and participants. Through these shared gods and festivals, Greeks cultivated a common identity that transcended local differences and hostilities. According to Herodotus (8.144.2), Greek identity revolved as much around religious practice as around language or kinship.

Judeans similarly fostered a collective identity around the shared reverence of their ancestral god, Yahweh, who was believed to have contracted a covenant of exclusivity with their common ancestor, Abraham (Genesis 15:18). Yet, the best historical reconstructions suggest that Israelites continued to worship the traditional Canaanite deities of their ancestors in addition to Yahweh; the prohibition of worshipping other gods reflects the position of a minority within the pre-exilic community in Judah, but that minority is the one responsible for compiling the Torah, whose worldview it represents.[57] This adherence to strict monotheism, what Morton Smith dubbed the "Yahweh-alone party," was codified and written into the Hebrew Scriptures just prior to and during the Babylonian exile (597–538 BCE) as the defining characteristic of a holy community. With the rebuilding of the temple (516 BCE) and the adoption/imposition of monotheism as the official religion of Judea during the Persian and Hellenistic periods, Judaism emerged as a distinct religion defined by the worship of a single and particular deity who required certain special observances and prohibited pollution of the community through intermarriage.

The previous two examples reflect the formation of collective identities around the worship of deities at the familial, tribal, city-state, or national/ethnic level. Deities could also have strong relationships with particular social classes and serve a prominent role in the expression and maintenance of class identity as Barbette Stanley Spaeth shows in the case of Ceres, Roman goddess of grain and fertility. In one of her cults, the goddess Ceres was closely identified with the plebeian social order in Roman tradition. Her temple was built on the Aventine Hill, the district in Rome most closely identified with the *plebs* (common people), and served as the headquarters for the plebeian magistrates, including the aediles and tribunes of the *plebs*, and likely as their treasury as well.[58] The sanctity of the tribune of the *plebs* was protected by Ceres, to whom an oath was sworn to protect the tribunes and to whom the confiscated property of anyone who harmed a tribune was given (Dionysius of Halicarnassus, *Antiquitates Romanae* 6.89.3). Thus, the goddess was explicitly allied with plebeian interests and political rights. Furthermore, Dionysius (*Antiquitates Romanae* 6.17.2, 6.94.3) dates the consecration of her temple in Rome to the year of the first plebeian secession (493 BCE), further linking the rise of her cult to the political rise of this order. Whether this dating is accurate or not, Spaeth argues that it reflects the strong association in later Roman imagination between the goddess and the *plebs*.[59] Spaeth demonstrates the importance of Ceres as an "integrative symbol" for the emergence of the plebeians as a social order in opposition to the patricians (ruling class); her festivals, games, and temple were explicitly contrasted with those of the patrician gods Jupiter, Juno, and Minerva, as well as Magna Mater, who was imported from Phrygia, a region in Asia Minor, by patricians and competed with Ceres for jurisdiction over fertility.

Spaeth reveals that another cult of Ceres played a prominent role in the inculcation of gender norms and social values for women; men were barred from participation in these rites. Ironically, it seems, these festivals of Ceres were celebrated primarily by noble women and served to dramatize symbolically, ritually, and mythically the two primary roles of upper-class women: virgin and mother.[60] The cult consequently reinforced and inculcated the cardinal virtues of noble women in ancient Rome: chastity and fertility. In this way, Spaeth demonstrates, this cult of Ceres promoted a particular type of female identity that supported patriarchy and male control over female sexuality.[61]

Topography

Religion and identity were also enmeshed in the orientation of individuals to the physical world in which they lived or the idealized world they imagined. Many ethnic groups living across the Roman Empire maintained a sense of identity based on allegiance to their ancestral homeland and sacred sites. Judeans living in the Diaspora, for example, continued to pay an annual tithe and make pilgrimages to the temple in Jerusalem as long as it stood.[62] They also took their collective name in Greek, *Ioudaioi*, from their homeland, Judea. Epitaphs from Israel indicate that many wealthy Judeans in the Diaspora sent their bones to be buried in Jerusalem, indicating a continuing identification with their sacred city as well as probable eschatological expectations tied to predictions that the kingdom of God would descend there.[63] Judith Lieu notes that narrative descriptions of Jerusalem and the temple enabled those in the Judean Diaspora to experience the temple vicariously and take pride in it.[64] For example, the Letter of Aristeas (99), most likely written in Alexandria, provides a vivid description of the temple and the sacrifices performed there. Its rich narrative detail and emphasis on the power and significance of the temple demonstrates the ongoing importance of this symbol for Diaspora Judeans, even while their cultic life (with the exception of sending tribute to the Jerusalem temple) was directed toward the local community where they read scripture, celebrated festivals, and observed certain traditional practices.[65]

Evidence of geographically defined identity is also indicated by two Samaritan inscriptions from Delos, the island birthplace of Apollo.[66] They attest to the presence of a Samaritan community and, possibly, a Samaritan synagogue, on the sanctified island as early as the third century BCE. Both inscriptions identify the commissioning group as "Israelites" who make offerings to sacred Mount Gerizim. T. A. Kraabel points to the excellent Greek of the inscription and its inclusion of a customary Greek form of honoring patrons with gold wreaths as evidence that those who commissioned this inscription were fully at home with Greek language and customs.[67] Yet, in both inscriptions the community that commissioned it self-identifies with a geographically remote location, indicating the continuing importance of their homeland for collective self-understanding even while they adopted Greek language and customs.[68] Significantly, these inscriptions stipulate Mount Gerizim, which is located in Israel near the ancient city of Shechem, as the sacred focal point of worship, distinguishing the commissioning group from Judeans, who worshipped the same God in Jerusalem. These inscriptions, therefore, not only identify the geographic orientation of the community but reveal competition with Judeans over the name Israel, and the sacred history of their shared eponymous ancestor.

Sacred topography plays a significant symbolic role in the cult of Isis as well, evidence for which is found scattered across the Greek and

Roman world. In contrast to Judeans and Samaritans, who looked back to their land of origin, a large percentage of devotees of Isis were native Greeks and Italians, who were attracted to the foreign goddess and sometimes underwent initiation into her mysteries (Apuleius, *Metamorphoses* 11.19).[69] The worship of Isis was originally brought by Egyptian slaves, freedmen, and merchants to the shores of Greece and Italy in the second century BCE; Delos, especially, seems to have been the point of entry, where non-Egyptian merchants encountered the goddess and imported her cult back home.[70] Through this process of dissemination and assimilation, the Greco-Roman cult of Isis fused Greek and Egyptian concepts and aesthetics in its decorative arts and devotional statuary, as well as sacrificial techniques and temple architecture.[71] While Egyptian artifacts and decorative themes were widely popular in the Late Republic and Imperial Rome – indicating that their presence in private homes does not necessarily prove devotion to the Egyptian deities – Egyptian iconography and decorative motifs contributed a distinctly Egyptian character to the rites, visually recalling Isis' exotic origins and her sacred mythology, which revolved around the life-sustaining waters of the Nile.[72] In more elaborate temples, such as the temple of Isis in Rome's Campus Martius, for example, Egyptian motifs included sphinxes and obelisks. Egyptian themes in Isiac temples thus expressed a strong identification between the goddess and her homeland, cultivating the sacred atmosphere of Egypt and thereby enhancing the devotee's experience and sense of proximity to the goddess.[73] Onomastica (the study of names) also indicates an identification with Egypt among non-Egyptian devotees; Roman initiates adopted names derived from Isis or Memphis, linking themselves publicly with the goddess and her sacred geography.[74]

In contrast to the previous examples, which oriented communities toward specific geographic regions, early Christians mapped a collective identity onto the breadth of the Roman Empire; Christian writers, beginning with Paul, express the notion that Christians, wherever they are located, belong to a geographically dispersed network of believers, united through their common worship of Jesus Christ.[75] Christian identity was not bound by any location, but realized through the performative act of worship: as Paul states, "calling on the name of our Lord Jesus Christ *in every place*" (1 Corinthians 1:2). Tertullian reaffirms both the geographic spread of Christianity and the universal nature of Christian identity when he boldly claims at the beginning of the third century that he belongs to a race that covers the whole world (*Apologeticus* 37.4–6).

A shift in geographic orientation from Jerusalem to Rome, evident in some early Christian writings, reflects a corresponding shift in self-conception for the early Christian movement from predominantly Judean to predominantly Gentile. Acts of the Apostles, for example, relocates the dramatic focus of the plot from Jerusalem to Rome, reflecting a dramatic ideological transformation at the center of Christianity's collective identity: from orientation toward Jerusalem, the sacred capital of Judaism, to Rome, the sacred capital of a Gentile empire. This transfer of interest from Judaism and Judea toward Gentiles and Rome is reinforced in the Pentecost event (Acts 2), where the grieving disciples of Jesus are said to have suddenly fallen into ecstatic foreign speech, their different tongues mirroring the different nations of the Mediterranean world and signaling the movement's mission to preach the gospel throughout these diverse regions. In Acts of the Apostles and the Apocryphal Acts, Christianity's new self-understanding as a global mission was represented spatially in narratives describing missionary travels.[76]

In addition to geographically oriented collective identity (associated either with a particular locale or conversely with a universal community), identity could be shaped by the built environment through which ancient bodies moved. In these human-created spaces art and architecture contributed to defining social identity in intriguing ways. Rome, for example, was delineated by a sacred boundary, the *pomerium*, that marked off and sanctified the heart of the city. According to legend, the city's eponymous founder, Romulus, murdered his twin brother, Remus, for leaping over the *pomerium* and violating the boundary of his newly founded city (Ovid, *Fasti* 4.833–48; Livy 1.7.2; Dionysius of Halicarnassus, *Roman Antiquities* 1.87.4; Cassius Dio 1.5.3). Since that time, according to Roman history, the *pomerium* served as a sacred and inviolate boundary symbolically protecting the city and delimiting the threshold of sacred and profane activities. During times of danger or inauspicious omens, for example, this symbolic border required reinforcement with purifications; it also marked the limits of political, religious, and military power.[77] Traditionally, it has been understood that only temples of native Roman gods were allowed to be built inside the *pomerium*, differentiating legitimate Roman cult from foreign intruders (Cassius Dio 53.2.4). Yet it is known that foreign cults were welcomed within the *pomerium*; Magna Mater's temple, for example, is still evident on the Palatine. Eric Orlin intriguingly proposes that the Aventine Hill, where most of the city's new cults were situated, should not be understood as excluded from the *pomerium* and thus from Roman acceptance, but rather as a liminal location, both inside the protective city walls of Rome yet outside the ancient sacred perimeter marked by the *pomerium*. Thus, new cults were welcomed within the city and located in a transitional zone associated with the *plebs*, relative newcomers to political power in Rome's history.[78] Orlin's study indicates how space could be demarcated architecturally to articulate ideas about identity and hybridity in an increasingly cosmopolitan city. As the empire grew and incorporated foreign deities and their cults into the religious topography of the capital city (as emblems of Rome's divine mandate to conquer and expand), Rome needed a symbolic way to integrate these newcomers (human and divine) into the fabric of the city.[79]

Seth Schwartz draws our attention to a contrasting situation in Roman Palestine, where religious identity is negotiated within a built environment imposed by an occupying power – an environment in which foreign deities and cults are regarded not as invited guests and signs of divine favor, but as unwelcome intruders. Schwartz investigates a narrative from the rabbinic legal compilation on idolatry, Mishnah Avodah Zarah (3:4), in which the famous Rabban Gamliel engages in a legal discussion with a Hellenistic philosopher, Proklos ben Philosophos, about bathing in a public bath in Akko that was dedicated to and decorated with a statue of Aphrodite.[80] Proklos questions the rabbi's presence in the bathhouse and suggests that he is committing idolatry. Significantly, Rabban Gamliel accuses the goddess of invading his territory: "I did not come within her boundaries; she came into mine." The Gemarrah, which comments on the Mishnah, understands Gamliel to be referring to the goddess's presence in a place designed for public use and hence permitted to Jews as long as they do not benefit from worship there (Babylonian Talmud, *Avodah Zarah* 44b). Boundaries of proper religious practice are thus spatially defined as well as violated by the intrusion of this pagan goddess into the profane territory of a bath. Next, Rabban Gamliel attempts to dissociate the bathhouse from idolatry by severing the bathhouse's cultic and practical functions: "One does not say 'let us make a bathhouse as an ornament for Aphrodite.' Rather one says 'let us make Aphrodite as an ornament for the bathhouse.'" The pragmatic utility of the bathhouse is primary; the attachment of it to Aphrodite is secondary and decorative, not integral to its use and purpose.[81] Finally, he distances the bathhouse and practices that occur in it from proper religion: "Another thing: if they gave you a large sum of money you would not enter to worship your goddess naked, impure from seminal emission, and urinating in front of her! And yet, here she stands above the drain and everyone urinates in her presence." This narrative about Rabban Gamliel's negotiation of religious identity in a public space increasingly occupied by foreign deities can be read as a strategy of resistance to Roman occupation and the increasing paganization of civic space during the second and third centuries CE.

Drawing Boundaries

In Rabban Gamliel's attack on the religious character of Aphrodite's bath he reaffirms the boundaries of Jewish identity based on proper religious practice. While mythic legends and narrative histories provided stories around which collective identities coalesced, the boundaries between groups in the ancient world were often reinforced or marked off by performative acts, such as distinctive clothing, bodily alteration, and dietary practices. Priests of Isis, for example, were identifiable by their shaven heads and white robes; they also observed a prohibition on eating pork and fish and drinking wine. These distinctive observances earned respect from their fellow devotees and ridicule from outsiders.[82] More extreme in many people's eyes were the priests of Cybele, who castrated themselves as an act of devotion to the Mother of the Gods, wore flamboyant clothing and jewelry, and flagellated themselves in an ecstatic frenzy (Apuleius, *Metamorphoses* 8.27). The actions of the priests were regarded as so extreme and insalutary by the Roman senate that Roman citizens were banned from becoming priests or participating in processions (Dionysius of Halicarnassus, *Antiquitates Romanae* 2.19.5). Here we see cultic boundaries erected by religious outsiders to prevent participation in religious performances regarded as too foreign and antithetical to conceptions of Roman identity, based, as Dionysius of Halicarnassus emphasizes (*Antiquitates Romanae* 2.18), on laws of good governance, temperance, and self-control, established by the founder of Rome himself.

Judeans also were well known for their distinctive practices, which set them apart from their neighbors and earned either respect for self-restraint or calumny for a separatist attitude regarded by some as a form of misanthropy.[83] Tacitus (*Historiae* 5.5), for example, describes Jewish practices such as observing the Sabbath, fasts, and circumcision, as well as eating separately and avoiding the beds of foreign women, as aberrant. Tacitus understood these practices to express hatred of mankind; they marked Judeans apart from others in the Mediterranean world and self-consciously served as boundary-marking devices, intended to keep the nation separate and pure. In the ancient world, as in the modern, social relationships were cemented through conviviality – hosting and being hosted, breaking bread and sharing a libation to a god. Jewish dietary restrictions thus complicated Jewish participation in Gentile society; numerous texts from the Hellenistic era attest to this concern and express the importance of adherence to divine law (Philo, *On the Migration of Abraham* 92; Josephus, *Contra Apion* 173–174).[84] Observance of the Sabbath and holidays constituted very public performances of Judean identity that both differentiated Jews from others in the ancient city and fostered cohesion of the community through shared meals, study of the Torah, and narration of the myth that provided the basis for their distinct ethno-religious identity (Josephus, *Contra Apion* 175–181). Rest on the Sabbath was the most public and problematic of Jewish customs; since Jews were unable to engage in normal business on the Sabbath it affected not just social integration, but legal, financial, and political relationships as well (Philo, *On the Migration of Abraham* 91).[85] Many outsiders consequently resented the practice as a form of religiously sanctioned indolence (Tacitus, *Historiae* 5.4) or just plain folly.[86]

Circumcision constituted the most private yet highly charged of these observances. It was denounced as perverse and disgusting by Tacitus (*Historiae* 5.5), mocked by Martial (*Epigrammata* 11.94) and Juvenal (*Satires* 5.14.96–106), and said to have been banned by Hadrian (*Scriptores historiae Augustae: Hadrian* 14.2). Simultaneously, it functioned as the essential mark of Jewish identity (for males at least) and was required of all male converts. If 1 Maccabees (1:15) is to be believed, removing the marks of circumcision was one of the acts that provoked the Maccabean revolt; it was regarded as the ultimate rejection of Jewish identity and violation of the covenant with Yahweh. Under the Hasmonean Dynasty (140–37 BCE) non-Jewish residents of Judea were forcibly converted and compelled to circumcise, demonstrating the significance of this ritual for ethnic-religious identity. Later, rabbinic narratives continued to situate circumcision at the center of Judean identity performance: in one midrash (homiletic exegesis) on Genesis imagines Joseph to have proved himself to his brothers by showing them his circumcision (*Genesis Rabbah.* 93.8). In another story, the Roman emperor Antoninus Pius undergoes circumcision in order to convert to Judaism (Palestinian Talmud, *Megillah* 3:2).[87]

These observances had a performative function for Jews, fostering a sense of ethno-religious solidarity based on shared customs and history. They also functioned to distinguish Jews from outsiders and maintain boundaries between Jews and their neighbors. Josephus remarks, for example, that circumcision was intended to keep the nation from mixing with others (*Antiquitates Judaicae* 1.192); Philo expresses this sentiment more explicitly, when he writes that it was intended to prevent "foreign seed" from being sown (*Quaestiones et Solutiones in Genesin* 3.61). Early Christians practiced these boundary-marking strategies, but they quickly became sites of contest as the movement attracted Gentiles. As early as the mid-first century CE, Paul's letter to the Galatians attests to competing opinions about the necessity of circumcision for Gentile believers. Paul rejected circumcision and observance of dietary restrictions as essential for salvation (Galatians 2:16; Romans 2:25–26); in his anticipation of an imminent apocalypse, he argued that everyone must remain as they are (1 Corinthians 7:26). The Apocalypse of John, in contrast, stridently threatens eschatological violence against those Christians who waiver in their observance of separationist dietary practices (2:14, 20). This debate over observing practices that could be identified as Jewish strategies of religious differentiation continued well into the fourth century, when John Chrysostom (*Against Judaizers*) virulently attacked Jews and Christians who violated what John conceived to be clear boundaries between the two communities.

While early Christians largely abandoned circumcision, dietary restrictions, and the celebration of Jewish holidays as identity markers, they performed their identity in a variety of other ways. Baptism, derived from Jewish purity practices, functioned as an initiation ritual into the Christian community. The earliest extant witness to the practice of baptism, Paul, not only describes it as an initiation ceremony, but also as a total soteriological transformation of the individual, who is changed from a body of sin and death to a new body, Christ's body, which is resurrected and redeemed from sin. With baptism, Paul writes (Romans 6:3–11), the neophyte participates in the death and resurrection of Christ; she is buried with Christ and with Christ dies to sin. But, as Christ was resurrected, so too the Christian is assured resurrection and life in Jesus Christ. Elsewhere Paul describes the individual members of the community as belonging to a single body, Christ (1 Corinthians 12:12; Romans 12:5). Judith Lieu proposes that the practice of nude baptism effected a powerful sense of discontinuity between one's previous life and one's identity as a Christian after baptism.[88] Paul's language of dying and becoming one with Christ – envisioned as a new collective body of believers – signaled a sharp division between insiders and outsiders, between one's old self (either as a polytheist or Judean) and one's new redeemed self, which was imagined as a spiritual body put on at baptism, transforming one from sinful and dead to pure and alive. So absolute was this understanding of forming a new body and taking on a completely new identity that some early writers/apologists claimed Christians formed a new race (*genos*) or people (*ethnos*).[89]

A more radical performance of identity, but one that quickly came to define Christian self-understanding, at least for a sizeable number of

Christians, is martyrdom. Paul describes putting on the body of Christ in baptism, and thereby participating in Christ's death and resurrection. Very early on, this also was understood to include participating in Christ's suffering. Ignatius, for example, proclaims that by extinguishing his corporeal existence between the teeth of wild beasts, he will attain a new identity – that of Christian; through his suffering he will be emancipated by Jesus and resurrected in him (*Pros Romaious* 3–4). For Ignatius and others who shared his line of thinking, martyrdom was the quintessential act of being Christian and the only one that made one worthy of the name.

The significance of martyrdom for early Christians was, however, contested. To the questions, "Did Christ suffer and die?" and "Was he physically resurrected?" there were some Christians who answered affirmatively and others negatively (Ignatius, *Smyrnaeans* 2, 5). This theological debate was inextricably bound up with the formulation of Christian identity and the role of martyrdom in it.[90] Justin, for example, refused to grant Christian identity to those who rejected belief in the resurrection of the body (*Dialogue with Trypho* 80.3). Martyrdom only made sense if predicated on a belief in and an expectation of resurrection. Martyrdom not only performed this understanding of Christian identity, but did so in defiance of Roman social hierarchy and conceptions of civic identity. Roman law categorized people according to social rank, which assumed concrete importance through the rights and honors that accrued to individuals in a judicial setting. As Peter Garnsey and others have pointed out, the elite were protected from physical punishment and public humiliation while lower rank citizens and, especially, slaves were subject to gruesome displays of imperial power inflicted on their physical persons.[91] In the act of martyrdom Christians resisted Roman interpretations of judicial violence as humiliation; they performed a new self-understanding as triumphant victors, conquering cosmic forces of depravity and evil.[92] In revering the broken, mutilated martyr's body through martyr acts and martyrology, Christians codified this counter discourse and challenged Roman social categories, shaping a distinctive Christian self-understanding for centuries.[93] Ironically, martyrdom both drew boundaries between Christians and others by asserting their uncompromising identity in opposition to Rome, and dissolved the hierarchical boundaries imposed by Roman law with a democratizing discourse that treated all bodies as equal and deserving of justice.[94]

Blurring Boundaries

Despite these various ways to denote identity and reinforce boundaries, much recent scholarship has emphasized the great degree to which religious practices and identities in the ancient world were blurred. Drawing on the language of post-colonial theorists such as Homi Bhabha,[95] scholars have recently begun to investigate hybrid identities that straddled competing cultures in the large kingdoms and even vaster empires of the ancient Mediterranean. Provincial subjects of the Roman Empire, for example, understood themselves to be both members of a large sprawling empire – whose military successes signaled divine sanction and whose legal system and stability were coextensive with civilization – and citizens of their local city or region. According to Clifford Ando, residents could not imagine civilized life beyond the boundaries of Roman control.[96] Membership in this extensive community, sometimes described as a single body with the emperor at its head, was actualized in the course of various bureaucratic actions such as registering the birth of children, paying taxes, and taking legal matters to Roman courts for fair judgment. In these tiny, insignificant acts, individuals experienced themselves as citizens of Rome and participants in a vast imperial network that blanketed every aspect of their lives. While to the modern observer these actions may have to do with political or civic identity, Ando demonstrates that they were intimately bound up with religious identity as well, in expressions of the imperial cult; each action required an oath on the Genius (divine spirit) of the emperor, recognizing him as the manifestation of the divine force supporting and sustaining the empire.[97]

The imperial cult thus played a significant role in creating a shared Roman identity that traversed the empire. While it provided a common unifying element, it was also incorporated into particularly local forms of reverence and celebration that honored the cultural diversity of the empire.[98] The insights of post-colonial theory enable us to better understand how the imperial cult contributed to the construction of hybrid identities: denizens of the colonized provinces felt at once to be members both of a large unified empire through their contacts with Roman imperial bureaucracy and emperor cult, and ethnically distinct members of their provincial communities, which continued age-old traditions and customs.

Recent work on material culture brings to light subtle ways that individual families negotiated hybrid identities in local contexts. Phillip Harland, for example, examines funerary inscriptions from the necropolis at Hierapolis in modern Turkey and discovers that many Judeans living in Hierapolis in the second and third centuries CE publicly identified themselves as Judean with symbolic images, such as the menorah, or by explicitly declaring a connection to the Judean community.

One family, for instance, describes themselves as "of the Judeans" and designates as beneficiaries of a tomb-violation penalty "the people of the Judeans."[99] Other tombs use different language to communicate the idea of a community of Judeans, suggesting that Judeans formed some kind of organized association. Yet, this Judean community is clearly not culturally isolated or insular. Harland points out that common use of Phrygian/Greek names and reliance on civic institutions to enforce protection of their tombs indicate a high degree of integration into the Hellenistic structures of the city even while maintaining clear ethnic/religious self-identity.[100] One tomb in particular, the family tomb of P. Aelius Glykon and Aurelia Amia, demonstrates the difficulty of defining individuals or families based on rigid conceptions of religion, ethnicity, or cultural identity. The use of the Roman *tria nomina* (traditional set of three names) to designate P. Aulius Glykon indicates that he held Roman citizenship and proudly displayed it.[101] His Greek cognomen, Glykon, was very common in Phrygia, suggesting that he was born in the region rather than arrived as an immigrant. In which case, Harland argues, his name reflects both Roman and Phrygian dimensions of his identity. Unlike in the previous inscription, Glykon does not explicitly self-identify as a Judean. Rather, he leaves money to two guilds, the purple-dyers and carpet weavers, to perform the customary Roman grave-crowning ceremonies at Passover and Pentecost, two Judean holidays. This suggests that if Glykon and his family were Judean, they had integrated sufficiently to practice local funerary customs. On the other hand, if Glykon and his family were not Judeans, they appear to revere the god of Judea and celebrated Jewish holidays either as converts, "God-Fearers" or, possibly, Christians. Complicating the classification of this family's identity, their epitaph stipulates that the grave-crowning ceremony also be performed at the Roman festival of Kalends, which marked the start of the new year in January with an exchange of sweet gifts and vows for the well-being of the empire.[102]

Nicola Denzey's research on Roman catacombs also reveals ample evidence for hybrid identities, mixed families, and the blurring of religious and cultural boundaries. For example, one family sepulchre, dating to the fourth century CE, indicates that the parents (whose names are now lost) were pagan, but their unmarried daughter was Christian; her tomb is decorated with biblical themes such as Noah's Ark, Jesus raising Lazarus, and Daniel in the lion's den. The mother's crypt, on the other hand, is decorated with pagan symbols and a portrait of Ceres, demonstrating her dedication to the Roman goddess of agricultural abundance.[103] As Denzey adroitly describes, these sepulchres – richly decorated with religious images and themes – were "memory theatres" where the living could situate their beloved deceased in sacred history and perform their religious convictions beyond death's final curtain.[104] They also attest to the religious pluralism within families that embraced multiple faiths both in life and in death.

CONCLUSION

Religious identity in the ancient world was thus multiform, ambivalent, and contingent. Identity emerged from narratives received and recited throughout one's life, which situated one in a sacred history and geography. Identity was further constructed through public and private performances, which moved bodies through space and time, inscribing those narratives into living flesh and the eternal memory of stone. As the constructed and ephemeral nature of ancient religious identities becomes increasingly apparent through studies such as those cited previously, a better and more nuanced understanding of contemporary religious identity is possible.

FURTHER READING

Gruen 2011 examines the complexity of identity across the ancient world – his study is erudite and broad. Lieu 2004 provides a comprehensive and theoretically sophisticated discussion of Christian identity against the backdrop of Judean and Graeco-Roman culture. Cohen 1999 provides an excellent examination of the emergence of Jewish identity in the Roman period, focusing on Palestine and rabbinic evidence. This can be complimented by Gruen 2002 on Diaspora Judaism. Finkelstein and Silberman 2002 present an engaging and clear introduction to material evidence for the emergence of Israelite identity in the context of ancient Near Eastern political history and offers one possible interpretation of the biblical narrative against this background. Dever 2003 offers a similar but alternative view. Mullen 1993 focuses on the formation of Israelite identity through collective memory constructed and idealized by the Biblical narrative.

GLOSSARY

Apocrypha: Early Christian and Jewish writings not included in the Bible.

Dead Sea Scrolls: Sectarian Jewish writings from the Hellenistic and Roman periods, which were hidden in a cave in the Judean Desert during the Roman conquest of Jerusalem in 70 CE.

God-Fearers: A class of people believed to have been affiliated with ancient synagogues, but who were not ethnically Judean or full converts to Judaism. The existence of such a group is disputed.

Israel/Israelite: The collective name of the people who inhabited the central highlands of what is modern Israel/Palestine in the Iron Age (1200–539 BCE). Originally a federation of tribes living in small hamlets, they eventually organized into two monarchic states: Israel in the north and Judah in the south.

Judah/Judean: Refers to the southern Israelite kingdom with its capital in Jerusalem during the Biblical period; often contrasted with Israel, the northern Israelite kingdom based in Samaria. Judea refers to the region, its people, customs, and religion during the period following the Babylonian exile (597–538 BCE) and is the root of the word Judaism. The term "Judean" is also often a better translation of Greek *Ioudaios* than "Jew," which is too closely associated with later rabbinic Judaism to correctly describe the ethnic and geographic orientation of the Greek term.

Hasmonean: The ruling dynasty of Judea (c. 140–37 BCE) established by Simon Macabbaeus, following a successful revolt against Seleucid rule.

Mishnah: Earliest redaction of legal rulings in the rabbinic tradition. Codified around 216 CE in Roman Palestine.

Mount Gerizim: Site of a temple to Yahweh built by the Samaritans in the fifth century BCE but destroyed in the second century BCE by the Hasmonean king, John Hyrcannus, cementing animosity between Jews and Samaritans.

Samaritan: Descendants of Israelites who survived the conquest of the northern Israelite kingdom based in Samaria. According to the Bible, these people intermarried with foreign populations brought by the Assyrians to resettle the region and were therefore considered impure.

Talmud: A commentary on the Mishnah that explains and expands the earlier and more abbreviated law code. There are two Talmudim: one codified in Palestine around 450 CE and one codified in Babylonia around 550 CE. The second is more authoritative and regarded as "the" Talmud by most Jews.

Torah: The Hebrew term for the Pentateuch, the first five books of the Hebrew Bible (Genesis, Exodus, Leviticus, Numbers, and Deuteronomy), believed to have been given to Moses on Mt. Sinai.

Notes

1   Evidence for Mithraic burials: Beard, North, and Price 1998:308; Christian: Denzey 2007:32; Isiac: Tran Tam Tinh 1984:1726–7; Judean: Williams 1998:60.

2   Boyarin 2003:71, building on the arguments of Schwartz 2001a:179.

3   Asad 1993; McCutcheon 1997; and Fitzgerald 2000.

4   Bhabha 1994.

5   Kerby 1991:1.

6   Hall, J. M. 1997:23.

7 Pindar *Isthmian Odes* 2; Herodotus 7.161.3; Euripides *Ion* 589–592; and Aristophanes *Wasps* 1075–1080, among others. See discussions in Gruen 2011:236; Loraux 1984, 2000; Rosivach 1987; and Isaac 2004:114–24.

8 Rosivach 1987:305; Hall, J. M. 1997:53; and Isaac 2004:114 n. 220.

9 Lape 2010:18–19.

10 Killebrew 2005:149; Dever 2003:167; and Finkelstein and Silberman 2002:118.

11 Killebrew 2005:184.

12 Machinist 1994:38–40.

13 Killebrew 2005:184.

14 Machinist 1994:49.

15 Finkelstein and Silberman 2002:302, 311.

16 Machinist 1994:50–1.

17 Gruen 2011.

18 Ibid., 235.

19 Ibid., 236.

20 Ibid., 338–42.

21 Lincoln 1989:20.

22 Gruen 2011:305.

23 Ibid., 306.

24 Apollodorus, *Epitome* 5.21; Livy, *Ab Uurbe Condita* 1.1; Virgil, *Aeneid* 2:634–804.

25 Virgil, *Aeneid* 2.296; Ovid, *Fasti* 1.527–8, 3.30; Dionysius of Halicarnassus, *Antiquities* 2.65.2, 2.66.5.

26 Galinsky 1969:7.

27 Ibid., 6.

28 Lincoln 1989:24–26.

29 Mullen 1993:7–11.

30 Ibid., 12–16.

31 Murray 1993: 282–3.

32 Hall, E. 1989:59 and Lape 2010:19.

33 Loraux 1986:155–171 on funeral orations and Parker 2005:401, 447–8, 462, 470 on festivals and cultic celebrations.

34 Ober 1989:83.

35 Gunderson 1996 and Futrell 1997.

36 Castelli 2004 and Aitken 2004.

37 VanderKam 2011.

38 Hall, E. 1989:80–3.

39 Ibid., 53.

40 Ibid., 35.

41 Stratton 2007:54, 62.

42 Standard Akkadian Version, Tablet Eleven.

43 Hendel 2005:26.

44 Ibid., 28, 29.

45 Ibid., 33.

46 Wiesehöfer 2005:114.

47 Nasrallah 2003.

48 Knust 2006:9.

49 Stratton 2007:131–4.
50 Butler 1999, 1993; Bourdieu 1977; and Bell 1992.
51 Parker 2005:13–14.
52 Ibid., 22.
53 Ibid., 23.
54 Ibid., 43.
55 Aeschylus *Agamemnon* 1277; Parker 2005:21.
56 Parker 2005:170–1.
57 Smith, Morton 1971:15–56; Smith, Mark 2002:19–31; and Finkelstein and Silberman 2002:246–9.
58 Spaeth 1996:83.
59 Ibid., 91.
60 Ibid., 109.
61 Ibid., 111.
62 Gruen 2002:246–7.
63 Williams 1998:75–6.
64 Lieu 2004:223.
65 Gruen 2002:243–4.
66 Bruneau 2006:605–475.
67 Kraabel 1984:45.
68 Bruneau 2006:475–479.
69 Malaise 1984:1634.
70 Takács 1995:5.
71 On temples: Malaise 1984:1639, and on cult images: Tran Tam Tinh 1984:1722.
72 Malaise 1984:1638–39, and on the symbolism of the Nile: Alvar 2008:314–16.
73 Swetnam-Burland 2007:119, 122–3, 128 and Alvar 2008:311–12.
74 Leclant 1984:1705.
75 Lieu 2004:231.
76 Nasrallah 2010:117–8.
77 On auspices: Varro, *De lingua Latina* 5.143. Tribunician powers were extended beyond the *pomerium* for Augustus and all following emperors: Cassius Dio 51.19.6. On lustrations: Tacitus, *Annals* 13.24; *Historiae* 1.871, 4.53; Beard, North, and Price 1998:178.
78 Orlin 2002:8–13.
79 Ibid., 15.
80 Schwartz 2001b:353–61.
81 Ibid., 355.
82 Beard, North, and Price 1998:264 and Malaise 1984:1633.
83 Gruen 2002:45–46.
84 Barclay 1996:436.
85 Ibid., 440.
86 Gruen 2002:49.
87 Cohen 1999:39–49.
88 Lieu 2004:163.
89 Buell 2005 and Lieu 2004:239–68.
90 Perkins 2009:242.

91 Garnsey 1970:127 and Bauman 1996:133.
92 Lieu 2004:200–1; Perkins 2009:254; and Castelli 2004:41.
93 Castelli 2004:1–9.
94 Perkins 2009:255.
95 Bhabha 1994.
96 Ando 2000:55–56.
97 Ibid., 232.
98 Price 1984:62–64.
99 Harland 2009:126.
100 Ibid., 141.
101 Ibid., 132.
102 Ibid., 133.
103 Denzey 2007:51–52.
104 Ibid., 34.

Works Cited

Aitken, Ellen Bradshaw. 2004. *Jesus' Death in Early Christian Memory*. Göttingen.

Alvar, James. 2008. *Romanising Oriental Gods: Myth, Salvation and Ethics in the Cults of Cybele, Isis and Mithras*. Ed. and Trans. Richard Gordon. Leiden and Boston.

Ando, Clifford. 2000. *Imperial Ideology and Provincial Loyalty in the Roman Empire*. Berkeley.

Asad, Talal. 1993. "The Construction of Religion as an Anthropological Category." In *Genealogies of Religion: Discipline and Reasons of Power in Christianity and Islam*, 27–54. Baltimore, MD, and London.

Barclay, John M.G. 1996. *Jews in the Mediterranean Diaspora: From Alexander to Trajan (323 BCE–117 CE)*. Edinburgh.

Bauman, Richard. 1996. *Crime and Punishment in Ancient Rome*. London and New York.

Beard, Mary, John North, and Simon Price. 1998. *Religions of Rome: Volume 1, A History*. Cambridge.

Bell, Catherine. 1992. *Ritual Theory, Ritual Practice*. New York and Oxford.

Bhabha, Homi K. 1994. *The Location of Culture*. London and New York.

Bourdieu, Pierre. 1977. *Outline of a Theory of Practice*. Trans. Richard Nice. Cambridge Studies in Social Anthropology 16. Cambridge.

Boyarin, Daniel. 2003. "Semantic Differences: Or, 'Judaism'/'Christianity'." In *The Ways That Never Parted: Jews and Christians in Late Antiquity and the Early Middle Ages*. Ed. Adam H. Becker and Annette Yoshiko Reed, 65–85. Tübingen.

Bruneau, Philippe. 2006. Études d'Archéologie Délienne. Bulletin de Correspondance Hellénique Supplément 47. Athens.

Buell, Denise Kimber. 2005. *Why This New Race: Ethnic Reasoning in Early Christianity*. New York.

Butler, Judith. 1993. *Bodies That Matter: On the Discursive Limits of "Sex."* New York.

———. 1999. *Gender Trouble: Feminism and the Subversion of Identity*. New York and London.

Castelli, Elizabeth A. 2004. *Martyrdom and Memory: Early Christian Culture Making*. Gender, Theory and Religion. New York.

Cohen, Shaye J. D. 1999. *The Beginnings of Jewishness: Boundaries, Varieties, Uncertainties*. Berkeley and Los Angeles.

Denzey, Nicola. 2007. *The Bone Gatherers: The Lost Worlds of Early Christian Women*. Boston.

Dever, William G. 2003. *Who Were the Early Israelites and Where Did They Come From?* Grand Rapids, MI.

Finkelstein, Israel and Neil Asher Silberman, 2002. *The Bible Unearthed: Archaeology's New Vision of Ancient Israel and the Origin of Its Sacred Texts*. New York and London.

Fitzgerald, Timothy. 2000. *The Ideology of Religious Studies*. New York and Oxford.

Futrell, Alison. 1997. *Blood in the Arena: The Spectacle of Roman Power*. Austin, TX.

Galinsky, G. Karl. 1969. *Aeneas, Sicily, and Rome*. Princeton, NJ.

Garnsey, Peter. 1970. *Social Status and Legal Privilege in the Roman Empire*. Oxford.

Gruen, Erich S. 2002. *Diaspora: Jews amidst Greeks and Romans*. Cambridge, MA.

———. 2011. *Rethinking the Other in Antiquity*. Martin Classical Lectures. Princeton, NJ.

Gunderson, Erik. 1996. "The Ideology of the Arena." *Classical Antiquity* 15: 113–51.

Hall, Edith. 1989. *Inventing the Barbarian: Greek Self-Definition Through Tragedy*. Oxford.

Hall, Jonathan M. 1997. *Ethnic Identity in Greek Antiquity*. Cambridge.

Harland, Philip A. 2009. *Dynamics of Identity in the World of the Early Christians: Associations, Judeans, and Cultural Minorities*. New York.

Hendel, Ronald. 2005. "Genesis 1–11 and Its Mesopotamian Problem." In *Cultural Borrowings and Ethnic Appropriations in Antiquity*. Ed. Erich S. Gruen, 23–36. Oriens et Occidens 8 Geschichte. Stuttgart.

Isaac, Benjamin. 2004. *The Invention of Racism in Classical Antiquity*. Princeton, NJ.

Kerby, Anthony Paul. 1991. *Narrative and the Self*. Studies in Continental Thought. Bloomington, IN.

Killebrew, Ann E. 2005. *Biblical Peoples and Ethnicity*. Atlanta.

Knust, Jennifer Wright. 2006. *Abandoned to Lust: Sexual Slander and Ancient Christianity*. New York.

Kraabel, A. T. 1984. "New Evidence of the Samaritan Diaspora Has Been Found on Delos." *The Biblical Archaeologist* 47: 44–46.

Lape, Susan. 2010. *Race and Citizen Identity in the Classical Athenian Democracy*. Cambridge and New York.

Leclant, Jean. 1984. "Aegyptiaca et milieus isiaques. Recherches sur la diffusion du matérial et des idées égyptiennes." In *Aufstieg und Niedergang der römischen Welt* 2.17.3: 1692–1709.

Lieu, Judith M. 2004. *Christian Identity in the Jewish and Graeco-Roman World.* Oxford.

Lincoln, Bruce. 1989. *Discourse and the Construction of Society: Comparative Studies of Myth, Ritual, and Classification.* New York and Oxford.

Loraux, Nicole. 1984. *Les enfants d'Athéna.* Paris.

———. 1986. *The Invention of Athens: The Funeral Oration in the Classical City.* Trans. Alan Sheridan. Cambridge, MA, and London.

———. 2000. *Born of the Earth: Myth and Politics in Athens.* Trans. Selina Stewart. Ithaca, NY.

Machinist, Peter. 1994. "Outsiders or Insiders: The Biblical View of Emergent Israel and Its Contexts." In *The Other in Jewish Thought and History: Constructions of Jewish Culture and Identity.* Ed. Laurence J. Silverstein and Robert L. Cohn, 35–60. New York.

Malaise, Michel. 1984. "La diffusion des cultes égyptiens dans les provinces euro-péennes de l'Empire romain." In *Aufstieg und Niedergang der römischen Welt* 2.17.3: 1615–91.

McCutcheon, Russell. 1997. *Manufacturing Religion: The Discourse on Sui Generis Religion and the Politics of Nostalgia.* New York and Oxford.

Mullen, E. Theodore. 1993. *Narrative History and Ethnic Boundaries: The Deuteronomistic Historian and the Creation of Israelite National Identity.* Atlanta.

Murray, Oswyn. 1993. *Early Greece.* 2nd ed. Cambridge, MA.

Nasrallah, Laura. 2003. *An Ecstasy of Folly: Prophecy and Authority in Early Christianity.* Cambridge, MA.

———. 2010. *Christian Responses to Roman Art and Architecture: The Second-Century Church amid the Spaces of Empire.* Cambridge and New York.

Ober, Josiah. 1989. *Mass and Elite in Democratic Athens: Rhetoric, Ideology, and the Power of the People.* Princeton, NJ.

Orlin, Eric M. 2002. "Foreign Cults in Republican Rome: Rethinking the Pomerial Rule." *Memoirs of the American Academy in Rome* 47: 1–18.

Parker, Robert. 2005. *Polytheism and Society at Athens.* Oxford and New York.

Perkins, Judith. 2009. "Early Christian and Judicial Bodies." In *Bodies and Boundaries in Graeco-Roman Antiquity.* Ed. Thorsten Fögen and Mireille M. Lee, 237–59. Berlin and New York.

Price, S. R. F. 1984. *Rituals and Power: The Roman Imperial Cult in Asia Minor.* Cambridge.

Rosivach, Vincent J. 1987. "Autochthony and the Athenians." *Classical Quarterly* n.s. 37: 294–306.

Schwartz, Seth. 2001a. *Imperialism and Jewish Society: 200 B.C.E. to 640 C.E.* Princeton, NJ.

———. 2001b. "The Rabbi in Aphrodite's Bath: Palestinian Society and Jewish Identity in the High Roman Empire." In *Being Greek Under Rome: Cultural Identity, the Second Sophistic, and the Development of Empire.* Ed. Simon Goldhill, 335–61. New York.

Smith, Mark S. 2002. *The Early History of God: Yahweh and the Other Deities in Ancient Israel.* Grand Rapids, MI.

Smith, Morton. 1971. *Palestinian Parties and Politics That Shaped the Old Testament.* Lectures on the History of Religions 9. New York.

Spaeth, Barbette Stanley. 1996. *The Roman Goddess Ceres*. Austin, TX.

Stratton, Kimberly. 2007. *Naming the Witch: Magic, Ideology, and Stereotype in the Ancient World*. New York.

Swetnam-Burland, Molly. 2007. "Egyptian Objects, Roman Contexts: A Taste for Aegyptiaca in Italy." In *Nile into Tiber: Egypt in the Roman World. Proceedings of the Third International Conference of Isis Studies, Faculty of Archaeology, Leiden University, May 11–14, 2005*. Ed. Laurent Bricault et al. Leiden.

Takács, Sarolta A. 1995. *Isis and Sarapis in the Roman World*. Leiden and New York.

Tran Tam Tinh, Vincent. 1984. "Etat des études iconographiques relatives à Isis, Sérapis et Sunnaoi Theoi." In *Aufstieg und Niedergang der römischen Welt* 2.17.3: 1710–38.

VanderKam, James C. 2011. "The Wicked Priest Revisited." In *The "Other" in Second Temple Judaism: Essays in Honor of John J. Collins*. Ed. Daniel C. Harlow et al., 350–367. Grand Rapids, MI.

Wiesehöfer, Josef. 2005. "Rūm as Enemy of Iran." In *Cultural Borrowings and Ethnic Appropriations in Antiquity*. Ed. Erich S. Gruen, 105–20. Oriens et Occidens 8 Geschichte. Stuttgart.

Williams, Margaret, ed. 1998. *The Jews among the Greeks and Romans: A Diasporan Sourcebook*. Baltimore, MD.

12   The Body

ELIZABETH A. CASTELLI

> In a sense, of course, "the body" is the wrong topic.
> It is no topic or, perhaps, almost all topics.
>
> Caroline Walker Bynum[1]

For the last thirty years, scholarship on the body across disciplines, historical periods, and archives has flourished at the same time as a series
of interlocking theoretical frameworks has emerged for interpreting the
body's significance. This work explores the body along a variety of tra-
jectories: as a metaphor for social organization, as the locus of the senses
and perception, the performative space of identity, the site for political
conflict, the mediation of religious and symbolic claims, and the working out of the ethical. The category of "the body" is also central to the
study of ancient Mediterranean religions and, indeed, trying to frame a
survey of the field is a particular challenge because the relevant evidence
is so diffuse and ubiquitous. But although "the body" is everywhere in
the ancient world – no topic or almost all topics, as Caroline Walker
Bynum has put it – it is also by no means an essentialized category,
nor is it reducible to a monolithic and self-evidently natural entity.
The body, in other words, is not a pre-existing material fact, but a shifting figure produced and reproduced through a vast array of ideological,
figurative, and symbolic gestures and practical, ritual, habitual enactments. As James Porter makes the point in the introduction to his state-
of-the-field anthology on the classical body a decade ago, "There is no
singular body in the classical world but only a series of embodiments,
hegemonic constructions, discriminations, and materializations, which
together produce the fantasy of 'the (classical) body.'"[2] The body is the

I wish to thank Todd Berzon, Assistant Professor of the History of Christianity at Iliff School
of Theology, who, in his role as my research assistant for this project while a doctoral can-
didate in Religions of Late Antiquity at Columbia University, helped enormously in developing the bibliography for this essay and discussing with me the contours of the essay's
argument.

product of complex and not-always commensurate histories, histories still being documented after decades of theoretically sophisticated and critical research.³ This essay cannot therefore pretend to be an exhaustive survey of every possible instantiation or permutation of the body in ancient Mediterranean religions, but rather it seeks instead to offer some exemplary soundings to mark the contours of the field and to suggest some arenas for further study. This discussion will cut back and forth between representations of the body (the body as signifier, metaphor, and ideological construction) and bodily enactments (performances, rituals, and other embodiments), noting some of the places where the two overlap or intersect.

THE BODY OF GOD(S)

One might well start with the question of the delimitation of the field: that is, which bodies are relevant for this discussion? When speaking of the body in ancient religion, does one include the bodies of gods, angels, demons, humans, and animals? Are all these bodies straightforwardly species or instantiations of the same genus? Moreover, is the body necessarily reducible to corporeality and to the material, and if so, do all bodies share in the same materiality? What is the relationship of various representations of bodies to living bodies – is it mimetic, performative, or idealizing? And what of the body as an empirical, historical, and material entity? Such questions are not only questions for our time; they also engaged philosophers, the writers of religious texts, and theologians in antiquity. Indeed, how different societies answered these questions became an element of ethnographic interest as well as a fault line dividing one religious worldview from another.

Two decades ago, historian of Greek religion Jean-Pierre Vernant explored the Greek vocabulary for the body, beginning with the Presocratics and traveling through Hesiod, reformulating the question of human and divine bodies in relational terms: how does the analogy of the human body, mapped onto divine subjects, allow for certain modes of comparative thinking to come into play?⁴ Vernant begins with a series of fragments attributed to the Presocratic philosopher Xenophanes, all preserved in the *Miscellanies* of the second-century Alexandrian Christian scholar, Clement. These fragments blend theology with anthropology. According to Clement, Xenophanes correctly teaches that there is "one god, greatest among gods and humans, in no way similar to mortals either in body (*demas*) or in thought" (Xenophanes, fr. 23; Clement, *Stromateis* 5.109.1),⁵ yet he also reports that it is nevertheless common for people to attribute human qualities to the gods. Hence, people think that "the gods are born and that they have clothes and speech and bodies like their own" (Xenophanes, fr. 14; Clement, *Stromateis* 5.109.3).[6] Meanwhile, different ethnic groups imagine their gods to resemble them phenotypically: "The Ethiopians say that their gods are snub-nosed and black, the Thracians that theirs have light blue eyes and red hair" (Xenophanes, fr. 16; Clement, *Stromateis* 7.22.1)[7] and even animals, were they able to draw, would portray the divine in species-specific identity with themselves (Xenophanes, fr. 15; Clement, *Stromateis* 5.109.3).[8] Although Clement is obviously using these quotations to critique pagan belief in order to lift up Christian notions of the incorporeal nature of God, Vernant cites these fragments and tacks back to the Greek context, arguing that, if the difference of the human body is marked primarily by its mortality, it "cannot be understood except in reference to what it presupposes: corporeal plenitude, a super-body, the body of the gods."[9] The bodies of gods are apparitional, invisible, "pure luminosity," disguised or veiled, brought into the vocabulary and experience of humans only through approximation, distortion, and metaphor.[10] Codified into a kind of theological orthodoxy by Hesiod's *Theogony*, the divine body in its fullness comes to reflect the idea of orderliness and beauty (cosmos), and "the gods" emerge as individuated subjects of narrative.[11]

In the Roman context, debate over the embodiment of the gods took place primarily in the context of theoretical engagement with Greek philosophical schools.[12] The debate staged in Cicero's *On the Nature of the Gods* is exemplary of some of the main positions taken: the three participants in the dialogue (Velleius, Lucilius, and Cotta) represent three major philosophical schools. The Epicurean Velleius argues that "all people of all races" naturally conceive of the divine in human form, and that the gods' form resembles the human but is "not corporeal but only resembles bodily substance; it does not possess blood, but the semblance of blood" (Cicero, *De Natura Deorum* 1.49). In response, Cotta the skeptical academic argues that the attribution of human form to the divine serves only instrumental purposes either as a means for philosophers to divert "the ignorant" away from immorality and toward proper religious observance or in the service of "superstition," to convince worshippers that their devotions to statues constitute true proximity to the divine (1.77). Contrasting Roman practice to that of Egyptians, Syrians, and "almost any of the uncivilized races," Cotta critiques the Roman arbitrariness of assuming that the gods share human form (1.81–82) when there are so many other (equally parochial) examples of deities incorporated in, for example, animal form.

Even as intellectuals engaged in ongoing debates about the relative merits of anthropomorphizing the gods, including debates over the likelihood that the gods actually have bodies, in both Greek and Roman contexts, the bodies of the gods materialized, as it were, in a rich program of artistic representations: cult statues in which the deities took idealized human form, reliefs in which the deities participated with human practitioners in ritual, and vase paintings and frescoes remediating myths and narratives associated with the gods. These modes of representation were not necessarily understood or received literally,[13] and indeed a literalist reading of such bodily representations was commonly read by elites as a form of superstition, even if an expedient one. (In the *City of God*, for example, Augustine mocks Scaevola the Pontiff and Varro for their insistence that there are religious matters upon which it is best to deceive the general public. "What are the elements which are harmful, if divulged to the general public? ... [Scaevola:] 'The allegation that communities do not have true images of those who really are gods, because the true God has neither sex nor age, nor has he a defined bodily form.' ... Thus he held that it was expedient for communities to be deceived in matters of religion, and Varro himself had no hesitation in saying as much, even in his books on 'Divine Affairs'" [Augustine, *De civitate Dei* 4.27].) Yet the presence of the divine was evoked routinely by statuary and other artistic representations, offering to the gods an occasion for embodiment, even if that embodiment remained analogical and metonymic.[14]

Meanwhile, ancient Israelite, Jewish, and Christian sources raise the problem of the body of God in a somewhat different vein: the biblical Genesis declares that human beings are made in the image of God, and so the question of God's embodiment emerges as a matter of theological anthropology.[15] With the recognition that the human body is material and mortal, Jewish and Christian writers have to contend with the incoherency of the analogy between the image of God, on the one hand, and the lived material fact of human existence, on the other, since God is immortal, unchanging, and perfect whereas human beings – human bodies – are mortal, characterized by changeability and the capacity to decay. In ancient Israelite and Jewish sources, God's perfection inspires a series of distancing pieties: the name of God cannot be spoken nor can humans gaze upon the face of God. That said, as recent scholarly work has shown, one can discern fissures in the wall of separation between the divine and human and see textual hints of corporeal knowledge of God in biblical texts. In a groundbreaking study of this textual tension, Howard Eilberg-Schwartz explores the biblical tradition's complex relationship to the body of God – a masculine-gendered body in intimate relationship with a feminized Israel. As Eilberg-Schwartz demonstrates, in the biblical tradition, when various figures report seeing God, almost all of them avert their gaze from his face and the front of his body, "those parts of the deity's body that play a critical role in our judgments about a human figure's sex."[16] Eilberg-Schwartz argues further that the aniconic impulse within the Hebrew Bible epitomizes the discomfort with "the nakedness of the father," a discomfort that results in the aversion of the gaze and the suppression of the very ideas of both the sex and the body of God. In a more recent contribution to the discussion of ancient Israel, Benjamin Sommer argues for the notion of a "fluidity of divine selfhood" manifest in a "multiplicity of divine embodiment" – a notion present, he argues, in both the broader Near Eastern context and the more narrowly construed monotheistic Israelite context, particularly in the older strands of tradition preserved in the Pentateuch, the first five books of the Hebrew Bible.[17] Operating with an expansive and abstracted definition of "body" – "something located in a particular place at a particular time, whatever its shape or substance"[18] – Sommer seeks to complicate and diversify the traditional understanding of God in the Hebrew Bible as manifest only in God's name or God's glory, the dominant argument of two of the four underlying sources of the Pentateuch, the Deuteronomist (whose work is preserved in the book of Deuteronomy) and the Priestly source (whose contents appear throughout the Pentateuch and are concerned with regulating elements of communal life relevant to ritual and the Temple). Sommer's approach highlights tensions and debates within Israelite traditions, especially traditions that make claims about theophany.

As the tradition developed into the rabbinic period, attention returned to the question of the human body as the image of God: Adam's body before his sin against God is "not necessarily the physical body with which we are acquainted. Adam's body is a body of light."[19] What this claim has to say about the body of God remains a source of controversy and contention as, even when staying within the corpus of Hebrew mystical literature, with its emphasis on the luminosity of the divine, "it is still impossible to sidestep the issue of God's having an actual body whence the light derives, very similar in form to the human body."[20] Moreover, in spite of the biblical prohibition against representations of the divine (e.g., idolatry), in ordinary religious observance – in prayer, for example – some of the rabbis urged "proper intentionality in prayer ... predicated on the iconic visualization of the divine within the imagination," in short, a mental conjuring of an image of the embodied divine in the service of directing the heart toward God.[21]

Christians meanwhile took the question of the body of God in a radically different direction – the New Testament asserts that God's word itself "became flesh," as the prologue to the Gospel of John puts it, and suffered a bodily death by public crucifixion, as all the gospels' passion narratives and Paul's epistles and other New Testament writings commonly assert.[22] As Christian theology expanded on the scriptural characterization of Jesus as the literal son of God, a full-blown theology of incarnation emerged, where the body of Jesus functions homeopathically to neutralize human sin, which itself is corporealized in the human experience of pain and mortality. The theology of the incarnation was not universally embraced by all early Christian thinkers, to be sure: The notion of an embodied god, especially one subject to the ordinary vicissitudes of suffering and mortality, was for some theologically incoherent, hence the counter-theologies of "docetism" (in which the divine Jesus only *seemed* to suffer) and the miraculous splitting of the divine and bodily aspects of Jesus at the crucifixion, whereby the mortal body suffered and died but the Christ-essence separated from the body in advance. Just so, for example, in the second century Irenaeus, who wrote voluminously against "heresy," attributed to the Christian teacher Basilides the (for Irenaeus, false) doctrine of Jesus' merely apparent embodiment: "[according to Basilides] For since he was an incorporeal power, and the Nous [mind] of the unborn father, he transfigured himself as he pleased, and thus ascended to him who had sent him, deriding them, inasmuch as he could not be laid hold of, and was invisible to all … so that it is not incumbent on us to confess him who was crucified, but him who came in the form of a man, and was thought to be crucified, and was called Jesus, and was sent by the father, that by this dispensation he might destroy the works of the makers of the world.… Salvation belongs to the soul alone, for the body is by nature subject to corruption" (Irenaeus, *Adversus Haereses* 1.24, 4–5). Meanwhile, Valentinian texts – gnostic sources associated with the early Christian teacher Valentinus – negotiate the problem of the divine embodiment in a variety of ways:[23] the *Tripartite Tractate*, for example, calls the Son "the body of the incorporeal" (*Tripartite Tractate* 66.14)[24] and the Savior "in fact … a bodily image of something unitary, namely the All" (*Tripartite Tractate* 116.30).[25] The *Excerpts of Theodotus* report that Jesus clothed himself in the invisible psychic Christ, whose invisibility required the creation of a sensible body introduced into the sensible world (Clement, *Excerpts of Theodotus* 59, 1–4). And at the moment of the crucifixion, the spirit withdrew temporarily from the physical body of Christ in order to trap death in the body, which is then dispatched by the Savior producing a body from which the passions have fallen away (61, 6–8).

Christian theology of salvation through the physical suffering of an embodied god soon drew on a series of other associations that are relevant to a consideration of the body: Jesus' death configured as an atoning sacrifice imaginatively translates the human body of Jesus into the body of a sacrificial lamb. The notion of creation in the image of God meanwhile feeds into an ethical imperative of the imitation of Christ – an imitation focused particularly on the suffering of Jesus, hence the repeated mapping of the figure of the crucified Christ onto the bodies of suffering martyrs. One thinks, for example, of the miraculous transformation of the slave girl, Blandina, in the *Martyrs of Vienne and Lyon*, whose degraded and violated body shape-shifted before the eyes of her fellow martyrs so that she came to embody the figure of Christ crucified.

COSMOLOGY AND THE CREATION OF THE HUMAN BODY

If theorization of the divine body occupied a central place in ancient philosophical and religious texts, so too did the matter of cosmology and the elaboration of a notion of creation as a matter of the body. Moreover, ancient theorists articulated the relationship between the cosmos and the creaturely as a matter of harmonious recapitulation – the macrocosm of the cosmos replicated in the microcosm of the human body and its senses. Plato's *Timaeus*, a theological account of creation, emphasizes the embodied character of everything that comes into existence: "Now that which has come into existence must needs be of bodily form, visible and tangible" (*Timaeus* 31b; see also 28b–c). The cosmos, constituted of all the fire, water, air, and earth in existence – without remainder – is itself a body characterized by completeness, perfection, sphericality, and immortality (*Timaeus* 32c–34b): "smooth and even and equal on all sides from the center, a whole and perfect body compounded of perfect bodies" (34b). As the text moves on to describe the creation of humanity, the demiurge (creator) takes the remnants of the material comprising the soul of the universe and creates many souls from it, implanting them by necessity into bodies, which are comprised of the same material as the cosmos (earth, air, water, and fire). Yet these bodies, unlike the body of the universe, "are subject to influx and efflux," from which follows a series of effects that will come to characterize all human life in its embodied form: first, "sensation that is innate and common to all proceeding from violent affections"; second, "desire mingled with pleasure and pain"; and "fear and anger and all such emotions as are naturally allied thereto, and all such as are of a different and opposite character." Those who gain mastery over the senses, over desire, and over all other strong passions will live justly (*Timaeus* 42a–b). The text goes on to reflect at some length on the experience of the soul in the body, analogizing it to being swept up by a powerful river (of sensation): "Still greater was the tumult produced within each creature as a result of the colliding bodies, when the body of a creature happened to meet and collide with alien fire from without, or with a solid lump of earth or liquid glidings of waters, or when it was overtaken by a tempest of winds driven by air, and when the motions due to all these causes rushing through the body impinged upon the soul" (*Timaeus* 43c). The senses of vision and hearing constitute embodied experiences of the world that offer the soul access to the rational organization of the cosmos and its harmonies.

Plato's framing of creation as a process of embodiment recapitulating the structures of cosmic perfection is remediated centuries later in Alexandria at the hands of the Jewish philosopher Philo, whose allegorizing project vis-à-vis the Hebrew Bible channels a Platonic worldview. Philo recapitulates Plato's understanding of the microcosmic/macrocosmic relationship between the cosmos and the human form: "Every person, in respect of his mind, is allied to the divine reason, having come into being as a copy or fragment or ray of that blessed nature, but in the structure of his body he is allied to all the world, for he is compounded of the same things, earth, water, air, and fire, each of the elements having contributed the share that falls to each, to complete a material absolutely sufficient in itself for the creator to take in order to fashion this visible image" (Philo, *De opificio mundi* 146). Philo also takes up the image of the raging river of sensation to describe the experience of the rational soul, buffeted by passions, always in danger of being swept away (e.g., Philo, *De fuga et inventione* 91; *De confusione linguarum* 23, etc.).

The *Timaeus* extends its narrative about the creation of the human body by differentiating its various elements, organs, and functions. The human head, for example, in its roundness, imitates the spherical shape of the cosmos and is "the most divine part and reigning over all the parts within us" (*Timaeus* 44d). Philo echoes this hierarchicalizing of the body, calling the face (where God breathed life into the human being) "the lordliest part of the body, where the senses are stationed like bodyguards to the great king, the mind" (Philo, *De specialibus legibus* 4.123). The senses, too, are arranged hierarchically in this Platonic genealogy: sight is the loftiest of the senses, the mechanism by which the intellect is developed and the soul instructed (Plato, *Timaeus* 45b–d). Philo meanwhile distinguishes between sight and the four other senses, the four others conceptually aligned with slavery while sight "had the strength to stretch its neck upwards, and to look, and to find in the contemplation of the world and its contents pleasures far better than those of the world" (Philo, *De Abrahamo* 164). Allegorically linking the five senses to the five cities of Sodom (of Genesis 19), Philo argues that sight is the one city of the five that God did not destroy "because its range is not confined to mortal things, as theirs is, but it aspires to find a new home amid imperishable beings and rejoice in their contemplation" (*De Abrahamo* 165).

The Platonic concern over "influx and efflux" expressed in the *Timaeus* comes to be echoed in other religious texts from antiquity, marking a radical difference between the divine and the created worlds. The porousness of bodies, their capacity to consume and to expel, and the messiness and smelliness of these processes all come to occupy a large place in the religious imaginary of ancient, late ancient, and medieval cultures.[26] Rabbinic sources also worried about how the body and its functions might impinge on one's pursuit of the life of a sage.[27]

Gnostic sources (what Williams will call "biblical demiurgical" sources[28] – sources that blend biblical mythology with [neo-]Platonic philosophy) address this problem in a different way, splitting the occasion of the creation of the human body into two distinct parts. In the gnostic *Apocryphon of John*, for example, the body is created in two separate stages: the first body is the psychic body, created in the image of the divine human; the second body is the material body, cobbled together out of the four elements (earth, air, water, and fire). Glossing and expanding on Genesis 1:26 ("Let us make a human being in our image"), the text describes the creation of the elements of the soul of the body: "The powers began to create: The first one, goodness, created a soul of bone. The second, forethought, created a soul of sinew. The third, divinity, created a soul of flesh. The fourth, lordship, created a soul of marrow. The fifth, kingdom, created a soul of blood. The sixth, jealousy, created a soul of skin. The seventh, understanding, created a soul of hair" (*Apocryphon of John* 15.14–22).[29] From here, a throng of angels, receiving these seven psychical substances, begins to create the body, and the text carefully names each angel and its responsibility for creating parts of the psychic body of Adam: "The first one, who is Raphao, began by creating the head, Abron created the skill, Meniggesstroeth created the brain, Asterechme the right eye, Thaspomocha the left eye ..." and so on, working from head to toe (*Apocryphon of John* 15.29–17.6), followed by another series of angels who activate the limbs of the body (*Apocryphon of John* 17.10–26).[30] The physical body of Adam emerges in this context as a response by the archons and the angels to imprison the psychic Adam whose "ability to think was greater than that of all the creators" (*Apocryphon of John* 20.31).[31] "The rulers brought Adam into the shadow of death so that they might produce a figure again, from earth, water, fire, and spirit that comes from matter – that is, from the ignorance of darkness, and desire, and their own phony spirit. This figure is the cave for remodeling the body that these criminals put on the human, the fetter of forgetfulness. Adam became a mortal person, the first to descend and the first to become estranged" (*Apocryphon of John* 21.4–13).[32]

BODY AS METAPHOR AND ALLEGORY

Religious texts from the Roman period adapt reigning philosophical interpretations of the body for theological ends in a variety of examples. Notable among such adaptations is the adoption by Paul in 1 Corinthians of the figure of the body as a metaphor for the Christian community (1 Corinthians 12:12–31). The passage comes in the midst of an extended argument that Paul is mounting against members of the Corinthian community who, from his perspective, have embraced too individualistic an ethic, paying insufficient attention to the communitarian commitments required of Christians. Hence, he adopts a Stoic notion of the body and translates it into a Christian idiom: "For just as the body is one and has many members, and all the members of the body, being many, are one body, so it is with Christ." Pointing out that the body would not function without its parts being differentiated nor would it function if all those different parts were not in full operation, Paul goes on to argue that the community *is* the body of Christ, made up of many different elements but all joined together in a single, unified body.

Paul's discourse of the body in 1 Corinthians is much more complex than this – the body figures not only as a symbol or metaphor for the community, but is the site where ordinary physical activity (e.g., eating, engaging in sexual activity), ritual life (e.g., the Eucharist), prophetic activity, and even the resurrection are theorized and analyzed. As with many sources from antiquity, the gendered body comes into full view in Paul's arguments, especially in his worrying over the disruption of conventional hierarchies through the inspirited enthusiasms of the Corinthian prophets (see 1 Corinthians 11:2–16), hierarchies that are simultaneously social and theological. In these passages, the individual body's activities reflect on the life of the social body.[33]

A slightly different take on the body as a metaphor or symbol emerges in the writings of first-century Jewish philosopher and biblical interpreter

Philo, who reads the history of Israel through allegorical lenses and interprets Egypt – a geographical region possessing a role of great significance
in the first five books of the Hebrew Bible – as itself "the land of the
body."[34] Philo follows the general framework of Platonic ideology, separating the soul and the body and viewing the body as a corpse, a tomb, a
prison of the soul. The image turns up at various points in Philo's biblical interpretation. See, for example, the end of Book I of his *Allegorical
Interpretation*: "For Heraclitus, following the teaching of Moses on this
point, says: 'We live their death, and are dead to their life,' which means
that now, when we are living, the soul is dead and has been entombed in
the body as in a sepulchre, but if we die, the soul lives its own life and is
released from the evil corpse to which it was tied, the body" (Philo, *Legum
allegoriae* 1.108 [translation adapted from the Loeb Classical Library]; see
Plato, *Gorgias* 493A, *Cratylus* 400B; see also *Legum allegoriae* 3.69: "For
he is well aware that the body ... is wicked and a plotter against the soul,
and is even a corpse and a dead thing. For you must make up your mind
that we are each of us nothing but corpse-bearers, the soul raising up and
carrying without toil the body which of itself is a corpse").

Throughout Philo's corpus, Egypt figures as the land of the body.
Exemplary of this treatment is his extended treatise on Genesis 12:1–
4, 6 in *On the Migration of Abraham*. Interpreting the Hebrews of the
Genesis text as the mind or the soul on a journey away from the passions, Philo interprets Moses as the guide who will lead "the population
of the soul away from Egypt, the body" (*De migratione Abrahami* 15). He
speaks of the historic exodus from Egypt as the abandonment of "all the
bodily region" (*De migratione Abrahami* 151), soon afterwards calling
Egypt again "the country of the body" (*De migratione Abrahami* 154). A
few paragraphs later, "the concerns of the body" appears in apposition to
the name Egypt (*De migratione Abrahami* 160). In this and other texts,
Philo takes advantage of the trope of travel and migration to emphasize
the ancients' role in his allegorical framing as "the soul" escaping from
the confines and demands of the body.

PURITY

Religion and the body intersect in ancient Mediterranean contexts at
many points, but nowhere more formatively than in the theorization
of purity and pollution and the practices surrounding them. Purity systems separate the material world into distinct categories, and they are
particularly concerned with the policing of the boundaries in between.
Whereas some elements of the purity system are concerned with

everyday life – as, for example, the kosher laws codified in the Mishnah and Talmud for Judaism – others affect the ritual life of the community, hence the extensive concern over ritual purity and its relationship to sacrificial culture found in Greek and Jewish sources. Although purity systems concern a wide variety of material elements, the human body figures prominently in these systems. One does not need to be a card-carrying follower of structural anthropologist Mary Douglas, whose canonical *Purity and Danger* has borne a heavy burden in purity discussions in antiquity and elsewhere,[35] to notice that purity regulations are often most highly articulated on occasions when boundaries are being crossed – the boundaries of the body (e.g., various forms of incorporation – eating, for example, or sexual activity), the boundaries separating one class of reality from another (e.g., human/divine), the boundaries between one mode of life and another (e.g., birth, marriage, death), and so on.

Purity concerns, even those deriving from the visceral and almost intuitive realms (e.g., what Robert Parker in his study of purity and pollution in early Greek culture calls "natural pollution" – birth and death),[36] are in antiquity most often still inscribed under the sign of the sacred or the religious. That is, these natural, inevitable, even routine elements of human embodied experience – reproduction and death – are simultaneously that which separates the mortal from the immortal and that which is "especially repugnant to the gods."[37] Pollution in these contexts is tactile and contagious, requiring rituals of washing, periods of exclusion from holy spaces, and interruptions in quotidian life. Failure to attend to the purity requirements circulating around death and birth could produce effects felt by a whole community. Parker cites the famous example of Sophocles's *Antigone*, where the material fate of the unburied corpse of Polyneices signals damnation for the city: "scraps of the corpse, dropped by birds of prey on the altars, doused the sacrificial fires, and doomed the city to godlessness" (see Sophocles *Antigone* 999–1015).[38]

Bodily purity impinges on communal religious life in different ways, but is perhaps most crucial in the maintenance of ritual purity. The biblical source for purity regulations – the book of Leviticus – concerns itself overwhelmingly with maintaining the holiness of the temple, where sacrifices take place. Hence, the regulations concerning purity focus on the body of the priest, who performs the sacrifices, who enters the holy of holies at the center of the temple once a year, and who stands in for the community as a whole in the temple cult. After the destruction of the temple in 70 CE, the rabbis took up the challenge of recreating an idealized, restored Jewish life organized around a temple that was no longer there, and ritual purity remained a centerpiece of their codification of the law and tradition in the Mishnah and the Talmud.

The body is not an essential, dehistoricized phenomenon, independent of the contexts that suffuse it with meaning, nor is it illuminating to view "purity" as a transhistorical abstraction, despite the strong history of structuralist anthropology in the theoretical framing of the matter. Levitical and rabbinic proscriptions of the behavior of the menstruating woman (*niddah*) are a case in point. In Leviticus, menstrual pollution appears in two distinct contexts: in Leviticus 15, menstruation is a matter of ritual pollution and purity, whereas in Leviticus 18, menstruation is addressed as an occasion for the prohibition of sexual relations between husband and wife – not a matter related (directly, at least) to matters of ritual purity but rather one of moral purity. Some have argued that Leviticus 15 lost its import and applicability upon the destruction of the Jerusalem temple, when matters of priestly purity to perform sacrifices were rendered irrelevant by historical events. That said, the rabbis continued to elevate the ritual purity side of the argument, even when discussing the prohibition of sexual activity by menstruating women with their husbands. In her extended discussion of rabbinic arguments about the pollution of menstruation and the purity requirements surrounding it, Charlotte Fonrobert emphasizes the discursive character of rabbinical argumentation, through which male and female bodies come to be constituted through figuration and metaphor (e.g., maleness as exteriority, femaleness as interiority, and so on).[39] As feminist critiques of ancient sources have often observed, the sources often use the female body as the site of rhetorical contestation. Just so, rather than providing a window onto the lived experience of embodied historical women, these texts more often offer insight into the logic of men's arguments about how the world is or should be. Hence, when discussing the rabbinical sources concerning the menstruating body, Fonrobert cautions against drawing facile historical conclusions about women's history even as she strives to unearth a counter-discourse produced within the text itself.

THE BODY OF THE EVERYDAY: THE SUFFERING BODY

At the beginning of his chapter on the body in gnostic (or, using his neologism, "biblical demiurgical") sources, Michael A. Williams cites a passage from the second-century Christian heresiologist, Irenaeus of Lyon, who offers a rare physical description of a person who has fallen under the sway of Valentinianism.[40] This person is "one puffed up to such an extent, that he thinks he is neither in heaven nor on earth, but that he has passed within the Pleroma; and having already embraced his angel, he walks with a strutting gait and a supercilious countenance, possessing all the pompous air of a cock. There are those among them who assert that that man who comes from above ought to follow a good course of conduct; wherefore they do also pretend a gravity [of demeanor] with a certain superciliousness" (*Adversus Haereses* 3.15.2). Irenaeus's description is neither neutral nor uninterested; it emerges from a long polemical discussion of forms of Christian practice and belief that Irenaeus finds objectionable. Still, Williams notes that the passage is noteworthy precisely because of its relative rarity: how often does the body's appearance and movement in an ordinary social frame come to be described in ancient sources, especially in testimony about how religious conviction produces bodily gestures that communicate?

The body that moves through and occupies space, the body shaped by appetites and desires, the body whose boundaries are breached through acts of ordinary physicality (e.g., eating and drinking), the body whose postures in relation to society and the divine come to be ritualized in all sorts of ways – this body also occupies a critical place in our understanding of corporeality in relation to the religious. So, too, the body that ails.

If the developed world with its forms of medical technology and pharmacological interventions imagines the default of human existence to be health and wellness,[41] it is important to remember that for most other periods of history and for many developing societies, pain and physical suffering and illness and disease are far more the norms than the exceptions. In the ancient Mediterranean, the realms of medicine and religion, magic and miracle all offered a variety of forms of relief to those who were injured or ill. The boundaries between these specialized domains were often fluid and often open to contestation as practitioners depended upon different modes of specialist training, theories of the body and disease, and sometimes competing structures of authority to undergird their practices. But what is most striking is not the creation of boundaries among these potentially competing domains, but rather how the injured or ill body became the site for the complicated mixing of disciplinary understandings and techniques of intervention. The names for practitioners of the healing arts as they appear in Greek sources suggest some of the variety involved: magicians (*magoi*), root-cutters (*rhizotomoi*), priests (*hiereis*), doctors (*iatroi*), doctor-prophets (*iatromanteis*), purifiers (*kathartai*), and drug-vendors (*pharmakopolai*) all appear in the ancient sources as participants in the work of treating illness and relieving physical and mental suffering.[42] With the emergence of medicine as a distinct field of practice – a *techne* – in the fifth century BCE comes an ever more refined theorization of the body, debates over the potential sources of disease and illness, and a wide range of modalities for addressing their effects.[43] The Hippocratic corpus offers evidence of conflict and competition between the practitioners of medicine and other healing practitioners over both the aetiologies of illnesses and their treatments. This conflict takes place largely on theological terrain, as the anonymous Hippocratic treatise *On the Sacred Disease* makes clear. The writer distinguishes the efforts of "magicians, purifiers, charlatans, and quacks" and those of doctors, arguing that the former seek to conceal their inability to help the sufferers of a particular disease (in this case, epilepsy) by attributing the cause of the disease to the divine. The author goes on to assert that such aetiologies are in fact impious, as are any claims that one might be able to manipulate the divine into changing the course of an illness (*De morbo sacro*1.3 = 6.354–358L).[44] On the other hand, other Hippocratic sources (e.g., *Regimen*) suggest that certain religious performances (e.g., prayer) can be fruitfully included in a regimen of healing practices.[45] Moreover, the medical handbooks from the fifth century routinely urged physicians to turn away those patients who could not be successfully treated, leaving a significant number of suffering bodies ready to seek relief from other sources, including healing sanctuaries.

Although there were numerous deities and cults to which the ill would turn, the Asklepios cult dominated the scene from the fifth century BCE until the Christian suppression of the cult culminating in the sixth century CE.[46] Overwhelmingly, the physical ailments for which people sought relief at the Asklepios sanctuaries were chronic or recurring illnesses.[47] The cures and healings experienced at the sites were publicized by inscribed narratives,[48] and the success of the cult caused physicians, especially in the Roman period, to lay claim to association with Asclepius.

The blending of the medical and the devotional among the chronically ill comes into clear relief in the autobiographical narratives written by Aelius Aristides, the second-century Greek orator who preserves in his *Sacred Tales* a detailed account of his chronic illness and the help he received from Asklepios, physicians, and other practitioners of the healing arts.[49] That individuals suffering from illness and pain could and would seek help from multiple sources is not surprising. The ancient disciplines of healing – medicine, ritual healing, magic (on which more in a moment) – offered different accounts of the nature of the body and its capacity for health. What the Asklepios sanctuary offered Aristides was less a *techne* for healing than an explanatory framework for making sense of his suffering.[50] Physical suffering, when set in a narrative framework, also provided Aristides an ongoing occasion for engagement with the divine, the renarration of his body's frailties as an opportunity to escape them: "The body, susceptible to pain, disease, old age, and death, seems to be a sign of distance from the divine world, but the creation of a story from the minute details of its physicality paradoxically seek to transcend its materiality and make it into a sign of divine favor."[51]

Aristides's narrative about his experiences of chronic illness and his search for healing incorporates yet another important element of the body's participation in ancient religious activity: with its sanctuaries scattered around the Mediterranean (Epidauros, Trikka, Olympia, Aegina, Athens, Corinth, Eleusis, Delphi, Euboea, Crete, Balagrae in North Africa, Tarentum in southern Italy, various cities in Asia Minor, and Rome),[52] the Asklepios cult required travel – or, in the language of religious performance, pilgrimage. Moreover, as art historian Alexia Petsalis-Diomidis shows, pilgrimage was not only about travel (the movement of the body from one location to another) but also a highly articulated sensory experience once the pilgrim had arrived at his or her destination. Exploring the archaeological and architectural remains of the Asklepieion in Pergamon, Petsalis-Diomidis argues "that the architectural context and the system of rules [the *lex sacra*, rules that structured the pilgrim's experience in the sanctuary] provided the physical and conceptual frameworks in which pilgrims experienced the process of sickness and healing."[53] The regulations themselves focused on the pilgrims' bodies, prescribing fasting, (temporary) sexual abstinence, required ritual performances, and even obligatory constraints on clothing and bodily ornamentation.[54] The pilgrim also interacted with the temple environment, not only its topography and architecture but also its iconography; Petsalis-Diomidis argues that this relationship of the pilgrim to the built environment of the sanctuary emphasized a tension at its heart: "A perilous struggle of order and chaos lay at the core of healing pilgrimage to this sanctuary: between order expressed in the architecture and in the regulated bodies of pilgrims, and the chaos of illness and miracle."[55]

If one approach to the problem of illness and disease involved the body of the afflicted traveling to a sanctuary for healing, another approach made healing portable through the production of "magical" remedies, often worn on the body in the form of amulets and other material objects. The widespread evidence for such practices demonstrates just how blurry the line was between "religion" and "magic" in ancient Mediterranean cultures. The Greek magical papyri (*PGM*) contain numerous recipes for treating a wide range of symptoms and maladies: for relief from a scorpion sting (*PGM* 7.193–196; *PGM* 28a.1–7; *PGM* 28b.1–9; *PGM* 28c.1–11), for migraine headaches (*PGM* 7. 199–202), for coughs (*PGM* 7.203–207), for hardening of the breasts (*PGM* 7.208–209), for swollen testicles (*PGM* 7.209–210), for fever (*PGM* 7. 211–214, 218–221; *PGM* 43.1–27, and numerous others), for childbearing (*PGM* 123a.48–50), and other forms of illness.[56] Likewise, Coptic magical sources include a significant collection of healing spells, such as the "Book of Ritual Spells for Medical Problems,"[57] which offers recipes for the relief of "gout, eye disease, pains from teething, fevers, pregnancy and childbirth, abdominal problems, malignancy, skin disease, headaches, toothaches, earaches, hemorrhoids, … constipation, foot disease, mental problems, and the like."[58]

The healing of disease and illness plays an important role in the establishment of religious authority in the Christian tradition. The canonical gospels contain numerous stories of miraculous healing (though it is also striking how often Jesus seeks to distance himself from attributions of miraculous power, repeatedly informing the recently cured that it is their faith and not his intervention that has produced the desired result). Meanwhile, other early Christian sources – the second- and third-century *Apocryphal Acts of the Apostles*, for example, and fourth- and fifth-century hagiographical literature – often attribute healing abilities to the apostles and to various saints. Present in these sources is also an undercurrent of professional competition between religious healers and physicians. For example, in a famous gospel story, which appears in all of the first three New Testament gospels, about the woman who suffers from a twelve-year flow of blood and who seeks a cure by touching Jesus' garment (Mark 5:21–34; Matthew 9:18–22; Luke 8:43–48), two of the three versions of the story draw attention to the inability of others to provide the woman relief. In the earliest version of the story (found in the Gospel of Mark), the woman's desperate condition is signaled by both the suffering she has endured at the hands of doctors and her abject poverty from having spent all her money on failed cures: "And a woman having a flow of blood for twelve years and having suffered a great deal from many doctors and having spent all that she had and was not better but worse" (Mark 5:25–26). Matthew is silent on these details while Luke's text is complicated by scribal variations: "And a woman having a flow of blood for twelve years [(some manuscripts add) who had spent all her living on doctors and who could not be healed by anyone]" (Luke 8:43). Both Mark and (some versions of) Luke thus distinguish between the costly and ineffective quality of care from physicians, on the one hand, and the free, instantaneous, and efficacious healing power of Jesus (though all three versions of the story end with Jesus' trademark "your faith has made you well" [Mark 5:34; Matthew 9:22; Luke 8:48]).

The reception of this story led in different directions. In the first systematic history of the Church written by the fourth-century Christian historian Eusebius of Caesarea, one finds an extended description of a monument erected in Caesarea Philippi, the woman's reported city of origin, to commemorate the story (Eusebius, *Historia ecclesiastica* 7.18.1–4). Eusebius notes that the woman's house was recalled as a local site of significance and that "marvelous memorials of the good deed, which the Savior wrought upon her still remained" there (*Historia ecclesiastica* 7.18.1). He offers a detailed description of a particular monument that represents the woman and Jesus, including the report that "at his [Jesus'] feet on the monument itself a strange species of herb was growing, which climbed up to the border of the double cloak of brass, and acted as an antidote to all kinds of diseases" (*Historia ecclesiastica* 7.18.2). Eusebius is ambivalent about the monument, which he claims to have seen himself on a visit to the city, because he considers artistic representations of its sort to be vestiges of a "pagan habit" (*Historia ecclesiastica* 7.18.4). Nevertheless, his description preserves an important detail about material religion and the belief that divine healing power is contagious (traveling seamlessly and across time from Jesus to a representation of Jesus to the herb that touches the image to the sufferer's body) and efficacious.

Athanasius's fourth-century *Life of Antony*, the founder of desert monasticism, also contains many stories of miraculous healing, including one that references the gospel story of the woman with the issue of blood. In this text, the parents of a girl with a terrible affliction (that caused her eyes, nose, and ears to run with a liquid that, when it fell to the ground, turned into worms) knew and "believed on" the story of Jesus' healing of the woman with the issue of blood, and asked monks to request an audience for their daughter with the hermit Antony. When the monks approach him, Antony already knows the girl's illness and he refuses her admission to see him, declaring himself unworthy: "'Go, and if she be not dead, you will find her healed: for the accomplishment of this is not mine, that she should come to me, wretched man that I am, but her healing is the work of the Savior, who in every place shows His pity to them that call upon Him. Wherefore the Lord has inclined to her as she prayed, and His lovingkindness has declared to me that He will heal the child where she now is'" (Athanasius, *Vita Antonii* 58).

If disease and healing offered occasions for illustrating the supernatural power of God, Jesus, and the saints, the language of disease and healing also operated as a significant metaphor for theological deviance or rectitude.[59] Hence, one of the most influential late-ancient heresiological manuals was entitled the *Panarion* [*The Medicine Chest*], in which the monk and bishop Epiphanius of Salamis detailed the failures and shortcomings of those he called "heretics," offering up the medicine of "orthodoxy" as the only effective cure.

ASCETICISM AND BODILY TRAINING

Bodily disciplines in the service of religious devotion emerge most prominently in the Christian context, where one encounters competing theories of embodiment: on the one hand, the body is a temple of God (1 Corinthians 6:19) but also the locus of desire and potentially uncontrolled appetite (1 Corinthians 7). The emergence of a wide repertoire of bodily renunciations – fasting, sexual renunciation, withdrawal from sociality, bodily mortifications, and so on – set the Christian adept on a complex path toward the angelic life: asceticism is paradoxically a thoroughly embodied practice, and the ascetic needs the body in order to police it and renounce it, even when the goal of asceticism is to shed the earthly body and to take on a different kind of body – what Paul calls in 1 Corinthians (15:35–41) the pneumatic body of the resurrection, what Christian ascetical theorists call the angelic body. For ascetics, daily practices of self-formation were theorized in a wide array of essays on virginity and continence, lionized in hagiographies (saints' lives), while the more ordinary struggles of the ascetic against the pull of the flesh and the world can be discerned in monastic handbooks and rules that address the practical demands of the ascetical life.[60]

Of course, Christians were not the only ascetical practitioners in antiquity, though bodily renunciations under other auspices were not always simple parallels to Christian ascetical virtuosity. In the Roman context, for example, the virginity of Vestal Virgins, who tended the household fire of the goddess Vesta for a period of thirty years' service, linked individual religious functionaries' sexual renunciation with the well-being of the city.[61] Hence, the sexual purity implied by the status as a Vestal Virgin focused not on the spiritual virtuosity of the individual practitioner but rather enabled her to undertake her ritual and ceremonial duties properly. To give another example, priestesses of the goddess

Ceres are traditionally noted for their celibacy during the performance of their duties, and the requirement seems to be practical rather than in the service of personal spiritual advancement.[62] Likewise, in Greek ritual contexts, temporary acts of abstention (from eating and from sexual activity), linked to particular religious observances and to notions of ritual purity, were common but were not aimed at the moral refinement of the practitioner but rather at the assurance that ritual activities would be efficacious.[63]

Meanwhile, Graeco-Roman philosophical schools promoted a range of ascetical practices, practices that aimed at elevating the rational, ensouled qualities of the practitioner and suppressing the material, desire-driven elements of the person. The Neoplatonist philosopher Porphyry, for example, focused on the theme of food and eating in his *On Abstinence from Killing Animals*, the fullest non-Christian text on asceticism surviving from antiquity.[64] Most immediately a treatise that seeks to reconvert his friend Castricius back to a vegetarian diet, *On Abstinence* offers a theory of embodiment that focuses on the effects of certain bodily practices (e.g., eating heavy food). According to Porphyry, the philosophical life requires a light diet since foods that fatten the body strengthen the bond between the body and the soul, restraining the rational soul from its proper activities.[65] Anyone who succeeds in abstaining from excessive or heavy eating escapes "an Iliad of evils" (Porphyry, *On Abstinence* 1.46.2):[66] " a condition of somnolence, intense and frequent illnesses, need for doctors, provocation of sexual desire, heavier exhalations, lots of residue, a heavy chain, robustness that prompts to action" (*On Abstinence* 1.47.2).[67] Elsewhere in Porphyry's body of writing, in his letter on the philosophical life addressed to his wife, he addresses the need for abstinence from both meat and sexual activity as prerequisites for a life of contemplation (Porphyry, *Letter to Marcella* 28).

Meanwhile, the Stoic school laid the groundwork for an asceticism focused on the control of interior drives, pursued through the creation of disciplined habits and performances. Musonius Rufus, the teacher of Epictetus, theorized this mode of living, distinguishing between two forms of practice or training (*askesis*), one focused on the soul alone and the other focused on the soul and the body together (Musonius 6).[68] For Musonius, the cardinal rule for such philosophical training, focused on the integrated character of body and soul, was the principle of moderation (*sophrosyne*), a term that will eventually be taken up by Christian theorists of asceticism to signify "chastity," just as other stoic virtues will make their way rather seamlessly into the Christian ascetical vocabulary. Likewise, the literary genre of lives of philosophers and of holy men, which collected tales of exemplary ascetical discipline – such as Philostratus's *Life* of the Pythagorean holy man Apollonius of Tyana, which records his habits of renunciation, fasting, and bodily mortification,[69] or the earlier *Lives of the Philosophers* collected by Diogenes Laertius – became templates for Christian ascetical hagiographies and collections recording occasions of monastic virtuosity.

Meanwhile, Jewish sources from the turn of the common era preserve important examples of emergent ascetical traditions: ascetical narratives,[70] the Essenes, the Qumran community of the Dead Sea Scrolls,[71] and the Egyptian-Jewish community of the Therapeutae and Therapeutrides documented in Philo's *On the Contemplative Life*.[72] These groups, on one reading, might be categorized as marginal relative to the more mainstream biblical and rabbinical traditions. Yet some scholars have fruitfully refocused their research apparatus to take in a broader frame, finding the ascetic imperative, as literary critic Geoffrey Harpham once called it, scattered throughout Jewish traditions of the Roman period.[73] Steven Fraade's definition of asceticism has become determinative for the study of ancient Jewish asceticism and is cited widely in the literature: "(1) the exercise of disciplined effort toward the goal of spiritual perfection (how ever understood), which requires (2) abstention (whether total or partial, permanent or temporary, individualistic or communalistic) from the satisfaction of otherwise permitted earthly, creaturely desires."[74] Working with this definition and Harpham's capacious notion of the "ascetic imperative," Eliezer Diamond argues that Judaism's requirements of "detailed and extensive self-restriction of all its adherents in matters of sex and diet ... might be said to have an inherently ascetic temperament."[75] Diamond goes on to argue that ascetical abstention, in particular as instantiated in the example of fasting, can either be instrumental and incidental (as he asserts is the case for rabbinic Judaism) or essential (as is the case for Christianity). The instrumental mode of asceticism, he argues, need not frame the body in negative terms but can frame the body as a site for productive religious expression.

Asceticism is one arena where the body operates as a locus for rigorous and often uncompromising religious enactments, but there are others as well. Priests devoted to the cult of Cybele were widely reported to engage in ritual self-castration,[76] and the controversial example of the Christian teacher Origen, who also reportedly undertook to materialize his renunciation through self-mutilation (Eusebius, *Historia ecclesiastica* 6.8.1–3), is but one example in a broader frame of Christians embodying the biblical call to "become eunuchs for the sake of the king-dom of heaven" (Matthew 19:12).[77] Meanwhile, other forms of cutting and marking the body – circumcision,[78] tattooing,[79] stigmatization[80] – are all examples of body-modification in a religious frame.

RESURRECTION OF THE BODY – THE BODY IN THE AFTERLIFE

What happens to the body in the afterlife? In the Christian context, the suffering body of Jesus and ongoing debates concerning its nature as a body intersected with disputations over the character of bodily resur-rection that flourished in the second century among Christian theorists who increasingly posited that the body that is resurrected is the same body of flesh and blood that the resurrected person inhabited in his or her earthly life.[81] Moreover, arguments about bodily resurrection mark the faultlines of religious difference. Those Christians who embraced and taught the resurrection of the body characterized those Christians who did not share this belief as heretics. As Judith Perkins puts it succinctly, "In the second century A.D., belief in the full humanity and material-ity of Jesus' body and its mandate for a material human resurrection was becoming a determinate in establishing Christian identity."[82] Just so, master heresiologist Irenaeus not only posits the resurrection of the body as the *sine qua non* of theological propositions distinguishing true Christians from heretics, he explicitly mobilizes the creation and resur-rection of the body as evidence to support an incontrovertible argument about the power of God: "For if He does not vivify what is mortal, and does not bring back the corruptible to incorruption, He is not a God of power.... Numbers would fail to express the multiplicity of parts in the human frame, which was made in no other way than by the great wis-dom of God. But those things which partake of the skill and wisdom of God, do also partake of His Power" (Irenaeus, *Adversus Haereses* 5.3.2; see also 5.7.1–2).

So thoroughly was the notion of the resurrection of the dead taken up by Christians that it is sometimes surprising to remember that groups within ancient Judaism – notably the Pharisees – also embraced a robust theology of resurrection.[83] Claudia Setzer's exploration of resurrection of the dead as a marker of religious difference emphasizes the absence of a clear position on the character of the body that will be resurrected, according to the Pharisees and the rabbis. "The sources do not use the phrase 'resurrection of the *body*' at all. The only information about the fate of the body is negative, that is, the understanding of resurrection that the Sadducees ridicule in Mark [and the parallel text in Matthew] as still gendered and still sexually active ('Whose wife will she be?'). Now what the Pharisees thought about the continuation of sexual difference and activity we cannot know. In Luke's version he says that sexuality and sexual difference will be erased. Those worthy to attain resurrection neither marry nor are given in marriage. The description in *The Jewish War* (2.5.14 §§162–163) sounds like a form of reincarnation, but most scholars think that Josephus is packaging the Pharisees for his Roman audience."[84] Hence, in these sources the resurrection functions primarily as a social marker in this world, and the body operating as a site for theological reflection, for the moment, recedes materially even as its signifying potential increases.

CONCLUSION

The body as image, as metaphor, as prison, as corpse, as historical artifact, as empirical fact occupies a central place in the religious imagination and religious repertoire of the ancient Mediterranean world. Still, without it, there would be no cosmology, no theology, no ritual, no system of purity, no space for the negotiation of the problem of finitude. But the body is also produced through an endless series of articulations, rearticulations, gestures, habits, theoretical and artistic framings, ritual performances, intentional and unintentional modifications, and more. Bodies marked and resignified by gender, ethnicity, age, status, relative state of health, religious identity and practice, role in family and community and in relation to the state and the created world – all products of complex and layered histories too diffuse and ubiquitous to narrate comprehensively. And so the body remains "no topic or, perhaps, almost all topics."[85]

FURTHER READING

The literature on the body in ancient Mediterranean religions is vast. For theoretical overviews and approaches see Bynum 1995a, Feher with Naddaff and Tazi 1989, Juvin 2010, Roy Porter 1991, and Sullivan 1990. For surveys of the field see Fögen and Lee 2009, Haines-Eitzen and Frank 2009, Montserrat 1998, and James I. Porter 1999. More specialized studies include the following. On Greece: Holmes 2010, Temkin 1991, and Vernant 1989. On Judaism: Boyarin 1993; Eilberg-Schwartz 1990, 1992, 1994; Hoffman 1996; Cohen 2005; and Sommer 2009. On Christianity: Brown 1988; Glancy 2010; Miller 2009; Perkins 2002, 2007, 2009; Seim and Økland 2009; Setzer 2004; and Shaw 1998. On religious healing:

Behr 1968, Edelstein and Edelstein 1945, King 1999, LiDonnici 1995, Temkin 1991, and Wickkiser 2008. On purity and piety (e.g., asceticism): Beard 1980, 1995; Brown 1988; Clark 2001; Diamond 2003; Fraade 1986; Francis 1995; Harpham 1992; and Wills 2006.

Notes

1 Bynum 1995b:1.
2 James Porter 1999:6.
3 See, e.g., Feher et al. 1989; Sullivan 1990; Roy Porter 1991; Bynum 1995a:2, Richlin 1997; Montserrat 1998; and Holmes 2010.
4 Vernant 1989:23.
5 Kirk, Raven and Schofield 1983:fr. 170.
6 Ibid., fr. 167.
7 Ibid., fr. 168.
8 Ibid., fr. 169.
9 Vernant 1989:24.
10 Ibid., 34–39.
11 Ibid., 41.
12 Feeney 1998:76–114.
13 Gordon 1979.
14 Tanner 2001.
15 Moore 1996.
16 Eilberg-Schwartz 1994:77.
17 Sommer 2009:13, 19.
18 Ibid., 2.
19 Gottstein 1994:195.
20 Aaron 1997:313.
21 Wolfson 1996:152.
22 Moore 1996.
23 See Williams 1996:125.
24 Meyer 2007:68.
25 Ibid., 92.
26 See Cuffel 2007.
27 Schofer 2005.
28 Williams 1996.
29 Meyer 2007:119.
30 Ibid., 119–121.
31 Ibid., 125.
32 Ibid., 125.
33 See Martin 1995.
34 Pearce 2007, esp. 81–127.
35 Douglas 1966.
36 Parker 1983:33.
37 Ibid.
38 Ibid., 44.
39 Fonrobert 2000.

40   Williams 1996:116–117.
41   Juvin 2010.
42   Wickkiser 2008:10.
43   Wickkiser 2008 and Holmes 2010.
44   See Wickkiser 2008:24, 30–31.
45   Wickkiser 2008:33.
46   Literary evidence: Edelstein and Edelstein 1945; inscriptional evidence: LiDonnici 1995; and archaeological evidence: Riethmüller 2005 and Melfi 2007.
47   Wickkiser 2008:58 and Wickkiser 2006.
48   See LiDonnici 1995.
49   Behr 1968:169–170.
50   King 1999:279.
51   Ibid., 282; see also Perkins 2002.
52   See Wickkiser 2008:35–37.
53   Petsalis-Diomidis 2006:185.
54   Ibid., 205.
55   Ibid., 218.
56   Betz 1986.
57   *p. Mich.* 136; Worrell 1935:17–37; and Meyer and Smith 1994:83–90.
58   Meyer and Smith 1994:83.
59   Burrus and Vessey 1996 and Reed 2008.
60   Brown 1988; Valantasis 2000; Wimbush 1990; and Brakke 1995.
61   Beard 1980, 1995.
62   Spaeth 1996:115 and Schultz 2006:75–79.
63   Finn 2009:14–18.
64   Clark 2001:41.
65   Ibid., 42.
66   Ibid., 43.
67   Ibid., 43.
68   Lutz 1947:55.
69   Francis 1995:83–129.
70   Wills 2006.
71   Newsom 1992.
72   Taylor 2003.
73   Harpham 1992; see, e.g., Weitzman 2005.
74   Fraade 1986:257.
75   Diamond 2003:11.
76   Roller 1999.
77   Kuefler 2001:245–282.
78   Eilberg-Schwartz 1990; Hoffman 1996; and Cohen 2005.
79   Jones 1987, esp. 144–145, and Burrus 2003.
80   Elm 1996, 1999.
81   Bynum 1995b:26.
82   Perkins 2009:242.
83   See Setzer 2001.
84   Setzer 2001:78–79.
85   Bynum 1995a:2.

Works Cited

Aaron, David H. 1997. "Shedding Light on God's Body in Rabbinic Midrashim: Reflections on the Theory of a Luminous Adam." *Harvard Theological Review* 90: 299–314.

Beard, Mary. 1980. "The Sexual Status of Vestal Virgins." *Journal of Roman Studies* 70: 12–27.

———. 1995. "Rereading (Vestal) Virginity." In *Women in Antiquity: New Assessments*. Ed. Richard Hawley and Barbara Levick, 166–177. New York.

Behr, Charles A. 1968. *Aelius Aristides and The Sacred Tales*. Amsterdam.

Betz, Hans Dieter, ed. 1986. *The Greek Magical Papyri in Translation including the Demotic Spells. Vol. 1: Texts*. Chicago.

Boyarin, Daniel. 1993. *Carnal Israel: Reading Sex in Talmudic Culture*. Berkeley.

Brakke, David. 1995. "The Problematization of Nocturnal Emissions in Early Christian Syria, Egypt, and Gaul." *Journal of Early Christian Studies* 3: 419–460.

Brown, Peter. 1988. *The Body and Society: Men, Women, and Sexual Renunciation in Early Christianity*. New York.

Burrus, Virginia. 2003. "Macrina's Tattoo." *Journal of Medieval and Early Modern Studies* 33: 403–417.

Burrus, Virginia and Mark Vessey, eds. 1996. *The Markings of Heresy: Body, Text, and Community in Late Ancient Christianity*. Special Issue of *Journal of Early Christian Studies* 4: 403–513.

Bynum, Caroline Walker. 1995a. "Why All the Fuss About the Body?: A Medievalist's Perspective." *Critical Inquiry* 22: 1–33.

———. 1995b. *Resurrection of the Body in Western Christianity 200–1336*. New York.

Clark, Gillian. 2001. "Fattening the Soul: Christian Asceticism and Porphyry on Abstinence." *Studia Patristica* 35: 41–51.

Cohen, Shaye. 2005. *Why Aren't Jewish Women Circumcised?: Gender and Covenant in Judaism*. Berkeley.

Cuffel, Alexandra. 2007. *Gendering Disgust in Medieval Religious Polemic*. Notre Dame, IN.

Diamond, Eliezer. 2003. *Holy Men and Hunger Artists: Fasting and Asceticism in Rabbinic Culture*. Oxford.

Douglas, Mary. 1966. *Purity and Danger: An Analysis of Concepts of Pollution and Taboo*. London.

Edelstein, Ludwig and Emma J. Edelstein, eds. 1945. *Asclepius: Collection and Interpretation of the Testimonies*. Baltimore, MD.

Eilberg-Schwartz, Howard. 1990. *The Savage in Judaism: An Anthropology of Israelite Religion and Ancient Judaism*. Bloomington, IN.

———, ed. 1992. *People of the Body: Jews and Judaism from an Embodied Perspective*. Albany, NY.

———. 1994. *God's Phallus and Other Problems for Men and Monotheism*. Beacon.

Elm, Susanna. 1996. "'Pierced By Bronze Needles': Anti-Montanist Charges of Ritual Stigmatization in their Fourth-Century Context." *Journal of Early Christian Studies* 4: 409–439.

———. 1999. "'Sklave Gottes': Stigmata, Bishöfe, und anti-häretische Propaganda im vierten Jahrhundert." *Historische Anthropologie* 8: 345–363.

Feeney, Denis. 1998. *Literature and Religion at Rome: Cultures, Contexts, and Beliefs.* Cambridge.

Feher, Michel, with Ramona Naddaff and Nadia Tazi, eds. 1989. *Fragments for a History of the Human Body, Parts I–III.* New York.

Finn, Richard. 2009. *Asceticism in the Graeco-Roman World.* Cambridge.

Fögen, Thorsten and Mireille M. Lee, eds. 2009. *Bodies and Boundaries in Graeco-Roman Antiquity.* Berlin.

Fonrobert, Charlotte Elisheva. 2000. *Menstrual Purity: Rabbinic and Christian Reconstructions of Biblical Gender.* Stanford.

Fraade, Steven. 1986. "Ascetic Aspects of Ancient Judaism." In *Jewish Spirituality: From the Bible Through the Middle Ages.* Ed. Arthur Green, 253–288. New York.

Francis, James A. 1995. *Subversive Virtue: Asceticism and Authority in the Second-Century Pagan World.* University Park, PA.

Glancy, Jennifer A. 2010. *Corporal Knowledge: Early Christian Bodies.* Oxford.

Gordon, Richard. 1979. "The Real and the Imaginary: Production and Religion in the Greco-Roman World." *Art History* 2: 5–34.

Gottstein, Alon Goshen. 1994. "The Body as Image of God in Rabbinic Literature." *Harvard Theological Review* 87: 171–195.

Haines-Eitzen, Kim and Georgia Frank, eds. 2009. *Bodies and Boundaries in Late Antiquity.* Special issue of *Journal of Early Christian Studies* 17: 167–307.

Harpham, Geoffrey Galt. 1992. *The Ascetic Imperative in Culture and Criticism.* Chicago.

Hoffman, Lawrence A. 1996. *Covenant of Blood: Circumcision and Gender in Rabbinic Judaism.* Chicago.

Holmes, Brooke. 2010. *The Symptom and the Subject: The Emergence of the Physical Body in Ancient Greece.* Princeton, NJ.

Jones, C. P. 1987. "Stigma: Tattooing and Branding in Graeco-Roman Antiquity." *Journal of Roman Studies* 77: 139–155.

Juvin, Hervé. 2010. *The Coming of the Body.* Trans. John Howe. New York.

King, Helen. 1999. "Chronic Pain and the Creation of Narrative." In *Constructions of the Classical Body.* Ed. James I. Porter, 269–286. Ann Arbor, MI.

Kirk, G. S., J. E. Raven, and M. Schofield. 1983. *The Presocratic Philosophers,* 2nd ed. Cambridge.

Kuefler, Mathew. 2001. *The Manly Eunuch: Masculinity, Gender Ambiguity, and Christian Ideology in Late Antiquity.* Chicago.

LiDonnici, Lynn R. 1995. *The Epidaurian Miracle Inscriptions: Text, Translation, and Commentary.* SBL Texts and Translations 36; SBL Graeco-Roman Religions 11. Atlanta.

Lutz, Cora E. 1947. "Musonius Rufus: The Roman Socrates." *Yale Classical Studies* 10: 3–150.

Martin, Dale B. 1995. *The Corinthian Body.* New Haven, CT.

Melfi, Milena. 2007. *I sanctuary di Asclepio in Grecia.* Vol. 1. Rome.

Meyer, Marvin, ed. 2007. *The Nag Hammadi Scriptures: The International Edition.* San Francisco.

Meyer, Marvin and Richard Smith, eds. 1994. *Ancient Christian Magic: Coptic Texts of Ritual Power*. San Francisco.

Miller, Patricia Cox. 2009. *The Corporeal Imagination: Signifying the Holy in Late Ancient Christianity*. Philadelphia.

Montserrat, Dominic, ed. 1998. *Changing Bodies, Changing Meanings: Studies on the Human Body in Antiquity*. London.

Moore, Stephen D. 1996. *God's Gym: Divine Male Bodies of the Bible*. London.

Newsom, Carol A. 1992. "The Case of the Blinking I: Discourse of the Self at Qumran." *Semeia* 57: 13–23.

Parker, Robert. 1983. *Miasma: Pollution and Purification in Early Greek Religion*. Oxford.

Pearce, Sarah K. 2007. *The Land of the Body: Studies in Philo's Representation of Egypt*. Wissenschaftliche Untersuchungen zum Neuen Testament 208. Tübingen.

Perkins, Judith. 2002. "The 'Self' as Sufferer." *Harvard Theological Review* 85: 245–272.

———. 2007. "The Rhetoric of the Material Body in the Passion of Perpetua." In *Mapping Gender in Ancient Religious Discourse*. Ed. Todd Penner and Caroline Vander Stichele, 313–332. Leiden.

———. 2009. "Early Christian and Judicial Bodies." In *Bodies and Boundaries in Graeco-Roman Antiquity*. Ed. Thorsten Fögen and Mireille M. Lee, 237–259. Berlin.

Petsalis-Diomidis, Alexia. 2006. "The Body in Space: Visual Dynamics in Graeco-Roman Healing Pilgrimage." In *Pilgrimage in Graeco-Roman and Early Christian Antiquity: Seeing the Gods*. Ed. Jaś Elsner, 183–218. Oxford.

Porter, James I., ed. 1999. *Constructions of the Classical Body*. Ann Arbor, MI.

Porter, Roy. 1991. "History of the Body." In *New Perspectives on Historical Writing*. Ed. Peter Burke, 206–232. University Park, PA.

Reed, Annette Yoshiko. 2008. "Heresiology and the (Jewish-)Christian Novel: Narrativized Polemics in the Pseudo-Clementine *Homilies*." In *Heresy and Identity in Late Antiquity*. Ed. Eduard Iricinschi and Holger M. Zellentin, 273–298. Texts and Studies in Ancient Judaism 119. Tübingen.

Richlin, Amy. 1997. "Toward a History of Body History." In *Inventing Ancient Culture*. Ed. Mark Golden and Peter Toohey, 16–35. London.

Riethmüller, Jürgen W. 2005. *Asklepios: Heiligtümer und Kulte*. 2 vols. Heidelberg.

Roller, Lynn E. 1999. *In Search of God the Mother: The Cult of Anatolian Cybele*. Berkeley.

Schofer, Jonathan. 2005. "The Beastly Body in Rabbinic Self-Formation." In *Religion and the Self in Antiquity*. Ed. David Brakke, Michael L. Satlow and Steven Weitzman, 197–221. Bloomington, IN.

Schultz, Celia E. 2006. *Women's Religious Activity in the Roman Republic*. Chapel Hill, NC.

Seim, Turid Karlsen and Jorunn Økland, eds. 2009. *Metamorphoses: Resurrection, Body and Transformative Practices in Early Christianity*. Berlin.

Setzer, Claudia. 2001. "Resurrection of the Dead as Symbol and Strategy." *Journal of the American Academy of Religion* 69: 65–101.

———. 2004. *Resurrection of the Body in Early Judaism and Early Christianity: Doctrine, Community, and Self-Definition*. Leiden.

Shaw, Teresa M. 1998. *The Burden of the Flesh: Fasting and Sexuality in Early Christianity*. Minneapolis, MN.

Sommer, Benjamin D. 2009. *The Bodies of God and the World of Ancient Israel*. Cambridge.

Spaeth, Barbette S. 1996. *The Roman Goddess Ceres*. Austin, TX.

Sullivan, Lawrence E. 1990. "Body Works: Knowledge of the Body in the Study of Religion." *History of Religions* 30: 86–99.

Tanner, Jeremy. 2001. "Nature, Culture, and the Body in Classical Greek Religious Art." *World Archaeology* 33: 257–276.

Taylor, Joan. 2003. *Jewish Women Philosophers of First-Century Alexandria: Philo's 'Therapeutae' Reconsidered*. Oxford.

Temkin, Otto. 1991. *Hippocrates in a World of Pagans and Christians*. Baltimore, MD.

Valantasis, Richard, ed. 2000. *Religions of Late Antiquity in Practice*. Princeton, NJ.

Vernant, Jean-Pierre. 1989. "Dim Body, Dazzling Body." In *Fragments for a History of the Human Body, Part I*. Ed. Michel Feher with Ramona Naddaff and Nadia Tazi, 19–47. New York.

Weitzman, Steven. 2005. "Sensory Reform in Deuteronomy." In *Religion and the Self in Antiquity*. Ed. David Brakke, Michael L. Satlow, and Steven Weitzman, 123–139. Bloomington, IN.

Wickkiser, Bronwen L. 2006. "Chronicles of Chronic Cases and Tools of the Trade at Asklepieia." *Archiv für Religionsgeschichte* 8: 25–40.

———. 2008. *Asklepios, Medicine, and the Politics of Healing in Fifth-Century Greece*. Baltimore, MD.

Williams, Michael Allen. 1996. *Rethinking "Gnosticism": An Argument for Dismantling a Dubious Category*. Princeton, NJ.

Wills, Lawrence M. 2006. "Ascetic Theology before Asceticism? Jewish Narratives and the Decentering of the Self." *Journal of the American Academy of Religion* 74: 902–925.

Wimbush, Vincent L., ed. 1990. *Ascetic Behavior in Greco-Roman Antiquity: A Sourcebook*. Minneapolis, MN.

Wolfson, Elliot. 1996. "Iconic Visualization and the Imaginal Body of God: The Role of Intention in the Rabbinic Conception of Prayer." *Modern Theology* 12: 137–162.

Worrell, William H. 1935. "Coptic Magical and Medical Texts." *Orientalia* 4: 1–37, 184–194.

13 Gender

ROSS SHEPARD KRAEMER

INTRODUCTION

Gender as both a concept and a topic of inquiry within the study of the ancient Mediterranean is relatively recent.[1] Both the first and second waves of Euro-American feminism produced increased inquiry into aspects of women and ancient Mediterranean religions, primarily couched in terms of the "roles," "status," and "images" of women, or of male writers' "attitudes" toward women.[2] In the mid-1970s, anthropologists, historians, literary scholars, and those in what was then called women's studies had begun to focus on gender as a category of analysis.[3] By the late 1980s, these insights and arguments began to infiltrate the scholarship both on the ancient Mediterranean generally, and on the study of religions more specifically.[4] Yet at the same time, defining and theorizing gender was highly contested, and remains so.[5] As Haraway pointed out some years ago, gender itself is "a concept developed to contest the naturalization of sexual difference in multiple arenas of struggle," and thus is itself liable to contestation.[6]

With full recognition of the complexity of these questions, for the purpose of this essay, gender designates culturally constructed meanings assigned to or associated with biological sex that vary considerably from one cultural context to another, whether in difference places, different communities, or different historical periods. Gender is the product of human activity, something humans create, sustain, reinforce, and reinterpret, even while in the ancient Mediterranean these meanings are almost always taken to be "natural" rather than "cultural." Further, gender is necessarily relational: ideas about femininity and masculinity never stand in isolation, but are always integrally linked to one another. Feminine is a category that has no meaning except in relation

Portions of this essay are condensed from Kraemer 2008, 2011, with permission of Oxford University Press; with occasional material from Kraemer 1992, 1998.

to masculine, and vice versa.[7] Class, ethnicity, and other components of social location may produce further distinctions. Although gender constructions may themselves be perceived and experienced differently by women and men, the limited amount of evidence from women of any social location in the ancient Mediterranean makes it particularly difficult to determine this.

Several decades of scholarship have illuminated the prevailing constructions of gender and associated constructions of sexuality in the ancient Mediterranean, as well as the centrality of gender in the organization and structure of ancient social life.[8] Central to these constructions are the notions that men are properly active (and penetrating): women are properly passive (and penetrated); gender is always hierarchical, and is an overarching means of expressing hierarchy in other domains (e.g. slavery; human/divine relations, etc.). Gender difference permeated all aspects of ancient social life: meals and foods, dress, sexual practices, bodily comportment, war, education, politics, commerce, and those practices we categorize under the label of religion.[9] Further, in the ancient Mediterranean, the terms we generally translate as woman or women usually encode numerous and complex elements of social identity, including distinctions of physical and social maturity, of rank and class, of licit marriage and so forth: to a considerable degree, this is also true of terms for man and men.[10]

Religions in antiquity are inextricably enmeshed in ancient understandings and contestations of gender. This has enormous consequences for the study of Mediterranean religions. For instance, what seem to be relatively useful source material about women's religions may instead be instances of male authors telling stories about women that invoke gender constructions for a range of ideological purposes, as the case of Livy's account of the Bacchanalia exemplifies. Even the somewhat more reliable evidence for particular practices, drawing, for instance, on epigraphical materials,[11] has illuminated the extent to which religious rites and beliefs performed and authorized prevailing gender constructions, even if they also, at least occasionally, seem to critique them.

WOMEN'S AND MEN'S RELIGIOUS PRACTICES IN THE ANCIENT MEDITERRANEAN

Men and women alike engaged in the range of practices examined throughout this volume. They sought the favor of the gods for themselves, their families, and their cities. They slept in the temples of healing gods and left records of their dreams and cures; they prayed for the health of their loved ones, and fulfilled the vows they had made for such healings with gifts ranging from the modest to the extravagant. They sought the assistance of religious specialists who knew the precise language with which to adjure the various powers to bring them lovers, fame, fortune, and justice. They celebrated agricultural civic festivals. They beseeched the gods for victory against their enemies, and thanked the gods when they were victorious. They supplicated their ancestors regularly, in household rites and mortuary rites; they invoked the wrath of the gods against those who violated the tombs of their families. All too aware of human mortality, they sought the blessings of the immortals after death.

Still, in the ancient Mediterranean, religious practice, like many other aspects of social life, was often gender-specific. Women's particular devotions take center stage in Greek plays such as Euripides' *Bacchae* and Aristophanes' *Thesmophoriazusai*. Pausanius' *Description of Greece* contains numerous accounts of women's festivals of Demeter and Artemis, games in honor of Hera, and a sanctuary to Sosipolis.[12] Ovid's *Fasti* contains accounts of Roman matrons' celebration of the *Matralia* (and its exclusion of enslaved women) and their tending to the statue of Venus.[13] Plutarch's *Moralia* purports to explain a wide range of women's practices: the founding of the temple of Carmenta; the offering of milk, but not wine, to the goddess Rumina; and women washing their heads on the Ides of August.[14] Juvenal's *Satires* includes a scathing depiction of women's devotions to goddesses like Bona Dea and Isis, while the various so-called Hellenistic novels contain rich and considerably less polemical accounts of women's devotions to various deities, including Artemis, Helios and others.[15] Inscriptions from various cult sites prescribe particular rites, such as those for brides and pregnant women worshipping Artemis: a papyrus from Egypt specifies the ritual equipment women need for a festival.[16] Many festivals (some Dionysian rites, the Thesmophoria, the Adonia, the Arkteia, the Matralia, and the sacra Cereris) were celebrated primarily, if not exclusively, by one sex or the other, as suggested not only by accounts in literary sources but also to some degree by extant inscriptions.[17] Rites performed on behalf of the body politic were particularly the domain of men, although the converse is not as true as many might think: domestic religion was similarly the domain of men, even while women's devotions were frequently focused on the health and welfare of the more immediate family and household.[18]

Animal sacrifice, however, was generally the domain of men, although there is some evidence for priestesses performing animal sacrifice, and women could sometimes eat the meat.[19] Such rites, and the meals attendant on them, were a major component of most ancient Mediterranean religions, with some significant exceptions. Judeans[20] had regularly engaged in animal sacrifices at the Jerusalem temple until its destruction by the Romans in 70 CE. Some philosophical schools disdained animal sacrifice on principle. Christians, too, abstained from animal sacrifice, although some of their early opposition appears due more to their rejection of deities other than the God of Israel, than to an inherent opposition to animal sacrifice.[21]

Religious practice in ancient Israel in particular was often gender-specific. The ancient Israelite priesthood, which had sole responsibility for the animal sacrifices in the temple in Jerusalem, was a hereditary male institution, passed from father to son. The Hebrew Bible mandates only the participation of adult men in the key festivals of Pesach, Sukkoth, and Shavuot.[22] Much of the biblical law is couched in language that explicitly envisions male actors (the sons of Israel) or subsets of male actors, such as the priests and their assistants. Yet elsewhere biblical authors envisioned or mandated the presence of women as well (e.g., the account of the receipt of the Torah in Deuteronomy 31:12, or the reading of the reconstituted law in Nehemiah 8:2ff., after the return to the land of Israel from Babylonian exile). In the first century CE, the Judean author Flavius Josephus describes the second Temple, expanded and renovated under Herod the Great in the late first century BCE, as having a series of courtyards progressively restricted by both gender and ethnicity, with women excluded from the courtyard open to all ritually pure Judean men, and of course from the innermost priestly courtyard.[23]

In the Hellenistic and early Roman periods, women may have attended major Judean festivals as well, although the extent of their participation, especially in the associated sacrifices, particularly the Passover lamb, is less clear. The early Christian gospels of Mark, Matthew, and Luke depict Jesus eating the Passover seder only with male disciples, although how accurately they depict first-century practices is uncertain. Rabbinic regulations and accounts collated from the third century CE on often seem to envision the Passover seder as restricted to males, although rabbinic accounts, too, are often unreliable evidence for actual Judean practices, particularly practices other than those of the rabbis themselves.[24] Some rabbinic regulations explicitly forbid women to assemble on their own to celebrate the Passover (they also forbid slaves and minors to do so).[25] There is virtually no evidence for Jewish festivals observed only by women.

Rabbinic sources of the third century CE on clearly presume that the entire law given to Moses (both in its written form, and in additional oral tradition) was binding only on free adult "sons of Israel." All others, including free adult "daughters of Israel," were exempt to varying degrees from various obligations and observances: Gentiles were excluded from all but a handful of generic obligations to refrain from things like killing. Rabbinic sources justify these differences in their classification of the commandments into negative and positive precepts (themselves either time-sensitive or not). Negative precepts were binding on women and men alike. Although the rabbis generally seem to think women were exempt from time-sensitive positive precepts, they also held women responsible for several key time-bound obligations, including the lighting of candles before the onset of the Sabbath.[26]

In the rabbinic view, men, but not women, were expected to wear a fringed garment called *tzitzit* under their outer clothing, and to pray daily, wearing special shawls called *talit* and phylacteries (*tefillin*). Women were obligated to recite the blessing after meals but did not count for the quorum of adults required for saying a communal grace.[27] Rabbinic elaborations of the biblical kosher laws (to refrain from eating certain animals, and from cooking a kid in its mother's milk) were binding on women as well as men, and women were apparently expected to ensure that the food eaten, the cooking pots, the storage jars, and food preparation itself all conformed to rabbinic norms. Married women were also expected to scrupulously observe divinely ordained menstrual purity regulations, including checking themselves regularly for menstrual blood and guaranteeing that they were free from menstrual bleeding for seven days before engaging in sexual intercourse with their husbands. The rabbis expected women and men to observe the Sabbath and its restrictions on work, particularly as the rabbis defined it, as well as numerous festivals.

Most crucially, the rabbis considered women exempt from the obligation to study Torah, which the rabbis deemed the most central of all God's commandments. Whether women ever read Torah in ancient synagogues, or engaged in Torah study, has been of considerable contemporary interest, although rabbinic sources actually devote little attention to this question. In the Mishnah, rabbis said to have lived in the early second century CE take somewhat different stances over whether a father may teach his daughter *torah* concerning the ritual prescribed in the biblical book Numbers 5.11–31 for a wife suspected of adultery,[28] a rite that could no longer have been performed. It required an accused woman to drink an unpleasant concoction that would only harm her if she was guilty.

The three rabbis cited in the text are concerned that previous meritorious deeds can nullify the effects of the drink. One proposes that a father should teach his daughter *torah* so that if she is suspected, rightly, of adultery, yet suffers no harm from the drink, she will know her merits have saved her. Another responds that teaching a daughter *torah* is effectively teaching her sexual impropriety. Knowing other merits will protect them, women may then engage in illicit sex. This same rabbi is said elsewhere to have said that it is better to burn the teachings of Torah than convey them to women.[29] Later rabbinic sources cite Deuteronomy 11:19 to demonstrate that it is not obligatory to teach daughters Torah, since it says only, "you shall teach them to your sons," meaning sons, but not daughters.[30] Another relatively early rabbinic Jewish compilation, the Tosefta, contains the position that while women may be included in the quorum of seven persons necessary for the public reading of Torah on the Sabbath, "one does not bring a woman to read [the Torah] in public."[31] Rabbinic understandings ultimately became normative for the majority of Jewish communities from late antiquity through the early modern period. Many if not most Judeans living in the ancient Mediterranean outside the land of Israel do not appear to have spoken either of the languages of rabbinic writings, Hebrew and Aramaic. Rather, Greek (or occasionally Latin) was probably their first, and perhaps their only, language. Until the end of late antiquity and the early medieval period, there is virtually no evidence that Jews in these areas were aware of the rabbis and their particular interpretations of Jewish practice. Because virtually no literary sources survive from these communities after the late first or early second centuries CE, the only evidence we have for differences in women's and men's practices comes from inscriptions and other archaeological remains.[32]

None of the numerous ancient synagogues excavated in the last century has yielded evidence for the gendered seating that comes to be normative in later Jewish synagogues (and is still observed in contemporary Orthodox synagogues). No evidence for women's balconies has been found, or evidence for other forms of gender segregation. At the same time, little evidence of synagogue seating survives apart from some stone benches, and we actually know very little about how people sat or stood in such spaces. Inscriptions from women donors, with and without male relatives, have been found in many synagogues outside the land of Israel, while those within the land of Israel generally lack such evidence.

Most of the religious practices surveyed thus far are closely linked with particular ancient ethnicities (Greeks, Romans, Egyptians, Israelites, and later Judeans) even when they come to be practiced by others, such as worship of Isis outside Egypt in the Hellenistic and Roman periods, worship of Cybele in Rome and elsewhere, or even the practice of philosophy. Unusually, then, for the religions of the ancient Mediterranean, Christian ritual practice does not appear to differ for women and for men, with the significant exception of the eventual explicit exclusion of women from priestly offices. The seeming lack of gender specificity in Christian practices might relate, in some ways, to constructions of Christianity as trans-ethnic, or as the formation of a new, universalizing ethnicity, but this requires further consideration.[33]

In the letters of Paul, the earliest depictions of Christ devotees (whom he does not call Christians, nor should we, yet) provides little explicit evidence of gender-differentiated practices, despite his famous insistence in 1 Corinthians 11:3–16 that women who pray and prophesy in the communal assembly should cover their heads while doing so, while men should not. Ordinary and festival devotions and sacraments were not, at least in idealized form, gender-specific, but were incumbent on women and men alike: (pre-baptismal) instruction, baptism, communal and individual prayer, hymning, prophecy, consumption of the Eucharist, charity, as well as many ascetic practices, and so forth. In his description of practices by then explicitly called "Christian," little more than a half-century later than Paul, Pliny the Younger, then governor of Pontus and Bithynia in Asia Minor, seems to suggest no distinction by sex. Writing to Emperor Trajan to ask whether his response to those accused of being Christians is correct, Pliny notes that persons of both sexes are involved: indeed, he claims to get his information about them particularly by torturing two female slaves (*ancillae*) called *ministrae* (usually translated as deaconesses).[34] All Pliny gets from his (former) Christian witnesses is that they met regularly on a fixed day before dawn, sang hymns responsively to Christ, as to a god, and bound themselves by an oath "not to commit fraud, theft, or adultery, not falsify their trust, nor to refuse to return a trust when called upon to do so." They also assembled for a communal meal.[35] Notably, though, Pliny characterizes these practices as "depraved, excessive superstition," clearly feminizing language, since the Romans often associated superstition and depravity with women.

Particularly because of its potential implications for contemporary practices, women's performance of various cultic offices has garnered considerable attention. Inscriptions as well as literary sources demonstrate that women routinely served as priestesses and other cult functionaries in the service of numerous ancient deities, both female and male. In Roman Asia Minor, many women are attested epigraphically as high priestesses of Asia, an office that carried considerable responsibility (and expense).[36] At the same time, it has become clear that the prestige, authority, power, and economic consequences of such appointments differed greatly and were often less for women than for men.

Although some scholars have debated how to understand occasional inscriptional references to Jewish women with priestly titles,[37] it seems a fair conclusion that only men served as priests in the Jerusalem Temple. There is considerable evidence for women called by ancient synagogue office titles, including *archisynagogos* (head of the synagogue), elder, and Mother of the Synagogue. A few scholars continue to think that such titles were "honorary" and do not designate women with actual synagogue functions.[38] But almost certainly some women did hold such positions in various synagogues throughout the Mediterranean diaspora in late antiquity, while such evidence is, interestingly, so far lacking for synagogues within the land of Israel itself. No literary sources of the period suggest that such practices were controversial, but the lack of writings from these communities makes this impossible to know (and rabbinic sources are silent on the subject).

In the New Testament, there are not yet actual Christian priests: the only priests are those of the Jerusalem Temple cult. Women are occasionally called deacon (Phoebe, in 1 Corinthians), apostle (Junia, in Romans 16), or disciple (Tabitha, in Acts), although what these terms designated at the time is debated. Women prophets are better attested: the four daughters of Philip in Acts 21:9; the women prophets in 1 Corinthians; and the excoriated prophet "Jezebel" in Revelation 1:20–23. Later Christian women are attested in inscriptions, and occasionally letters on papyrus, as prophets,[39] teachers, deacons, and elders,[40] while literary sources depict women as heads of female monastic communities both small and large. From the letters of Paul on, the question of women's authority over men and communal and cultic offices becomes a subject of contention. Concerns about women's authority also seem visible in the diverse and conflicting accounts of who first saw the resurrected Jesus, Mary Magdalene, Peter, or even someone else.

WHAT DIFFERENCE GENDER DIFFERENCE MAKES: REREADING THE EVIDENCE

Where religious practices differed between women and men, the significance of these differences was considerable. Religious practices regularly effected the production of properly gendered persons, both women and men. As Barbara Goff illuminates, ancient Greek religion was particularly concerned with the production of citizen wives who conformed to gender expectations.[41] Its "rituals aim at producing women who are equipped to perform successfully their roles within a patriarchal order and who have internalized a version of themselves that is useful to others."[42] Stories and visual images of transgressive females (wild worshippers of the Greek god Dionysos, witches, and others) served more as counterpoints to ideal female figures than as instances of actual persons. They served as models for what good Greek women should not do, and created other social categories of "not-wives," including slaves, prostitutes, and other marginalized categories. Much of Roman women's practices functioned similarly.[43]

One of the primary religious practices for the production of properly gendered men was animal sacrifice. As Nancy Jay argued before her premature death allowed her to develop and defend her arguments, the practice of animal sacrifice, a common feature of agricultural, urban societies, regularly produces male lineages purged of women. These lineages, which also then produce male community, were structured hierarchically. They were enacted in the killing, distribution, and consumption of meat, with the imagined participation of one or more divine beings, in a system of reciprocal but not identical gift-giving, a system in which women are generally themselves one kind of gift to be exchanged, and largely, although not entirely, excluded from engaging in such exchanges.[44] This system itself expresses, encodes, reinforces, and authorizes not only gender in general but also particular attributes of gender: masculinity as active, exterior, superior, self-controlled, hard, meat-eating, knife-wielding, speaking, and ruling, with femininity as the negative inversions of all these traits.

Masculinity could, of course, be produced in other ways and conflicting definitions of masculinity and femininity could be deployed to wage social and cultural battles and to differentiate social identifications.[45] Early Jewish rabbis concurred with the defining characteristics of elite Roman masculinity, including mastery over both the self and subordinate others, and public oral contestation and debate as a primary form of masculine competition.[46] At the same time, the rabbis refashioned these, positioning their own very specialized practice of Torah study as the ultimate act of masculinity. In doing so, they differentiated themselves from other components of Greek and Roman definitions of masculinity that emphasized the deliberate, controlled exercise of physical strength, athletic abilities, military prowess, and the selective use of violence.

Rabbinic constructions of masculinity would appear to have been equally differentiated from those of numerous other Judeans:

revolutionaries from the Maccabean fighters in the second century BCE to the anti-Roman Sicarii in the first century CE, to the various other groups known particularly from Josephus, and the men responsible for the early second-century anti-Roman revolts in Cyrene and Palestine (including the Bar Kokhba forces).[47] How much rabbinic redefinition of masculinity as Torah study and debate, as opposed to myriad other forms of masculine performance, was a response to the massive failure of the several revolts, and the loss of temple sacrifices, is impossible to determine, although certainly tempting to argue. At the very least, advocating such practices made, literally, a virtue of necessity.

Understanding ancient constructions of Torah study in rabbinic circles as the ultimate form of masculinity puts contemporary discussions of whether ancient Jewish women studied Torah, or read from Torah scrolls in public, into a very different light. Lavishly adorned, ordinarily secluded from sight, and displayed on occasion to its licit male viewers, a Torah scroll seems an obvious analogue to a woman's body, and reading the Torah analogous to the performance of sexual intercourse.[48] In rabbinic constructions of femininity and masculinity, women generally lacked much of the (masculine) capacity necessary for Torah study, including sufficient self-discipline, critical discernment, and so forth. For the rabbis, women reading Torah was always dangerous, for they, like Gentiles, lacked by definition the self-restraint necessary to do it properly.[49] Thus for women either to study Torah generally or read Torah scrolls specifically posed a fundamental contradiction in gendered terms.

Just as Greek and Roman divisions of (religious) labor by gender produced both proper free adult men and proper free wives, so, too, did rabbinic divisions produce proper rabbinic men and women. Even in the potentially transgressive case of teaching daughters some *torah*, its effect, if not also its purpose, seems to be to inculcate gender expectations in daughters, expectations themselves understood to be divinely authorized. The production of compliant, submissive women seems especially visible in the divine threats of death in childbirth some rabbis envisioned for women who deviated from rabbinically mandated practices of Sabbath candle lighting, separation of dough, and the observance of rabbinic versions of the menstrual purity regulations found in the Hebrew Bible.[50] What the daughters, wives, and other relatives of such rabbis actually did, and how they themselves construed these practices, is, regrettably, all but unavailable to us.

If strong gender difference in religious practices inculcates gender, the absence of strong gender difference in religious practices did not deter those practices from participating in the (re)production of gender, and the enforcement of gender conformity. Festivals and rites incumbent on all persons, or at least all free adults, frequently had gendered dimensions. In ancient Mediterranean domestic religions, male heads of families performed sacrifices on behalf of the whole household, while women might perform daily devotions whose very ordinariness contributed to their construction as lesser (and feminized). Ancient Christian devotional practices, prayer, prophecy, singing hymns of divine praise, being baptized, and baptizing are prime examples. All encoded gendered meanings, even when they were practiced by both women and men.

Prayer might seem to be the least gendered of early Christian devotional forms, a universal human practice before the divine, fitting for both men and women. Numerous ancient narratives in all religious traditions depict women as praying, and often narrate their actual prayers. Yet prayer may be especially appropriate for women precisely because it entails some degree of petition and subordination and constructs the petitioner as female in relation to the gods. To the degree that subordination is inevitably coded as feminine, prayer always has a feminine dimension to it. Even while it has the capacity to feminize, prayer is still regularly seen to be appropriate even for the most masculine men with tremendous amounts of authority, such as the high priest, or the Roman emperor (who, while praying to the gods, are still themselves somewhat inevitably feminized, given the power discrepancies between them and the gods). Still, because prayer in antiquity was largely performed aloud and in public, it intersects with the gendered associations of speech, which is regularly constructed as masculine. Women did pray aloud, partly because to pray silently raised the suspicion that one was praying for malicious or illicit favors, but it is not surprising to find fewer representations of women praying aloud in public, and more representations of women's prayers performed in private, and/or in the company of other women.

Prophecy, too, can be seen as a fundamentally gendered category: it relies on the notion of penetration of a human by a divine agent, and casts the prophet into the role of the passive, penetrated, god-possessed female, even when the prophet is, as is usually the case, male.[51] A more complex set of analogies involving speech and seed, knowledge and fertility, may be at work here: the god is to the prophet as the husband is to the wife, and the words of the god are to the prophet as the husband's seed is to his wife.[52] Although the vast majority of the prophets in the Hebrew Bible are clearly men, the handful of female examples, especially Miriam the sister of Moses and Aaron, were sufficiently well known in antiquity to authorize and legitimize women prophets in the Jesus movement.[53]

The attributes of women prophets in early Christian sources tend to confirm these associations, for such prophets are generally (if not universally) represented as celibate or chaste: the eighty-four-year-old widow Anna in Acts 2:36–37; the four virgin daughters of Philip in Acts 21:9; and the women prophets in 1 Corinthians who appear to be practicing celibacy.[54] Not being penetrated by human husbands or other male authorities, they are available to be penetrated by the male deity.

All these practices rely on a gendered paradigm of receptivity and passivity that was on the one hand deemed natural to women and, on the other, troubling, since it made women the potential vehicles of authoritative knowledge. Various writers from Paul and those who continued to write in his name, to later Christian authors such as Tertullian attempt to restrict these practices to celibate women. Such restriction not only coheres with the sexualized metaphors of inspiration but also, perhaps, solves the challenge to male hierarchy and authority posed if allegedly subordinate women receive such knowledge and transmit it to men: virgins, at least, if not also women who do not engage in penetrative intercourse, may not count as "subordinate" women. The characterization of women as passive transmitters of this knowledge, as opposed to active teachers, may further assuage the difficulties inherent in women's mediation of such knowledge. This seems implicit in Tertullian's later account of a female prophet in his New Prophecy church, who made sure to clear all her revelations with the appropriate (and presumably male) authorities before sharing them with a wider public.[55]

Baptism, too, was enmeshed in systems of hierarchy and prestige. Tertullian claimed explicitly that baptism (together with other priestly offices) is properly masculine and may not be performed by women.[56] The view that women may not baptize, or may at best baptize other women, was clearly rooted not in issues of modesty but in an implicit logic in which the baptizer is superior to the baptized, so that women baptizing men subverts the equation of superiority with masculinity, whereas women baptizing other women, while perhaps still problematic, at least does not fundamentally invert the implicit hierarchy.

Analyzing these practices in this manner also allows us to rethink debates about women's cultic offices, both those of modern scholars and those of ancient Christian writers. While the historical questions remain important (what offices did women hold, and what do we know about such women?), more productive is whether such offices were presumed to be gendered, and to require certain masculine characteristics of activity, self-control, exercise of authority over subordinates, and the like, as Tertullian and Epiphanius both explicitly argue. For them, baptism, teaching, performing the Eucharist, and other practices were inherently male actions whose performance by women was illogical and transgressive. Yet the advocacy of celibacy and virginity as ideal forms of Christian life seems at the same time to have created the possibility of persons who were female in their bodies yet whose abstinence from female sexuality made them male in their spirits, and thus able to exercise these masculine prerogatives.

Such cannot have been the mechanism by which non-Christian women held cultic offices, partly because none of these other religions seems to have advocated celibacy as an ideal form of life (although women did sometimes abstain temporarily from sexual activity in order to engage in particular cultic rites, such as those of the Roman Ceres) or valorized the construct of a person female in body but male in spirit (some philosophical schools being an important exception). There is no evidence that women office-holders in Jewish communities relied on distinctions between sexually inviolate women and women subject to male penetration for the legitimacy of their claims to office, although interestingly, many women office-holders in ancient synagogues appear to have been unmarried at the time. Elite married women in Roman Asia Minor were regularly able to hold and perform the functions of numerous offices and priesthoods. Their ability to do so seems integrally linked to the construction of those benefactions as the extension of the familial obligations of the extremely wealthy to the cities as a whole, overriding other potential cultural meanings.[57] Women office-holders in synagogues might conceivably have been understood in similar ways, particularly for those synagogues in the same cultural milieu of Roman Asia Minor, from which all but one of the known women heads of synagogue come.

Attention to gender allows us to rethink numerous other ancient religious practices. Women figure prominently in the earliest Christian narratives about martyrs, people executed in fairly gruesome ways for refusing to renounce their Christian affiliation.[58] In these accounts, the passivity, suffering, weakness, and inferiority widely thought to be inherent in the condition of being female are both masculinized (as in the martyr Perpetua, who becomes a man to fight in the arena of her death) and shown to be far more powerful than the seeming but ultimately false masculine power of the Roman authorities. Both the act and the rhetoric of martyrdom proved a particularly effective Christian attack on, and subversion of, imperial Roman power, all the more so if the representative of Christians was female. The weakest, most vulnerable, and

powerless women easily triumph, through God, over the most powerful human male authorities. Such stories may, of course, reflect some
historical realities that women became Christians at the cost of their
lives, but the utility of gender in the construction of these narratives
may explain both the prevalence of stories about women martyrs and
their appeal to Christians.

Ancient authors and modern scholars alike have portrayed women
as particularly prone to take on new and sometimes foreign religious
practices. The second-century critic of Christianity, Celsus, famously
accused Christianity of appealing largely to women, slaves, children,
and ignorant men.[59] It may, in fact, be true that certain new religions
do appeal disproportionately to women of various social standings by
virtue of new possibilities they make available to women and the critiques these religions sometimes offer of traditional gender values.[60]
Yet, at the same time, to say that women are particularly attracted to
new, foreign religions (or, as numerous ancient Christian writers do, to
associate women particularly with forms of Christianity the writer dis-
likes, e.g., "heresies")[61] is to say at least as much about the new, foreign,
or "heretical" religion, that is, to feminize and denigrate it, and all its
adherents, male and female.[62]

This strategy is clearly at work in the Roman annalist Livy, in his
account of the importation of certain rites of the Greek god Dionysos,
also known as Bacchus or Bakchos to Rome in the second century BCE.[63]
Gender is central to Livy's construction of the rites of the Bacchanalia as
antithetical to true Roman values. He claims that women were prominent among the god's worshippers and instrumental in the importation
of the rites into Rome itself (although he actually gives three conflicting accounts of these events). The rites of the Bacchanalia were foreign,
practiced by women and effeminate men. They were held at night, in
illicit gatherings where an improperly mixed group of men and women
engaged in lust, fraud, murder, madness, error, and impiety. Their performance emasculated unsuspecting young men, rendering them unfit
for masculine military service, perhaps by involving them in homoerotic
encounters. At the very least, they rendered soldiers unfit to defend the
chastity of the wives and children of the male citizenry. Once proper
Roman matrons engaged in wholly improper practices. Bacchic men
prophesied in a frenzied state that itself required a lack of proper masculine self-control.

In Livy's account, religion and truth are themselves gendered, with
predictable associations. True religion (that of the Roman state and its
pontiffs) is masculine. False religion is feminine (equivalences that many

Christian authors would later map onto their intra-Christian opponents, equating "heresy" with femininity and "orthodoxy" with masculinity). But true religion also affirms the authority of the masculine (here Roman) state, and a gendered moral order where women are subordinate and feminine and men are superior and masculine. False religion is not only feminine, it is feminizing, challenging the authority of the state, fostering military weakness, and inverting gender relations. It is accompanied by madness, disorder, and heinous crimes of all sorts. What attention to gender shows us, then, is that accounts of women's practices are rich sources for the relationships between religion and gender in antiquity, if also deeply problematic sources for women's actual practices, in these instances and many more.

GENDERING THE COSMOS

All ancient Mediterranean religious practices were embedded in rich, all-encompassing models of the cosmos. While there appear to have been diverse models, many persons in the ancient Mediterranean seem to have imagined the cosmos as a series of concentric spheres, with the upper levels inhabited by increasingly powerful beings, including the sun, moon, stars, and planets, while living humans remained in a lower realm and the dead resided within the earth. All these cosmologies were gendered in diverse ways, with attendant implications for the study of ancient religions.

Polytheist universes were unsurprisingly populated by male and female deities, and a wide range of subordinate beings of lesser power, prestige, and authority over the lives of humans, such as heroes, demigods, nymphs, satyrs, and generic daimones of all sorts. The major gods were regularly depicted as having the familial relations of elite humans, including father–son conflicts, power struggles between siblings, and a divine mother lamenting her inability to protect her divine daughters from the machinations of their divine male relatives (as in the story of Demeter and Kore).[64] Major male deities were also depicted as having the kinds of competitions typical of ancient men jockeying for position, even if the means at their disposal transcended those of ordinary humans, and their immortality meant that no conflict was ever permanently resolved (as in the conflict between Osiris and his brother Typhon in Egypt).

Ancient Israel and subsequent Judeans (Jews) might seem to be a major exception (perhaps along with the Nabateans, who are sometimes thought to have worshipped only a single deity, although the evidence is fairly modest). Ancient Israel is often popularly depicted as monotheistic, worshipping only a single male deity, Yahweh. But the reality on the ground appears far more complex. The Hebrew Bible contains numerous traces of conflict myths known elsewhere in ancient West Asia, where a masculine sky deity overpowers a female sea deity to create the earth, the heavens, and the seas. Numerous books contain evidence for beliefs in, and devotions to, Yahweh's consort, Asherah, perhaps also known as the Queen of Heaven, which are born out by various archaeological finds, including inscriptions to Asherah and cult images.[65] Yahweh is often imaged as a king presiding over a cosmic court comprised of various subordinate beings, imagery pervasive in ancient West Asian cultures.

Worship of Yahweh alone becomes the official ideology of the Jerusalem Temple. The shift to monolatry (worship of only one God), if not monotheism (the claim that there is only one God), has sometimes been seen as a correlate to the establishment of a pan-tribal monarchy: one God in his one temple with his analogue, one king in his one palace. Such a move would have had serious consequences both for women's ability to envision themselves in relation to the gods and for women's devotions to goddesses, particularly those associated with traditional women's concerns for fertility and family health. Perhaps unsurprisingly, the Hebrew Bible contains very little indication of such practices. Instead, the male God is seen to have control over women's fertility on an individual basis.

Numerous books of the Hebrew Bible and other ancient Judean writings feature a female figure, Wisdom. (In Hebrew, a gendered language, the word *Hokmah* is feminine, as it also is in Greek, *Sophia*.) Knowing how to make sense of the gender of Wisdom within ancient Israelite and later Jewish cosmologies is complicated. Rarely if ever does Wisdom seem to be a female aspect of God easily accessible to women, or concerned with the issues of fertility and well-being that numerous goddess cults offered ancient Mediterranean women. Instead, Wisdom is often depicted as an attractive woman who invites men to obtain divine truth and knowledge, and contrasted to the Wicked Woman, who lures men away into illicit behaviors.[66]

Later Jewish sources exhibit complex cosmologies with numerous angels who have control over various parts of the cosmos, or who form a divine army in the service of Yahweh against various evil forces. Whether in the Hebrew Bible or non-biblical texts from the Persian period on, the numerous para-divine figures are all male, whether on the side of Yahweh or arrayed against him: Gabriel, Michael, Raphael, Beli'al, and so on.

As gods differ from humans precisely in lacking the definitive human characteristics of mortality and limited knowledge, various deities exemplified ideal gender on the one hand, but often transcended it on the other. Most pantheons replicate ancient gender structures, with a powerful father or ruler figure at their head and the gendering of the gods replicating the gendered social relations of antiquity. Yet ancient gods are not perfect instantiations of gender ideals. Greek gods like Zeus, Hades, and Apollo do not exhibit perfect masculinity when, for instance, they yield to anger or lust, and fail to exercise sufficient masculine self-control and mastery over themselves. Goddesses like Demeter, Hera, and Aphrodite are often insufficiently passive (comparable, perhaps, to the most elite ancient women whose extreme wealth and prestige, at least in the Roman period, allowed them to disregard ordinary gender constraints). Yet they are often depicted as irrational and insubordinate to male authority. In the Greco-Roman Mediterranean, Isis models the marital fidelity and maternal devotion of the idealized wife and mother yet is also said to be the most powerful of deities, able to overcome even Fate, and to possess numerous masculine attributes.[67] Some deities flagrantly transgress gender norms, including both gods such as Adonis and Dionysos and goddesses like Athena and Artemis, who lack typical feminine attributes and possess masculine self-mastery together with the numerous skills of intellect, reason, and physical prowess, all of which may relate to their depiction as virgins unsubordinated to husbands (or even fathers).

Ancient cosmologies did more than model gender and gender relations, however imperfectly these models correlated with human ideals or social practices. They typically inscribed gender into the very creation, order, and fabric of the cosmos. In ancient West Asian conflict myths, order, both cosmic and human, comes about when female elements of the cosmos are subdued and subordinated to masculine elements, such as the story of the Babylonian Tiamat and Marduk, or the Genesis account of the *ruach* (the breath, or spirit) of God subordinating the waters. Gender plays a central role in the two Hebrew creation narratives in Genesis (Genesis 1:1–2:4a and Genesis 2:4b–3:24), if a more complex one than most readers recognize. In the earlier narrative, placed second (Genesis 2:4b–3:24), God creates the male, Adam, and then the female, Eve, out of the male after no other created being is a sufficient companion to him. Eve's famous disobedience of a divine order not to eat from the fruit of the Tree of Knowledge of Good and Evil results in their expulsion from the primordial paradise (to prevent them from eating of the Tree of Life and attaining divine immortality). In that expulsion all the conditions of human existence come into play, most especially gender difference. The male will henceforth labor to produce food, while the female will labor to produce children, and the female will be subordinated to the male. In the later narrative (Genesis 1:1–2:3), placed first, God confers with the heavenly council before creating a being, called "the adam," in the divine image and likeness that is at once male and female, in a narrative that will generate endless complex speculation by its subsequent readers. Rather than punish the primordial couple and banish them from paradise, in Genesis 1, God blesses them, commands them to be fruitful and multiply, and gives them authority over all the other created beings. Only by appending the older narrative of Genesis 2:4b–3:24 to this utopian account does a story of gender subordination acquire its full force.

Christians incorporate diverse ancient Mediterranean paradigms, including the Israelite creation account(s), into their own distinctive cosmologies. Most retain the model of a sole male God responsible for the creation of the entire cosmos, emphasizing his role as Divine Father of a unique only Son, Jesus, whose mortal mother never attains the status of her divine Son. This Christian cosmos continues to contain multiplicities of angels, all masculine, as well as malevolent demons, whose gender is somewhat complicated. They regularly appeared to pious Christian monks, for instance, in the guise of seductive women. Some Christians also came to think that the deities worshipped by non-Christians were actually demons who at least presented themselves in female and male form, whatever their own gendering. Christians then endeavored to exorcise and expel these demon deities from their temples, as both literary accounts and archaeological evidence indicates.[68]

In antiquity, some persons denied that the true Father was the creator of the imperfect present world. Some subscribed to a view of the cosmos in which sparks of light broke off from the Primordial divine light and fell through the layered cosmos, past numerous malicious beings (usually construed as male rulers and other *daimones*), until they came to be weighted down in mortal human bodies, losing all knowledge of their true identity. In such cosmologies, the Father sends his only Son, the Savior, to awaken the enmired souls from their slumber, and teach them their true identities and how to return to the heavenly Light from which they came.[69] Some ancient writings envision that the creation of the present universe comes about through the flawed couplings of deficient female emanations of the Godhead.

GENDER AND THE EFFECTS OF CHRISTIANIZATION IN THE ANCIENT MEDITERRANEAN

Both in the West and in the East, orthodox Christianity ultimately eliminated virtually all non-Christian competitors except for Jews and Samaritans (on whom it also put considerable constraints). Christianity rendered illicit the diverse polytheist devotions of the ancient Mediterranean and eliminated actual goddess worship, although many scholars would argue that it channeled at least some of this into Marian devotion, and into the cult of female saints. The location of saints' shrines on the sites of former pagan temples certainly contributes to this perception, as do the various practices associated with the veneration of female and male saints, including festivals that involve parading the elegantly dressed and decorated statues of saints; incubation practices; offerings of food and drink; and petitionary prayers for healing, safe travel, and redress of personal grievances.[70]

A disturbing text from the early fifth century CE (*The Letter of the Bishop Severus on the Conversion of the Jews of Minorca*)[71] depicts a Christian cleric who attempted to impose his understandings of gender and gender relations onto those forcibly converted to Christianity. In Severus' account of how, under duress and threats of violence, all the Jews of Minorca converted to Christianity in a single week, Jewish women are portrayed as irrational, impetuous, and disobedient wives who resist male authority until they accept Christ. At that point, they become paragons of gendered Christian virtue, docile and subordinate to their newly Christian husbands, the bishop himself, Christ, and, of course, God.

Yet at the same time, orthodox Christian constructions of gender contain the seeds of their own deconstruction. A saying found already in the writings of Paul (Galatians 3:28), perhaps an ancient baptismal formula, proclaims that "in Christ ... there is no male and female" – a quotation from Genesis 1:26, where God creates the primordial human "male and female." This reading, along with an early and enduring valorization of celibacy, undergirds a Christian conceptualization of gender as separable from the sex of the physical body. Some women, at least, are thus able to become male (like Perpetua in the arena) and "female men of God,"[72] even as masculinity remains the ideal, and the perfect image of God. Perhaps ironically, then, the most masculine of "monotheist" religions – Christianity, with its pervasive masculine imagery of God the Father, God the Son (and a neutered Holy Spirit), and a wholly male clergy – turns out to offer the most possibilities for the elimination and transcendence of gender, if through the elevation of celibacy and ascetic practices, and thus at the cost of the denial of the body and human sexuality. Still, the underlying gender constructions of the ancient Mediterranean lose none of their efficacy, and religion continues into Western modernity as a primary instrument of the inculcation and the authorization of gender.

FURTHER READING

In the last thirty years, there has been an explosion of research both on women and on gender relevant to the study of ancient Mediterranean religions. The following suggestions focus particularly on gender, rather than primarily on the history of women, and women's practices in particular religions. On Greek religion, one might begin with Lyons 1997, as well as Cole 2004 and Goff 2004. For the Roman period see McDonnell 2006, Spaeth 1996, Staples 1998, Takács 2007, and van Bremen 1996. For the Hebrew Bible and ancient Israel see Brenner 1997; on later Judean religion and ancient Judaism see Baker 2002, Fonrobert 2000, Matthews 2001, and Taylor 2003, as well as the articles by Satlow 1996 and Levinson 2001. There is perhaps the most extensive bibliography on ancient Christianity. For the New Testament see especially the anthology by Moore and Anderson 2003. Cooper 1996 provoked many subsequent rethinkings of how to read female characters in ancient Christian texts: on which see also the important work of Clark 1994 and especially Clark 2004. The work of Burrus, especially Burrus 2000, has been particularly influential. Other important studies include Castelli 2004, Cobb 2008, MacDonald 1996, Matthews 2001 (also cited previously), and Ringrose 2003 on early Byzantium. Of my own works, Kraemer 1992 is perhaps the most comprehensive: Kraemer 2011 revisits that work, with more intensive treatments of fewer instances, and Kraemer 2004 is an anthology of relevant ancient primary sources with introductions and some bibliography.

GLOSSARY

daimones: Plural of the Greek "daimon": non-human beings with counterintuitive properties and powers. Often translated in English as "demons," in ancient Greece daimones were not necessarily evil.

Eucharist: Literally "thanksgiving," a Christian rite commemorating Jesus' last dinner with his disciples, typically involving the blessing and sharing of bread and wine, representing the body and blood of Jesus.

Gentile: A Jewish term for all non-Jews; frequently used to translate Hebrew, Greek, and Latin terms meaning "the nations."

Mishnah: A collection of early (c. 200 CE) rabbinic Jewish teachings on a wide range of subjects, from agriculture to festivals to marital matters, engaging and elaborating on the laws set forth in the Hebrew Bible.

Nabateans: Inhabitants of the small kingdom of Nabatea, east of the Jordan River and the Dead Sea, in what is modern Jordan.

seder: The ritual meal for the Jewish festival of Passover.

Torah: A Hebrew term meaning "instruction" or "law," Torah often designates the first five books of the Hebrew Bible (Genesis, Exodus, Leviticus, Numbers, and Deuteronomy) and is sometimes also called by the Greek term, *Pentateuch.* More specifically, Torah may designate the commandments said to be given to Moses on Mt. Sinai; more generally, Torah may designate the subsequent study and interpretation of those commandments.

Notes

1 Katz 1995:36 claims that in the decade before her essay, the field has emerged from the study of the history of women to the study of the history of gender.

2 For a bibliography see Kraemer 1983; on the history and ideology of this framing see Katz 1995.

3 Rosaldo and Lamphere 1974, Reiter 1975, and especially Rubin 1975, who seems to have been the first to use the language of "the sex/gender system" (Haraway 2001). See also MacCormack and Strathern 1980 and Ortner and Whitehead 1981.

4 E.g., Winkler 1990; Rawson 1986; and Bynum, Harrell, and Richman 1986.

5 See, e.g., Wittig 1983; Bynum, Harrell, and Richman 1986; Scott 1986; Butler 1990, 1993, 2004; Boyarin 1998; Castelli 2001; Bourdieu 2001, and Kuefler 2001.

6 Haraway 2001:53.

7 This definition is similar in some respects to that of David Halperin: "socially and ideologically significant distinctions [mapped] onto biological differences between the sexes" (Halperin 1990:264).

8 The literature here is now extensive; for a sense of how the field looked in the 1970s and early 1980s see the bibliography in Pomeroy 1973, 1975:251–59 and Kraemer 1983; cf. the bibliographies in Kraemer 2008, 2011, etc.

9 For my own discussion of the category see Kraemer 2011.

10 Hanson 1990, 1999 and Kraemer 2011.

11 E.g., Cole 1992, 2004.

12 Demeter: Pausanius 2.35.6–8 (Corinth), 7.27.9–10 (Achaia), 4.17 (Messenia). Artemis: Pausanias 7.18.11–12 (Achaia). Hera: Pausanias 5.16.2–8 (Elis). Sosipolis: Pausanias 5.20.2–3 (Elis). See Kraemer 2004:no. 17

13 Ovid, *Fasti* 6.473–568 on the Matralia; *Fasti* 4.133–62 on Venus. See Kraemer 2004: no. 11.

14 Plutarch, *Roman Questions* 56 (*Moralia* 278) on Carmenta; *Roman Questions* 57 (*Moralia* 278) on Rumina; *Roman Questions* 100 (*Moralia* 287) on the Ides of August. See Kraemer 2004:no. 16.

15 Juvenal, *Satire* 6; Heliodorus, *Ethiopian Story* 5.15; 5.34; 6.13–15; Chariton, *Chareas and Callirhoe* 2.2; 3.7–9; 7.5; 8.8; Xenophon of Ephesus, *Ephesian Tale of Anthia and Habrocomes* 1.2; 4.3; 5.4; 5.10–13, 5.15; Achilles Tatius, *Leucippe and Clitophon* 7.13. For excerpts with introductions, see Kraemer 2004.

16 Kraemer 2004:nos. 4 and 10.

17 Cole 1992, 2004.

18 Cole 2004:95; see also Bodel and Olyan 2008.

19 Connelly 2007:165–196. Cole 2004:93–104 provides a detailed assessment of the epigraphical evidence for women's participation in feasts and sacrifices, including at least occasional evidence for women dining alone on sacrificial meat; see also 117–118. See also Jay 1992:53.

20 On the translation Judeans for Jews see Mason 2007 and Elliott 2007.

21 See Ullucci 2011.

22 Exodus 23:14, 23:17; Deuteronomy 16:16 (see also 1 Kings 9:25, where Solomon offers up burnt offerings and sacrifices three times a year).

23 *The Jewish War* 5.198–200; *Against Apion* 2.102–104, in Kraemer 2004:no. 15.

24 Rosenblum 2010.

25 Mishnah Tractate *Pesahim* 8:7; see Wegner 1988:148.

26 Babylonian Talmud Tractate *Kiddushin* 29A–B; 34A–36A; see also Kraemer 1992:97–98 and Wegner 1988.

27 Kraemer 1992:97 and Wegner 1988.

28 Babylonian Talmud Tractate *Sotah* 22B.

29 Jerusalem Talmud Tractate *Sotah* 3.4, 19A; see Ilan 1995:191.

30 *Sifre Deuteronomy* 46, p. 104, ed. Finkelstein, cited in Ilan 1995:191; also Babylonian Talmud Tractate *Kiddushin* 29A–B.

31 Tosefta Tractate *Megillah* 2.11: see Wegner 1988:158. On the relationship between Mishnah and Tosefta see Mandel 2006, with additional references.

32 Brooten 1982; Kraemer 1998:50–51, 1992; Horbury 1999; and Levine 2000.

33 On these general issues see Buell 2005, Konstan 1997, Mason 2007, and Elliott 2007.

34 See, e.g., Kraemer 1992:182.

35 Pliny, *Letters* 10.96–97.

36 Kraemer 2004:no. 84. See also Connelly 2007.

37 Kraemer 2004:no. 89 and Brooten 1982.

38 Rajak and Noy 1993.

39 Kraemer 1992:157–73, Kraemer 2004:nos. 66 and 97; Tertullian, *On the Soul* 9, Eusebius, *Ecclesiastical History* 5.16; Epiphanius, *Medicine Box* 48; 49.1.3.

40 Kraemer 2004:nos. 90, 91, 97, 98; Eisen 2000; and Madigan and Osiek 2005.

41 Goff 2004.

42 Ibid.,123.

43 Spaeth 1996, Takács 2007, and Staples 1998.

44 Jay 1992, 2001. For a lovely overview of animal sacrifice, including useful qualification of Jay's work, see Ullucci 2011; on women as exchange see Rubin 1975 and Strathern 1990.

45 See Kraemer 2011:Introduction.

46 Satlow 1996 and Levinson 2001.

47 On competing masculinities see Connell 1987, 2005.

48 Kraemer 2011. The lavish adornment of Torah scrolls may postdate antiquity, although already at Qumran some scrolls were found wrapped in expensive fabrics.

49 Satlow 1996:33, 36.

50 *Genesis Rabbah* 17.7–8; for other references and discussion see Kraemer 1992:95–105; see also Baskin 1984.

51 In Greek religion there were female oracles: the Pythia of Apollo at Delphi and the Sibyl of Cumae.

52 I owe this argument to Jesse Goodman, Brown '04; for details, see Kraemer 2011.

53 Miriam (Exodus 15:20), Deborah (Judges 4:4), Huldah (2 Kings 22:14), an anonymous woman prophet in Isaiah 8:2, and No'adiah (Nehemiah 6:14); three other texts mentioning women as prophets or among prophetic groups: Ezekiel 13:17–23, Joel 3:1–2, and 1 Chronicles 25:1–8: see Gafney 2008.

54 E.g., Schüssler Fiorenza 1983, Wire 1990, Mitchell 1993, Martin 1995, and MacDonald 1999; see also the various entries in Meyers, Craven, and Kraemer 2000.

55 Tertullian, *On the Soul* 9.

56 Tertullian, *On Baptism* 17; *On the Veiling of Virgins* 9, *On the Prescription Against Heretics* 41: see Kraemer 2011:115–20.

57 van Bremen 1996.

58 See, e.g., *The Acts of the Martyrs of Scilli, The Letter of the Churches of Lyons and Vienne* (Eusebius, *Ecclesiastical History* 5.1.3–63); *The Martyrdom of Saints Perpetua and Felicitas.*

59 Origen, *Against Celsus* 3.44.

60 See, e.g., Kitch 1989 on American utopian movements, especially the Shakers; see also Sered 1994 and Kraemer 1979, 1992, 2011.

61 Kraemer 1992:157–73.

62 Lieu 1998; see also MacMullen 1997.

63 Livy, *Annals of Rome* 39.8–18.

64 *The Homeric Hymn to Demeter.*

65 Olyan 1988, 2010; Wiggins 1993; and Ackerman 2000.

66 Camp 2000a, 2000b.

67 Plutarch, *On Isis and Osiris* 12–19; Kyme Aretalogy to Isis.

68 See, e.g., *The Life and Miracles of St. Thecla*; see also Hahn, Emmel, and Gotter 2008, and esp. Brakke 2008.

69 E.g., *The Hymn of the Pearl* in the apocryphal *Acts of Thomas.* The canonical Gospel of John has been read in a similar light. Another instance might be the work known as the *Ascension of Isaiah.*

70 See, e.g., MacMullen 1997 and Davis 2001.

71 Bradbury 1996 and Kraemer 2009.

72 Cloke 1995.

Works Cited

Ackerman, Susan. 2000. "Asherah, Asherim." In *Women in Scripture: A Dictionary of Named and Unnamed Women in the Hebrew Bible, the Apocryphal/Deutero-canonical Books and the New Testament*. Ed. C. Meyers, T. Craven and R. Kraemer, 508–11. Boston.

Baker, Cynthia. 2002. *Rebuilding the House of Israel: Architectures of Gender in Jewish Antiquity*. Stanford, CA.

Baskin, Judith. 1984. "The Separation of Women in Rabbinic Judaism." In *Women, Religion and Social Change*. Ed. Ellison Findly and Yvonne Haddad, 3–18. Albany, NY.

Bodel, John and Saul M. Olyan, eds. 2008. *Household and Family Religion in Antiquity*. Oxford.

Bourdieu, Pierre. 2001. *Masculine Domination*. Trans. Richard Nice. Stanford, CA.

Boyarin, Daniel. 1998. "Gender." In *Critical Terms for Religious Studies*. Ed. M. C. Taylor, 117–35. Chicago.

Bradbury, Scott. 1996. *Severus of Minorca: Letter on the Conversion of the Jews*. Oxford.

Brakke, David. 2008. "The Christianization of Pagan Temples in the Greek Hagiographical Texts." In *From Temple to Church: Destruction and Renewal of Local Cultic Topography in Late Antiquity*. Ed. J. Hahn, S. Emmel, and U. Gotter, 91–112. Leiden.

Brenner, Athalya. 1997. *The Intercourse of Knowledge: On Gendering Desire and 'Sexuality' in the Hebrew Bible*. Leiden.

Brooten, Bernadette J. 1982. *Women Leaders in the Ancient Synagogue: Inscriptional Evidence and Background Issues*. Brown Judaic Studies 36. Chico, CA.

Buell, Denise. 2005. *Why This New Race? Ethnic Reasoning in Early Christianity*. New York.

Burrus, Virginia. 2000. *"Begotten, not made": Conceiving Manhood in Late Antiquity*. Stanford, CA.

Butler, Judith. 1990. *Gender Trouble: Feminism and the Subversion of Identity*. London and New York.

———. 1993. *Bodies That Matter. On the Discursive Limits of "Sex."* London and New York.

———. 2004. *Undoing Gender*. London and New York.

Bynum, Caroline W., S. Harrell, and P. Richman, eds. 1986. *Gender and Religion: On the Complexity of Symbols*. Boston.

Camp, C. 2000a. "Woman Wisdom in the Hebrew Bible." In *Women in Scripture: A Dictionary of Named and Unnamed Women in the Hebrew Bible, the Apocryphal/Deutero-canonical Books and the New Testament*. Ed. C. Meyers, T. Craven and R. Kraemer, 548–550. Boston.

———. 2000b. "Woman Wisdom in the Apocryphal/Deutero-canonical Books." In *Women in Scripture: A Dictionary of Named and Unnamed Women in the Hebrew Bible, the Apocryphal/Deutero-canonical Books and the New Testament*. Ed. C. Meyers, T. Craven, and R. Kraemer, 550–552. Boston.

Castelli, Elizabeth. 2004. *Martyrdom and Memory: Early Christian Culture Making*. New York.

————, ed. 2001. *Women, Gender, Religion: A Reader*. New York.

Clark, Elizabeth A. 1994. "Ideology, History, and the Construction of 'Woman' in Late Ancient Christianity." *Journal of Early Christian Studies* 2: 155–84.

————. 2004. *History, Theory, Text: Historians and the Linguistic Turn*. Cambridge, MA.

Cobb, Stephanie. 2008. *Dying to be Men: Gender and Language in Early Christian Martyr Texts*. New York.

Cole, Susan G. 1992. "Gynaiki ou themis: Gender Difference in the Greek Leges Sacrae." *Helios* 19: 104–22.

————. 2004. *Landscapes, Gender and Ritual Space: The Ancient Greek Experience*. Berkeley, CA.

Cloke, Gillian. 1995. *This Female Man of God: Women and Spiritual Power in the Patristic Age, 350–450 A.D.* London and New York.

Connell, Robert. 1987. *Gender and Power: Society, the Person and Sexual Politics*. Oxford.

————. 2005. *Masculinities*. 2nd ed. Berkeley.

Connelly, Joan B. 2007. *Portrait of a Priestess: Women and Ritual in Ancient Greece*. Princeton, NJ.

Cooper, Kate 1996. *The Virgin and the Bride: Idealized Womanhood in Late Antiquity*. Cambridge, MA.

Davis, Stephen J. 2001. *The Cult of Saint Thecla: A Tradition of Women's Piety in Late Antiquity*. Oxford.

Eisen, Ute. 2000. *Women Officeholders in Early Christianity: Epigraphical and Literary Studies*. Collegeville, MN.

Elliott, J. H. 2007. "Jesus the Israelite was Neither a 'Jew' Nor a 'Christian': On Correcting Misleading Nomenclature." *Journal for the Study of the Historical Jesus* 5: 119–154.

Fonrobert, Charlotte. 2000. *Menstrual Purity: Rabbinic and Christian Reconstructions of Biblical Gender*. Stanford, CA.

Gafney, Wilda C. 2008. *Daughters of Miriam: Women Prophets in Ancient Israel*. Minneapolis, MN.

Goff, Barbara. 2004. *Citizen Bacchae: Women's Ritual Practice in Ancient Greece*. Berkeley, CA.

Hahn, Johannes, S. Emmel and U. Gotter, eds. 2008. *From Temple to Church: Destruction and Renewal of Local Cultic Topography in Late Antiquity*. Leiden.

Halperin, David M. 1990. "Why is Diotima a Woman?" In *Before Sexuality: The Construction of Erotic Experience in the Ancient World*. Ed. D. M. Halperin, J. J. Winkler and F. I. Zeitlin, 257–308. Princeton, NJ.

Hanson, Ann E. 1990. "The Medical Writer's Woman." In *Before Sexuality: The Construction of Erotic Experience in the Ancient World*. Ed. D. M. Halperin, J. J. Winkler, and F. I. Zeitlin, 309–28. Princeton, NJ.

————. 1999. "The Roman Family." In *Life, Death and Entertainment in the Roman Empire*. Ed. D. S. Potter and D. J. Mattingly, 19–66. Ann Arbor, MI.

Haraway, Donna. 2001. "'Gender' for a Marxist Dictionary: The Sexual Politics of a Word." In *Women, Gender, Religion: A Reader*. Ed. E. Castelli, 49–75. New York.

Horbury, William. 1999. "Women in the Synagogue." In *Cambridge History of Judaism* 3: 358–401. Cambridge.

Ilan, Tal. 1995. *Jewish Women in Greco-Roman Palestine. An Inquiry into Image and Status*. Texts and Studies in Ancient Judaism 44. Tübingen.

Jay, Nancy B. 1992. *Throughout Your Generations Forever: Sacrifice, Religion, and Paternity*. Chicago.

———. 2001. "Sacrifice as a Remedy for Being Born Female. In *Women, Gender, Religion: A Reader*. Ed. E. Castelli, 174–94. New York.

Katz, Marilyn A. 1995. "Ideology and 'The Status of Women' in Ancient Greece." *Women in Antiquity: New Assessments*. Ed. R. Hawley and B. Levick, 21–43. New York and London.

Kitch, Sally. 1989. *Chaste Liberation: Celibacy and Female Cultural Status*. Urbana, IL.

Konstan, David. 1997. "Defining Ancient Greek Ethnicity." *Diaspora* 6: 97–110.

Kraemer, Ross S. 1979. "Ecstasy and Possession: The Attraction of Women to the Cult of Dionysos." *Harvard Theological Review* 72: 55–80.

———. 1983. "Women in the Religions of the Greco-Roman World." *Religious Studies Review* 9(2): 127–139.

———. 1992. *Her Share of the Blessings: Women's Religions among Pagans, Jews and Christians in the Greco-Roman World*. New York and Oxford.

———. 1998. "Jewish Women in the Diaspora World of Late Antiquity." In *Jewish Women in Historical Perspective*. Ed. J. Baskin, 46–72. 2nd ed. Detroit, MI.

———. 2004. *Women's Religions in the Greco-Roman World: A Sourcebook*. Oxford and New York.

———. 2008. "Women and Gender." In *The Oxford Handbook of Early Christian Studies*. Ed. S. A. Harvey and D. Hunter, 465–492. Oxford.

———. 2009. "Jewish Women's Resistance to Christianity in the Early 5th Century: The Account of Severus, Bishop of Minorca." *Journal of Early Christian Studies* 17: 635–665.

———. 2011. *Unreliable Witnesses: Religion, Gender and History in the Greco-Roman Mediterranean*. New York and Oxford.

Kuefler, Matthew. 2001. *The Manly Eunuch: Masculinity, Gender Ambiguity and Christian Ideology in Late Antiquity*. Chicago.

Levine, Lee I. 2000. "Women in the Synagogue." In *The Ancient Synagogue: The First Thousand Years*, 471–90. New Haven, CT.

Levinson, Joshua. 2001. "Cultural Androgyny in Rabbinic Literature." In *From Athens to Jerusalem. Medicine in Hellenized and Jewish Lore and Early Christian Literature*. Ed. S. Kottek and M. Horstmanshoff, 119–40. Rotterdam.

Lieu, Judith. 1998. "The 'Attraction of Women' in/to Early Judaism and Christianity: Gender and the Politics of Conversion." *Journal for the Study of the New Testament* 72: 5–22.

Lyons, D. 1997. *Gender and Immortality: Heroines in Ancient Greek Myth and Cult*. Princeton, NJ.

MacCormack, Carol and M. Strathern 1980. *Nature, Culture, Gender*. Cambridge.

MacDonald, Margaret Y. 1996. *Early Christian Women and Pagan Opinion*. Cambridge.

———. 1999. "Reading Real Women Through the Undisputed Letters of Paul." In *Women and Christian Origins*. Ed. R. S. Kraemer and M. R. D'Angelo, 199–220. New York and Oxford.

MacMullen, Ramsay. 1997. *Christianity and Paganism in the Fourth to Eighth Centuries.* New Haven, CT.

Madigan, Kevin and C. Osiek, eds. 2005. *Ordained Women in the Early Church: A Documentary History.* Baltimore, MD.

Mandel, Paul. 2006. "The Tosefta." In *Cambridge History of Judaism* 4: 316–335. Cambridge.

Martin, Dale. 1995. *The Corinthian Body.* New Haven, CT.

Mason, S. 2007. "Jews, Judeans, Judaizing, Judaism: Problems of Categorization in Ancient History." *Journal for the Study of Judaism* 38: 457–512.

Matthews, Shelly. 2001. *First Converts: Rich Pagan Women and the Rhetoric of Mission in Early Judaism and Christianity.* Stanford, CA.

McDonnell, M. A. 2006. *Roman Manliness: Virtus and the Roman Republic.* Cambridge.

Meyers, Carol, Toni Craven, and Ross Kraemer, eds. 2000. *Women in Scripture: A Dictionary of Named and Unnamed Women in the Hebrew Bible, the Apocryphal/Deutero-canonical Books and the New Testament.* Boston.

Mitchell, Margaret M. 1993. "Review Essay on A. C. Wire's *The Corinthian Women Prophets.*" *Religious Studies Review* 19: 308–11.

Moore, Stephen D. and J. C. Anderson, eds. 2003. *New Testament Masculinities.* Atlanta, GA.

Olyan, Saul. 1988. *Asherah and the Cult of Yahweh in Israel.* Atlanta.

———. 2010. "What Do We Really Know About Women's Rites in the Israelite Family Context?" *Journal of Ancient Near Eastern Religions* 10: 55–67.

Ortner, Sherry and H. Whitehead, eds. 1981. *Sexual Meanings: The Cultural Construction of Gender and Sexuality.* Cambridge.

Osiek, Carolyn and M. Y. MacDonald. 2005. *A Woman's Place: House Churches in Earliest Christianity.* Minneapolis, MN.

Pomeroy, Sarah. 1973. "Selected Bibliography on Women in Antiquity." *Arethusa* 6: 125–57.

———. 1975. *Goddesses, Whores, Wives and Slaves: Women in Classical Antiquity.* New York.

Rajak, Tessa, and D. Noy. 1993. "Archisynagogoi: Office, Title and Social Status in the Greco-Jewish Synagogue." *Journal of Roman Studies* 83: 75–93. Reprinted in T. Rajak, *The Jewish Dialogue With Greece and Rome: Studies in Cultural and Social Interaction,* 393–430. London 2001.

Rawson, Beryl, ed. 1986. *The Family in Ancient Rome: New Perspectives.* Ithaca, NY.

Reiter, Rayna R., ed. 1975. *Toward an Anthropology of Women.* New York.

Ringrose, Kathryn. 2003. *The Perfect Servant: Eunuchs and the Social Construction of Gender in Byzantium.* Chicago.

Rosaldo, Michelle Z. and L. Lamphere, eds. 1974. *Woman, Culture and Society,* Stanford, CA.

Rosenblum, Jordan. 2010. *Food and Identity in Early Rabbinic Judaism.* Cambridge.

Rubin, Gayle. 1975. "The Traffic in Women: Notes on the 'Political Economy' of Sex." In *Toward an Anthropology of Women.* Ed. R. R. Reiter, 157–211. New York.

Satlow, Michael L. 1996. "'Try To Be A Man': The Rabbinic Construction of Masculinity." *Harvard Theological Review* 89: 19–40.

Scott, Joan W. 1986. "Gender: A Useful Category of Historical Analysis." *American Historical Review* 91: 1053–75.

Schüssler Fiorenza, Elisabeth. 1983. In *Memory of Her: A Feminist Theological Reconstruction of Christian Origins*. New York.

Sered, Susan. 1994. *Priestess, Mother, Sacred Sister: Religions Dominated by Women*. New York and Oxford.

Spaeth, Barbette Stanley. 1996. *The Roman Goddess Ceres*. Austin, TX.

Staples, Ariadne. 1998. *From Good Goddess to Vestal Virgins: Sex and Category in Roman Religion*. London.

Strathern, Marilyn. 1990. *The Gender of the Gift*. Berkeley.

Takács, Sarolta A. 2007. *Vestal Virgins, Sybils and Matrons: Women in Roman Religion*. Austin, TX.

Taylor, Joan E. 2003. *Jewish Women Philosophers of First-Century Alexandria: Philo's 'Therapeutae' Reconsidered*. Oxford.

Ullucci, Daniel. 2011. *The Christian Rejection of Animal Sacrifice*. New York and Oxford.

van Bremen, Riet. 1996. *The Limits of Participation: Women and Civic Life in the Greek East in the Hellenistic and Roman Periods*. Dutch Monographs on Ancient History and Archaeology 15. Amsterdam.

Wegner, Judith. R. 1988. *Chattel or Person: The Status of Women in the Mishnah*. New York and Oxford.

Wiggins, Steve. 1993. *A Reassessment of 'Asherah': A Study According to the Textual Sources of the First Two Millenia B.C.E.* Kevelaer, Germany.

Winkler, John. 1990. *The Constraints of Desire: The Anthropology of Sex and Gender in Ancient Greece*, 188–209. New York.

Wire, Antoinette C. 1990. *The Corinthian Women Prophets: A Reconstruction through Paul's Rhetoric*. Minneapolis, MN.

Wittig, Monique. 1983. "The Point of View: Universal or Particular." *Feminist Issues* 3: 63–69.

14 Visuality

ROBIN M. JENSEN

INTRODUCTION: VISUALITY AND THE HISTORY OF RELIGIONS

According to Augustine of Hippo (354–430 CE), the eyes play the lead role among the senses in acquiring knowledge. Indeed, he adds, the work of the eye – "seeing" – is a way to speak of intellectual comprehension (*Confessiones* 35.54). Thus, sight is the faculty most associated with understanding or mental perception. Even those ideas or conceptions that humans discern inwardly by imagination or cogitation are grounded in visual experience. Just like Doubting Thomas, humans depend upon visual evidence (John 29:25). Seeing is believing.

In the past half-century or so, historians of religion have become more aware of the importance of material and visual culture for their research. Whereas once the study of texts dominated the field, now the analysis of physical artifacts has attained nearly equal footing in academic religious studies. Analysis of archaeological or art historical materials is no longer regarded as subsidiary, supportive, or simply illustrative. Meanwhile, new methods and theories have been generated for its evaluation and interpretation. What was once an occasional cross-disciplinary experiment has now become a widely utilized approach that can produce a fuller and richer perspective of ancient religion than could have been achieved by documentary study alone. Objects and their viewers are now as central to religious studies as books and their readers.[1]

The images, spaces, objects, clothing, and furnishings associated with ritual practice can be juxtaposed with the documents that describe ceremonies, explain their purpose, and reveal their underlying mythology or meaning. Physical remains have the advantage that, even if fragmentary or no longer in situ, they are firsthand witnesses to religious rites. Texts do not have this privilege, for they have come down through the centuries as transcriptions, translations, and parts of edited collections. Yet, material evidence is difficult to interpret independently. Without the relevant documents, historians can be at a loss for understanding what they are looking at. When taken together, and without subordinating one type of evidence to the other, both images and texts give historians a more complex understanding of ancient religious belief and practice.

Along with a burgeoning interest in material evidence broadly (including architecture and even landscape) is the recognition that images may hold religious content and serve religious functions; they are both reflective and performative instruments.[2] Whereas in earlier decades art historians tended to concentrate on the aesthetic, stylistic, and technical characteristics of ancient art, at the end of the twentieth century they began to attend more and more to its social power and purpose. Adapting those methods, historians of religion now consider the religiosity of religious art. They raise questions of how, when, and where viewers actually perceived sacred images and what those images might have meant in a particular context, time, or place; they study the ways that devotees as well as religious authorities judged the images' value (or lack thereof); and they note the ways that ancient viewers even attributed different types of agency to images: as mediators of divine presence, as objects of veneration, as possessing and wielding supernatural powers (e.g., to heal or to repel enemies as in the case of miracle-working icons), or even being occasionally animate (e.g., talking statues or weeping portraits).[3] Thus, methodologically, historians have progressed, first from being primarily reliant on documents and, second, from producing a simple identification or description of an artifact's iconographic content (i.e., labeling). Analysis of an object's possible purpose or meaning generates an enriched understanding of religion as including significant visual dimensions and practices.

Simultaneously, reception traditions as well as post-modern attention to the ways readers respond to texts have spurred new ways of evaluating the objective role and power, as well as the subjective perception, of religious visual art.[4] Studies on the rhetorical use of words related to "seeing" and "vision" have appeared, as have examinations of visual piety in religious ritual and investigations of the relationship between viewers and their subjects, posing questions about the activity of seeing or the dynamics of perception.[5] Thus, analysis has now turned toward the spectator or the gaze, no longer regarding the artifact as if it were an autonomous object.[6] In other words, this innovative, enriched direction in the academic study of religion has led scholars to speculate about what ancient artisans intended their objects to mean or how ancient viewers might have perceived, understood, and responded to what they beheld. Those speculations presume that the viewing process is dynamic; that it includes perception, assessment, and reaction, and that viewers are informed and affected by what they see.

These subject-oriented wonderings are impossible to resolve in any conclusive sense. Whether craftspersons or viewers, individuals differ from one another. Every experience of viewing is subjective and contextualized, and it may change even from moment to moment for the same viewer. Of course, text historians encounter the same problems, for they cannot know how any set of words were understood by those who read or heard them at any particular time. Yet, despite such obstacles, scholars strive to assess what these things communicated to those who attended to them and how their ancient audiences or observers experienced or received them. Simultaneously and self-consciously, they are not only working across large quantities of time and space but must also reckon with their own subjectivity. The selection of evidence is, itself, a process affected by personal interest, taste, or inclination. The evaluation of that evidence is influenced either by acknowledged or unacknowledged presuppositions or by partially formed hypotheses.

Scholars may offset some of these inherent problems by assessing ancient artifacts in their broadest possible cultural settings. After all, viewers and objects ordinarily come together in a common space. Even if one or the other (subject or object) is out of place (away from home, removed, or imported), the two still occupy a shared physical environment that influences the viewing experience. In addition, viewer and object are hardly ever alone. They are affected by environmental stimuli of all kinds, often competing for attention, sometimes harmoniously adding to or enhancing the meaning communicated, transmitted, or received, sometimes clashing with or contradicting it. Changing any of these environmental factors can make a subtle or significant difference to the seeing process and, consequently, the way the object is regarded. Looking at an object in a museum in one's home city, amidst a collection of disparate artifacts, is a very different experience from seeing the same object in its original setting half a world away.

As crucial as environmental surroundings are the spectator's own history and background. Past experiences, expectations, and assumptions all affect the viewing process. Along with these individually formed distinctions are even more fundamental differences of gender, social status, religious identity, ethnicity, and intellectual formation. In every new instance, perception is shaped by what observers find familiar or, conversely, do not recognize. The object will be either comprehensible or puzzling; it may fit or it may seem out of place. The sense a viewer makes of an object has everything to do with previous encounters, whether imagined or actual, whether in life or in art. And with each new sighting the subject's comprehension of the object is adjusted, challenged, or reinforced. Understanding evolves through a recurring cycle of observation, recollection, and conceptualization.

Most people have difficulty recalling and evaluating what they saw after the fact. Historians have a much more challenging task: to envision what an ancient spectator might have perceived and then to determine how or what she or he subsequently thought about it. It would be naïve to think that all observers were consistently attentive or equally conscious of all that they might have seen on any occasion.

Because of these problems of perception and perspective, access to extant ancient documents can be crucially helpful. Ancient writers sometimes offer illuminating descriptions (*ekphraseis*) of sacred images and even reflect on how, when, or where they saw them, as well as how they assessed their worth.[7] Among the best examples of these are found in the *Imagines* of Philostratus (c. 170–250 CE), a collection of brief essays that describe paintings based on classical myths. As the narrator guides his protégée through a Naples art gallery, he describes the works and interprets them, pointing out the ways they narrate the stories in a visual, rather than a verbal, mode. Although these are just as likely to be artificially constructed rhetorical pieces, they nevertheless offer a contemporary witness to an object in its place.

As Philostratus' essays demonstrate, texts both refer to material images and objects or provide the content of narrative scenes. As much as possible, coordinating such textual descriptions with relevant, surviving material evidence offers both balance and control. Narrative art requires some familiarity with the story, whether heard or read. Simultaneously, giving adequate consideration to material objects requires that they be viewed independently, rather than simplistically subjecting them to relevant textual evidence. A careful study includes detailed observation of an artifact, attention to relevant similarities to or differences from comparable objects, and careful evaluation of its context and surroundings.

By practicing an informed and attentive analysis of visual artifacts, scholars may better reconstruct the conditions of the viewing event (its religious situation) and more helpfully speculate about the content of the experience (what it communicated), and the ways a viewer may have responded to or recalled the encounter (any lasting outcome). While the tools of an art historian are crucial, this process is more akin to the task of an anthropologist or a ritual specialist. The object is not important per se; its value is in the role it plays in structuring religious worldviews or in shaping and supporting ritual practices. Although art objects may compose the majority of examples to be considered, not of interest for their own sakes but, rather, as components of a larger enterprise.

This essay begins with a consideration of ancient theories of sight and the reliability of the senses. It continues with an examination of the ways in which ancient Mediterranean people perceived the visual images of their gods, followed by a discussion of how the gods were imagined to look. It then turns to the problem of divine visibility or invisibility and the question of visual art in Judaism and Christianity. Finally, the essay considers the production of pictorial narratives and the ways in which sacred stories are transmitted and interpreted through visual art.

THE RELIABILITY AND MECHANICS OF SIGHT: THE FORMATIVE POWER OF VISION

The question of reality and illusion is central to any discussion of religious visual practice. From antiquity, philosophers and theologians alike regarded the act of seeing (or the organs of sight) as unreliable. The bodily eye did not necessarily see what was real or true; it was easily deceived. The most influential thinker on this subject, Plato (429–347 BCE), believed that mental images that arise from sensory apprehension of external things (the realm of appearances) are the most likely to be defective, the least truthful. For Plato, truth was only comprehended by the soul or mind, as distinct from the eye, and bodily observation was more a hindrance to knowledge than a source of it. Plato had a famous suspicion of appearances, which he believed not only differed from reality but often could be patently false illusions (cf. *Respublica* 10.601c).[8]

Plato's distrust of the senses – especially sight – was well known in Late Antiquity and was adapted for both pagan and Christian critiques of idolatry. For example, in his treatise *On the Soul*, Tertullian (*fl.* 200 CE) cites Plato's disparagement of sensory experience in the search for truth, noting the famous example of the oar that looks bent when immersed (*De anima* 17, citing Plato, *Timaeus* 44d–47e). Tertullian concedes a distinction between corporeal and spiritual things and between objects manifest to bodily sight and objects hidden from it that are accessible only by the rational faculty. Yet, he continues, both classes of objects are grasped by the soul, which exercises both sensation and intellect. Citing Romans 1:20, Tertullian insists that truths can be perceived in palpable, visual things; in other words, that invisible realities are comprehended through sensible experience and, therefore, that the intellect should not be preferred above the senses (*De anima* 18).

The first-century Jewish philosopher Philo (c. 20 BCE–50 CE) objected to religious images on much the same basis as Plato. Arguing that artisans who fashioned images out of earthly materials had led humans into error about the proper conception of the ever-living God, he added blasphemy to the error of deception. Image-makers not only attempted to attribute divine powers to created things but also came dangerously close to hubristically claiming the role of the Creator. He claimed that it made more sense to deify the sculptors than to attribute divine attributes to their products or for artists to worship their tools or their hands than the things that they made (*De Vita Contemplativa* 1.7; *De Decalogo* 14.65–72). The great Moses, he says, condemned sculptures and paintings in his laws because they were deceitful, imitative snares that aimed, through the agency of the eyes, to beguile souls and lead them into sin and error (*De Gigantibus* 13.59–59).

The impact of these ideas on the ancient assessment of visual art was enormous. Art objects were judged to be imitative and, thus, pretending to be something other than what they were. Portraits were deemed particularly deceitful. They presented merely outward manifestations, revealing only how their subjects looked from a certain angle and at a single moment in time; they could not fully or truthfully represent an inward nature, character, or essence. According to his biographer Porphyry, the Neoplatonist philosopher Plotinus (c. 205–270 CE) refused to allow his portrait to be made, insisting that it would be no more than an image of what was already only an image: his physical appearance (*Vita Plotini* 1). A parallel story comes from Clement of Alexandria, *Strom.* 4.13, reporting on the teachings of Valentinus.

The apocryphal *Acts of John*, probably compiled from a Christian source in the late second or early third century, recounts a similar disparagement of portraiture. John had healed the wife of the Ephesian praetor, Lycomedes. Wishing to show his appreciation, Lycomedes commissioned the apostle's portrait, set the image up in his bedroom, decked it out with garlands, and lit lamps before it. When he showed it to John, the apostle was flattered by its beauty but repudiated the object, not as an idol, but as a deceitful thing. He explained that an imperfect copy of his outward appearance could never be a true likeness. A true image would display the saint's virtues: his faith, reverence, tranquility, kindness, and knowledge (*Acts of John* 27–29).

Despite this distrust of sensory perception and the argument that artistic representations were not only imitations of external facades, philosophers conceded potential spiritual value to superior works of art. As signs, they could direct the viewer to higher realities: the invisible forms or ideals. For example, Plotinus believed that a concept, conceived in the mind of a skilled artist, could become visible in a worked block of marble. The artist's idea existed independently of the work but was also revealed through it. Certain art objects were, thus, more than merely imitative renderings of worldly things; they assisted both makers and viewers in comprehending higher realities. Attentive observation of the natural world's order and structure led artists to recognize universal, transcendent order and structure in the realm of forms that was, after all, the basis for all sensory knowledge. Extended contemplation of beautiful art objects – sometimes made more lovely than they were in nature – would nurture this awareness of pure intellectual beauty (*Enneades* 5.8.9).

Similar arguments can be found in the works of Augustine, who otherwise has little use for visual art in religious practice. Augustine allowed that artists had a power to externalize a form or image that they only conceived inwardly, in their minds. The results are the imposition of inward vision on an external object. The inward vision, the materials the craftsperson utilized to make it visible, and the bodily senses that allowed viewers to appreciate its beauty all had their ultimate source in God (*Confessiones* 11.5.7).

These evaluations of artists as proceeding from an image in the mind or imagination to the externally visible work contradicted older assertions that artists only reproduce what they saw in the sensible realm. The process by which images arise in the mind – or move from being exterior to being interior – introduced a more complicated problem. Different theories about the mechanics of seeing (optics) have bearing on how ancient thinkers valued the viewing process. Whether an object was the active agent, producing rays to be received by the viewer's eye, or vice versa (the eye as the sending organ and the object as its receptor) was debated in antiquity. Plato, for example, assumed that the eye emits a beam of light that reaches out to external objects, while Aristotle held the opposite: that vision was a response to a stimulus or light that emanated from objects. While the former theory (emission) depended on the idea that visual rays were analogous to human touch, the latter theory (intromission) relied on the idea that an object projected replicas of itself (*simulacra*) that passed through space to enter the eye.[9]

In a famous passage from a sermon preached on the feast of St. Vincent, Augustine outlined his theory of vision, which was largely derived from Plato's theory, in which the viewer is the active agent rather than the receptive participant. Discussing the corporeal nature of the resurrected body, Augustine uses the example of sight as evidence of how it might move about with great speed, unburdened by the sluggishness of earthly flesh. Eyesight, he says, is a way that we touch what we behold, but with a ray of light rather than a fingertip. It can travel great distances from its origin (the eye); it can even reach the sun itself and in the "twinkling of an eye" (*Sermones* 277.10).

In his treatise *On the Trinity*, Augustine gives a fuller elaboration of his theory of vision. He distinguishes three parts of the seeing process. First is the thing seen, which existed prior to the act of seeing; second is the act of seeing, which did not have a prior existence; and third is the conscious intention of the viewer to sustain the gaze. Here, however, he makes a slight shift in his idea of agency and process. He concedes that while sight proceeds from the viewer to the object (like a blind man's cane), it is the viewer's attention that shapes the outcome: what he or she actually perceives and then how he or she responds to the perception. Moreover, the object has a kind of agency as well. Vision is derived from the visible thing as it emanates a likeness of itself that passes to the seer (*De Trinitate* 11.2–6).

Thus, Augustine posits a unified and reciprocal idea of vision: a jointly produced – or willed – product that exists within an external body, is sought by the eye, impressed upon the mind, preserved by the memory, and impinges on the soul. The result can be positive or negative. As an example of this formative power of vision, Augustine cites the ancient belief that the things pregnant women looked at, and the ways those viewing experiences imprinted on their souls, could shape or change their unborn babies. Similarly, the state of one's soul will affect what is seen and how it is judged. A propensity to violence, covetousness, or lust will change the nature of the gaze, just as love and compassion will change what and how a person sees. Furthermore, certain things attract attention, appear unbidden to the eye, occasionally even against the wishes or intention of the viewer or in response to piqued curiosity or carnal desire (cf. the lust of the eyes, 1 John 2:16; *Confessiones* 10.55). Similarly, the world is filled with things, good and bad, that people overlook, sometimes to their peril. The benefits and dangers of visual practice are, thus, fundamentally important to religious practice and moral formation. Among all the senses, vision has a distinct ability to delude and harm as well as to instruct and heal.

GAZING – OR NOT GAZING – AT THE GODS

Roman traditional, polytheistic religion was based on rituals that usually were performed in the physical presence of gods' images (*simulacra deorum*).[10] Such images were everywhere, as centerpieces in private gardens, humble objects on family altars, official cult statues in public temples, and votive offerings for local shrines. They might have been crafted from valuable materials or merely stamped on pottery lamps. They were undoubtedly valued as high-status decoration by some while piously cherished by others. They could be colossal or diminutive, commissioned one-of-a-kind pieces or mass-produced and sold in markets (cf. Acts 19:24). Their functions were as varied and eclectic as their makers, owners, circumstances, or settings; and not all of them had clear cultic purpose. Undoubtedly, some statues simply had aesthetic or decorative value.[11] Others were treated as if they were alive; they were bathed, dressed, and coiffed.[12] Nevertheless, despite the accusations of Christian critics, the majority of educated Roman citizens did not regard the images as gods per se. It was obvious that the images were manufactured out of mundane materials, even if by extraordinarily skilled artisans.

For example, in one of his sermons, Augustine of Hippo acknowledges that better-educated pagans claimed that they did not worship the actual images but what the images signified. For example, they realized that Neptune's statue was not Neptune, for Neptune was completely other; he was the sea, in fact. Thus, the gods' images portrayed the anthropomorphic deities described by Homer or Hesiod, which were, themselves, only symbols of vast, transcendent divine forces (*Sermones* 198 or Dolbeau 26.16–24). Thus, a figure of Tellus as a bare-breasted mother represents the divine earth (Fig. 8.1); a statue of Juno represents the element of air. Vulcan is fire and Mercury represents genius (an invisible, mental reality). Augustine wonders, why then should anyone need a statue? Why not simply offer worship or veneration to the earth, the air, the water, or fire directly? Why offer adoration to an image of the sun when the actual sun is right before one's eyes? One might answer Augustine's query by stressing the importance of visual focus. The devotee wishes to turn his or her eyes toward a recognizable figure, something that could inspire veneration, affection, or simply be a reminder of the god whose patronage one might seek.

Augustine's question echoes that of an earlier, fourth-century, Christian critic of pagan images, Arnobius of Sicca (d. c. 337 CE). In his treatise *Against the Nations*, Arnobius admits being baffled about the motivation for polytheists' skillfully fashioning and piously tending images and statues; he cannot discern whether they do these things in earnest, out of pretense of worship, or simply for sly amusement (*Adversus Nationes* 6.8–9). Recognizing that polytheists believe that the immortal gods live in a distant heavenly realm and cannot be seen by mortal eyes, he wonders why they then pray to images instead of the deities themselves. He provides a possible answer: because they cannot see the gods, polytheists worship and serve them by means of their images. In feigned confusion, Arnobius asks why the immortal gods should require third-party intermediaries (the images) to receive such benefits on their behalf. From a worshiper's perspective, is this not like acknowledging one set of gods but offering supplication to a group of others?

For their part, traditional polytheists apparently found the absence of images of the Christian god slightly suspicious. In his dialogue, *Octavius*, Minucius Felix (*fl.* 200 CE) records a probably fictional exchange between the pagan Caecilius and the Christian Octavius. Prompted by Octavius' objection to Caecilius' throwing a kiss toward a statue of Serapis, the two agreed to a debate. Among other arguments against the Christian god is his lack of images. Caecilius suggests that Christians try to hide and conceal their god for some shameful or even criminal purpose. Furthermore, Christians believe their god – whom they are unable to see for themselves or show to others – oversees everyone else, constantly spying on mortals as they go about their daily lives (*Octavius* 10.2–5).

In defense, Octavius asks what kind of image he could fashion for God, seeing that humans are, themselves, rightly considered to be the true image (cf. Genesis 1:26). Moreover, the most persuasive reason for believing in this Christian God is the fact that he neither can be seen nor shown, yet can still be perceived in creation – the works of creation, the ordering of the cosmos, and deep within the human soul (cf. Romans 1:20). Moreover, even if it were possible, trying to gaze at this God would be like staring at the sun and being blinded by its brilliance. Truly, he allows, this God is the observer of everything on earth; humans live their lives in his gaze, not vice versa (*Octavius* 32.1–7).

A few decades later (c. 245–250 CE), the Christian teacher Origen similarly engaged the writings of the pagan philosopher Celsus against various Christian teachings. Celsus' (now lost) work, *The True Word*, written in the last quarter of the third century, prompted Origen's much later refutation, *Against Celsus*. Although he attacked Christian resistance to statues and temples, Celsus' position on divine images was strikingly different from Caecilius'; he did not defend them. Rather, Celsus insisted that the Christian resistance to idolatry was a commonly shared view among polytheists. In response, Origen readily admitted that one could find plenty of evidence for philosophically based aniconism, but then suggested that this proved that the Christian God had been at work, changing hearts, even among ancient Greeks and Persians (*Contra Celsum* 1.5).

Thus, in his critique of Christian attitudes toward images, Celsus identified what he found to be a contradictory aspect of Christian teaching: its tendency to conceive (although not depict) their god in a human form while yet eschewing temples, altars, or divine images. In their intolerance, he claimed, Christians are like tribes who worship no god at all. By contrast, he pointed to the Persians, who similarly considered images and altars illicit because they explicitly denied that the gods have human nature or likeness. Claiming to agree with the ancient teachings of Heraclitus, who thought it was absurd to offer prayers to statues, Celsus explained that such images were meant only to honor the Divine Being. Who, he asks, would be so utterly naïve as to take the images for actual gods rather than pious representations that were consecrated to divine service? Yet, he continues, Christians clearly recognize this, since what they object to are the gods themselves (whom they regard as demons) and not, actually, to their images as such (*Contra Celsum* 7.62, 66; and cf. 6.63).

Thus, the fact that many pre-Christian philosophers and even many contemporary polytheists held carefully nuanced or even negative assessments of divine images was widely recognized among Christians. Origen's own teacher, Clement of Alexandria (c. 160–250 CE), had noted that Pythagoras had enjoined his followers to repudiate likenesses of the gods out of respect for them, recognizing that offering worship to an immaterial being by means of matter was to dishonor it (*Stromateis* 5.5). Here Clement credits Moses with teaching this to Pythagoras. Certain Christian apologists even allowed that pagan idols were a relatively new invention. One of these, Athenagoras (c. 175), had claimed that prior to Homer and Hesiod, the Greeks lacked representations of the gods (*Legatio pro Christianis* 6). Such images, he argued (inaccurately), did not appear until the invention of drawing, which he dated to the late third century BCE.

Other Christian writers claimed that the Roman king Numa (sixth century BCE) prohibited human-made images of the gods. According to Clement of Alexandria, Numa was not only following Pythagorean philosophy but was also cognizant of and influenced by Moses' injunctions against idolatry. Clement added that Numa's efforts were successful and lasted, at least for the first 170 years of Rome's history. Numa's most important legacy was to teach Romans that the Best of Beings could be apprehended only by the mind alone (*Stromateis* 1.15).

Plutarch (c. 46–120 CE) may have been Clement's source for this information, since his *Life of Numa* gives a roughly parallel version of the story, excluding the influence of Moses (Plutarch credited only

Pythagorean influence). He asserted that in that first 170 years after Rome's foundation, Romans continually built temples and shrines but never put an image of the deity in them, as they were truly convinced that it was both impious and impossible to apprehend a deity except through the mind (*Numa* 8.8). Other Christian authorities, including Tertullian (*Apologeticus* 25), also cited this evidence of Numa's image-free polytheism. Augustine actually attributed his information about Roman aniconism to a no longer extant treatise of the first-century Roman antiquarian Varro (*De Civitate Dei* 4.31). According to Augustine, Varro believed that divine images only led people to disrespect religion and he praised Judaism as a positive example of a religion without images.[13]

RECOGNIZING THE GODS

Assuming that one could fashion images of immortal beings, what could serve as models? How did artists determine the gods' appearances? Apart from certain rare aniconic exceptions, such as the plank representing Hera at Samos; the Phyrgian black stone representing Cybele, brought to Rome from Phyrgia in 204 BCE during the height of the Punic wars (cf. Arnobius, *Adversus Nationes* 7.49); or Elagabalus' conical black meteorite that was interpreted as an unwrought image of the sun (cf. Herodian, *Historia*, 5.3.5), most images were anthropomorphic; the gods were represented in human form.[14] As these were not exactly portraits, or believed to be actual likenesses, they also needed to be extraordinary in some respect. As symbolic replacements for gods who were otherwise out of sight, the images usually were idealistically beautiful and often larger than life. Additionally, they possessed particular attributes (e.g., Jupiter's thunderbolt and eagle or Minerva's aegis), by which a viewer could easily recognize them (Fig. 14.1).[15] Such attributes may have been derived from literary descriptions, the works of Homer and Hesiod in particular, or it might be that the visual images preceded their verbal counterparts.

In regard to this question, the *Olympic Discourse* of Dio Chrysostom (c. 40–120 CE) delineates the four bases for human conception of the gods: 1) that known innately, 2) that gleaned from the poets, 3) that derived from the lawgivers, and 4) that observed in the works of artists who make their statues and likenesses. Dio goes on to explain that those painters and sculptors who regarded themselves as worthy of such a task ordinarily made their images conform to the descriptions given by the myth-makers. Most were not inclined to innovation, but occasionally one would include something distinctive (a personal touch) in the work.

Figure 14.1. Statue of Minerva, known as the Athena Giustiniani. Antonine era copy of a fourth-century BCE Greek original. Now in the Vatican Museum, Rome. Photo: Vanni/Art Resource, NY.

Although their intent was only to honor the divine beings by interpreting their physical attributes for the sake of their cultured viewers, such originality, Dio says, makes them fellow craftspersons and even rivals to the poets (*Orationes* 12.44–47).[16]

In contrast to this appreciative approach to artistic originality, the Christian apologists cited it as evidence of folly. Minucius Felix's title character Octavius invites his pagan companion to admit that Vulcan's lameness, Janus' two faces, and Juno's cowlike eyes are laughable. He notes that sometimes Diana is depicted as a hunter in a short tunic, and other times as burdened with dozens of pendulous breasts; that Jupiter sometimes has a beard and sometimes horns. He wonders how anyone could respect gods who are represented so ignominiously (*Octavius* 22–23). A century later, in his apologetic treatise, Arnobius asks how artisans could know whether their creations actually resembled the otherwise unseen immortals. He notes common inconsistencies in their representations. Sometimes a god has a beard and at other times is clean-shaven. Sometimes one is fair and blue-eyed and at other times dark and swarthy. How can it be reverent, he continues, to fashion a supposed likeness that could not possibly be derived from an actual model? Even observable heavenly beings, like the sun and moon, are given human faces and bodies, when everyone can see that they are perfectly round disks of pure light (*Adversus Nationes* 6.10).

Not every polytheist thought that these images were worthy or true. Cicero (106–43 BCE), for instance, ridiculed the practice of making the gods in human form, of picturing Jupiter with a thick, full beard or Minerva wearing a helmet. He added that the unlettered multitude at least assigned symbols of each god's activities to the images, in addition to human physical features. This way they at least recognize that divinities are known by their actions or characteristic deeds, not simply by their visual representation (*De Natura Deorum* 1.36.101–2). Pliny the Elder (23–79 CE), an acknowledged agnostic, asked how anyone could know what god (or the gods) looked like. He asserted that human forms of the gods were mere condescension to human weakness (*Naturalis Historia* 2.14).

The images also varied from place to place, a testimony to their adaptability but also, according to some, to their inconsistency. Lucian of Samosata (c. 125–180 CE) wrote a humorous account of the Celtic version of Hercules. Instead of heroically youthful and muscular, the Celtic Hercules was, apparently, old, balding, and wrinkled. Lucian is assured that this figure was meant to be Hercules, by his props (lion's skin and club), and so assumed that the Celts had made the offensive image in order to spite the Greek gods (*Hercules* 1).[17] In another place, Lucian explains a geographically distinct representation of Apollo. In Hierapolis, he says, one can see a statue of the god showing him as mature and bearded and robed, rather than youthful and nude. The Syrians do this, he says, because they believe it is stupid to portray gods as youths (*De Syria Dea* 36).[18]

Thus representations, especially three-dimensional statues, acted as proxies for the divine presence. They mediated an encounter between the devotee and the god; they made a vast or distant reality accessible. Devotees may have heard or read the stories told by Homer and Hesiod, but they did not encounter the gods primarily through sacred texts; rather, they sought audiences with the gods and addressed them through their sacred images. In lieu of honoring the gods themselves, their statues could also be treated as if they were animate beings that both needed and appreciated physical care. They could be bathed and dressed, paraded in wagons around the circus, covered with garlands, delighted by smoky incense, or anointed with perfumes. They might be addressed in court, entertained with stories, told the time of the day, or had their hair dressed (Augustine, *De Civitate Dei* 6.10, quoting Seneca, *De superstitione*, fr. 35–37). Some of them were even made to speak.[19]

Nevertheless, one can assume that ancient viewers realized that the statues were inanimate, liable to fall down and break, get corroded or rotten, or provide a perch for pigeons. What is clear is that, as images, they gave visual direction or focus to religious rituals. As Arnobius noted (*Adversus Nationes* 6.9), devotees gazed at them when performing oblations, making sacrifices, or offering prayers, and polytheists believed that the gods appreciated this respectful viewing and pious service. The gods presumably noticed who paid appropriate attention and rewarded them with their patronage or special consideration. The gazers were, in turn, prompted to reverence and awe. Polytheists clearly related to the gods by means of their visual representations. They certainly never thought that they were honoring insignificant, inanimate objects. Porphyry, Plotinus' biographer, wrote a treatise on images in which he defended the gods' anthropomorphic depictions, arguing that no one actually mistook a statue for a divine being (*Peri agalmaton* 1). Similarly, the emperor Julian argued that the one who loves the gods and delights in gazing upon their images understands that the images (like the images of emperors) are not the gods themselves, but neither are they merely lumps of wood, stone, or metal (*Fragmenton epistolae* 293–4).

SEEING THE DIVINE IN JUDAISM AND CHRISTIANITY

Most Christians and Jews insisted that God is inaccessible to bodily vision, but not all of them thought of God as incorporeal or invisible by nature. Key biblical passages assert that no one has ever seen God (e.g., Deuteronomy 4:15–18; John 1:18; 1 Timothy 6:16); that God in God's fullness is hidden from human sight (e.g., Isaiah 45:15); and that God cannot be confined in temples or served, like a statue, by human hands (Acts 17:24–29). Others indicate that God deigns to appear in some limited, provisional, or incarnationally mediated way (e.g., Exodus 33:23; Isaiah 6:1; Ezekiel 1:26; John 14:8; Colossians 1:15). Such scripture passages undoubtedly prompted readers or hearers to imagine what the Divine Being might look like, even if they could not see it.

Jews and Christians alike can say that God could have a body, even a human-like one, with some justification. It is, after all, one way to interpret the Genesis creation story, when God says, "Let us make humankind in our own image, according to our likeness" (Genesis 1:26; cf. Genesis 5:1, 9:6). If humans are theomorphic, then God might be anthropomorphic. And as Celsus' writings had pointed out to Origen, the account of human creation in the image of God led some Christians to imagine God with human features. Origen, however, demurred, insisting that it only meant that humans possessed the *imago dei* in their souls, and certainly not in their bodies (*Contra Celsum* 6.63, cf. also *De Principiis* 1.1, and *Homiliae in Gen.* 1.13). Later theologians would insist that the human likeness to God is found in their ability to discern good from evil, or in their rational faculties.[20]

Jews, like Christians, held a variety of viewpoints on God's human likeness. Some Jews maintained that humans are like God in an ethical sense: they can distinguish good from evil (cf. Genesis 3:5); others that they looked like angels, who are sometimes called "gods" in the Hebrew Scriptures (cf. Genesis 18). Still others, like Philo, reading the scriptures allegorically, insisted that the archetypal Divine Mind is the basis for the human likeness (cf. *De Opificio Mundi* 23). In addition, for Philo, God's appearance or theophany was comprehended by the intellect, drawn upwards by a reasoning process that was prompted by a love of knowledge and beauty. That process was started in the eye, but concluded in the inner eye (*De Specialibus Legibus* 3.189).[21]

Nevertheless, ancient documents show that some rabbis thought that humans looked, physically, like God. Jewish sacred literature continued and even developed these anthropomorphic depictions of the Deity in rabbinic commentaries (*midrashim*), in apocalyptic texts, and in

Figure 14.2. Vision of Ezekiel. Wall painting from the Dura Europos Synagogue, c. 239 CE. Now in the National Museum, Damascus. Photo: SEF/Art Resource, NY.

mystical treatises.[22] Moreover, in Jewish art, as in the synagogue at Dura Europos, the hand of God appears, presumably a symbol for an otherwise inaccessible being, but nevertheless a human hand in form (Fig. 14.2).[23]

A famous controversy about the corporeality of God blew up in the early fifth century among Egyptian monks, when the Bishop of Alexandria, Theophilus, denounced their habit of imagining God as anthropomorphic, with a face, arms, lap, feet, and hands. According to John Cassian (c. 360–435 CE), many of the monks resisted, and at least one, Serapion, responded with a cry from the heart. Bursting into tears, he threw himself on the ground and wailed that he could no longer pray, that without his image of God he had no one to address or to adore (*Collationes* 10.2–5).

Augustine of Hippo considers the problem of God's human appearance in several different places in his extant writings. Among these is a treatise-length reply to a certain Paulina who had asked him if God is invisible or can be seen with bodily eyes. Responding that God can only be perceived with the gaze of the mind, Augustine acknowledges that some biblical figures had, indeed, been granted a kind of theophanic revelation (*Epistulae* 147). Later he takes the question up again, in the *City of God*. Here he presses the question of visuality itself. It is possible, he allows, to comprehend invisible things in and through material, created beings and objects (*De Civitate Dei* 22.29). As in Paul's Epistle to the Romans, God's invisible eternal power and divine nature can be seen in the marvels of earthly creation and the wonderful structure of the cosmos (Romans 1:20).

Within Christian teaching, of course, the invisible (but not altogether unimaginable) God also becomes personally present in the visible form of the Incarnate Christ. In his lifetime, Jesus was said to be the living image of God (John 14:9), the visual revelation of the One whose face reveals the glory of God (2 Corinthians 4:6). In his treatise *On the Incarnation*, Athanasius of Alexandria (c. 300–373 CE) compares the Incarnate Logos to an art restorer. By his appearance as a human, he displayed the original state of the human soul, so that it could be recognized and renewed. The likeness that was effaced over time by stains (sins) could be redrawn and restored (*De Incarnatione* 14).

Yet, painting actual pictures of Jesus was subject to the same suspicion of copies and reproductions that deemed such portraits to be fundamentally untrue. According to orthodox Christology, Jesus was acclaimed to have two distinct natures (divine and human). This raised unique questions about the possibility of making true visual representations of him. While in life he could be seen with the eye (he wasn't invisible), how or whether one could see a true image of him after his death and ascension was controversial. Moreover, those who argued against the possibility of making images of Jesus asserted that no image could portray his essential divinity. Nevertheless, by the late fourth century, representations of the ascended Christ, seated on a heavenly throne as judge or (new) lawgiver, came into prominence (Fig. 14.3). However, those opposed to such images continued to insist that the visible external appearance could not, by itself, incorporate or transmit the divine nature.[24]

JEWISH AND CHRISTIAN ATTITUDES TOWARD VISUAL ART

Although Christian apologists tended to focus on what they believed was the patent foolishness of making or worshipping images (and, in

Figure 14.3. Jesus enthroned with apostles. Apse mosaic from the Church of Sta. Pudenziana, c. 400–410 CE. Rome. Photo: Robin M. Jensen.

this, agreed with many ancient philosophers), the biblical prohibition of graven images has always been seen as central to the discussion of ancient Jewish and Christian aniconism. Through the millennia, this prohibition, usually referred to as the "Second Commandment" (Exodus 20:4; Deuteronomy 5:8), has been construed as a blanket condemnation of any figurative, representational art: "You shall not make for yourself an idol, whether in the form of anything that is in heaven above, or that is on the earth below." However, the injunction has been interpreted in more or less restrictive senses in different times, places, and communities. According to many readings, the prohibition is aimed only at idols (Hebrew = *pesel* and Greek = *eidolon*) and is qualified by the next line, "you shall not bow down to them or worship them." Thus, a more liberal reading understands the commandment only as an injunction against human-made objects that might attract worship or veneration. Visual art (figurative or not) would therefore be permissible, so long as it did not lead to idolatry (making or venerating cult images of divine beings, or engaging in polytheism).[25]

Historically, while the commandment may have inhibited some Jews (and, later, Christians) from making pictorial art, its observation evolved and changed according to time and place. Scholars have surmised the prohibition itself may date no earlier than the religious reforms of King

Josiah in the seventh century BCE.[26] In any case, biblical descriptions of the tent of meeting (tabernacle) refer to heavenly beings with wings and faces (cherubim) overshadowing the mercy seat (Exodus 25:1–22), and to the Israelites gazing at the bronze serpent in the wilderness as a cure for snakebite (Numbers 21:8–9). Solomon's temple included rich embellishments of lions, cherubim, and molten oxen (cf. 1 Kings 6:23–29, 7:25, 27). In the first centuries of the Common Era, both Christians and Jews decorated their tombs and places of worship with figurative art. The evidence includes the famous synagogue and house church at Dura Europos (Fig. 14.6), both dated to the mid-third century.

The Christian teacher Origen of Alexandria, praised Jewish repudiation of visual images, citing the Decalogue injunction.[27] Although he might have been speaking from knowledge of contemporary Judaism, his comments seem to have been drawn from an anachronistic picture of biblical Jews. Origen insisted that Jews denied citizenship to makers of images and expelled all pictorial art from their land. Therefore, Jews were a people without art, and thus the eyes of the soul could not be dragged from contemplation of God by worldly distractions (*Contra Celsum* 4.31).

Yet, as in the tabernacle or temple, the inclusion of religious art in synagogues appears to have been tolerated by at least some Jewish religious authorities. For example, according to the Jerusalem Talmud, Rabbi Johanan allowed two-dimensional images painted on walls, and Rabbi Abun permitted images on mosaic pavements, so long as these images did not prompt worship or veneration as such (*Abodah Zarah* 3.1, 42b–c).[28] That caveat makes a crucial distinction between permissible images and prohibited idols, which was based partially on the religious origins of the objects in question. Both scriptures and chronicles recount stories of pious Jews consistently resisting images of other nations' gods, particularly if they were required to bow down to them by foreign occupiers. This is evident in the judges' polemics against idols of Baal and Astarte (Judges 2), the resistance of the Hebrew youths to Nebuchadnezzar's golden image (Daniel 3), accounts of the Maccabees' cleansing the desecrations of Antiochus IV Epiphanes (1 Maccabees 4:36–51), and in Josephus' first-century CE chronicle of Jewish refusal to tolerate statues of the Roman emperor in their holy places (*Antiquitates Judaicae* 17.3–4, 18.3.1; *BJ* 2.9.2). Thus, Jews in antiquity specifically condemned images associated with polytheists and, for the most part, not figurative art made for their own places of worship.

Early Christians similarly aimed their condemnations of idols against the images of Greco-Roman gods and not, usually, at figurative art per se. For example, in his treatise against idolatry, Tertullian cites the biblical prohibition as directed against anything manufactured specifically for the purpose of veneration (*De Idolatria* 4). He defines images as representations of deities, fashioned out of ordinary materials and transformed by ritual consecration into objects of worship. He mocks those who pay homage to statues, for they are inanimate counterparts to their dead originals (*Apologeticus* 12). A century later, Arnobius of Sicca, in his discourse *Against the Nations*, likewise ridicules those who bow down to images made of base materials, baked in kilns, forged in furnaces, or whittled by knives. Is it not folly, he asks, to kneel down in supplication to an object that you, yourself, made with your own hands? (*Adversus Nationes* 6.16). Clearly, for most early Christians, as for some Jews, idols were images of someone else's gods – not representations of their own.

Although Christian critics normally attacked the images of polytheistic religion, some surviving documents suggest that figurative depictions of saints or Jesus bothered for certain Christian authorities, at least to the extent that such depictions might be misunderstood as objects of veneration. Eusebius of Caesarea (c. 260–309 CE) noticed that converted Gentiles sometimes set up likenesses of Peter, Paul, and Jesus in order to pay honor to them (*Historia Ecclesiastica* 7.18). Eusebius' disapproval was offset by the acceptance of something that he saw as inevitable: habits are hard to break. A more hostile condemnation dates a few decades later, toward the end of the fourth century, and comes from the heresy-fighting bishop, Epiphanius of Salamis (c. 315–403 CE). Objecting to representations of saints painted on walls or woven into curtains and recalling ancient authorities' denunciation of pagan idols, he asked how anyone could dare to plaster church walls with false images invented from the ignorant inclinations of mortal artists.[29]

Official censure of such church decoration was codified by the early Christian Council of Elvira (c. 305 CE), which prohibited pictures on the walls of churches for fear that viewers would be tempted to offer them reverence or adoration: "There shall be no pictures in churches, lest what is reverenced and adored be depicted on the walls."[30] The need for the Council's prohibition, of course, indicates that such pictures were, in fact, appearing on church walls and that groups of Christians were offering prayers or veneration in their presence. The decorated walls of the mid-third-century Christian house church in Dura Europos serves as a possible example. Yet, here the iconography mostly presents biblical narrative scenes; for example, the Samaritan woman at the well, and Jesus healing the paralytic or walking on the water (Fig. 14.4). They were not iconic representations of God, Christ, or the saints.

Figure 14.4. Jesus walking on the water. Wall painting from the Christian baptistery in Dura Europos, c. 240 CE. Now in the Yale University Art Gallery. Photo:
Yale University Art Gallery, Dura-Europos Collection.

This local council seems to have had little long-range or long-term
influence on the decoration of churches. Beginning in the mid- to late
fourth century, images of saints, apostles, angels, the Virgin, and Jesus
began to appear as part of the décor of Christian churches, imperial mausolea, and martyrs' shrines. Among the oldest of these, Old St. Peter's
Basilica, built sometime in the second quarter of the fourth century,
probably had an apse mosaic of Jesus giving the law to Peter and Paul.[31]
The Basilica of St. Paul on the Via Ostiense, built in the mid-380s, had
an original figural mosaic in the apse and on the triumphal arch that
depicted Christ, the apostles, and the elders mentioned in Revelation
4; Pope Leo adorned its nave with a biblical pictorial cycle sometime
around 450. The basilica of Santa Pudenziana was furnished with an
apse mosaic of Jesus surrounded by his apostles at the beginning of the
fifth century (Fig. 14.3), and the basilica of Santa Maria Maggiore (built
in the 430s) had a triumphal arch showing scenes from the infancy of

Figure 14.5. Apse mosaic from the Church of Ss. Cosmas and Damian, c. 526–30 CE. Rome. Photo: Robin M. Jensen.

Jesus and nave mosaics depicting scenes from the Old Testament. Its now-lost apse mosaic most likely held an image of the Virgin, probably seated with the baby Jesus in her lap. Perhaps the best example is the apse mosaic from the Church of Ss. Cosmas and Damian in Rome, dated to c. 526–30 CE, which depicts Jesus in the middle, with St. Peter, St. Cosmas, and St. Theodorus on the right and St. Paul, St. Damian, and Pope Felix IV on the left (Fig. 14.5).

Textual evidence gives some explanation for these developments. At the beginning of the fifth century, Bishop Paulinus of Nola (355–431 CE) commissioned artists to decorate the basilica dedicated to St. Felix with paintings of scenes from the Old Testament including the heroics of Joshua, the Israelites entering the Promised Land, and Ruth with Naomi. In an extant poem, Paulinus explains that he agreed to these visual embellishments (mere "empty figures") in hopes of enticing the flocks of pilgrims coming to Felix's shrine to keep sober vigils rather than holding rowdy feasts. The colorful paintings, he says, attract them as well as instruct them. Because the images are enhanced with explanatory inscriptions, visitors are able to identify the images and even read the captions to one another. By seeing and reading accounts of ancient heroes of the faith, they are encouraged to be more pious and virtuous themselves (*Carmina* 27.511–595).[32]

Figure 14.6. West wall and Torah niche from the Dura Europos Synagogue, c. 239 CE. Now in the National Museum, Damascus. Photo: Princeton University Press/ Art Resource, NY.

Possibly the earliest recorded official action against images (after the Council of Elvira's stipulation against pictures on the walls of churches) comes at the beginning of the seventh century. Two letters from Gregory the Great (pope from 590 to 604) to Bishop Serenus of Marseilles reveal that Serenus had practiced iconoclasm by removing or destroying images of the saints, possibly sculpted as well as painted, from the churches under his jurisdiction (*Epistulae* 9.105, 11.13). Gregory admonished Serenus against this action. While conceding that images could be misused and lead to idolatry, Gregory's defense is somewhat like Paulinus': art also serves a useful religious function. In a famously quoted line, he says that pictures can serve as sacred texts for the unlettered, helping them to read on the walls what they cannot read in books.[33]

Images of biblical heroes were not limited to Christian religious contexts. The mid-third-century synagogue at Dura Europos also was decorated richly with biblical scenes, here on all four walls and on three separate registers (Fig. 14.6). These wall paintings include scenes from the life of Moses, the visions of Ezekiel, the binding of Isaac, the competition between Elijah and the priests of Baal, and Samuel anointing David. Notably, the hand of God is depicted, perhaps as a way of simultaneously displaying and concealing God's presence in sacred history (Fig. 14.2). From the fourth through sixth centuries, synagogues in Galilee were decorated with figurative mosaics that included the figures of Abraham and Isaac, as well as animals, birds, temple implements, and even zodiacs (Fig. 14.7).[34] Although the evidence for other Jewish art is

Figure 14.7. Zodiac mosaic floor panel from the Beth Alpha Synagogue, sixth century CE. Beit Alpha, Israel. Photo: Art Resource, NY.

scarce and limited mostly to tomb decorations instead of synagogues, worries about idolatry did not necessarily or universally inhibit the production of narrative or symbolic figurative art.

Both the stipulations that would prohibit and those that would permit religious iconography in Judaism and Christianity are based on a repudiation of idolatry, whether that be the misplaced worship of inanimate objects or the veneration of foreign gods. So long as the art was not created for or subject to idolatrous use, it might be permitted. Nevertheless, in the Greco-Roman period, most philosophers and theologians worried about the temptation to idolatry posed by images, realizing that their beguiling beauty could sometimes lead viewers away from the pure worship of God in spirit and in truth (John 4:23). They argued that intellectual comprehension was far more reliable than sensory perception and emphasized the inherent invisibility and incomprehensibility of the Divine Being.

GAZING AT MYTHOLOGICAL NARRATIVES OR SACRED STORIES

Pictorial representations of divine or semi-divine figures presented as characters in episodes from classical mythology, or depictions of heroes, saints, and angelic or divine beings as they appear in Jewish or Christian sacred narratives, contribute to a different kind of religious visual practice. Unlike images or portraits of the gods that were intended primarily to invite veneration, inspire devotion, or prompt prayer, narrative images transmit their content or meaning in a form quite different from texts; they have a syntax that is grasped, either by the eye or mind, and in figures rather than in words. Although all cognition may be constructed of mentally envisioned signs, narrative art plays a special role in shaping the ways that stories are told, remembered, and recounted. Illustrations never contain the same information as verbal presentations of narratives; they are both more and less. They add visual details not specified in the texts, but also present only selected passages. They further interpret the narrative, emphasizing certain aspects by means of composition, color, technique, and context.

Furthermore, looking at pictures is different from reading texts or hearing them read; the information is received and comprehended panoptically rather than sequentially. The gaze does not move in a single trajectory, from beginning to end. Stories unfold; images present themselves. The eye sees all at once or observes small sections one at a time, moving through a picture in almost any possible direction. Pictures also relate to other images that surround them, embedded as they are in unrelated groups, intentional programs, and various physical settings (e.g., tombs, shrines, and synagogues). Thus the relationship of image to text is more that of a juxtaposed mode of interpretation than of dependence or subordination. Although its meaning necessarily relies on some knowledge of its source (the story itself), an illustration never slavishly conforms to narrative but functions exegetically. It focuses, abridges, elaborates, and diverges from its origin. It can offer visual cues to the religious significance of the story or point to related narratives.[35] The artist has become the storyteller but the story unfolds in a constitutively different format.

Figure 14.8. Wall paintings from the Villa of the Mysteries, first century CE. Pompeii. Photo: Robin M. Jensen.

Scenes from classical mythology were well represented in both private and public buildings of antiquity. Such scenes appeared in floor pavements and in wall paintings throughout the Mediterranean world. The houses of Pompeii and Herculaneum alone have a wide repertoire of mythological motifs.[36] Some of the images are clearly identifiable episodes of those stories. Others, like the wall paintings of the Villa of the Mysteries at Pompeii, appear to be combinations of mythological characters and their mortal devotees, engaged in a ritual of some kind (Fig. 14.8). Although not necessarily viewed as "sacred" in the same way as illuminations in later Christian Bibles, for example, many may have been intended to inspire or edify viewers while still decorating such spaces as private dining rooms, public baths, family tombs, and simple altars. Their ability to arouse emotions of pity or affection is evident in Philostratus' ekphrastic treatise, *Imagines*. Among the images the author describes is that of Marsyas. Looking at the hero of the tragic tale, he notes the way the man's facial features betray his awareness of his doom. Having lost a contest with Apollo over who was the better musician, he realizes that he has played his flute for the last time. He stands near the pine tree from which he will be hung as punishment for his hubris in challenging the god, and he glances toward the barbarian who is preparing to flay him alive (*Imagines* 2).

Despite the long tradition of narrative art in Greco-Roman culture, the appearance of narrative art in both Judaism and Christianity appears relatively late. The earliest extant evidence seems to date to the second century CE. Nevertheless, the examples of the synagogue and house church at Dura Europos demonstrate that places of worship were, at least occasionally, adorned with scriptural scenes by the 240s or 250s. The Christian building had a baptismal room enhanced with wall paintings that depicted scenes that alluded to the rite (e.g., the Samaritan woman at the well and Jesus walking on the water – cf. Fig. 14.4) while the much more elaborately decorated synagogue had an impressive series of narrative images that depicted scenes from the Hebrew scriptures (e.g., the Israelites crossing the Red Sea, Saul anointing David), along with portraits of prophets and representations of Jewish liturgical objects (cf. Fig. 14.6).

As mentioned previously, Paulinus of Nola clearly understood the value of narrative images to attract and to entrance. He also believed that they could educate and form both minds and morals. Paulinus justified the paintings in his basilica by claiming that they could reform the behavior of visiting pilgrims and inspire viewers to imitate saintly virtues (*Carmina* 27.511–595). He was obviously convinced that looking at pictures of heroic deeds was at least as effective as hearing them retold in sermons. He did note, however, that the explanatory inscriptions were necessary to reveal the themes of the illuminations.[37]

Gregory the Great similarly believed that pictures could have a pedagogical function. He asserted that people might learn from paintings what they could otherwise read in books.[38] He argued that those who were illiterate could be especially aided by sacred images, so long as they were only discerning the things they should adore, rather than adoring the things they saw. Furthermore, he added, the images could do more than educate; they could move viewers, out of love and humility, to bow down in adoration to the Holy Trinity. He supported his contention by pointing out that narrative images (histories) had long existed, and for these good reasons (*Epistulae* 11.13).

The Cappadocian theologian Gregory of Nyssa (c. 331–395 CE) gave an example of such iconographic inspiration. In admiration for the artist's skill, he described the emotional impact he felt whenever he saw a certain painting depicting Abraham about to sacrifice his son, Isaac, as described in Genesis 22:9–10. As Gregory gazed at the vividly rendered depiction of this terrifying scene, he was moved to tears (*De deitate Filii et Spiritus Sancti*).[39] A related incident comes from an epistle of Cyril, the fifth-century bishop of Alexandria. Having just recounted the same story of Abraham binding his son for sacrifice from Genesis 22, he asked his readers how an artist might depict it. Recognizing the problem that an artist faced trying to capture several different episodes from a longer

Figure 14.9. Abraham's hospitality, offering of Isaac. Sanctuary mosaic from the Church of San Vitale, c. 547 CE. Ravenna. Photo: Robin M. Jensen.

narrative, he asks whether his listeners would have preferred to see the same figure (Abraham) enacting all the moments simultaneously, or in a sequential series of illustrations. He concludes that it would not be reasonable or possible for an artist to try to show everything at once. Thus, the viewer must be able to recognize Abraham, appearing in different guises in various parts of the painting (*Epistulae* 16).[40]

A survey of early Christian art demonstrates the exceptional popularity of this scene. Surviving representations appear in Christian catacomb paintings; on sarcophagus reliefs; on precious metals, gold, glass, and gems; and on pottery lamps, bowls, and tiles. It even appears as a series of sequential scenes above the main altar in Ravenna's sixth-century basilica of San Vitale (Fig. 14.9). The binding of Isaac also appears in Jewish iconography: over the Torah niche in the Dura Europos synagogue (cf. Fig. 14.6) as well as on the pavements of fifth- and sixth-century Jewish synagogues.[41] Whether other ancient viewers experienced Gregory of Nyssa's emotional response to the scene is impossible to know. The image may have had other purposes than arousing pity. Depending on its context, it also transmitted its possible theological significance. Juxtaposed with a representation of Jesus' arrest and trial, it could symbolically refer to the crucifixion (Jesus as the innocent son, willingly sacrificed – Fig. 14.10). When set over the Torah niche or on the floor of a synagogue, it could refer to the covenant with Abraham and the shift from temple cult to synagogue worship.

Thus visual narratives served many different functions. Even when they were directly juxtaposed with the texts that they alluded to (as

Figure 14.10. The so-called Two Brothers Sarcophagus. Now in the Pio-Cristiano Museum, Vatican, mid-fourth century CE. Rome. Photo: Robin M. Jensen.

in Paulinus' captions or, later, in illuminated manuscripts), they went beyond a simple pictorial presentation of an episode. They were interpretive, guiding understanding of a narrative's possible meaning or significance, and they were also able to evoke emotions from viewers in a visceral way. Episodes incorporated into pictorial cycles or programs also became part of new religious or theological narratives that might have little to do with the original story.

CONCLUSION

Visuality in the Greco-Roman religions of Late Antiquity is constituted by far more than pictorial art, of course. Rituals are complex visual events in which all the participants are images, along with their garments, their surroundings, the ceremonial objects and furniture that they use, and the gestures and movements that they follow. Furthermore, the visual dimension of these religions includes invisible and imagined images as well as those that others can also see, expressed in paint, glass, stone, or wood. In the long run, however, it is the material that survives. The temples, synagogues, churches, altars, statues, paintings, terra-cotta lamps, glass mosaics, funeral stele, and sarcophagi have a permanency and continuing social presence that mental conceptions, spoken words, or even written texts do not possess. They still exist, standing in the midst

Figure 14.11. Ara Pacis Augustae, 13–9 BCE. Ara Pacis Museum, Rome. Photo: Robin M. Jensen.

of modern civic landscapes as testimonies to the distant past. Modern viewers still gaze upon the ancient and ancient Roman rituals when they visit the Emperor Augustus' Ara Pacis, now enclosed in a contemporary glass reliquary that sits along the banks of the ancient Roman Tiber River, for example (Fig. 14.11). Tomb inscriptions in all parts of the Mediterranean world, whether in situ or in museums still bid us to pray for their occupants and call attention to our own mortality.

The receptive practice of observing or viewing (seeing or recognizing), as well as the active work of visualizing (describing or making images) are central elements of religious expression, then and now. These elements are fundamental for comprehending, encountering, venerating, or explaining both present and absent beings, essential concepts, and core values. In this sense, images are as cognitive and discursive as texts, but just work in a different way. Visual images both narrate and interpret stories. They shape and give focus to private prayers and communal rites. Some may even have agency (acting for themselves). Their function and their power are, however, a language that is embedded in, shaped by, and reflective of their particular time, place, and circumstance. As such, they are nuggets of precious firsthand data for historians of religion.

FURTHER READING

The study of visual and material culture has been developing, expand-ing, and becoming more central to historical and religious studies over the past thirty or forty years. Some of the most important contributors in the areas of religion and art of Late Antiquity have been Paul Zanker, Richard Brilliant, Jas Elsner, John Clarke, and Peter Stewart in Greco-Roman art and religion; Mary Charles Murray, Paul Corby Finney, Thomas Mathews, Herbert Kessler, Hans Belting, and Robin M. Jensen in ancient and early Byzantine Christian art; and Steve Fine, Rachael Hachlili, Zeev Weiss, and Lee Levine in Jewish art and architecture. For readers who wish for accessible introductions the following would make excellent choices: Elsner 1998, Jensen 2000, Stewart 2003, and Fine 2005. Elsner's work, in particular, bridges Roman art and visual culture of Late Antiquity with the rise of Christianity and the transi-tion of images, themes, styles, and religious contexts engendered in that fourth- and fifth-century religious revolution. The major exhibition cata-logue published by the Metropolitan Museum of Art in 1979, *The Age of Spirituality*, edited by Kurt Weitzmann, was a fundamental resource for generations of scholars who sought new approaches to the study of reli-gion and art in Late Antiquity. This catalogue has recently been matched in importance by one edited by Jeffrey Spier, *Picturing the Bible* (2007), which offers a combination of overview essays by many of the above-mentioned authors, exceptional photographs, clearly written entries on a wide range of important artifacts, and an extensive bibliography.

Notes

1   Examples of religious studies scholars who use these new methods include Miles 1985, Finney 1994, Elsner 1998, Fine 2005, and Nasrallah 2010.
2   Pioneers of this new methodology include Freedberg 1989, Belting 1994, Morgan 2005, and Elsner 2007.
3   Barasch 1992:36–39 gives some instances of this.
4   See the seminal study of Freedberg 1989.
5   See, e.g., Elkins 1996 and Elsner 1995:51.
6   See, e.g., Elsner 2007.
7   On the topic of ekphrasis see Elsner 2007:67–109.
8   A brief, good summary is Ando 2008:27–31; see also Camille 1996:31–33.
9   Plato's theory of vision probably was derived from earlier (fifth-century BCE) thinkers, including Pythagoreans and the Presocratics (e.g., Alcmaeon of Croton, Democritus, or Empedocles). Plato's theory is best summarized in *Timaeus* 45b–d, while Aristotle's appears, principally, in his treatises *De anima* and *De sensu*. For a summary see Lindberg 1976:1–9.

10 See Stewart 2003:184–222, with a good discussion of terms; also Camille 1996:31–33.
11 As an example see Pliny the Younger, *Epistle* 3.6.
12 See Barasch 1992:34–36, and later.
13 On ancient Roman aniconism see Taylor 1931.
14 On aniconism in ancient Greek religion see Gaifmann 2008.
15 See Rüpke 2007:69–74.
16 See Stewart 2008:130–38.
17 See Elsner 2007:59.
18 Ibid., 61.
19 See Stewart 2003:192–93 and Barasch 1992:34–36.
20 See Jensen 2005:103–15.
21 See Elsner 1995:94–5.
22 See Aaron 1997.
23 See Hachlili 1998:59–70, esp. 66; Jensen 2005:36; Kessler 2000:5–6.
24 This is summarized in Besançon 2000:123–31.
25 Here see Jensen 2005:101–103, 131–34.
26 See Gutmann 1977:5–25.
27 On the use of the Decalogue see Grant 1947 and Murray 1977.
28 See Fine 2005:97–102.
29 This comes from a fragment of Epiphanius' *Testament*, published in Mango 1986:41.
30 Translation by author. Latin text and translation in Hefele 1894:151. See Jensen 2005:20 for a discussion of an alternative rendering of the text.
31 Based, in part, on medieval sketches of the building before its reconstruction in the sixteenth century. See discussion in Hellemo 1989:70.
32 See De Nie 2005.
33 See Chazelle 1990 and Kessler 1994:2–5.
34 See Fine 2005:196–205 and Hachlili 1988:301–10.
35 A brief discussion of narrative imagery, with a good bibliography, is found in Kemp 1996:58–69. See also Brilliant 1984:15–20 and Elsner 1995:249–87 (a study of visual exegesis).
36 See Elsner 1995:49–87 and Clarke 1991, 2006.
37 See the previous discussion of Paulinus' arguments for church decoration.
38 See the previous discussion of Gregory's letters to Bishop Serenus.
39 See Mango 1986:34.
40 Ibid.
41 See Hachlili 1988:288–92, 1998:239–46, and Jensen 2000:143–48.

Works Cited

Aaron, David. 1997. "Shedding Light on God's Body in Mirashim: Reflections on the Theory of a Luminous Adam." *Harvard Theological Review* 90: 299–314.

Ando, Clifford. 2008. *The Matter of the Gods: Religion and the Roman Empire.* Berkeley.

Barasch, Moshe. 1992. *Icon: Studies in the History of an Idea.* New York.

Belting, Hans. 1994. *Likeness and Presence: A History of the Image before the Era of Art*. Chicago.

Besançon, Alain. 2000. *The Forbidden Image: An Intellectual History of Iconoclasm*. Trans. J. M. Todd. Chicago.

Brilliant, Richard. 1984. *Visual Narratives: Story Telling in Etruscan and Roman Art*. Ithaca, NY.

Camille, Michael. 1996. "Simulacrum." In *Critical Terms for Art History*. Ed. R. Nelson and R. Shiff, 31–44. Chicago.

Chazelle, Celia. 1990. "Pictures, Books, and the Illiterate: Pope Gregory I's Letters to Serenus of Marseilles." *Word and Image* 6: 138–53.

Clarke, John. 1991. *The Houses of Roman Italy, 100 B.C.–A.D. 250: Ritual, Space and Decoration*. Berkeley.

———. 2006. *Art in the Lives of Ordinary Romans: Visual Representation and Non-Elite Viewers in Italy, 100 B.C.–A.D. 315*. Berkeley.

De Nie, Giselle. 2005. "Paulinus of Nola and the Image within the Image." In *Reading Images and Texts: Medieval Images and Texts as Forms of Communication*. Ed. M. Hageman and M. Mostert, 261–89. Turnhout.

Elkins, James. 1996. *The Object Stares Back: On the Nature of Seeing*. San Diego, CA.

Elsner, Jas. 1995. *Art and the Roman Viewer: The Transformation of Art from the Pagan World to Christianity*. Cambridge.

———. 1998. *Imperial Rome and Christian Triumph*. Oxford.

———. 2007. *Roman Eyes: Visuality and Subjectivity in Art and Text*. Princeton, NJ.

Fine, Steven. 2005. *Art and Judaism in the Greco-Roman World*. Cambridge.

Finney, Paul Corby. 1994. *The Invisible God: The Earliest Christians on Art*. Oxford.

Freedberg, David. 1989. *The Power of Images*. Chicago.

Gaifman, Milette. 2008. "The Aniconic Image of the Roman Near East." In *The Variety of Local Religions of the Ancient Near East*. Ed. T. Kaizer, 37–72. Leiden.

Grant, Robert. 1947. "The Decalogue in Early Christianity." *Harvard Theological Review* 40: 1–17.

Gutmann, Joseph. 1977. "Deuteronomy: Religious Reformation or Iconoclastic Revolution. In *The Image and the Word*. Ed. J. Gutmann, 5–25. Missoula, MT.

Hachlili, Rachel. 1988. *Ancient Jewish Art and Archaeology in the Land of Israel*. Leiden.

———. 1998. *Ancient Jewish Art and Archaeology in the Diaspora*. Leiden.

Hefele, Karl Joseph. 1894. *History of the Christian Councils*. Trans. W. Clark. London.

Hellemo, Geir. 1989. *Adventus Domini: Eschatological Thought in 4th-Century Apses and Catecheses*. Leiden.

Jensen, Robin M. 2000. *Understanding Early Christian Art*. London.

———. 2005. *Face to Face: Picturing the Divine in Early Christianity*. Minneapolis, MN.

Kemp, Wolfgang. 1996. "Narrative." In *Critical Terms for Art History*. Ed. R. Nelson and R. Shiff, 58–69. Chicago.

Kessler, Herbert. 1994. *Studies in Pictorial Narrative*. London.

———. 2000. *Spiritual Seeing: Picturing God's Invisibility in Medieval Art*. Philadelphia.

Lindberg, David. 1976. *Theories of Vision from Al-Kindi to Kepler*. Chicago.

Mango, Cyril. 1986. *The Art of the Byzantine Empire 312–1453*. Toronto.

Miles, Margaret. 1985. *Image as Insight: Visual Understanding in Western Christianity and Secular Culture*. Boston.

Morgan, David. 2005. *The Sacred Gaze: Religious Visual Culture in Theory and Practice*. Berkeley, CA.

Murray, Mary Charles. 1977. "Art in the Early Church." *Journal of Theological Studies* 43: 685–90.

Nasrallah, Laura Salah. 2010. *Christian Responses to Roman Art and Architecture*. Cambridge

Rüpke, Jörg. 2007. *Religion of the Romans*. Trans. Richard Gordon. Cambridge.

Spier, Jeffrey, ed. 2007. *Picturing the Bible: The Earliest Christian Art*. New Haven, CT.

Stewart, Peter. 2003. *Statues in Roman Society: Representation and Response*. Oxford.

———. 2008. *The Social History of Roman Art*. Cambridge.

Taylor, Lily Ross. 1931. "Aniconic Worship among the Early Romans." In *Classical Studies in Honor of John C. Rolfe*. Ed. G. D. Hadzlits, 305–19. Middletown, CT.

Weitzmann, Kurt, ed. 1979. *The Age of Spirituality: Late Antique and Early Christian Art, Third to Seventh Century*. New York.

Index

Page numbers in *italics* reference illustrative materials. Specific works will be found under their authors unless they are anonymous, in which case they will be listed under their title.

Aaron and Aaronite priesthood, 84–85, 92

Abraham (biblical patriarch), 82, 203, 222, 224, 229, 232, 332, 336, *337*

Academicism, 169, 170

Achaemenids, 125, 126, 128, 129, 134, 204, 205. *See also* Iran and Zoroastrianism

Achilles Tatius, *Leucippe and Clitophon*, 302n15

Acts of John, 314

Acts of Paul, 190

The Acts of the Martyrs of Scilli, 303n58

Acts of Thomas, 180, 303n69

Adad (Mesopotamian deity), 37, 67

Adonis (Greek deity), 138, *152*, 297

Aeschylus: *Agamemnon*, 247n55; *The Persians*, 228; *Prometheia* (plays on Prometheus), 146–47

Aesculapius/Asclepius (Roman deity), 158, 266. *See also* Asklepios/Asclepius

afterlife. *See* life after death; underworld gods

age as discriminating factor: in Greece, 145; in Iran and Zoroastrianism, 122, 124; in Israel and Judaism, 86–87; in Rome, 163, 168–69

Agni/Atar (Iranian deity), 117

agnosticism, of Pliny the Elder, 322

Ahiqar, story of, 69

Ahriman (Iranian deity), 120–21, 126, 134

Ahura Mazda [Ohrmazd] (Iranian deity), 117, 118, 119, 120–21, 123, 124, 125, 126, 127, 132, 134

akh (transfigured spirit), 17, 30

Akkadians, 33, 48, 62. *See also* Mesopotamia

Alaca Höyük, 95, 103

Alcmaeon of Croton, 340n9

Alexander the Great, 71, 125, 126, 132–33, 138, 152, 204, 229–30

alimentary sacrifice, 63, 85, 100–01, 141, 164, 284

allegory and metaphor, 259–62

alterity and otherness narratives, 227–31

Amarna theology, Egypt, 26, 27

Amenemope (Egyptian deity), 15

Amenemope[t] (author), "Instructions of Amenemope[t]," 14, 58

Amesha Spentas (Bounteous Immortals), 117, 123

Ammonites, 68

Ammuna (Anatolian ruler), 106

Amorites, 33, 55, 56, 60, 66

Amos (biblical prophet), 87–88

amphictyony, 103, 104, 106

Amun (Egyptian deity), 14, 15–16, 19, 21, 22, 23, 30, 67

Amun-Re (Egyptian deity), 15, 19

Anahita (Iranian deity), 118, 125, 132

Anat (Syro-Canaanite deity), 14, 58, 59, 60, 61

Anath (Syro-Canaanite deity), 80

Anathyahu (Israelite deity), 80

Anatolia, 3, 95–110; belief systems in, 97–100; chronology, 110–11; cities, association of particular deities with, 98; connections to and borrowings from religions in other cultures, 96–97, 106; cosmology and eschatology, 99–100; deities, 97–99; feasts and festivals in, 103, 106; gender in, 104; glossary, 111; Greece and, 138; Hattians, 95, 96, 98, 99–100, 105, 109; historical development

Anatolia (*cont.*)
  of religion in, 95–97; Luwians, 95,
  96, 98, 104; philosophy and ethics
  in, 107–8; politics and religion in,
  96–97, 98, 103–4, 105–8; practice
  of religion in, 100–05; research and
  further reading, 108–10; ritual in,
  100–02; sacred space in, 102–3;
  sacred time in, 103; social context
  of religion in, 105–8; structural
  organization of religion in, 103–4,
  105. *See also* Hittites
ancestor worship, 61, 68, 139–40,
  162, 231
ancient Mediterranean religions, 1–7;
  as academic discipline, 2–3; the
  body and, 6, 252–75 (*see also* body);
  comparative study of, 4–5; concept
  of religion and, 1, 136, 220; gender
  and, 6, 281–300 (*see also* gender);
  identity in, 5–6, 220–44
  (*see also* identity); interdisciplinary
  approach to, 1–2, 7; map of
  Mediterranean world, *xii–xiii*, 4;
  regional approach to, 3–4; topical
  approach to, 4; violence and, 5, 199–
  213 (*see also* violence); visuality in,
  6–7, 309–40 (*see also* visuality).
  See also *specific cultures and religions*
Ando, Clifford, 175n16, 242
angels, 89, 183, 205, 253, 260–61, 265,
  270, 296–97, 298, 324, 330, 334
aniconic representations of gods, 320
aniconism, Jewish and Christian,
  326–34
animal sacrifice: Abraham's sacrifice of
  ram in place of son Isaac, 82, 203,
  336–37, *337*; abstention from, 284;
  alimentary sacrifice, 63, 85, 100–01,
  141, 164, 284; in Anatolia, 97,
  100–01; burnt offerings, 101, 141,
  302n22; Christianity and, 181; in
  Egypt, 19–20; gender and, 283–84,
  289; in Greece, 141–42, 146, 149,
  150; holocaust sacrifice, 141–42,
  149; as identity performance,
  231; in Iran and Zoroastrianism,
  117; in Israel, 82–83, 85, 284;
  meat avoidance and, 141; in
  Mesopotamia, 35; in Rome, 163,
  164; in Syria-Canaan, 63, 64
animals representing or associated with
  gods, 15, 59, 95, 99

anthropomorphism: in Anatolia, 95,
  99; bodies of gods and, 253–58; in
  Egypt, 15; in Greece, 139, 147; in
  Mesopotamia, 34; in Rome, 160; in
  Syria-Canaan, 59; visual images of
  gods and, 317, 320, 323, 324–25
Antoninus (C. Arrius Antoninus), 191
Antony the Hermit, 269–70
Anu (Mesopotamian deity), 34, 36
Anum (AN) god list, 36
Anzû Epic, 40, 57
Aphaia (Greek deity), 137
Aphrodite (Greek deity), 138, 139, 145,
  237–38, 297. *See also* Venus
Apis (Egyptian deity), 14, 30
apocalyptic beliefs. *See* eschatological
  beliefs
Apocrypha, 236, 244.
  See also specific texts
Apocryphal Acts of the Apostles, 268
Apocryphon of John, 260–61
Apollo (Greek/Roman deity), 137, 139,
  142, 144, 146, 158, 165, 232, 287,
  303n51, 323, 335
Apollodorus: *Bibliotheca*, 224; *Epitome*,
  246n24
Apollonius of Tyana, 272
Apollos of Alexandria, 188
Apology of Hattusili III, 106
Apuleius, *Metamorphoses*, 235, 238
Aqhat, Ugaritic story of, 60, 61, 62,
  65, 68
Ara Maxima, Rome, 157
Ara Pacis, Rome, 160, *161*, *339*
Arameans, 33, 55, 62, 63, 68, 70
Ardashir I (Iranian ruler), 125–26, 134
Aredwi Sura (Iranian deity), 120
Aristides (Aelius Aristides), *Sacred
  Tales*, 266–67
Aristophanes: *Thesmophoriazusai*, 283;
  Wasps, 246n7
Aristotle: *De anima* and *De sensu*,
  340n9; Golden Mean of, 127; on
  vision, 315, 340n9
arkuwar prayers, 102
Arnobius of Sicca, *Adversus Nationes/
  Against the Nations*, 317–18, 320,
  322, 323, 329
Arsacids, 123, 129, 131, 133, 134.
  See also Iran and Zoroastrianism
Arslan Tash, 55, 57, 62
Artaxerxes I (Iranian ruler), 124
Artaxerxes II (Iranian ruler), 125, 132

Artemis (Greek deity), 97, 137, 138,
 143, 149, 159, 180, 283, 297.
 See also Diana
Ascension of Isaiah, 303n69
asceticism: as bodily training, 270–73;
 defined, 272; in Egypt, 22, 23;
 gender issues and celibacy rules,
 292–93; healing and, 269–70; self-
 castration, 272, 287, 320; violence,
 mortification of the flesh as form
 of, 206–8, *208*
Asclepius. *See* Aesculapius/Asclepius;
 Asklepios/Asclepius
asherah (pole or stylized tree), 79
Asherah (Syro-Canaanite/Israelite
 deity), 58, 59, 60, 62, 68, 69, 70, 72,
 79–80, 91, 296
Ashtar. *See* Astarte
Asklepios/Asclepius (Greek deity),
 62, 65, 137, 152, 266–67.
 See also Aesculapius/Asclepius
Assmann, Jan, 17–18, 26, 27
Assur (Mesopotamian deity), 38, 39,
 43, 45
Assyrians, 33, 56, 92n2, 205.
 See also Mesopotamia
Astarte [Ashtar, Athtart] (Syro-
 Canaanite deity), 14, 58–60, 64–65,
 71–72, 138, 165, 328
astral religions, 34, 46, 59
astrology, 65, 66, 159, 332, *333*
Atar/Agni (Iranian deity), 117
Aten/Aton (Egyptian deity), 15, 26
Athanasius of Alexandria: *De
 Incarnatione/On the Incarnation*,
 326; *Vita Antonii/Life of Antony*,
 269–70
atheism, in Israel, 89
Athena (Greek deity), 97, 118, 137, 139,
 145, 146, 160, 222, 225, 232, 297.
 See also Minerva
Athena Giustiniani (statue), 320, *321*
Athens. *See* Greece and Greeks
Athirat. *See* Asherah
Athtart. *See* Astarte
Atrahasis Myth, 37
attraction rituals, 101, 122
Atum (Egyptian deity), 15, 16, 30
augury. *See* divination
Augustine of Hippo: *Confessiones*,
 309, 315, 316; *De civitate Dei/
 City of God*, 255, 320, 323, 326;
 De Trinitate, 184, 316; on divine

bodies, 255; *Epistulae*, 326; just war
 theory of, 203; as Manichaean, 134;
 Sermones, 315–16, 317; Trinitarian
 theology and, 184; visuality and,
 309, 315–16, 317, 320, 323, 326
Augustus (Roman emperor), 160, 165,
 204, 225, 247n77
Aulus Gellius, 166
authority structures. *See* structural
 organization of religion
autochthonous peoples, 222, 223
Avesta, 117, 119, 122, 123, 125, 128,
 129, 130
Avestan sources for Iran and
 Zoroastrianism, 122, 128, 130, 132,
 133, 134

ba (spirit), 19, 30
Baal (Syro-Canaanite deity), 14,
 58–62, 64, 66, 71, 72, 76–78, 80, 88,
 328, 332
Baal Cycle, 57, 58, 61, 64
Baal Hadad (Syro-Canaanite deity), 58,
 59, 60, 72
Baal-Hammon (Syro-Canaanite
 deity), 60
Baal-Samad (Syro-Canaanite deity),
 62–63
Baal-Shamayn (Syro-Canaanite deity), 62
Baal-Shamem (Syro-Canaanite deity),
 60, 68
Baalat (Syro-Canaanite deity), 60
Babylonians, 33, 205.
 See also Mesopotamia
Bacchus (Roman deity), 141, 159, 294.
 See also Dionysos
Balaam son of Beor, 68
baptism, 185–86, 189, 240, 241, 287, 292
Bar Kochba Revolt (132–35 CE), 180, 290
Basilides of Alexandria, 180, 192, 257
Bat (Egyptian deity), 15
Behistun inscription, 124
Bel (Syro-Canaanite deity), 66, 67
belief, concept of, 150
belief systems. See under *specific
 cultures and religions*
Bendis (Thracian deity), 138
Beth Alpha Synagogue, Israel, zodiac
 mosaic, 332, *333*
Bibel-Babel Debate, 46
Bible: aniconism in, 327, 328; *Avesta*
 compared, 128; Baal in Israel and,
 59–60, 76–77, 78, 80, 88, 328, 332;

Bible (*cont.*)
    body of God in, 255–56; bronze
    serpent *nehushtan* of Moses in,
    65; on child sacrifice and *herem*,
    63–64; on circumcision, 65, 82;
    cosmology and eschatology, 81,
    296–98; Cyrus the Persian in, 117,
    123; development of monotheistic
    worship of Yahweh in, 76–81;
    discovery of books of, 77, 82;
    on exile and redemption, 80–81;
    identity narratives in, 221, 222, 224,
    225–26, 228–29; legal corpora in,
    81–82, 83, 88–89; on *marzeah* feast,
    67; offerings and animal sacrifice
    in, 63; Philo's allegorical approach
    to, 259–60, 262; philosophy and
    ethics in, 88–89; on practice of
    religion, 81–86; prophecy in, 67–68,
    85–86; Proverbs and "Instructions
    of Amenemope[t]," 14, 58; on
    purification rituals, 64; as research
    source, 69, 89–90; scapegoat rite,
    97; social context of religion in,
    86–89; Syo-Canaanite mythological
    corpus and, 57–58; on visibility/
    invisibility of God, 324; Wisdom,
    principle of, 183, 296. *See also* New
    Testament
body, 6, 252–75; asceticism as training
    for, 270–73; cosmology and creation
    of human body, 258–64; divine and
    human bodies, 253–58; healing
    suffering bodies, 258, 264–70;
    image of God, human body as,
    255, 256, 324; as metaphor and
    allegory, 261–62; modification of,
    273; mortification of the flesh, as
    form of violence, 206–8, 208; purity
    of, 262–64; research and further
    reading, 274–74; resurrection of the
    body, 241, 273–74. *See also* purity
    and purification rituals; *specific
    cultures and religions*
Bona Dea (Roman deity), 168, 283
boundary performance through
    distinctive appearances and
    observances, 238–41
Boyarin, Daniel, 209, 213, 220, 274
Buddhism, 125, 126, 127, 128, 134
Bundahishn, 120, 127, 133, 134
burials. *See* funerary beliefs and
    practices

burnt offerings, 101, 141, 302n22
Bynum, Caroline Walker, 252, 274

Caesar (Gaius Julius Caesar), 213n20
calendar. *See* feasts and festivals;
    sacred time
Cambridge Ritualists, 149
Canaan. *See* Syria-Canaan
Capitoline Temple of Jupiter Optimus
    Maximus, Rome, 164
Carthage, 56, 60, 64, 165, 191
Cassius Dio/Dio Cassius, 160, 213n16,
    236, 247n77
Castelli, Elizabeth A., xi, 3, 6, 209, 213,
    252, 300
Castor and Pollux (Greek/Roman
    deities), 158
Cato, 163, 229
celibacy. *See* asceticism; purity and
    purification rituals
cellae, 102, 143, 152, 164
Celsus, *The True Word*, 294, 318–
    19, 324
Ceres (Roman deity), 160, 167, 220, 233,
    243, 271, 293. *See also* Demeter
Chariton, *Chareas and Callirhoe*,
    302n15
Chemosh (Syro-Canaanite deity), 60,
    64, 90
child sacrifice, 63–64, 82, 203
Christianity, 177–94; animal sacrifice,
    abstention from, 284; baptism,
    185–86, 189, 240, 241, 287, 292;
    belief systems in, 182–84; the body
    and, 257–58, 261, 268–70, 271–72;
    chronology, 194; cosmology/
    cosmogony, 298; deities in, 182;
    diversity, heterodoxy/heresy, and
    orthodoxy, 177, 184, 190, 193,
    230–31, 257, 294, 295; divinely
    sanctioned conquest in, 204;
    Dura Europos house church and
    baptistery, 186, 328, 330, 336;
    eschatology, 177–78, 182–83,
    240; Eucharist/Lord's Supper,
    185, 186, 189–90, 230, 261, 287,
    293, 300; extension of movement
    to non-Jews, 179, 189, 236,
    240; first attested use of term,
    180; gender concepts affected
    by Christianization of ancient
    Mediterranean, 299–300; gender
    in, 189, 190, 287–88, 291–95, 298;

geographic orientation of, 235–36; glossary, 194; "God-Fearers," 179, 243, 245; Greek and Roman gods, use of, 139; Greek religion suppressed by, 136; healing in, 268–70; historical development of, 177–82; identity narratives, 221, 226–27, 230–31; identity performances, 239–41, 243–44; Iran and Zoroastrianism, 117–18, 126, 127; Isis and Horus and Madonna and Child iconography, 14; Jesus Movement, 178–80, 185, 194, 227, 236, 292; Jewish beliefs and practices, 182, 185, 239–40; law in, 179, 241, 326, 330; life after death in, 241; literature of, 181–82; meat avoidance and animal sacrifice, 141; mortification of the flesh in, 208; persecution of, 127, 159, 173, 179, 180–81, 191, 194, 209–11, 211; philosophy and ethics, 191–92; politics and religion in, 190–91; practice of, 185–88; religious functionaries and authority structures in, 187–88, 288; research and further reading, 192–94; ritual in, 185–86; in Roman Empire, 159; sacred space in, 186; sacred time in, 186–87; social context of, 180–81, 188–92; structural organization of, 187–88, 288; Trinity, 183–84. *See also* asceticism; Jesus. martyrdom; New Testament; Paul; visuality

Christmas, 187

chthonic beliefs. *See* funerary beliefs and practices; life after death; underworld gods

Cicero (Marcus Tullius Cicero): *De Divinatione/On Divination*, 158, 170; *De Fato/On Fate*, 170; *De Natura Deorum/On the Nature of the Gods*, 158, 162, 170, 254, 322; *Epistulae*, 168; as philosopher, 169–70; *Pro Balbo*, 167

circumcision, 64–65, 82, 239–40, 273

cities, association of particular deities with: in Anatolia, 98; in Egypt, 16; in Greece, 137, 138, 139, 144, 145, 146; as identity performance, 232; in Mesopotamia, 38; in Roman sphere, 157; in Syria-Canaan, 99

city-state, Greek, rise of, 137

Civilis (leader of Batavian revolt), 205, 213n20

class, social. *See* social context of religion

Clement of Alexandria: on date of birth of Jesus, 187; *Excerpts of Theodotus*, 257; *Exhortation to the Greeks*, 149; *Stromateis/ Miscellanies*, 253–54, 314, 319

collective memory and identity, 225–27

Collins, Billie Jean, xi, 3, 95, 109

colonialism and identity, 220–21

communal meals. *See* meals

comparative study of ancient Mediterranean religions, 4–5, 150, 172

connections to and borrowings from religions in different cultures: to and from Anatolia, 96–97, 106; to and from Egypt, 14, 15–16, 58, 59; gender and, 294–95; geographically defined identity and, 234–35; to and from Greece, 97, 137, 138–39, 234–35; to and from Iran, 117–18; to and from Israel, 77–78; to and from Mesopotamia, 35–36; to and from Rome, 157–60, 165, 234–35, 235–36; to and from Syria-Canaan, 36, 58, 59, 97. *See also* syncretism

Constantine I the Great (Roman emperor), 177, 187, 204

cosmology, creation, and creator-Gods: in Anatolia, 98–100; Christian, 298; Egyptian, 15, 16–17; gender and, 295–98; Greek, 140; human body, creation of, 258–64; in Iran and Zoroastrianism, 117–21; in Israel, 81, 295–98; Mesopotamian, 34, 38–40, 46, 297; Syro-Canaanite, 59

Creation Epic (Mesopotamian narrative), 36, 37, 39, 40

curses. *See* magic

Cybele [Kybele/Magna Mater/Great Mother] (Phrygian deity), 1, 137, 142, 152, 158, 159, 165, 233, 236, 238, 272, 320

cylinder seals, 34–35, 69

Cynics, 192

Cyprus, 14, 65, 70, 138

Cyril of Alexandria, *Epistulae*, 336–37

Cyrus (Persian king), 71, 77, 92, 117, 124, 132

daena, 117, 121, 134
Dagan (Syro-Canaanite deity), 60, 66, 72
Darius I the Great (Iranian ruler), 92,
    124–25, 127, 128, 132
David (Israelite king), 81, 84, 87, 91,
    100, 182, 336
daxma, 122
De morbo sacro/On the Sacred Disease
    (Hippocratic text), 266
Dea Syria (Syro-Canaanite deity), 159
Dead Sea Scrolls and Qumran
    community, 85, 92, 178, 185, 227,
    244, 272, 303n48
death. See funerary beliefs and practices;
    life after death; underworld gods
deconstructionist theory and
    identity, 220
Deir Alla inscription, 68
deities: in Anatolia, 97–99; Christianity
    See (Jesus); in Egypt, 15–17; Greek,
    139–40; in Iran and Zoroastrianism,
    118–19; in Israel and Judaism,
    78–81 (see also Yahweh); in
    Mesopotamia, 37–38; Roman,
    160–62; in Syria-Canaan, 58–60.
    See also pantheons; specific deities
Delphi, oracle at, 142, 146, 232
Demeter (Greek deity), 97, 141, 142,
    145, 283, 295, 297, 303n64.
    See also Ceres
Democritus, 340n9
demons, 40, 61, 62, 107, 117, 118,
    121, 122, 124, 125, 126, 136, 190,
    211, 213n6, 253, 298, 300, 319.
    See also magic; specific demons
    by name
Denkard (ninth-century Zoroastrian
    encyclopedia), 126, 128, 133, 134
Dever, William G., 70, 79, 244
di manes (Roman deities), 162
Diana (Roman deity), 157, 322.
    See also Artemis
Diaspora Judaism, 234, 243–44, 288
Didache, 181–82, 186
dietary restrictions, 141, 238–40, 263,
    271, 285
dii familiares (Roman deities), 167
dingir (god classifier in
    Mesopotamia), 37
Dio Cassius/Cassius Dio, 160, 213n16,
    236, 247n77
Dio Chrysostom: Olympic Discourse,
    320; Orationes, 322

Diogenes Laertius, Lives of the
    Philosophers, 272
Dionysius of Halicarnassus:
    Antiquitates Romanae/Roman
    Antiquities, 225, 229, 233, 236, 238,
    246n25; description of early Rome,
    157; on eunuch priests of Cybele,
    159; on Roman fetiales, 166, 225
Dionysos [Dionysus] (Greek deity): in
    Anatolia, 97; Bacchic mystery cults,
    141; biennial festivals, association
    with, 144; Christian use of, 139;
    distinction of Christian women
    from worshipers of, 189; dramatic
    festivals and, 142, 152; gender and,
    283, 289, 297; maenadism in cult
    of, 142, 152, 189, 283, 289; spheres
    of influence, 139; transgressive
    behavior, association with, 139,
    142, 289. See also Bacchus
divination: in Anatolia, 101–2; in Egypt,
    25; Greco-Roman forms, eventual
    dominance of, 66; in Greece, 142–
    43, 146; haruspicy, 158, 163, 174;
    Roman, 157, 158, 162, 163, 164,
    165–66, 169; in Syria-Canaan, 65–66
divinities. See deities
djet (linear time in Egypt), 21
docetism, 257
Dodona, oracle at, 142–43
Dolansky, Shawna, xi, 3, 55
Donatists, 214n32
dramatic festivals, in Greece, 142
dreams, interpretation of. See divination
Drimios (Greek deity), 137
dualism, 17, 119, 120–21, 125, 126, 127
Dura Europos: house church and
    baptistery, 186, 328, 330, 336;
    synagogue, 66, 325, 328, 332,
    336, 337

Ea (Mesopotamian deity), 36, 39
Eanna temple complex, Uruk, 34
early Christianity. See Christianity
Easter, 186–87
Ebla (city). See Syria-Canaan
Eblaite literature, 41, 48, 56, 60, 61
economic life and religion, 107–8, 146
Eflatun Pinar (Anatolian site), 99
Egypt, 13–27: Amarna theology, 26, 27;
    belief systems in, 14–18; body, as
    land of, 262; chronology, 27–30;
    cities, association of particular

deities with, 16; connections to and
borrowings from religions in other
cultures, 14, 58, 59; Coptic magical
texts, 268; cosmology/cosmogony,
16–17; deities, 15–17; eschatology,
16–18; gender in, 23; glossary,
30; Greece and, 13–14, 138, 140,
152; historical development of
religion in, 13–14; Isis worship
and identification with, 234–35;
Israelite enslavement in and
exodus from, 80, 222–23, 262;
mummification of animals in, 20;
personal piety in, 18, 26; philosophy
and ethics in, 25; politics and
religion in, 23–25, 24; practice of
religion in, 18–22; research and
further reading, 25–27; ritual in,
18–20; sacred space in, 20–21;
sacred time in, 21; social context
of religion in, 22–25, 24; structural
organization of religion in, 21–23;
Syria-Canaan and, 58, 69; Syro-
Canaanite gods imported to, 14
Eilberg-Schwartz, Howard, 255–56, 274
El (Syro-Canaanite deity), 58, 59, 60, 62,
64, 65, 67, 68, 71, 72
Elamatum (Mesopotamian deity), 36
Elephantine, 13, 16, 80, 82
Eleusinian mysteries, 141, 145, 152
Elijah (biblical prophet), 67–68, 76–77,
88, 332
Elkunirsa (Anatolian deity), 58
Elvira, Council of (305), 329–30
Empedocles, 340n9
Enki (Mesopotamian deity), 39
Enlil (Mesopotamian deity), 36, 38,
39, 40
Enuma Elish, 37, 57
Ephesus/Ephesos, temple and statue of
Artemis at, 97, 137, 138, 159, 180
Epictetus, 191
Epicureanism, 147, 152, 169–70, 254
Epiphanius of Salamis: on gender, 293;
Panarion/The Medicine Chest, 270,
302n309; *Testament*, 341n29; on
visual representations of saints, 329
epulones (Roman college of public
priests), 166
Erechtheus (ancestor-deity), 222
Ereshkigal (Mesopotamian deity), 38
Erra (Mesopotamian deity), 38
eschatological beliefs: in Anatolia, 100;

in Christianity, 177–78, 182–83,
240; in Egypt, 16–18; in Greece,
140–41, 151; insurrectionary
counter-violence/Millennial revolt,
201–2, 205–6, 207; in Iran and
Zoroastrianism, 120, 121; in Israel,
81, 230, 234; in Mesopotamia,
40–41; in Rome, 162; in Syria-
Canaan, 60–61. *See also* life after
death. underworld gods
Eshmun (Syro-Canaanite deity), 60, 62
Essenes, 178, 272
ethics. *See* philosophy and ethics
ethnicity: in Anatolia, 109; Christianity
and, 177, 189, 287; gender and, 282,
284, 286–87; in Greece, 139, 144,
145; of human and divine bodies,
254, 274; identity and, 221, 223,
233, 239, 242, 243; in Israel, 76;
Latin, as ethnic designation, 174;
pan-Babylonism versus, 46–47;
Panhellenism versus, 137, 143, 144,
148, 152, 232; religion as marker
of, 4; in Rome, 158, 174; in Syria-
Canaan, 55, 67; visuality and, 311
Etruscans, 138, 139, 157–58, 163,
171, 174
Eucharist/Lord's Supper, 185, 186,
189–90, 230, 261, 287, 293, 300
Euripides: *Bacchae*, 283; on barbarian
origins of Medea, 228; critiques of
traditional religion, 147; *Ion*, 246n7
Eusebius of Caesarea, *Historia
Ecclesiastica/Ecclesiastical
History*, 90, 179, 269, 272, 302n39,
303n58, 329
Evil Eye. *See* magic
exile and redemption in Israel and
Judaism, 80–81, 222–23,
225–26, 262
Exodus, 80, 222–23, 262
exorcism, 35, 36, 62, 105, 177, 190, 298
The Exploits of Ninurta, 37, 40
exported gods. *See* connections to
and borrowings from religions in
different cultures; syncretism
extispicy, 25, 41, 43, 44, 46, 65, 66, 101.
See also divination

Fate goddesses, 99, 100, 140, 297
feasts and festivals: in Anatolia, 103,
106; in Egypt, 21; gender and, 283,
284, 287, 291; in Greece, 144;

feasts and festivals (*cont.*)
    as identity performance, 232; in
    Iran and Zoroastrianism, 123; in
    Israel, 83; in Mesopotamia, 42, 43,
    45; in Rome, 162, 163, 164, 166,
    167, 168; in Syria-Canaan, 61,
    66–67. *See also* sacred time; *specific
    events, e.g.* Passover
feminist studies, 281, 301n1
fertility, 58–59, 62, 65, 72, 100, 104, 149,
    162, 233, 291, 296
fetiales (Roman college of public
    priests), 166
Finkelstein, Israel, 223, 244
First Jewish Revolt (66–70 CE), 179, 190
flamines (Roman priests), 166
Flavius Josephus. *See* Josephus
Floralia (Roman festival), 168
food. *See* dietary restrictions; meals
foreign gods, importation of.
    See connections to and borrowings
    from religions in different cultures;
    syncretism
foreign/mixed origins, narratives of,
    222–24
Fortuna (Roman deity), 160, 164–65
Fortuna Virilis (Roman deity), 168
Frankfurt School, 172
frawashi (Iranian guardian spirit), 121
Frazer, Sir James G., *The Golden Bough*,
    149, 172
Freudian analysis and identity, 220
funerary beliefs and practices: in
    Anatolia, 100; Christian, 186;
    in Egypt, 16–18, 21; identity
    proclaimed through, 220, 242–44;
    in Iran and Zoroastrianism, 122; in
    Mesopotamia, 41; in Rome, 162; in
    Syria-Canaan, 60–61, 62, 63, 64
further reading. *See* research and further
    reading

Galen, 191, 192
games: Olympic Games, 142, 144, 145;
    Roman and Plebeian Games, 166
Gamliel (rabbi), 237–38
Gathas, 119, 127, 128–29, 130, 132, 134
Gaumata the Magu, 125
Geb (Egyptian deity), 16
Gemarrah, 237
gender, 6, 281–300; in Anatolia, 104;
    animal sacrifice and, 283–84, 289;
    bodies of gods and, 255–56; in

Christianity, 189, 190, 287–88,
    291–95, 298; Christianization
    of ancient Mediterranean and,
    299–300; connections to and
    borrowings from religions in other
    cultures and, 294–95; cosmology
    and, 295–98; cultic office and,
    287–88, 292–93; defined, 281–82;
    education and ministry, restriction
    of women regarding, 285–88, 290,
    292–93; in Egypt, 23; feminist
    studies and, 281, 301n1; glossary,
    300–01; gods reinforcing and
    transgressing rules of, 297; in
    Greece, 145, 231–32, 283, 289, 297;
    heterodoxy/heresy and orthodoxy,
    gendering of, 294, 295; in Iran
    and Zoroastrianism, 121, 124; in
    Israel and Judaism, 79–80, 85–86,
    255–56, 284–88, 289–90, 291–92,
    296–98; luxury, superstition, and
    depravity associated with women,
    229, 287, 294–95; martyrdom
    and, 293–94; monotheism and
    polytheism, 295–97; personal piety
    and, 283, 291; practice of religion
    and, 282–88; properly gendered
    persons, religious practices
    producing, 288–95; purity and, 264;
    research and further reading, 300;
    resurrection of the body and, 274; in
    Rome, 167, 168–69, 229, 283, 289,
    294–95, 297; sexuality and, 281–83,
    285–87, 290, 292–93, 299–300,
    301n3, 301n7; social identity and
    gender difference, 231–32, 233, 282;
    Yahweh and, 79–80, 296–97
genius (Roman protective spirit), 167
geographic/topographic identity,
    performance of, 233–38
Gilgamesh epic, 40, 228
Girra and Elamatum (Babylonian
    myth), 36
Glykon (Publius Aulius Glykon), 243
Gnosticism: the body in, 257, 260, 264;
    defined, 194; Egyptian religious
    tradition and, 14; Manichaeanism,
    125, 126, 134, 208; mortification of
    the flesh in, 208; research on, 193,
    194; women and, 190
Göbekli Tepe, 33–34, 55
"God-Fearers," 179, 243, 245
god lists, 35–36

gods and goddesses. *See* deities
Goff, Barbara, 288–89, 300
Golden Fleece, 97
Golden Mean of Aristotle, 127
Gospel According to Judas, 191
Gospel of Mary Magdalene, 190
Gospel of Thomas, 181, 183
Great Dionysia of Athens, 142
Great Mother. *See* Cybele
Greece and Greeks, 136–51; Anatolia
    and, 97; belief systems in, 139–41,
    150; the body, 253–54, 255, 258–60,
    263, 265–67, 271–72; chronology,
    151–52; cities, association of
    particular deities with, 137, 138,
    139, 144, 145, 146; city-state,
    rise of, 137; connections to and
    borrowings from religions in
    other cultures, 97, 137, 138–39,
    234–35; cosmology/cosmogony,
    140, 295, 297; deities, 139–40;
    divinely sanctioned conquest in,
    204; Egypt and, 13–14, 138, 140,
    152; eschatology, 140–41; four
    metallic ages, 120; gender issues,
    145, 231–32, 283, 289, 297; glossary,
    152; healing cults, 265–67; heroes
    and hero-gods, 136, 138, 139–40,
    142; historical development of
    religion in, 136–39; identity
    narratives, 222, 224, 226, 228;
    identity performances, 231–32;
    minor deities, 139; Panhellenism,
    137, 143, 144, 148, 152; philosophy
    and ethics in, 146–47; politics and
    religion in, 145–46, 146–47; practice
    of religion in, 141–45; research and
    further reading, 147–51; ritual in,
    141–43; Roman borrowings from,
    158, 160; Roman identity and,
    229; sacred space in, 137, 143–44;
    sacred time in, 144; social context
    of religion in, 144, 145–47; structural
    organization of religion in, 144–45.
    See also visuality
Gregory I the Great (pope), *Epistulae*,
    332, 336, 341n38
Gregory of Nyssa: *De deitate Filii et
    Spiritus Sancti*, 336, 337; trinitarian
    theology of, 184
Gruber, Mayer I., ix, 3, 76, 78
Gruen, Erich, 223–24, 244
Gudea stele, 35

Gulses (Anatolian fate goddesses),
    99, 100
Gutium (Mesopotamian place name), 36

Hadda/Hadad (Syro-Canaanite deity),
    58, 59–60, 61, 63, 66, 72
Hades (Greek deity), 141, 297
Hamath inscription, 67
Hanigalbat (Mesopotamian place
    name), 36
haoma (sacred drink), 116, 117, 122, 123
Hapantaliya (Anatolian deity), 98
Hapy (Egyptian deity), 15
Harland, Phillip, 242–43
haruspicy, 158, 163, 174
Hasmoneans, 227, 239, 245
Hathor (Egyptian deity), 15, 23, 58
Hattians, 95, 96, 98, 99–100, 105, 109
Hattusa, Great Temple at, 102, 107–8
Hattusili I (Anatolian ruler), 96, 106
Hattusili III (Anatolian ruler), 106
healing cults, 38, 41, 60, 62, 65,
    160, 161–62, 264–70, 268–70.
    See also Asklepios; Aesculapius
Hebat (Hurrian deity), 98
Hebrew Bible. *See* Bible
Hegel's master-slave dialectic, 199
Heliodorus, 302n15
Heliopolis, Egypt, Jewish temple at, 82
Helios (Greek deity), 283
helots, 145, 152
hemerologies, 46, 48
henotheism, 26
Hephaistos (Greek deity), 145.
    See also Vulcan
Heptad (the "Seven"), 99
Hera (Greek deity), 136, 144, 151, 160,
    224, 283, 297, 320. *See also* Juno
Heraclitus, 262, 319
Herakles (Greek hero-god), 138, 139
Hercules (Roman deity), 152, 157, 158,
    160, 168, 322–23
herem (war spoils, sacrifice of), 64
heresy/heterodoxy, orthodoxy and
    Christian diversity, 177, 184, 190,
    193, 230–31, 257, 294, 295
Hermes (Greek deity), 140.
    See also Mercury
Herodian, *Historia*, 320
Herodotus, *Histories*: on Egypt, 13, 19,
    26; Greek deities and, 139, 145,
    146; Greek identity and, 222, 232,
    246n7; on Iran and Zoroastrianism,

Herodotus, *Histories* (cont.)
123, 125, 127, 128, 129; on Persian
Wars, 226; on Syria-Canaan, 64,
66, 69
heroes and hero-gods, 37, 38, 69, 136,
138, 139–40, 142
heroön, 138, 152
Hesiod: the body, Greek vocabulary
for, 253; representations of gods
and, 317, 319, 320, 323; as research
source, 148; on theodicy, 146–47;
Theogony, 14, 140, 151, 254; *Works
and Days*, 144, 146
Hesiodic Hymn to Demeter, 97
heterodoxy/heresy, orthodoxy and
Christian diversity, 177, 184, 190,
193, 230–31, 257, 294, 295
Hierapolis, 64, 242–43, 323
Hinduism, 122, 125, 126, 127
Hippocratic texts, 266
historical development of religion.
See under *specific cultures and
religions*
Hittites: Greece and, 138; Israel and, 58;
Mesopotamia and, 36, 48; Syria-
Canaan and, 55, 57, 58, 60, 64.
See also Anatolia
holocaust sacrifice, 141–42, 149
Homer, *Iliad* and *Odyssey*, 140, 142,
148, 199, 222, 317, 319, 320, 323
Homeric Hymn to Demeter, 303n64
Horus (Egyptian deity), 14, 15, 19, 23
human sacrifice: Abraham's sacrifice of
ram in place of son Isaac, 82, 203,
336–37, *337*; child sacrifice, 63–64,
82, 203; in Egypt, 19; in Syria-
Canaan, 63–64
Hurrians, 36, 95, 96, 98, 99, 101, 107,
109, 111
huwasi (standing stone), 103
Hyakinthos (Greek deity), 137
Hyksos, 58
hypostasis, 36, 48, 59
hypostyle halls in Egypt, 20–21

iconography. See visuality
identity, 5–6, 220–44; alterity and
otherness narratives, 227–31;
autochthonous peoples, 222,
223; blurred/hybrid identity
performances, 241–44; boundary
performance through distinctive
appearances and observances,
238–41; built environment, 236–38;
collective memory narratives, 225–
27; common descent narratives,
222–23; defining characteristics,
delineation of, 226–27; ethnicity
and, 221, 223, 233, 239, 242, 243;
fictitious kinship narratives,
224–25; gender and social identity,
231–32, 233, 282; glossary, 244–45;
god[s] worshiped as form of identity
performance, 231–33; martyrdom as
identity performance, 241; narrative
and, 221–31; outsider origin
narratives, 222–24; performance
of identity, 231–44; research and
further reading, 244; sacred space,
236–37; topographic/geographic
identity, performance of, 233–38
idolatry, 247, 256, 313, 318, 319,
326–34, *327*, *330–33*
Idrimi Stele of Alalakh, 65
Ignatius of Antioch: *Epistle to the
Romans*, 191; *Epistle to the
Trallians*, 188; *Letter to the
Magnesians*, 180; *Smyrnaeans*, 241
ilib (god of the father or divine
ancestor), 61
Illuyanka myth, 97, 103
images. See visuality
imperial cult, Roman, 159–60, 166, 169
imperial narrative, martyrological
inversion of, 209–11, *211*
importing gods from other cultures.
See connections to and borrowings
from religions in different cultures;
syncretism
Inanna (Mesopotamian deity), 34, 35,
36, 37, 40, 43, 80. See also Ishtar
*Inanna's/Ishtar's Descent to the
Netherworld*, 40
Inara (Anatolian deity), 98
incarnation theology, Christian, 257–58
India: Buddhism in, 127; Christianity in,
177, 180; Hinduism, 122, 125, 126,
127; Vedic literature of, 118, 122,
128, 130
Indo-Aryans, 116–17, 128
Indra/Werethraghna (Iranian deity),
117, 118
initiation rituals: baptism, 185–86,
189, 240, 241, 287, 292; Greek
mystery cults, 141; in Iran and
Zoroastrianism, 122, 124

"Instructions of Amenemope[t]" and
Proverbs, 14, 58
Instructions of Shuruppak, 45
intermarriage: Israelite fear of
contamination via, 223, 232;
patrician and plebeian divide
in Rome softened by, 168; of
Samaritans, 245
Iran and Zoroastrianism, 116–32;
Avestan sources, 122, 128, 130,
132, 133, 134; belief system in,
118–21; chronology, 132–33;
connections to and borrowings
from religions in other cultures,
117–18; deities, 118–19; divinely
sanctioned conquest in, 204, 205;
gender in, 121, 124; glossary, 134;
Greek identity and, 226, 227;
historical development of religion,
116–18; Indo-Aryans, 116–17, 128;
Islam eclipsing Zoroastrianism,
116, 126–27; Israelite counter-
teachings, 78; Pahlavi sources, 120,
124, 127, 128, 129, 130, 131, 132,
133, 134; philosophy and ethics,
127–28; politics and religion,
124–27; practice of religion, 122–23;
research and further reading,
128–32; ritual in, 122; Roman
borrowings from, 158; sacred space,
122, 123; sacred time in, 121,
122–23; social context of religion,
123–28; structural organization
of religion in, 123, 125, 126;
Zarathushtra (Zoroaster/Zardusht),
117, 118, 119, 121, 127, 128–29,
130, 131, 132, 134; Zurvanism, 121,
127, 134
Irenaeus of Lyon: *Adversus [Contra]
haereses/Against Heresies*, 187,
194, 230, 257, 265, 273; on Basilides
and Valentinus, 180, 264–65; on
names of canonical gospels, 182; on
Trinity, 183–84
Isaac (biblical patriarch), 82, 203, 222,
332, 336, *337*
Isaeus, 231
isfet (cosmic disorder), 17
Ishkhara (Mesopotamian/Syro-
Canaanite deity), 36, 60.
See also Ishtar
Ishkur (Mesopotamian deity), 38
Ishmael (biblical patriarch), 82

Ishtar (Mesopotamian deity), 14, 34,
36, 38, 40, 43, 71, 78, 80, 98, 106,
118, 138
Isidore of Seville, 78
Isis (Egyptian deity): Christian Madonna
and child iconography and, 14;
deceased depicted as, 220; Egyptian
identification of worshipers of,
234–35; in Egyptian pantheon, 16;
gender rules and, 297; in Greek
islands and Ephesus, 14, 138, 152,
234–35; headdresses identifying,
15; Isidore of Seville and, 78; *On
Isis and Osiris* (Plutarch), 302n14;
priests, distinctive appearance
and observances of, 238; rise of
Mediterranean-wide cult of, 1, 14,
26, 30; Roman worship of, 159,
234–35; women's devotion to, 283
Isitemkheb D (Egyptian queen), 31n16
Islam, 116, 123, 126–27, 221
Israel and Judaism, 76–91; Baal in,
59–60, 76–77, 78, 80, 88, 328, 332;
Bar Kochba Revolt (132–35 CE),
180, 290; belief systems in, 78–81;
the body in, 255–56, 259–60, 262,
272; body of God in, 255–56; child
sacrifice in, 63–64, 82; chronology,
91–92; circumcision in, 65, 82;
connections to and borrowings from
religions in other cultures, 77–78;
cosmology/cosmogony, 81, 295–98;
deities, 78–81 (*see also* Yahweh);
Diaspora, 234, 243–44, 288;
dietary restrictions, 238–39,
263, 285; divinely sanctioned
conquest in, 205; early Christian
beliefs and practices, 182, 185,
239–40; eschatology, 81, 230, 234;
exile and redemption in, 80–81,
222–23, 225–26, 262; extension
of Christianity to non-Jews, 179,
189, 236, 240; First Jewish Revolt
(66–70 CE), 179, 290; gender in,
79–80, 85–86, 255–56, 284–88,
289–90, 291–92, 296–98; glossary,
92; "God-Fearers," 179, 243, 245;
historical development of religion
in, 76–78; identity narratives in,
221, 222–23, 225–26, 227, 228–29;
identity performance in, 232, 234,
238–39; Iran, Jews in, 126; Jesus
Movement and, 178–80, 185, 194,

Israel and Judaism (*cont.*)
227, 292; Jewish or Hebrew Biblical
Theology, 90; law in, 81–82, 86, 88,
89, 179, 263, 264, 284–85, 314; life
after death in, 273–74; martyrdom
and, 209, 214n30; minimalist
theories of ancient Israel, 91, 93n23;
Minorca, forcible conversion of
Jews of, 299; monotheism and
polytheism, 76–81, 89, 229, 232;
mortification of the flesh in, 208;
multicultural influences on, 76–78;
philosophy and ethics in, 88–89;
politics and religion in, 87–88;
practice of religion in, 81–86;
prophets and sages in, 85–86; purity
and purification rituals, 77, 84, 185,
263–64; rabbinic Judaism, 208, 245,
272; relationship between ancient
Israel and Judaism, 76; research
and further reading, 89–91; ritual
bathing, 185; ritual in, 82–83;
in Roman Empire, 159; Roman
paganization of civic space in, 237–
38; Sabbath observance, 83, 86, 239;
sacred space in, 82–83; sacred time
in, 83, 86; Second Jewish Revolt
(Bar Kochba Revolt; 132–35 CE),
180, 290; social context of religion
in, 86–89; structural organization of
religion in, 83–86, 284, 288; treaty
formats and divine covenants, 58;
Yahweh, 59–60, 76–81, 82, 88, 90,
91, 232, 296–97; Zoroastrianism
and, 117–18, 127. *See also* Bible;
Jerusalem temple; Mishnah.
synagogues and synagogue worship;
Talmud; Torah and Torah study
Israel, kingdom of, 67, 76–78, 81, 86, 87,
89, 90, 91

Jacob (biblical patriarch), 82, 92,
222, 224
James, brother of Jesus, 178, 179
Jeh (Iranian whore demoness), 121, 124
Jensen, Robin M., xi, 3, 6–7, 194,
309, 340
Jeremiah (biblical prophet), 88
Jerusalem temple: Babylonian
destruction of Solomon's temple,
71, 80; biblical descriptions of, 328;
discovery of books of Bible in, 77,
82; festivals of pilgrimage to, 83;

rebuilding of, 232; restriction of
ritual worship of Yahweh to, 77,
82; Roman destruction of Second
Temple, 185, 226, 263–64, 284
Jesus: death and resurrection of, 178,
183, 190, 226–27, 240–41, 257–58;
diversity of attractions to, 184;
ethical teachings of, 191; as
healer, 268–69; as image of God,
and images of, 326; incarnation
theology and, 257–58; life of,
177–78; nature and relationship to
God, 182–84, 192, 257, 326; social
and class background, 188–89.
See also Christianity
Jesus Movement, 178–80, 185, 194, 227,
236, 292. *See also* Christianity
Jews. *See* Israel; Judaism
Jezebel (female prophet in Book of
Revelation), 288
Jezebel (Israelite queen), 76
John Cassian, *Collationes,* 325
John Chrysostom, *Against
Judaizers,* 240
John the Baptist, 177, 185
Josephus: *Antiquitates Judaicae/Jewish
Antiquities,* 190, 195n3, 224, 239,
328; *Bellum Iudaicum/Jewish
Wars,* 226, 274; *Contra Apion,* 239;
Jewish religious groups recorded by,
290; religious literature of ancient
Near East, preservation of, 90; on
Second (Herodian) Temple, 284
Josiah (king of Judah), 77, 82, 91,
225, 328
Judah, kingdom of, 60, 66–67, 77–78,
80–81, 86–90, 91–92
Judaism. *See* Israel and Judaism
Judea and Judeans. *See* Israel and
JudaismJudah, kingdom of
judges or deliverers in Israel, 87
Julian (Roman emperor), *Fragmenton
epistolae,* 323
Julius Africanus, 187
Julius Caesar. *See* Caesar
Juno (Roman deity), 158, 160, 164, 165,
167, 233, 317, 322. *See also* Hera
Juno Sospita (Roman deity), 158, 160
Jupiter (Roman deity), 14, 157, 160,
163–66, 174, 233, 320, 322.
See also Zeus
just war theories, 166, 203
justice, judgment, and judicial systems.

See philosophy and ethics; politics and religion; theodicy

Justin Martyr: *Apologia*, 180; arrival in Rome, 194; on baptism, 185; *Dialogue with Trypho*, 183, 241; on gospels, 182; martyrdom of, 191; as philosopher, 192; teaching career, 186

Juvenal: on Egyptian religion, 26; on luxury and unchastity, 229; *Satires*, 239, 283, 302n15

Kalends, 167, 243
Kamish (Syro-Canaanite deity), 60
Karatepe Stele, 62
Karnak, temple at, 21, 22
Kassites, 33. *See also* Mesopotamia
katabasis, 140, 152
Khirbet el-Qom, 60, 79
Khnum (Egyptian deity), 15, 16
Khonsu (Egyptian deity), 21, 24
Kilamuwa of Zincirli (Syro-Canaanite king), 62–63
kingship and religion. *See* politics and religion
Kirder (Iranian chief priest), 126, 129, 133
Kirta story, 62, 64, 65, 68–69
Kizzuwatna (Hurrian place name), 96, 101, 106, 111
Kore (Greek deity), 145, 295
Kothar (Syro-Canaanite deity), 60
Kraemer, Ross Shepard, xi, 3, 6, 281, 300
Kubaba (Anatolian deity), 36
Kuntillet 'Ajrud inscriptions, 60, 79
kursa (goatskin hunting bag), 97
Kuşaklı-Sarissa (Anatolian town), 102, 103
Kushan Empire, 125, 129, 134
Kybele. *See* Cybele

Lady of Byblos (Syro-Canaanite deity), 60, 66, 68
Lamashtu (Mesopotamian demon-deity), 35, 62
LAMMA deities, Anatolia, 98
lararia, 167–68
Lares (Roman deities), 167
Larson, Jennifer, ix, 3, 136, 151
law: in Anatolia, 107; in Christianity, 179, 241, 326, 330; in Egypt, 25; human conception of gods derived from, 320; identity and, 224, 228,

238–39, 241; in Israel and Judaism, 81–82, 86, 88, 89, 179, 263, 264, 284–85, 314; in Mesopotamia, 45; in Rome, 158, 166, 169, 171, 241; Torah and Torah study, 88, 232, 239, 245, 284–86, 289–90, 301, 303n48; violence and, 204

Lemuria (Roman festival), 162
Lent, 187
Leo I the Great (pope), 330
Letter of Aristeas, 234
Levites, 84–85, 86, 92
lex sacra/leges sacrae, 171, 267
Liber (Roman deity), 167
Lieu, Judith, 234, 240, 244
life after death: in Anatolia, 100; in Christianity, 241, 273–74; democratization of, 17; in Egypt, 16–18; in Greece, 140–41; in Iran and Zoroastrianism, 121, 122; in Judaism, 273–74; in Mesopotamia, 40–41; resurrection of the body, 241, 273–74; in Rome, 162; in Syria-Canaan, 60–61. *See also* funerary beliefs and practices; salvation/redemption; soul; underworld gods

Lincoln, Bruce, xi, 3, 5, 199, 213, 225
Livy: *Ab Urbe Condita*, 229, 246n24; *Annals of Rome*, 303n63; description of early Rome, 157; on Dionysius cult, 159, 282, 294; on outsider origins of some Roman religion customs, 158; on *pomerium*, 236; on Roman priestly colleges, 166

logos (Word), Jesus as, 183, 192
Lord's Supper/Eucharist, 185, 186, 189–90, 230, 261, 287, 293, 300
Lucian of Samosata: *De Syria Dea*, 64, 66, 69, 323; on Egyptian religion, 26; *Heracles*, 322–23
Lucretius, *De Rerum Natura/On the Nature of the Universe*, 169
Lugal-e, 57
Lullubu (Mesopotamian place name), 36
Luwians, 95, 96, 98, 104
Lyon and Vienne, martyrs of, 258, 303n58

maat (cosmic balance and order), 17–18, 24–25, 27, 30
Maat (Egyptian deity), 14, 24–25, 27, 30, 58

Machinist, Peter, 223
Macrobius, *Saturnalia*, 165, 167
Magi, 117, 123, 125, 126, 132
magic: in Anatolia, 104–5; in
    Christianity, 230; in Egypt, 26; in
    Greece, 151, 228; healing and, 267–
    68; in Mesopotamia, 35; in Rome,
    172, 174; in Syria-Canaan, 62–63
Magna Mater. *See* Cybele
Malandra, W. W., ix, 3, 116, 130, 131
Man and his God (Babylonian poem), 45
mana, 172, 174
Mani and Manichaeanism, 125, 126,
    134, 208
Manual of Discipline (Qumran
    text), 185
Marathon, Battle of, 226
Marcion and Marcionites, 184, 190, 194
Marcus (early Christian leader), 230
Mardan Farrox, *Shikand-gumani-
    wizar*, 127
Marduk (Mesopotamian deity), 34, 36,
    37, 39, 40, 43, 45, 78, 213n14, 297
marriage: as boundary between one
    mode of life and another, 263;
    Christianity and, 190, 274; gender
    and, 282, 285, 293; gender divisions
    in Roman religion and, 168; identity
    and, 223, 231, 232; installation
    of high priestess in Mesopotamia
    analogous to, 43; of patriarch Joseph
    and Asenath, daughter of Potiphera
    the priest of On, 84; of priests and
    priestesses in Egypt, 22, 23; *rex*
    and *regina sacrorum* in Rome, 167;
    Sacred Marriage (hierogamy) of
    Mesopotamian rulers and Inanna/
    Ishtar, 43; in Syria-Canaan, 65.
    See also intermarriage
Mars (Roman deity), 160, 166
Martial, *Epigrammata*, 239
martyrdom: as alternative form of
    power, 211, 212, 293–94; authority
    conferred by, 187, 188; crucifixion
    of Jesus and, 226–27, 241, 258;
    defined, 209; gender and, 293–94; as
    identity performance, 241; imperial
    narrative inverted by, 209–11, 211,
    241, 293–94; interplay between
    Jewish, Roman, and Christian
    traditions of, 209, 214n30;
    persecution of early Christians,
    127, 159, 173, 179, 180–81, 191,

194, 209–11, 211; research and
    further reading, 213; sacred space in
    Christianity and, 186; zeal for, 191
Mary (mother of Jesus) and Marian
    devotion, 14, 298, 299
Mary Magdalene, 189, 190, 288
marzeah (Syro-Canaanite feast), 61,
    67, 72
Matralia (Roman festival), 168, 283
Matthias (rabbi), 190
Maximilla (Montanist), 184, 190
Mazdak (Iranian religious leader), 126
meals: alimentary sacrifice and, 63, 85,
    100–01, 141, 164, 284; Anatolia,
    communal and sacrificial meals in,
    100, 104; dietary restrictions, 141,
    238–40, 263, 271, 285; Eucharist/
    Lord's Supper, 185, 186, 189–90,
    230, 261, 287, 293, 300; funerary
    meals in Christianity, 186; gender
    and, 282, 284, 285; Greece, meals
    and animal sacrifice in, 141, 148;
    Judaism, shared meals in, 239;
    marzeah feast in Syria-Canaan,
    61, 67, 72; meat avoidance and
    animal sacrifice, 141; Mesopotamia,
    religious personnel's use of offerings
    and sacrifices in, 44; Passover *seder*,
    185, 186, 284, 301; Rome, meals
    and animal sacrifice in, 165; Syria-
    Canaan, sacrificial meals in, 61, 67,
    68, 72; *yasna* feast in Iran, 122, 123,
    129. *See also* feasts and festivals
mean, doctrine of the, 127–28
medicine. *See* healing cults
Medinet Habu, Egypt, 15, 18
Mediterranean world, ancient religions
    in. *See* ancient Mediterranean
    religions
Melammu Project, 47
Melanippos (Greek hero-god), 146
Melchizedek (king of Salem), 82, 84
Melqart (Syro-Canaanite deity), 60, 66,
    67, 138
men. *See* gender and ancient
    Mediterranean religions
menologies, 46, 48
menstrual blood, 122, 124, 264, 268,
    285, 290
Mercury (Roman deity), 317.
    See also Hermes
Mesha Moabite stele, 64, 90
Mesopotamia, 33–47; Anatolia and,

95; belief systems in, 37–41; chronology, 48; cities, association of particular deities with, 38; connections to and borrowings from religions in other cultures, 35–36; cosmology, 38–40; deities, 37–38; divinely sanctioned conquest in, 205; eschatology, 40–41; glossary, 48; historical development of religion in, 33–36; Israelite identity and, 228–29; Israelites, Babylonian exile of, 80–81, 223, 225–26; philosophy and ethics in, 45–46; politics and religion in, 39–40, 42, 43, 44–45; practice of religion in, 41–44; research and further reading, 46–47, 90; ritual in, 41–42; sacred space in, 34, 41, 42–43; sacred time in, 42; social context of religion in, 37, 44–46; structural organization of religion in, 43–44; Syria-Canaan and, 36, 57

metaphor and allegory, 259–62

Metis (Greek deity), 14, 27

Micah (biblical prophet), 88

Milan, Edict of (313), 194

Min (Egyptian deity), 15

Minerva (Roman deity), 159, 160, 164, 233, 320, 321, 322. *See also* Athena

minimalist theories of ancient Israel, 91, 93n23

Minorca, forcible conversion of Jews of, 299

Minucius Felix, *Octavius*, 318, 322

Miriam (sister of Moses and Aaron), 291

Mishnah, 237, 245, 263, 264, 285, 301, 302n25, 302n31

Mithra/Mitra (Iranian deity), 117, 118, 132

Mithras (Roman deity), 158, 245n1

mixed/foreign origins, narratives of, 222–24

Moabites, 57, 60, 64, 70, 71, 90

Moirai (Greek divinities of fate), 140

monotheism: in Egypt, 26; gender and cosmology, 295–97; in Iran and Zoroastrianism, 119, 127; in Israel, 76–81, 229, 232; Mesopotamian religion and, 46, 47

Montanus and Montanism (New Prophecy movement), 184, 188, 190, 292

Montu (Egyptian deity), 19, 21

mortification of the flesh. *See* asceticism

Moses (biblical patriarch), 65, 76, 77, 84, 87, 89, 92, 192, 222, 245, 285, 301, 314, 319, 332

Mot (Syro-Canaanite deity/death), 58, 60, 61, 72

Mount Gerizim, 234, 245

mouth-washing rituals in Mesopotamia, 41

mummification of animals, in Egypt, 20

mushkhushshu -dragon, 37

Musonius Rufus, 191, 271

Mut (Egyptian deity), 21

Muth (Syro-Canaanite deity), 60

Muwatalli II (Anatolian ruler) and Muwatalli's Prayer to the Assembly of Gods, 106, 112n20

Mycenaeans, 137, 138, 148

mystery religions, 14, 30, 141, 145, 149, 152

myth: Anatolian, 97–99, 103, 108–9; bodies, human and divine, and, 255, 260; concept of, 225; Egyptian, 14, 16, 17, 25; gender and, 296, 297; Greek, 146, 149; identity and, 6, 221–22, 224–25, 228–29, 233, 235, 238–39; in Iran and Zoroastrianism, 119–21, 127; Mesopotamian, 34–40, 44, 46–47; Roman, 160, 172; Syro-Canaanite, 57–60; violence and, 205; visuality and, 309, 312, 320, 334–38

Nabateans, 66, 67, 295–96, 301

Nabu (Mesopotamian deity), 37, 38

Nabu (Syro-Canaanite deity), 66

Nag Hammadi library, 184

Nanna (Mesopotamian deity), 36

narrative and identity, 221–31. *See also* identity

narrative art, 329, 331, 332, 334–38, *335, 337*

Nasu/Nasu Druj (Iranian demon of putrefaction), 121, 123

natural features or phenomena personified as gods, 15, 42, 59, 98–99, 119, 139

Nazareans, 126

Nebuchadrezzar II (Babylonian king), 80, 85, 87, 92

nehe (cyclic time in Egypt), 21

Neoplatonism, 271, 314

Nephthis (Egyptian deity), 16
Neptune (Roman deity), 317.
    See also Poseidon
Nergal (Mesopotamian deity), 38, 63
Nero (Roman emperor), 159, 173,
    180, 191
netherworld. See life after death;
    underworld gods
Nevalı Çori, 33–34
New Prophecy movement (Montanism),
    184, 188, 190, 292
New Testament: belief systems in,
    182, 183; chronology, 194; on
    ecclesiastical authority structures,
    187, 188; gender in, 287, 288,
    292; geographic orientation of
    Christianity and, 235, 236; healing
    in, 268–69; historical development
    of, 181–82; philosophy and ethics
    in, 191–92; practice of religion
    in, 185, 186; resurrection of the
    body in, 274; Rome in Book of
    Revelation, 191, 230; social and
    political context of, 189, 190, 191;
    spread of Christianity documented
    by, 180; on visibility/invisibility of
    God, 324, 326. See also Bible
New Year festivals, 43, 45, 66, 67, 83,
    123, 144, 243
Nicaea, Council of (325), and Nicene
    Creed, 183, 184, 194
Ninurta (Mesopotamian deity), 37, 40,
    44, 50n62
Nippur, temples of, 40
Nisaba (Mesopotamian deity), 38
Nofertari, tomb of, 16
Nofertum (Egyptian deity), 15
Nubia, Egyptian gods worshiped in, 14
Numa Pompilius (Roman king), 157,
    166, 319
Nun (undifferentiated primordial mass),
    14, 16
Nut (Egyptian deity), 16

offerings: in Anatolia, 100; burnt
    offerings, 101, 141, 302n22; in
    Egypt, 18–19; in Greece, 142;
    in Mesopotamia, 41; in Rome,
    163; in Syria-Canaan, 60–61, 63.
    See also animal sacrifice; human
    sacrifice; votive offerings
ogdoad (group of eight gods), 14
Ohrmazd. See Ahura Mazda

Old St. Peter's Basilica, Rome, 330
Old Testament. See Bible
Olympic Games, 142, 144, 145
omen, 25, 38, 44–46, 65, 101–2, 104,
    143, 213n16, 236
Opening of the Mouth, 20
Opet (Egyptian deity), 21
Opet (Egyptian festival), 21
oracles. See divination; specific oracles
Origen: Contra Celsum/Against Celsus,
    303n59, 318–19, 324, 328; De
    Principiis, 324; Homiliae in Genesi,
    324; reputed self-mutilation of, 272
Orpheus and Orphic mysteries, 141
orthodoxy, heterodoxy/heresy, and
    Christian diversity, 177, 184, 190,
    193, 230–31, 257, 294, 295
Osiris (Egyptian deity), 14, 15, 16, 17,
    21, 23, 30, 295, 302n14
otherness and alterity narratives, 227–31
outsider origins, narratives of, 222–24
Ovid: Fasti, 165, 172–73, 236, 246n25,
    283, 301n13; Metamorphoses, 224

Pahlavi sources for Iran and
    Zoroastrianism, 120, 124, 127, 128,
    129, 130, 131, 132, 133, 134
paidaia, 221
Palaians, 95, 98, 111
Palladium, 225
Palmyra inscriptions, 67
pan-Babylonism, 46–47
Panathenaia, 232
Panhellenism, 137, 143, 144, 148,
    152, 232
pantheons: in Anatolia, 96, 97–99;
    in Egypt, 16; gender and, 297;
    Greek, 136–37, 138; Iran, 117; in
    Mesopotamia, 36, 38; Phoenician,
    60; in Syria-Canaan, 57, 59–60
Parthenon, Athens, 146, 152
Parthian Empire, 48, 118, 125, 133, 134.
    See also Iran and Zoroastrianism
Passover, 83, 178, 186–87, 243, 284
paterfamilias, 167
patrician/plebeian social class divide in
    Rome, 168, 174, 233
Paul of Tarsus (Paul the apostle): on
    asceticism, 270; on authority
    figures and ecclesiastical structures,
    188; on baptism, 240, 241; belief
    system of, 182, 183; on the body,
    261; on circumcision and dietary

restrictions, 240; on crucifixion, 227; on gender, 287, 288, 299; Jesus Movement and, 178–79, 194, 227; letters of, 180, 181, 194; as philosopher and ethicist, 191–92; on practice of religion, 185, 186; social context of Christianity and, 189–90; on universal nature of Christianity, 235

Paulinus of Nola, *Carmina*, 331, 332, 336, 341n37

Pausanias, *Description of Greece*, 138, 146, 149, 153n26, 224, 283, 301n12

pax deorum (peace of the gods), 162, 163, 168, 174

Pegasos (Greek mythological creature), 97

Peloponnesian War, 146, 222

Penates (Roman deities), 167

performance of identity, 231–44. *See also* identity

performance, ritual, in Greece, 142

Pergamon, Asklepieion at, 267

Perikles/Pericles, 146, 222

Perpetua (martyr), 188, 191, 194, 293, 299, 303n58

Persephone (Greek deity), 141

Persia. *See* Iran and Zoroastrianism

Persian Wars (499–449 BCE), 226, 227

personal piety: in Anatolia, 98, 104, 109; in Egypt, 18, 26; gender and, 283, 291; in Greece, 145; in Mesopotamia, 45; in Rome, 167–68

Peter (apostle), 178, 187, 189, 192, 288

Pharisees, 273–74

Philistines, 60

Philo of Alexandria: on cosmology and human body, 259–60; *De Abrahamo*, 260; *De confusione linguarum*, 259; *De Decalogo*, 314; *De fuga et inventione*, 259; *De Gigantibus*, 314; *De migratione Abrahami/On the Migration of Abraham*, 239, 262; *De opificio mundi*, 259, 324; *De specialis legibus*, 259, 324; *De Vita Contemplativa/On the Contemplative Life*, 272, 314; *Legum allegoriae/Allegorical Interpretation*, 262; *Quaestiones et Solutiones in Genesin*, 192, 239

Philo of Byblos, *Phoenician History*, 60, 69, 70

philosophy and ethics: in Anatolia, 107–8; animal sacrifice, abstention from, 284; Christianity and, 191–92; in Egypt, 25; Greek, 146–47; in Iran and Zoroastrianism, 127–28; in Israel, 88–89; in Mesopotamia, 45–46; Roman, 169–70; in Syria-Canaan, 69. *See also specific philosophers and schools of philosophy*

Philostratus: *Imagines*, 312, 335; *Life of Apollonius of Tyana*, 272

Phoenicians: in Carthage, 56, 60, 64, 165; child sacrifice by, 63, 64; cultic personnel, 67; demons/Evil Eye/curses, 62, 63; feasts and festivals, 67; Greece and, 138; on life after death and funerary practices, 60, 62, 63; pantheons in different cities of, 60; research sources, 70; in Syria-Canaan, 55, 56; temples, 66

pilgrimage, 20, 83, 232, 234, 267, 331, 336

Pindar, *Isthmian Odes*, 246n7

Plato: Christianity and, 184; conception of the divine, 147; on cosmology and the body, 258, 259, 260, 262; *Cratylus*, 262; *Gorgias*, 262; historical development of Hellenistic Greek philosophy following, 169; *Leges*, 231; Neoplatonism, 271, 314; *Respublica/Republic*, 138, 147, 313; *Timaeus*, 194, 258–60, 313, 340n9; on visuality, 313, 315, 340n9; on worship of ancestral gods, 231

plebeian/patrician social class divide in Rome, 168, 174, 233

Pliny the Elder, *Naturalis Historia*, 322

Pliny the Younger, *Epistulae*, 168, 180–81, 191, 194, 287, 302n35, 341n11

Plotinus, *Enneades*, 314, 315

Plutarch: *De Herodote malignitate*, 226; *On Isis and Osiris*, 302n14, 303n67; *Lives*, 158, 213n20, 319–20; *Moralia*, 283, 302n14; *Roman Questions*, 302n14

Pluto (Greek deity), 60

polis. *See* city

politics and religion. *See* under *specific cultures and religions*

pollution. *See* purity and purification rituals

Polycarp, 187
polytheism: in Egypt, 14–16, 26;
    gender and, 295–96; in Greece,
    137; in Israel, 76–81, 90, 232; in
    Mesopotamia, 38, 47; in Rome,
    160; visual images of gods and,
    316–23, 328
pomerium, 163–64, 174, 236–37, 247
Pongratz-Leisten, Beate, xi, 3, 33, 47
pontifices and *pontifex maximus*
    (Roman college of public priests),
    166, 167
Porphyry of Tyre: *Abstinence from
    Killing Animals*, 271; *Letter to
    Marcella*, 271; *Peri agalmaton*, 323;
    Vita Plotini, 314
Poseidon (Greek deity), 136, 145, 151.
    See also Neptune
post-colonialism and post-modernism,
    220–21
practice of religion: in Anatolia,
    100–05; Christianity, 185–88; in
    Egypt, 18–22; gender and, 282–88;
    in Greece, 141–45; in Iran and
    Zoroastrianism, 122–23; in Israel,
    81–86; in Mesopotamia, 41–44;
    performance of identity and, 231–44
    (*see also* identity); in Rome, 161,
    163–68; in Syria-Canaan, 63–68.
    See also ritual
Praeneste, sanctuary of Fortuna
    Primigenia at, 164–65
prayer: in Anatolia, 97, 99, 102, 109,
    112n20; the body and, 256, 266;
    in Egypt, 25; gender and, 287,
    291, 299; in Greece, 151; identity
    and, 220; in Iran, 120; in Israel,
    82; in Mesopotamia, 41, 44, 46; in
    Rome, 163, 172; in Syria-Canaan,
    61–62; visuality and, 319, 323, 329,
    334, 339
Presocratics, 147, 253, 340n9
Priestly Code, 88–89, 256
priests, priestesses, and priesthoods.
    See structural organization of
    religion
primitivism, 149, 172
Priscilla (Montanist), 184, 190
Prithivi/Spenta Armaiti (Iranian deity),
    117, 118
procession: in Anatolia, 101; in Egypt,
    20, 21, 25, 26; in Greece, 141, 142,
    144, 145, 147; identity and, 232,

238; in Mesopotamia, 35, 43, 44, 45;
    in Syria-Canaan, 66
prodigies, 162, 163, 165, 174
prophecy, 67–68, 85–86, 291–92
prostitutes, 77, 145, 168, 289
prostitution, sacred, 23, 67, 79
psyche (soul), 140–41
Ptah (Egyptian deity), 15–16, 21
Ptah-Sokar-Osiris (Egyptian deity), 15
purity and purification rituals, 262–64;
    baptism, 185–86, 189, 240, 241,
    287, 292; in Egypt, 19; in Greece,
    143, 145–46, 263; in Iran and
    Zoroastrianism, 122; in Israel
    and Judaism, 77, 84, 185, 263–64;
    menstrual blood, 122, 124, 264,
    268, 285, 290; in Mesopotamia, 36,
    41–42, 45; in Rome, 163; in Syria-
    Canaan, 64
Pyramids, 16–17
Pythagoras and Pythagoreans, 141, 272,
    319–20, 340n9
Pythia (Apollo's oracle at Delphi), 142

Quartodecimans, 187
Qudshu (Syro-Canaanite deity), 14, 58
queen mothers, in Syria-Canaan, 68
quindecemviri (Roman college of public
    priests), 166
Quirinus (Roman deity), 166
Qumran community and Dead Sea
    Scrolls, 85, 92, 178, 185, 227, 244,
    272, 303n48

rabbinic Judaism, 208, 245, 272.
    See also Mishnah; Talmud; Torah
    and Torah study
Ramesses IV (pharaoh), Khonsu
    Relief, 24
rapi'uma (kings in afterlife), 61, 67, 72
Rashnu (Iranian deity), 118
Rashp/Rasap/Reshep[h] (Syro-Canaanite
    deity), 14, 60, 72
Re (Egyptian deity), 15, 16, 19
reading lists. *See* research and further
    reading
redemption. *See* salvation/redemption
religion, concept of, 1, 136, 220
religions of ancient Mediterranean.
    See ancient Mediterranean religions
religious functionaries. *See* structural
    organization of religion
representation. *See* visuality

Reshep[h]/Rashp/Rasap (Syro-Canaanite deity), 14, 60, 72
resurrection of Jesus, 178, 183, 190, 226–27, 240–41, 257–58
resurrection of the body, 241, 273–74
reversion offerings, 18
rex and *regina sacrorum* (king and queen of rites), 167
Rig Veda, 128
ritual: in Anatolia, 100–02; attraction rituals, 101, 122; in Christianity, 185–86; in Egypt, 18–20; in Iran and Zoroastrianism, 122; in Israel and Judaism, 82–83; in Mesopotamia, 41–42; in Rome, 163; in Syria-Canaan, 63–66. *See also* initiation rituals; purity and purification rituals; *specific rituals, e.g.* divination
Roman and Plebeian Games, 166
Rome and Romans, 157–73; belief systems, 160–62; the body, 254–55, 270–72; in Book of Revelation, 191, 230; Christian identification with, 235–36; Christianity in Rome, 179; chronology, 173; cities, association of particular deities with, 157; connections to and borrowings from religions in other cultures, 157–60, 165, 234–35, 236–37; cosmology/cosmogony, 295, 297; deities, 160–62; divinely sanctioned conquest in, 204, 205; Egypt and, 14; eschatology, 162; Etruscans, 138, 139, 157–58, 163, 171, 174; gender issues, 167, 168–69, 229, 283, 289, 294–95, 297; glossary, 174–75; historical development of religion, 157–60; identity narratives, 224–25, 229; identity performances, 236–37, 238, 242–44; imperial cult, 159–60, 166, 169; imperial narrative, Christian martyrological inversion of, 209–11, 211, 241, 293–94; Latin, defined, 174; martyrdom tradition of, 209, 214n30; as other in literature and traditions of opponents and subjects, 229–30; paganization of civic space in territories of, 237–38; patrician/plebeian social class divide, 168, 174, 233; *pax deorum* (peace of the gods), 162, 163, 168, 174; philosophy and ethics, 169–70; politics and religion, 159–60, 162, 165, 168, 169; *pomerium*, 163–64, 174, 236–37, 247; practice of religion, 161, 163–68; research and further reading, 170–73; ritual in, 163; sacred space, 163–65; sacred time in, 164; Senate and Senate House (Curia), 148, 159, 162, 164, 165, 168, 169, 238; social context of religion, 168–70; structural organization of religion, 157, 165–67, 169; Trojan origin stories, 166, 173, 224–25. *See also* visuality
Romulus (founder of Rome), 157, 158, 163, 166, 173, 229, 236
rta (principle of order and truth), 118
Rumina (Roman deity), 283
Rüpke, Jörg, 167, 173, 175n16

Sabbath, 83, 86, 239
sacralization of violence, 202–6
sacred prostitution/temple sex, 23, 67, 79
sacred space: in Anatolia, 102–3; in Christianity, 186; in Egypt, 20–21; in Greece, 137, 143–44; identity and, 236–37; in Iran and Zoroastrianism, 122, 123; in Israel, 82–83; in Mesopotamia, 34, 41, 42–43; Roman, 163–65; in Syria-Canaan, 66
sacred texts. *See specific texts*
sacred time: in Anatolia, 103; in Christianity, 186–87; in Egypt, 21; in Greece, 144; in Iran and Zoroastrianism, 121, 122–23; in Israel and Judaism, 83, 86; in Mesopotamia, 42; in Rome, 164; in Syria-Canaan, 66. *See also* feasts and festivals
sacrifice. *See* alimentary sacrifice; animal sacrifice; human sacrifice
sacrificial meals. *See* meals
Sadducees, 274
sages, in Israel, 85–86
Ss. Cosmos and Damian, Rome, apse mosaic, *331*
St. Paul's Basilica, Via Ostiense, Rome, 330
saints, Christian cult of, 186, 268, 270, 299, 329

salvation/redemption: in Christianity,
141, 227, 240, 257, 258; identity
and, 226, 227, 240; in Israel and
Judaism, 80, 91, 93n21, 226; in
Syria-Canaan, 62; violence and,
204, 205
Samaritans, 89, 92, 234–35, 245, 299
Samuel (prophet), 87, 332
San Vitale, Ravenna, sanctuary
mosaic, *337*
Sanballat (governor of Samaria), 78
"Sanctified Violence in Ancient
Mediterranean Religions"
(University of Minnesota, 2007), 2
sanctuaries. *See* sacred space
Sta. Maria Maggiore, Rome, 330–31
Sta. Pudenziana, Rome, apse mosaic,
326, 327, 330
Sarapis/Serapis (Egyptian deity), 14, 30,
138, 159, 318
Sassanids, 125–27, 129, 134, 204.
See also Iran and Zoroastrianism
Sausga (Anatolian deity), 98, 106.
See also Ishtar
Scaevola the Pontiff, 255
scapegoat rite, 97, 104–5
Schultz, Celia E., xi, 3, 157
seals, 95, 100, 108.
See also cylinder seals
Second Jewish Revolt (Bar Kochba
Revolt; 132–35 CE), 180, 290
Seleucids, 71, 129, 133, 134, 205, 245
Senate and Senate House (Curia),
Rome, 148, 159, 162, 164, 165, 168,
169, 238
Seneca the Younger: *De Superstitione*,
322; as Stoic, 170
Serapis/Sarapis (Egyptian deity), 14, 30,
138, 159, 318
Serenus of Marseilles, 332, 341n38
Servius, 163, 164
Seth (Egyptian deity), 16, 58, 59
Severus of Minorca, 299
sexuality: Aphrodite (Greek deity) and,
138; bodies, divine and human, and,
255, 256, 261, 264, 267, 270–71,
272, 274; creation and, 140; ethics,
taboos, and infractions, 46, 220,
264; gender and, 281–83, 285–87,
290, 292–93, 299–300, 301n3,
301n7; identity and, 230, 233;
ritual and, 19, 142, 143, 165, 267;
of Rome in Book of Revelation,

230; sacred prostitution/temple
sex, 23, 67, 79; violence and, 199.
See also asceticism; marriage
Shamash (Mesopotamian deity), 36,
44, 60
Shanidar cave, 33
Shapshu (Syro-Canaanite deity), 58, 72
Shapur I (Iranian ruler), 133, 134
Shawushka (Hurrian deity), 36
Shemesh (Syro-Canaanite deity), 60, 72
Shu (Egyptian deity), 16
Sibyls, 166, 213n20
Sicarii, 290
Silberman, Neil Asher, 223, 244
Simon Maccabee, 227, 245
Simon Peter. *See* Peter
sin: in Anatolia, 100, 107, 108; in
Christianity, 183, 185–86, 229,
240, 257, 326; in Israel and
Judaism, 88, 91, 93n21, 256, 314;
in Mesopotamia, 34; in Syria-
Canaan, 64
Sin (Mesopotamian deity), 36
Sinhue, tale of, 69
slavery: in Anatolia, 105; the body and,
258, 260; gender and, 282, 283, 284,
287, 289, 294; Hegel's master-slave
dialectic, 199; in Israel, 82, 83, 86;
Israelites' enslavement in Egypt, 80,
222; Naaman (Israelite slave girl),
77; in Rome, 167, 168, 171, 174,
241, 283; social death, as form of,
199; Spartan helots, 145, 152
snakes and snakebites, 34, 62, 65,
101, 328
Snyder, H. Gregory, xi, 3, 7, 177, 194
Sobek (Egyptian deity), 19
social context of religion: in Anatolia,
105–8; Christianity, 180–81,
188–92; class identity, 233; in
Egypt, 22–25; gender and social
identity, 231–32, 233, 282; in
Greece, 144, 145–47; in Iran
and Zoroastrianism, 123–28; in
Israel, 86–89; in Mesopotamia, 37,
44–46; patrician/plebeian social
class divide in Rome, 168, 174,
233; in Rome, 168–70; in Syria-
Canaan, 68–69
Socrates, 192, 214n30
Sogdia and Sogdian, 125, 134
Sokar (Egyptian deity), 15, 17
Sol Invictus (Roman deity), 159, 187

Solomon (Israelite king), 66, 82, 84, 87, 89, 91
Sommer, Benjamin D., 256, 274
Sons of Light and Sons of Darkness, 227
Sophocles, *Antigone*, 263
Sosipolis, sanctuary to, 283
soul: in Anatolia, 100; body, relationship to, 257–60, 262, 271; in Christianity, 211, 257, 313, 316, 318, 324, 326, 328; in Egypt, 17, 30; gender and, 298; in Gnosticism, 260; in Greece, 140, 258–59, 262, 271, 313–14; identity and, 211; in Iran and Zoroastrianism, 121–22, 123; in Israel and Judaism, 91, 93n21, 262, 314; in Rome, 162; in Syria-Canaan, 61; visuality and, 313–14, 316, 318, 324, 326, 328
Spaeth, Barbette Stanley, xi, 1, 232, 300
Spartacus, 205, 213n20
Spartans/Lacedemonians, 137, 138, 145, 152, 222, 224
Spenta Armaiti/Prithivi (Iranian deity), 117, 118
state cults. *See* politics and religion, *under specific cultures and religions*
Stoicism, 147, 152, 169–70, 208, 261, 271
Stratton, Kimberly B., xi, 3, 5–6, 220
structural organization of religion: in Anatolia, 103–4, 105; Christian, 187–88, 288; Cybele, eunuch priests of, 159, 238, 272; in Egypt, 21–23; gender and, 285–88, 292–93; in Greece, 144–45; in Iran and Zoroastrianism, 123, 125, 126; Isis, distinctive appearance and observances of priests of, 238; in Israel, 83–86, 284, 288; Magi, 117, 123, 125, 126, 132; in Mesopotamia, 43–44; in Rome, 157, 165–67, 169; in Syria-Canaan, 65, 67
Sul Minerva (Roman deity), 159
Sumerians, 33, 55, 80, 99, 111.
See also Mesopotamia
Šurpu (Mesopotamian purification ritual), 36, 45
Sutium (Mesopotamian place name), 36
synagogues and synagogue worship, 179, 234, 285–86, 288, 293, 325, 328, 332, 332–34, *333*, 336–38
syncretism (combinations of gods):

in Aleppo, 96–97; in Egypt, 14, 15–16; in Greece, 137, 139; in Mesopotamia, 36; in Roman sphere, 159; in Syria-Canaan, 60. *See also* connections to and borrowings from religions in different cultures
Syria-Canaan, 55–70; Anatolia and, 95, 97; belief systems in, 58–63; chronology, 70–71; connections to and borrowings from religions in other cultures, 36, 58, 59, 97; defined, 55; deities, 58–60; Egypt and, 58, 69; eschatology, 60–61; glossary, 71–72; Greece and, 138; historical development of religion in, 55–58; Israelite worship of deities of, 76–77; Mesopotamia and, 36, 57; philosophy and ethics in, 69; politics and religion in, 67, 68; practice of religion in, 63–68; research and further reading, 69–70; ritual in, 63–66; sacred space in, 66; sacred time in, 66; social context of religion in, 68–69; structural organization of religion in, 65, 67

Tabernacles, Festival of, 83
Tacitus: *Annals*, 180, 191, 247n77; *Germanica*, 213n20; *Historiae*, 213n20, 238, 239, 247n77
tākultu banquet-ritual, Mesopotamia, 45
Talmud, 84, 237, 239, 245, 263, 264, 302n26, 302n28–30, 328
Tanit (Syro-Canaanite deity), 60
Taru/Tarhuna (Anatolian deity), 98
Teeter, Emily, xi, 3, 13, 27
Tefnut (Egyptian deity), 16
Tel Ras Shamra, 56
Telipinu (Anatolian deity), 97
Telipinu (Anatolian ruler), 106, 110
Tell el-Farkha, Dynasty I deposit, 15, 19
Tell Fekherye, 61, 63
Tellus (Roman deity), 160, *161*, 317
temple sex/sacred prostitution, 23, 67, 79
temples. *See* sacred space
Ten Commandments, 81–82, 83, 88, 327, 328
Tertullian: *ad Scapulam*, 195n12; *Apologeticus*, 235, 320, 329; on baptism, 185; *On Baptism*, 303n56;

Tertullian: *ad Scapulam* (*cont.*)
    De Anima/On the Soul, 302n39,
    303n55, 313; *De Idolatria,* 328–29;
    *De prescriptione haereticorum/On
    the Prescription Against Heretics,*
    190, 192, 303n56; gender issues
    and, 190, 292–93, 302n39, 303n56;
    heterodoxy/heresy and, 184, 190;
    on philosophy, 192; on universal
    nature of Christian identity, 235;
    On the Veiling of Virgins, 303n56;
    visuality and, 313, 320, 328–29
Teshub (Anatolian deity), 97, 98
texts, sacred. *See specific texts*
Thanatos (Greek deity), 21
Thecla (follower of Paul), 190
theodicy (paradox of human suffering
    and omniscient, omnipotent, and
    benevolent God), 89, 127, 146–
    47, 204
theology: in Anatolia, 98, 100, 106, 108,
    109; bodies, divine and human, and,
    253–55, 257–58, 261, 266, 270, 273–
    74; Christian, 48, 181, 182, 184,
    193, 257–58, 261, 270, 273–74; in
    Egypt, 13, 16, 18, 26; identity and,
    241; in Iran and Zoroastrianism,
    117, 119, 120, 124–27, 134; in
    Israel and Judaism, 89, 90, 91; in
    Mesopotamia, 33, 39; Roman, 170;
    in Syria-Canaan, 57, 69; violence
    and, 205; visuality and, 313, 324,
    333, 336–38
Theophilus of Alexandria, 325
Therapeutae and Therapeutrides, 272
Theudas (teacher of Valentinus), 187
Thoth (Egyptian deity), 15, 19
Thucydides, 146, 222
Thvoreshtar/Tvashtar (Iranian deity),
    117, 118
Tiamat (Mesopotamian deity), 36
time, sacred. *See* sacred time
topographic/geographic identity,
    performance of, 233–38
Torah and Torah study, 88, 232, 239,
    245, 284–86, 289–90, 301, 303n48
Tosar (Iranian chief priest), 126, 134
Tosefta, 286, 302n31
transgressive behavior, gods associated
    with, 139
treaty formats and divine covenants, 58
Trinity and trinitarian theology, 183–84
Tripartite Tractate, 257

Tukulti-Ninurta Epic, 50n62
Tvashtar/Thvoreshtar (Iranian deity),
    117, 118
Two Brothers Sarcophagus, 337, *338*

Ugarit. *See* Syria-Canaan
underworld. *See* life after death;
    underworld gods
Underworld Books, Egypt, 25, 27
underworld gods: in Anatolia, 99–100;
    in Egypt, 15, 16–17; in Greece, 140,
    141; in Rome, 162; in Syria-Canaan,
    58, 60–61, 72
Unleavened Bread, Festival of, 83
Urnamma stele, 35
Uruk Vase, 35
urwan (soul), 121
Ushedar and Ushedarmah (Zoroastrian
    Saviors), 121
Utu (Mesopotamian deity), 36

Valentinus and Valentinianism, 180,
    187, 190, 194, 257, 264, 314
Valerius Maximus, 158
Varro: Augustine on, 255, 320; *De
    Lingua Latina,* 163, 247n77
Varuna (Vedic deity), 118
vassal states, 70, 92n2, 97, 111, 223
Vayu/Wayu (Iranian deity), 117
Vedic literature, 118, 122, 128, 130
Vendidad, 129
Venus (planet), 37
Venus (Roman deity), 283.
    See also Aphrodite
Vercingetorix, 205, 213n20
Vergil/Virgil: *Aeneid* and Aeneas,
    162, 163, 164, 166, 173, 224–25,
    246n24–25; description of early
    Rome by, 157
Vernant, Jean-Pierre, 149, 150, 151, 212,
    253, 254, 274
Vesta (Roman deity), 160, 167, 225, 270
Vestal Virgins, 157, 164, 167, 270
Victor (pope), 187, 188
Vienne and Lyon, martyrs of, 258,
    303n58
Villa of the Mysteries, Pompeii, wall
    paintings, *335*
violence, 5, 199–213; condemned
    by religions, 202–3; divinely
    sanctioned conquest, appropriate
    humiliation of the defeated, and
    Millennarian revolt, 203–6, *206,*

207; domination, relationship to, 201–2; immediate and mediate victims of, 200, 201; insurrectionary counter-violence, 201–2, 205–6, 207; mortification of the flesh as, 206–8, *208*; nature and definition of, 199–201; research and further reading, 212–13; sacralization of, 202–3. *See also* martyrdom; *specific cultures and religions*

visuality, 6–7, 309–40; academic interest in, 309–13; aniconic representations, 320; anthropomorphism and, 317, 320, 323, 324–25; attitudes of Jews and Christians toward visual art, 247, 256, 313, 318, 319, 326–34, *327*, *330–33*; bathing, dressing, and parading with statutes, 147, 323; context, importance of, 311–12; descriptions of sacred images, 312; determining and recognizing divine images, 320–23, *321*; image of God, human body as, 255, 256, 324; mediators, images of gods as, 323; monumental cult statues, development of, 147; narrative art, 329, 331, 332, 334–38, *335*, *337*; perception of visual images of gods, 316–20; polytheism and, 316–23, 328; research and further reading, 340; theories of sight and reliability of the senses, 313–16; visibility/invisibility of God in Jewish and Christian thought, 324–26, *325*, *327*

votive deposits, 174–75

votive offerings: in Egypt, 19, 27; in Greece, 142, 148; in Mesopotamia, 33–34, 41; in Rome, 161–62, 163, 164; in Syria-Canaan, 63

Vulcan (Roman deity), 317, 322. *See also* Hephaistos

War Scroll, 227

Wayu/Vayu (Iranian deity), 117

Weeks, Festival of, 83

Weil, Simone, 199

Wen-Amun/Wenamun, story of, 67, 69

Werethraghna/Indra (Iranian deity), 117, 118

White Temple, Mesopotamia, 34

Williams, Michael Allen, 260, 264–65

Wisdom, principle of, 183, 296

Wishtaspa (Iranian ruler), 117, 121

Woðanaz (Germanic deity), 213n20

women. *See* gender and ancient Mediterranean religions

Wurunsemu (Anatolian deity), 98

Xenophanes, 147, 253–54

Xenophon of Athens, *Memorabilia*, 147

Xenophon of Ephesus, *Ephesian Tale of Anthia and Habrocomes*, 302n15

Xerxes (Persian ruler), 124, 125, 128, 132, 228

Xʷarenah (impersonal force attaching itself to legitimate rulers), 118

Yahweh/YHWH (Israelite/Judean deity), 59–60, 76–81, 82, 88, 90, 91, 232, 296–97

Yamm (Syro-Canaanite deity/sea), 58, 60, 72

Yarikh/Yareah (Syro-Canaanite deity), 60, 72

Yashts, 117, 122, 128, 129

Yasna (collection of sacred texts), 127, 129, 131

yasna (ritual), 122, 123, 129

Zadok the priest, 84, 87

Zakkur (Aramean king), 62, 67, 68

Zarathushtra (Zoroaster/Zardusht), 117, 118, 119, 121, 127, 128–29, 130, 131, 132, 134

Zend-Avesta, 130, 131

Zeus (Greek deity), 14, 136, 139, 140, 142, 143, 146–47, 151, 160, 224, 232, 297. *See also* Jupiter

Zeus Ammon (Greek deity), 138, 152

Zevit, Ziony, 70, 78, 91

ziggurats, 34

Zithariya (Anatolian deity), 98

zodiacs, 66, 332, *333*

Zoroaster and Zoroastrianism. *See* Iran and Zoroastrianism

zukru rite, 66

Zurvanism, 121, 127, 134

CPSIA information can be obtained
at www.ICGtesting.com
Printed in the USA
LVHW050936310820
664595LV00016B/503

9 780521 132046